Legislative Power
in Emerging African
Democracies

Legislative Power in Emerging African Democracies

EDITED BY
Joel D. Barkan

LYNNE
RIENNER
PUBLISHERS

BOULDER
LONDON

Published in the United States of America in 2009 by
Lynne Rienner Publishers, Inc.
1800 30th Street, Boulder, Colorado 80301
www.rienner.com

and in the United Kingdom by
Lynne Rienner Publishers, Inc.
3 Henrietta Street, Covent Garden, London WC2E 8LU

© 2009 by Lynne Rienner Publishers, Inc. All rights reserved

Library of Congress Cataloging-in-Publication Data
Legislative power in emerging African democracies / Joel D. Barkan, editor.
    p.   cm.
  Includes bibliographical references and index.
  ISBN 978-1-58826-688-0 (hardcover : alk. paper)
  1. Legislative bodies—Africa, Sub-Saharan. 2. Legislative power—Africa, Sub-Saharan. 3. Africa, Sub-Saharan—Politics and government—1960–
I. Barkan, Joel D.
  JQ1877.L44 2009
  328.3'40967—dc22

                                                  2009026969

British Cataloguing in Publication Data
A Cataloguing in Publication record for this book
is available from the British Library.

Printed and bound in the United States of America

The paper used in this publication meets the requirements
of the American National Standard for Permanence of
Paper for Printed Library Materials Z39.48-1992.

5 4 3 2 1

such much!

Contents

Acknowledgments		ix
1	African Legislatures and the "Third Wave" of Democratization *Joel D. Barkan*	1
2	Kenya's Tortuous Path to Successful Legislative Development *Joel D. Barkan and Fred Matiangi*	33
3	The Rise and Ebb of Uganda's No-Party Parliament *Nelson Kasfir and Stephen Hippo Twebaze*	73
4	Benin: Legislative Development in Africa's First Democratizer *Ladipo Adamolekun and Mouftaou Laleye*	109
5	Co-optation Despite Democratization in Ghana *Staffan I. Lindberg with Yongmei Zhou*	147
6	Rules and Rents in Nigeria's National Assembly *Peter M. Lewis*	177
7	South Africa: Emerging Legislature or Rubber Stamp? *Joel D. Barkan*	205
8	Conclusion *Joel D. Barkan*	231
Bibliography		251
The Contributors		261
Index		263
About the Book		277

Acknowledgments

This study began while I was serving as senior consultant on governance at the Public Sector Reform Unit (AFTPR) in the Africa Region of the World Bank. Initial funding for the first round of field studies in Benin, Ghana, and Kenya in 2002 was provided by the World Bank through a combination of grants from four of its units: AFTPR, the World Bank's Research Council, the Poverty Reduction and Economic Management Unit (PREM), and the World Bank Institute (WBI).

Follow-up research by the principal investigators in Benin, Ghana, and Kenya was supported by the investigators themselves, their home institutions, USAID, and the World Bank. The study of the South African National Assembly was funded by the Democracy in Africa Unit (DARU) of the Centre for Social Science Research (CSSR) at the University of Cape Town and also by the Fulbright Senior Specialists fellowship program. The study of the Uganda National Assembly was supported by the Department of Government, Dartmouth College. The preparation of this volume was also facilitated by a Reagan-Fascel Fellowship awarded to me by the National Endowment for Democracy, where I was a resident fellow during the 2005–2006 academic year. The views expressed in this volume, however, are the authors' alone and do not represent any official or unofficial position of the World Bank, USAID, or the other institutions that supported the research reported herein.

I would also like to thank the following individuals for their support during various stages of this inquiry: Brian Levy, manager of AFTPR from 1999 to 2003, was especially supportive of what was a new exercise, as were Rick Messick of PREM and Frederick Stapenhurst of WBI. Sally Blair, Larry Diamond, Marc Plattner, Ed Kramon, and Joe Tucker of the International Forum for Democratic Studies at the National Endowment for Democracy; Michael Bratton, Michigan State University; Gerhard Loewenberg and Peverill Squire of the Center for Comparative Legislative Research at the University of Iowa; Robert Mattes, director of both DARU and CSSR at the University of Cape Town; Shaheen Mozaffar, Bridgewater State College; and Ben Turok, a political scientist and veteran member in the South Africa National Assembly, all encouraged and informed the study. Without their support and periodic advice, this volume would not have been possible. I also thank two anonymous readers of the manuscript for their helpful suggestions. The contributors to the book and I, however, are alone responsible for whatever limitations remain in the pages that follow.

—*Joel D. Barkan*

1

African Legislatures and the "Third Wave" of Democratization

Joel D. Barkan

Nearly two decades after the resumption of multiparty politics across Africa, the legislature is emerging as an institution to be reckoned with in some countries. Once the rubber stamp of the executive, or nonexistent during periods of military rule, these bodies have begun to assert their independence as players in the policymaking process, as watchdogs of the executive, and as organizations that respond to demands by civil society. Put simply, they are becoming institutions "that matter" in the politics of African countries—still weak, but increasingly significant.

Legislatures matter in the context of multiparty politics and democratization, because they are mechanisms for achieving both vertical and horizontal accountability of the rulers to the ruled. As the one institution explicitly established to represent society's diverse interests in government, legislatures promote vertical downward accountability of the state to the public at large, particularly to organized interests or civil society. As an emerging state institution, legislatures also promote "horizontal" accountability across and between other state and quasi-state institutions by scrutinizing the operations of the executive, including the civil service, as well as the operations of the judiciary, the military, independent agencies, and state-owned enterprises.

It is precisely because legislatures are both representative bodies and instruments for horizontal and vertical accountability that an institutionalized legislature is a defining attribute of *all* established democracies, and why they contribute to the overall process of democratization. While the development of the legislature into an autonomous and powerful branch of government will not occur without the holding of "free and fair" competitive elections, the emergence of civil society, and the emergence of a free press, the expansion of legislative power is also a driver of democratization. As such, the development of the legislature is both a dependent and an independent variable in relation to democratization. It is a dependent variable in the context of a typical emerging democracy, because the legislature rarely matters as an institution until *after* the second or third multiparty election, and thus after the transition from authoritarian to democratic rule has been under way for an extended period. It is an independent variable, because democratic consolidation—the highest stage of democratization—cannot be achieved without a developed and powerful legislature. As Steven Fish concluded from his examination of emerging legislatures in Eastern Europe: "stronger legislatures, stronger democracies" (Fish 2006; Fish and Kroenig 2009).

Legislatures in Africa

In terms of raw power, most African legislatures, like legislatures worldwide, remain weak in relation to the executive. Although more than half of Africa's forty-four legislatures have existed continuously or intermittently since the end of the colonial period, they are at best emerging institutions in terms of their capacity to foster horizontal and vertical accountability. A small number, probably no more than a dozen, have become real players in the policymaking process and thus institutions of countervailing power vis-à-vis the executive. Most have not. Yet African legislatures are arguably more powerful and autonomous today than at any time since independence a half century ago. That power is also likely to increase as several of these legislatures develop the capacity to expand their authority.

The extent of legislative capacity and power varies greatly from country to country. In some countries, the legislature remains very weak despite the return to multiparty politics, the holding of presidential and legislative elections at regular intervals, and even the alternation of power between rival political parties. In other countries, the legislature has asserted itself more forcefully, both as a check on the executive branch and as a contributor to the policymaking process and/or as a monitor of policy implementation. In still others, the reality lies somewhere in between—the legislature remains weak, but aspires to, and to a limited extent has achieved, a larger role.

Where the legislature has begun to emerge as an independent branch of government, as it has in Kenya, and to a lesser extent in Nigeria, Uganda, and South Africa, its impact on the governmental process can be profound. In the first, the legislature has asserted its independence from the executive and forced the executive to accept changes to its proposed legislation and budget that would have been unthinkable a decade ago. The Kenyan legislature has also exposed corrupt practices within the executive, and in some instances forced the executive to shut down these schemes. In South Africa, the legislature has refined legislation proposed by the executive and enabled the executive to achieve policy objectives that it would not have been able to achieve as effectively on its own.

Where, by contrast, the legislature has remained relatively weak, as in Benin and Ghana, its impact on the policymaking process and the operations of the state has been small.

These contrasting records of legislative performance raise the question of why the legislatures in some emerging democracies have enhanced their capacity and power while those in others have not. It is the main puzzle to which this book is addressed. Three subsidiary sets of questions guide this inquiry: (1) If democratization is not the prime determinant of legislative development and authority, what other factors shape this process? Put differently, if the development of the legislature is not the dependent variable in relation to those aspects of democratization such as elections that occur early in that process, what other variables drive the development of this critical institution? (2) What has been the varying impact of the legislature on the political process in a selected group of new and fragile African democracies? Does a strong and competent legislature contribute to or undermine the process of democratization? How has the legislature shaped the content of public policy and the nature of governmental operations? Put simply, does the legislature "make a difference," and if so, how and why? (3) Is it possible to answer these questions in terms of several meaningful generalizations and hypotheses that apply to the entire genre of emerging legislatures in emerging democracies—in Africa and more broadly across the developing world? Or, are the answers gleaned from this study sui generis to the legislative experiences of the individual countries considered in this volume? We explore these questions in the chapters that follow through an examination and comparison of the legislative experience in six African countries: Benin, Ghana, Kenya, Nigeria, South Africa, and Uganda. The studies reported from these countries are based mainly on original field research, a description of which is provided later in this chapter.

Democratic Studies and Comparative Legislative Studies

Although an institutionalized legislature is a defining attribute of all established democracies, the vast literature on the "Third Wave" of democratization has paid scant attention to the legislative process or to the development of this institution. Neither has the literature of comparative legislative studies devoted much attention to the development of the legislature in the context of emerging democracies, nor to its impact on democratization. Indeed, with few exceptions, this literature has focused overwhelmingly on the legislature in established democracies, particularly the United States (Gamm and Huber 2002), or tested theories derived from the study of the US experience in other political systems (Shepsle 2007; Loewenberg 2007). The result is not only a void in the literature, but also a regrettable disconnect between students of democracy and democratization and students of the legislative process—two communities of scholars within comparative political science that rarely address each other's concerns, and which largely ignore each other's work. This volume is also addressed to bridging the void between these two groups and the literature each produces.

Most contemporary students of democratization focus on the group of approximately eighty countries that have attempted transitions from authoritarian to democratic rule during the period that began in the mid-1970s and lasted for nearly three decades. Labeled by Huntington (1991) as "the Third Wave" of democratization, these countries and the historical period within which they attempted their transitions are distinguished from those countries that became democracies prior to World War I and those that attempted but largely failed to become democracies after the end of colonial rule. The beginning of the Third Wave is usually marked by the end of the António de Oliveira Salazar and Marcelo Caetano regime in Portugal and its transition to an elected government in 1974. There is less consensus about the end of this cycle, but most observers agree that the number of countries evolving from authoritarian rule to democratic regimes peaked during the mid- to late 1990s (Diamond 1996; Joseph 1998) and certainly by the early to mid-2000s. Democratic transitions in Africa, however, are confined to the second half of this thirty-year period. The first such transition occurred in Benin in 1990, followed by the end of one-party rule and democratic elections in Zambia the following year. The most recent occurred in Sierra Leone and Liberia following the end of civil wars in those countries in 2005 and 2006. For the purpose of this study, we shall therefore date the end of the Third Wave in Africa as occurring in 2006. During this period of only sixteen years, all but three of the forty-eight states that compose sub-Saharan Africa attempted *nominal* transitions by holding multiparty elections for the first time in twenty or more years.

A review of the literature during the second half of this period illustrates the extent to which students of democracy and democratization and students of legislatures pursued separate agendas of inquiry. From their inaugural issues in 1989 and 1993 through 2005, neither the *Journal of Democracy* nor *Democratization,* the two leading journals explicitly devoted to publishing work on democracy and democratization, published a single article whose principal subject was the legislature! This omission did not reflect an editorial aversion to work on legislatures as much as the failure by students of democratization and the legislative process to submit manuscripts that considered the relationship between the two. Yet one does wonder why no article addressing this relationship appeared in either journal until the publication of Fish's discussion of democratization and legislative development in Eastern Europe in the *Journal of Democracy* in 2006 (Fish 2006). My own article, "Legislatures on the Rise?" published in the *Journal of Democracy* two years later (Barkan 2008), was only the second. From 2006 through 2008, *Democratization* also published its first two articles that considered the legislature or its members (Ahmed 2006 and Sater 2007).

A review of the leading journals of political science as well as the more specialized journals on the legislative process presents the other side of the same coin. Gerald Gamm and John Huber reported in their 2002 review of the state of legislative studies that 85 percent of the 110 articles on legislatures that appeared in the *American Political Science Review* between 1993 and 2001 and in the *American Journal of Political Science* and the *Journal of Politics* between 1996 and 2001 were limited to the US experience (Gamm and Huber 2002). The pattern has moderated somewhat. Of the 100 articles published on legislatures by the same journals from 2002 through 2008, 60 percent were limited to the US experience but only seven considered the legislative process in the context of Third Wave democratizers. A similar pattern is found in the two leading journals on legislative research. Between 1995 and 2008, 75 percent of the 302 articles published by *Legislative Studies Quarterly (LSQ)* were concerned solely with the legislative process within the United States, while only 5 percent focused on legislatures in emerging democracies. By contrast, the *Journal of Legislative Studies (JLS)*, a journal edited by a member of the British House of Lords and less encumbered by the methodologies of legislative inquiry developed in the United States, has published a modest number of articles on the legislative experience in emerging democracies. However, like *LSQ,* its primary focus has been the legislative process in the context of established democracies, albeit with a European twist. Of the 400 articles published by the *Journal of Legislative Studies* from its inception in 1995 through 2008, 52 percent have considered some aspect of the legislative process in Western Europe, including the European Parliament, while 8 percent have considered the US experience. In addition, 68 articles or 17 percent have dealt with the new legislatures in Third Wave democratizers, but most of these have considered the legislative experience in Eastern and Southern Europe. Only three have dealt with the legislature in an African country (Burnell 2001; Nijzink, Mozaffar, and Azevedo 2006; and Schrire 2008). Another distinguishing feature of the literature on legislative studies is that very little of it, probably no more than 5 percent, is genuinely comparative in scope and approach.

This book seeks to bridge these two subfields of political science. It is also, to the best of our knowledge, the first comparative study of legislative development in Africa. Although there have been a smattering of case studies that have examined the legislature in the African context (Alderfer 1997; Barkan 1979; Burnell 2001; Djerekpo, Laleye and Tevoedjre 1998; Krafchik and Wehner 1998; Maforikan 1999; Tamale 1999; Murray and Nijzink 2002; Olum 2002; Hughes 2005; February 2005; Kazoora 2005; Thomas and Sissokho 2005) and two multicountry monographs (Salih 2005; Bauer and Britton 2006), this is the first comparative effort at theorizing about the process of legislative development on the continent based on a series of original and complementary field research studies.

African Democratizers

This volume also addresses a third subfield of comparative political studies—the politics of developing areas—because roughly 80 percent of Third Wave democratizers are developing countries that share five characteristics that shape their politics and distinguish them from most middle- and high-income countries. This is particularly true of African democratizers, where the majority of their populations are poor, live in the rural areas, and derive their livelihood from agriculture or related activities, although this is no longer the dominant pattern in Nigeria and South Africa. All but two of these countries are also former colonial states whose state structures, including the legislature, were established by the former colonial regime.

Nearly all are also plural societies populated by the members of two or more ethnic, linguistic, and/or religious groups that reside in different geographic regions of their countries. These regions often vary in their respective levels of economic development. This in turn means that different ethnic groups residing in different regions perceive themselves as relative "haves" and "have nots" in the context of the broader political system. This pattern of uneven economic development intertwined with ethnicity is particularly pronounced in sub-Saharan Africa. It is a pattern present in all of the countries considered in this study except South Africa.

This configuration of variables leads both politicians and citizens to define their political interests in terms of their ethnic and/or regional identities rather than in terms of different positions on issues that are shared by peoples of different regions and ethnic groups. Put differently, in plural and agrarian societies where most people are tied to the land and their local community, one's place of residence and the cultural and linguistic affinities one shares with one's neighbors often defines one's perspective of politics. This is especially true when political leaders and aspiring leaders mobilize the population on the basis of these identities during the run-up to an election or for other political objectives (Mozaffar, Scarritt, and Galaich 2003; Posner 2004, 2005). It is also a configuration of factors that encourages the formation of patron-client political organizations and retards the development and performance of the legislature.

The Four Core Functions of Modern Legislatures

Legislatures are unique institutions and contribute to the realization of vertical and horizontal accountability that are the hallmark of democratic political systems, because they perform four core functions.[1] First, legislatures are the institutional mechanism through which societies realize representative governance on a day-to-day basis. Regardless of the type of electoral system by which the members of the legislature gain their seats, the main purpose of individual legislators and the body to which they belong is to *represent,* that is to say, to *re*-present or mimic the varied and conflicting interests extant in society as a whole. The legislature is the institutional arena where representatives of competing interests articulate and strive to advance their respective objectives in the policymaking process. While the president in a democratic presidential system is also expected to "represent the people," she or he is not expected to articulate the diverse and competing interests of particularistic constituencies on a continuous basis. Rather, presidents, as heads of state, are expected to synthesize, balance, and aggregate interests into "the national interest." As heads of the executive branch of government, presidents are also expected to implement a single national public policy on an evenhanded basis vis-à-vis society's diverse constituent groups.

Second, legislatures obviously *legislate*—but at two levels. At a minimum, they pass laws, but such activity may merely rubber-stamp legislation handed down by the executive. More significantly, legislatures contribute to the making of public policy by crafting legislation in partnership with or independent of the executive and with input from civil society, and then pass such legislation into law. In the pages that follow, we shall refer to this level of legislating as *legislating in the broad sense.*

Third, legislatures exercise *oversight* of the executive branch to ensure that policies agreed upon at the time they are passed into law are in fact implemented by the state. Oversight is an essential function for any democratic legislature because it ensures both vertical accountability of the rulers to the ruled and horizontal accountability of all other agencies of government to the one branch whose primary function is representation. For the same reason, effective oversight requires a significant measure of transparency about the substance of governmental operations.

Fourth, legislatures, or more accurately, legislators acting individually, rather than as members of a corporate organization that engages in collective decisionmaking, perform the function of *constituency service.* In countries where members of the legislature (MPs)[2] are elected from single or small multimember districts, and especially in Africa where most countries remain agrarian societies despite continuous rural-urban migration, constituency service takes one of two forms: (1) regular visits by MPs to their districts to meet their constituents and assist some with their individual needs, or (2) involvement in small- to medium-scale development projects that provide various forms of public goods to the residents of their district, including roads, water supply systems, schools, health clinics, and meeting halls. In countries where MPs are elected by proportional representation (PR), constituency service is less important because members do not represent citizens on the basis of a shared place of residence.[3]

Although the performance of *all* four of these functions define the legislature and distinguish it from other institutions, it is important to appreciate two aspects of these functions that also distinguish the legislature from other political institutions. First, representation, legislating in the broad sense, and oversight, especially the latter two, are activities that occur *within* the legislature and require acts of *collective* action on the part of all MPs albeit those in leadership positions obviously play more prominent roles than others. Because these functions are performed collectively, they also require intense bargaining, compromise, and cooperation between rival claimants for government action (or inaction). By contrast, indeed in stark contrast, constituency service is performed by members on an *individual* basis back in their districts or by lobbying central government officials on their constituents' behalf.

Second, the four core functions that define the legislature exist in tension with each other.[4] There is tension between representation and legislating, because representation requires members to advocate the particular concerns of their respective constituencies, while legislating requires bargaining and compromise across these and other interests. Similarly, there is the tension between legislating and constituency service, because the first seeks to arrive at decisions that serve the entire nation, while constituency service is, by definition, addressed to a smaller subcommunity of society. Oversight may or may not exist in tension with representation, legislating, and constituency service depending on whose interests are at stake.

The tensions between the four core functions become even more apparent in respect to how individual legislators (and by extension the entire legislature) allocate their time. MPs elected from single and small multimember districts—especially in agrarian societies where political interests are often defined in local geographic and communal terms—are under constant pressure from their constituents to service their districts. This in turn leads MPs to spend far more time on constituency service than on legislating in the broad sense or on oversight, the two functions that legislators perform on a collective basis. But when members do not perform these functions and focus overwhelmingly on constituency service, the legislature exists in name only—a conglomerate of elected representatives from separate constituencies that rarely acts as a whole.

Given these realities, a fundamental challenge to the development of legislatures in emerging African democracies is how to restructure the incentives facing MPs so that they devote more time and effort to the functions of legislating in the broad sense, and to oversight, while ensuring that their reputations for constituency service are not compromised. This also means changing the way African legislatures do business from the practices established prior to the beginning of the democratic opening in the early 1990s.

African Legislatures in Historical Context

Legislatures in Africa, particularly Anglophone Africa, are not new. Indeed, their origins across most of the continent precede the end of the colonial period, and in many cases date to the early twentieth century or earlier. Although their structure and purpose has changed over time, some African legislatures, most notably in Kenya and South Africa, have been in existence in one form or another for more than a century.

The Colonial Legacy

A hallmark of British colonial practice was the establishment of the Legislative Council, or LEGCO. Initially appointed by the governor of each colony, its purpose was not to promulgate legislation but to provide a feedback mechanism for the colonial administration regarding how its policies were being received by local elites and the general public. Early appointments were limited to members of the colonial civil service and leading British notables in the colony (e.g., prominent businessmen, clergy, educators, etc.). The Legislative Council was established in Kenya as early as 1906, but the first Kenyan African was not appointed to serve in the body until 1944. LEGCOs were first appointed in Ghana (then the Gold Coast) in 1850, and they were partially elected in Nigeria and Sierra Leone as far back as 1924 and in Ghana in 1925 (Wight 1947).

Following World War II and especially during the 1950s after Britain determined that it must soon dismantle its colonial empire, the LEGCO was viewed as the basis for elected democratic government in the postcolonial era. Power would be transferred gradually and hopefully smoothly by increasing the size of the LEGCO through a series of direct (and in some instances indirect) elections of some members of the council. The number and thus the proportion of the LEGCO's elected members would rise over time by holding a series of elections until 80 to 90 percent or more of the seats were held by directly elected members. At that point, the colonial governor would invite the leader of the majority party, or majority coalition, to form a government to run the internal affairs of the colony. After a modest period, usually no longer than six months, total power was transferred to the new government and the colony became an independent state.

Although all former British colonies in Africa later adopted a presidential system of government, all became independent states as parliamentary systems in the Westminster tradition. Most members were elected from single-member districts as in Britain. The presiding officer was the Speaker, and the chief administrative officer the Clerk. Parliamentary rules of procedure were set forth in the Standing Orders as in Britain. Sessions of the legislature were thus opened with the laying of the ceremonial mace on the table before the Speaker, who wore a wig identical to his counterpart in London. In some colonies, Uganda for example, the British constructed a parliamentary chamber similar to that at Westminster as a lasting parting gift. The establishment of "Parliament" was viewed as the linchpin for both the transition to independence and the establishment of democratic governance. The notion of institutional transfer as the key to democracy weighed heavily in British thinking (Apter 1955).

British policy as the colonial era drew to a close also replicated five aspects of Westminster that were to have a long-term impact on the way legislatures evolved in Anglophone Africa. First, parliament was established primarily as a deliberative body rather than as an institution for the making of public policy, that is, legislating in the broad sense. Second, while the Standing Orders provided for a small number of "housekeeping" committees, there was no provision for permanent committees concerned with different areas of public policy to enable legislators to oversee governmental operations ministry by ministry. As Britain's African colonies transitioned to independence, the new parliaments were not provided with a well-defined and well-resourced system of portfolio committees to facilitate a division of labor among MPs, which was essential if they were to perform the core functions of the legislature. Although India revamped its committee system soon after independence (Morris-Jones 1957), it would be more than four decades before African legislatures began to strengthen this key component of modern legislative practice.

Third, members of the "government," that is, cabinet ministers, were drawn entirely from the ranks of the legislature. Although this practice is usually not an issue in legislatures where there is a clear division between governing and opposition parties, it became a problem in the African context as multiparty politics gave way to one-party rule, and then to neopatrimonial rule during the 1970s and 1980s. As one-party regimes proliferated across the continent, African presidents appointed more and more MPs, often a third or more of all members of the legislatures, to ministerial positions or to positions as deputy ministers to maintain their political support and that of their respective clients.

Fourth, the role of the legislature in the budgetary process was kept to a minimum—to briefly deliberate and then pass the annual budget drawn up entirely by the executive, particularly by the Ministry of Finance. Indeed, the constitutions that Britain bequeathed to its colonies typically forbade the legislature from passing any legislation that would raise the level of government expenditures. In marked contrast to the US Congress, the legislature was not to initiate money bills of any kind. Nor was the legislature permitted to reallocate expenditures proposed by the Treasury for the next fiscal year. Parliament could only accept or reject the budget in its entirety, and it was expected to do the former. Not surprisingly, MPs developed little or no understanding of the budget or the budgetary process. Economic illiteracy among African MPs was the norm and continued to be the norm through the 1990s.

Fifth, as Britain transformed the LEGCO from an appointed to an elected body, it did so through elections that were also based on the British practice of electing MPs from single-member districts on the basis of "first past the post." As the number of elected seats in the legislature increased, the average size of all constituencies became smaller and reinforced the tendency on the part of politicians and citizens to define their political interests in geographic and/or ethnic terms. In this context, the election of the legislature from single-member districts likewise raised the expectation for constituency service. Taken together, these five legacies of colonial practice probably retarded the development of the legislature after independence in most former British colonies—the exact opposite of what was intended at the time.

The colonial legacies in Francophone and Lusophone Africa were not any more supportive of the development of a legislature that could perform the four core functions. If anything, they were worse. Whereas Britain established quasi-legislative institutions in their colonies early in the colonial period and thus established the norm that the legislature was a basic component of government, France, consistent with its tradition as a centralized state, concentrated all decisionmaking in Paris. Colonial governors in what were to become the independent states of French West Africa and French Equatorial Africa took orders from the governor-générals in Dakar and Brazzaville, who in turn took their orders from Paris. There was no equivalent of the British LEGCO, and the election of Africans to territorial legislatures did not begin until 1946. France's colonies did, however, elect a small number of representatives to the French National Assembly in Paris. Some such as Léopold Senghor of Senegal and Félix Houphouet-Boigny of the Ivory Coast served in the cabinets of French governments. The assumption was that the inhabitants of the "overseas territories" would ultimately realize their full political rights and citizenship within a "greater" France. However, with the breakup of the French empire in 1960, a series of nascent legislative bodies were quickly set up, and a single round of elections was held to determine their membership before independence. This provided little time to get these bodies up and running or to lay the groundwork for their institutional development.

As in the former British colonies, the French drew on their own experience when establishing these bodies. Legislative procedures were set forth in the Règlement Intérieur, the equivalent of the Standing Orders, which were patterned on the procedures for the French National Assembly. The chief presiding officer was the president of the assembly. Perhaps most important, limits were placed on the proportion of cabinet ministers who could be appointed from members in the assembly—usually no more than half. Whether this subsequently limited the ability of the presidents of the former French colonies to use such appointments as patronage for the purpose of regime maintenance is difficult to assess. As in the former British colonies, the power of the legislature to participate in the budgetary process was limited. Members of the legislatures in most former French colonies are also elected from single-member districts. Where no candidate obtains a majority of the vote, a second-round runoff election is held to determine the winner of the seat. As in the former British colonies, MPs in Francophone Africa report that they are under intense public pressure to service their constituencies, and that much less emphasis is placed on performing the other core functions of the legislature (Thomas and Sissokho 2005).

Legislative practice in the former Belgian Congo and the Portuguese colonies of Cape Verde, Angola, and Mozambique was, for all practical purposes, nonexistent before independence. In the Congo, parliamentary elections were held for the first time just prior to independence in 1960. Little effort was made to establish the national legislature, and it soon collapsed, a victim of the political turmoil that followed in that country. The same was true in Lusophone Africa where Portugal hung onto its colonies until 1975, and where independence was followed by one-party rule and/or civil war. Only in Mozambique, where a transition to multiparty politics was part of the settlement to that country's civil war in the mid-1990s, has the legislature begun to emerge as an autonomous institution.

In summary, where the colonial experience with legislative practice was both the longest and deepest, for example, in the former British colonies, its significance for the emergence of the legislature as an autonomous branch of government was limited. However, the idea that "there should be a legislature" and the symbolism of legislative procedure were firmly planted and carry through to the present era. Conversely, where that colonial experience with legislative practice was limited or nonexistent—such as in Francophone and Lusophone Africa—only the formal structures continue in the present era. For all practical purposes, the legislatures in these countries did not begin to build their capacity for performing the core functions of the legislature until well after the transition to democracy in the early and mid-1990s. Compared to the legislatures in Anglophone Africa, they started "from scratch." It is therefore not surprising that the most-developed legislatures in Africa today appear to be concentrated in Anglophone Africa.

The Era of Neopatrimonial Rule

For a quarter century, from the second half of the 1960s through the late 1980s, Africa was not a hospitable place for democracy or legislatures. The nascent legislatures that emerged at independence were weak and soon swept aside or made weaker by the broader currents of African politics. This period became known as the era of neopatrimonial rule (Bratton and van de Walle 1997),[5] because nearly all African countries became ruled by a single leader who relied heavily on the distribution of patronage in the form of appointments to government positions and the distribution of rents to maintain themselves in office. Neopatrimonial leaders, or "big men" as they were popularly known, distributed patronage liberally to loyal subordinates, who in turn passed on a portion of their privileges to ensure the continued loyalty of their own clients and their clients' clients down the line. The opportunity "to eat" became the common description of the practice in what Jean-François Bayart called the "politics of the belly" (Bayart 1993) and Richard Joseph described as "prebendal rule" (Joseph 1987). A hierarchical web of patron-client relationships was the defining structure of these systems, as was the use of repression to remove those who would not play by neopatrimonial rules.

Neopatrimonial systems manifest themselves in both military (e.g., Idi Amin in Uganda, Sani Abacha in Nigeria) and civilian forms (e.g., Daniel arap Moi in Kenya, Paul Biya in Cameroon) or in combinations of the two (e.g., Mobutu in the former Zaire). Beginning in the mid-1960s, a spate of military coups pushed civilian governments aside and with them the legislatures in approximately half of the countries in sub-Saharan Africa. Although some countries such as Ghana made periodic efforts to return to civilian rule, the military ruled throughout most of this period. In the case of Nigeria, the country remained under military rule from 1966 until 1999 except for a brief interlude of four years in the 1970s when civilian rule including the legislature was restored.

The pattern in the remaining half of the continent was different and left a mixed legacy—ever weaker legislatures, but a continuity of legislative practice. For example, despite the onset of one-party rule in Kenya, Tanzania, and Zambia, the National Assembly continued to function in all three countries without interruption. Parliamentary elections for seats in the assembly were held at regular intervals every five years, and there was a modicum of competition similar to that in US primary elections—that is, there was a genuine contest between two or more candidates albeit only from the ruling party. These elections often resulted in a turnover of as many as half or more of all MPs, but never in the defeat of the regime.

The focus of these elections was purposely local. Leaders of the one-party states, including Jomo Kenyatta in Kenya and, to a lesser extent, Julius Nyerere in Tanzania, wanted to divert attention away from the national government yet use elections as a mechanism for legitimizing their regime. They urged MPs to focus their attention on the development of their constituencies rather than to deliberate or amend legislation proposed by the executive branch, or to propose legislation on their own. They likewise urged the public to evaluate their representative's performance in the same terms. In this setting, voters needed little encouragement to focus first on whether their MP regularly visited his/her district and brought home "pork-barrel" projects from the center (Barkan 1979).

The result was that parliamentary elections became effective mechanisms for holding MPs accountable for a narrow set of tasks, but did not hold regimes accountable for their overall performance. Elections became referendums on incumbents' ability to service their districts, but distorted the basis on which the legislature, as an institution, was held accountable for the performance of its four core functions. Time spent on constituency service meant less or little time spent on legislating and oversight.

A final but important incentive that oriented MPs to emphasize constituency service at the expense of legislating and oversight was the fact that they were poorly paid. Salaries for legislators were never high, with the result that MPs who were not appointed to positions in the cabinet or as deputy ministers, that is, "backbenchers," had a very difficult time paying for their living expenses in the capital city while the legislature was in session. More important, they had a difficult time paying for the cost of visiting their constituencies on weekends. Such visits were costly not only in terms of the required travel, but mainly because MPs were expected to provide favors and cash assistance to individual constituents while back home. MPs were typically "greeted" by long lines of constituents outside their homes hours after their return seeking help to pay their children's school fees, hospital bills, and so on.

Without such visits back to one's district, however, the prospects for reelection amongst backbenchers were low. Sixty-five to 80 percent of backbenchers were typically defeated in their bids for reelection (Barkan 1984). Poor pay thus meant that many backbenchers became heavily dependent on the presidential handouts or on other benefactors for their political survival. For example, in Kenya, during the presidency of Daniel arap Moi, MPs were encouraged to stop by the office of the president on Friday afternoons or make contact with an emissary of Moi to pick up a paper bag filled with cash so that they could travel back to their districts over the weekend. Such handouts in combination with poor pay made MPs increasingly compliant vis-à-vis Moi, and both practices were continued for that purpose. MPs were reluctant to criticize the president, or to oppose or amend legislation he or senior members of his government introduced in the National Assembly, or to exercise oversight of the executive branch. Others sang his praises in the hope that they would be appointed a minister or deputy minister in the next cabinet reshuffle and gain access to the perks of office.

This dual system of patronage—of appointing up to a third or more of all MPs to become ministers and deputy ministers, and keeping backbenchers compliant through the combination of poor pay and cash handouts—became the hallmark of neopatrimonial rule across Africa. The result was a vicious cycle of legislative dependence on the executive that few legislators could challenge. That said, the dual system of patronage ultimately unraveled, because the costs for maintaining it escalated while the resources available for doing so declined. By the end of the 1980s, neopatrimonial leaders came under increasing pressure to bring ever-larger numbers of MPs into the executive with the attendant costs that this entailed. In the period immediately after independence, the number of ministerial departments in a typical African government was no more than in a typical Western democracy—between a dozen and a dozen and a half. By the end of the 1980s, it had climbed to the low to mid-twenties, and by the end of the 1990s, it had risen still higher. Every time the number of ministries was increased, the pressure to do so again increased by those left out of the spoils. The official "sticker" costs of these positions—for example, the published salaries and benefits for individual ministers and deputy ministers, housing, and other specified allowances—were not the problem. Rather, it was the informal license to loot as granted by the head of state that posed the real cost: government ministries became riddled with corruption, because ministers and their deputies were encouraged to take whatever was necessary to maintain their respective clienteles.

The license to loot gave rise to a series of neopatrimonial "kleptocracies" of which Moi's Kenya and Mobutu's Zaire are the best-known examples—systems of governance based on patronage and theft that undermined the capacity of most African states to perform their basic functions, including the management of the economy, the collection of revenues, the delivery of social services, and the maintenance of law and order and defense. In the process, the economies of most African countries collapsed. By the end of the 1980s, per capita income in many countries actually declined as the dual system of patronage had become a system of "inflationary patronage" that bankrupted the state and necessitated the printing of money. As their resources dwindled, neopatrimonial rulers like Moi and Mobutu resorted increasingly to repression in addition to patronage to maintain their regimes.

In the process, African legislatures suffered by becoming little more than agglomerations of individuals whose principal activity was constituency service and the search for political survival. They existed in name only, unable to perform any of the core functions, particularly *legislating in the broad sense* and *oversight* that required collective action on the part of its members. As the economy declined, MPs and backbenchers in particular also became increasingly unable to engage in constituency service, because they could no longer serve as conduits for the extraction of government resources and/or services back to their districts. The high turnover of MPs from one election to the next further eroded the capacity of the legislature to perform its core functions.

The Return of Multiparty and Competitive Politics

The return of multiparty politics in the early 1990s stopped the downward spiral of conditions that had undermined African legislatures for a quarter century. It did not, however, result in an immediate rebirth of the legislature in most countries. Although the "Third Wave" of democratization swept across most of Africa at the beginning of the decade, the extent of the process was highly varied and remains so today. As Michael Bratton and Nicolas van de Walle documented in detail in their comparative study of democratic transitions in

Africa, the Third Wave was triggered by widespread public dissatisfaction with declining economic conditions and the mode of governance that produced that decline (Bratton and van de Walle 1997). This dissatisfaction manifested itself primarily through protests by selected elements of civil society that were no longer cowed by the threat of repression by authoritarian leaders determined to retain power. Civil society leaders demanded a transition to democratic rule beginning with the relegalization of multiparty politics, free and fair competitive elections, and accountable government that they hoped would result in the improvement of the economy. Authoritarian incumbents, by contrast, sought to maintain the status quo, and the battle—in many instances a protracted struggle—was joined. Not surprisingly, they resisted any effort to expand the legislative authority.

The result, by the mid-1990s, was a swift return to multiparty politics and the holding of multiparty elections in all but a handful of countries. Beginning with Benin in 1990 and Zambia in 1991, one African country after another amended their constitutions to permit the registration of opposition parties and the return of multiparty politics. Elections followed within a few months, but after the historic elections in Benin and Zambia where the incumbent authoritarian regime was forced out of office, the outcomes were decidedly mixed. By the end of the first round of multiparty elections in 1994, neopatrimonial leaders retained power in roughly half of the countries where multiparty elections had been held. In some countries, such as Ethiopia, Uganda, Rwanda, and the Democratic Republic of Congo, the process was limited. In these countries the authoritarian regime was displaced by a guerrilla insurgency, which later attempted to legitimize itself through multiparty elections, or, in the case of Uganda, competitive elections within the framework of a "no-party" system. In all of these latter cases, the progress toward democracy was more limited.

These mixed results continued through the end of the second round of multiparty elections held in the middle to late 1990s (Bratton 1998). Some additional advances in the levels of democratization occurred as a result of the third and fourth rounds of elections (Lindberg 2006), when a number of African presidents who had hung on to office in the first and second rounds of elections, including Jerry Rawlings in Ghana and Moi in Kenya, were forced to retire because of constitutional limits on the number of terms they could serve.[6] Some, such as Frederick Chiluba in Zambia, Bakili Muluzi in Malawi, and Olusegun Obasanjo in Nigeria tried but failed to overturn these bans. Others, including Yoweri Museveni in Uganda and Sam Nujoma in Namibia, succeeded and were reelected to a third or fourth term.

The impact of the return of multiparty politics on democratization and on the development of the legislature was thus decidedly ambiguous for the first ten years. As noted earlier, the extent of democratization varied greatly across the continent and remains so today. Whereas African regimes were relatively homogeneous from the mid-1960s to the end of the 1980s, the return of multiparty politics and the holding of multiparty elections in the early 1990s gave rise to a broad range of regimes from semiauthoritarian states to liberal democracies. Similarly, the return of multiparty politics gave rise to a broad range of legislative types. Whereas the legislature had been a rubber stamp or ceased to exist, some of these bodies remained very weak, while others began to build their capacity to perform the core functions that define this institution after the return of multipartyism.

But as the case studies in this volume make clear, legislative development where it has occurred, and like democratization itself, has been a slow and tortuous process. Legislative development does not occur at the earliest stages of democratization, but later—five to ten years into the process. This delay is entirely logical and one would be naïve to expect faster development given the ambiguous results of the first round of African multiparty elections. More fundamentally, democratization, and especially the consolidation of democracy, depends on the establishment of an array of institutions of countervailing power that force horizontal and downward accountability upon the executive, of which the legislature is but one. Having discussed the demographic and historical contexts within which the process of legislative development takes place, we turn now to an examination of the process itself.

The Argument and Hypothesis

The argument presented in this volume is that although the legislature cannot emerge as a politically important institution in the absence of some minimum level of democratization, other variables explain its development into an institution that can perform all four of its defining functions, particularly those performed collectively and within the legislature. More fundamentally, the emergence of the legislature is the result of changing the structure of incentives faced by individual legislators and is best understood from this perspective. As discussed earlier in this chapter, the demographic features of African society combined with the constitutional legacy of the colonial period created a structure of incentives that encouraged the rise of patron-client politics culminating in neopatrimonial regimes. The legislature was extremely weak in these regimes, because the structure of incentives (and disincentives) forced MPs to devote a disproportionate amount of their time to constituency service. These included very low salaries for MPs and insufficient professional staff to sustain modern legislative practice, especially a system of portfolio committees.

Of these three sets of factors, the first two, that is, the demographic and the constitutional, are the most difficult to change, though it is possible to rewrite the rules that have retarded the development of the legislature. It is also possible to change the terms of service for members. These possibilities, however, beg the question of how and under what conditions the structure of incentives facing MPs can be changed. The answer, for want of a better label, is when *a coalition for change* emerges within the legislature that is intent on changing these incentives. But this answer in turn begs the answer to a second question: What does a "coalition of change" consist of and what explains its emergence?

Coalitions for change are usually informal groups of legislators who are dissatisfied with the status quo, though not all members of these coalitions agree on all aspects of what needs to be changed to enhance legislative authority. These coalitions consist of both "reformers" and "opportunists." The two groups are distinguished from each other by the extent to which they support, oppose, or remain neutral on the goal of transforming the legislature into an institution that performs all four of its core functions well. "Reformers" are exactly what the name implies—members of the legislature who are intent on transforming their institution from a weak rubber stamp of the executive into a modern autonomous legislature. By contrast, "opportunists" are members who are primarily interested in improving their own terms of service, especially a raise in salary and other perks that sustain their political careers. They are less interested, though not opposed to, improving the institutional performance of the legislature, but the changes they do support are often essential for improved performance. In a typical "coalition for change," reformers are usually outnumbered by "opportunists" for obvious reasons: The latter represent the lowest common denominator for changes that buttress reform.

Opportunists' participation in coalitions for change, however, is crucial to the passage of major reforms. For example, because improvements in legislators' salaries, travel allowances, and other perks are often resisted by the executive branch, such changes are dependent on the passage of a constitutional amendment and/or other enabling legislation to formally delink the legislature from the executive branch. Once that is accomplished, as it was in Kenya in 2000, the legislature can set its own annual budget and recruit and deploy its own staff. Such legislation is also necessary before the legislature can expand and professionalize its staff to the point that it can effectively support and sustain a modern system of portfolio committees.

Both "reformers" and "opportunists" might therefore join in a coalition to pass the required enabling legislation, though their respective motivations for doing so are not the same. The same is true with respect to changing the internal procedures of the legislature, for example, its Standing Orders or Règlement Intérieur. Reformers view such changes, including the enactment of provisions to establish a system of departmental committees, as the key to reform, while opportunists support them more out of self-interest.

Finally, as the discussions in the chapters that follow reveal, the presence in the legislature of even a small group of reformers, as few as 5 to 10 percent of all MPs, is usually sufficient to bring in a much larger group of opportunists to support (but rarely initiate) a broader reform agenda. The experiences of the six legislatures considered in this volume suggest that (1) the size of these coalitions and the balance of their membership between reformers and opportunists vary greatly from one legislature to the next. The extent to which these legislatures have developed their capacity to perform the core functions is a direct function of the presence, power, and composition of these coalitions. (2) The size and composition of these coalitions within any given legislature where they have achieved reforms also varies over time. The coalitions are largest, and enjoy the greatest participation by opportunists, during the early stages of reform and during the second and third terms of these legislatures when the struggle for reform gets under way.

Because opportunists join coalitions for change to enhance their terms of service, and because improvements in the terms of service for members is necessary if they are to engage collectively in activities beyond constituency service, reformers and opportunists need each other at the outset of the reform process. However, as time passes and the reform agenda shifts toward more ambitious and complicated goals such as the establishment of a viable system of departmental committees or the revision of the internal rules of procedure, opportunists drop away. The coalition for change is gradually reduced to a hard core of committed reformers, many of whom lose their seats in the next election because they have a tendency to neglect the demands for constituency service in their districts. Reformers are also targeted for political extinction by executives who rightly regard reformers as legislators who are seeking to contain or reduce the authority of the executive. Presidents and senior strategists for ruling parties often seek to defeat reformers in the next election by denying them the party's nomination for reelection, or by liberally financing their opponents if they are members of opposition parties.

The Third Wave of democratization that swept the continent from the early to mid-1990s changed the opportunities for parliamentarians seeking to reform the legislatures to which they were elected. Multiparty elections accelerated the turnover of members and brought in new members willing to challenge the executive for the first time. The arrival of a new, younger and more professionally trained generation of political activists reinforced this willingness to challenge the executive. This was particularly true in countries where civil society is large and robust, as in Kenya, a condition that was itself a function of that country's high level of urbanization and the commercialization of selected rural areas.

Following the second and third rounds of multiparty elections in the late 1990s, civil society also began to expect more from parliament as a mechanism for holding the executive accountable to the public. In some countries, civil society organizations organized workshops and other events that brought civil society and parliamentarians together for the first time. The purpose of these workshops was to inform MPs about diverse issues, including the national budget, the concerns of women, HIV/AIDS, commercial farmers, and other interests, and to encourage parliamentarians to make greater efforts to strengthen their institution. In some instances, nongovernmental organizations (NGOs) offered to assist MPs in capacity-building initiatives. Members who participated in these sessions often formed the nucleus of what later became the coalition for change in their legislature.

The emergence of coalitions for change within a parliament may or may not be affected by the relative size of the ruling and opposition parties. Where the ruling party holds a very large majority, as in South Africa, the prospects for legislative reform are more limited than where the ruling party and opposition approach parity in terms of the number of seats each holds in the legislature. Parity alone, however, may or may not contribute to the emergence of a coalition for change. In some instances such as Kenya, it does. In others, such as Ghana, it has not. Perhaps more important are the changes in party cohesion. Where there is a decline of cohesion among members of the ruling party coupled with rising cohesion among the opposition, cross-party alliances are likely to emerge to strengthen the legislature. Coalitions for change were frequently coalitions of backbenchers from both the ruling and opposition parties. This was the pattern in Kenya during the last term of the Moi presidency (1997–2002). A variation of this pattern also occurred in Uganda, where MPs who were both supporters and opponents of President Museveni, albeit within the National Revolutionary Movement, joined together to strengthen the National Assembly before the return to multiparty politics in that country.

Where these conditions were present, members sought first to improve their own terms of service, including significant increases in salary and support for constituency service. Where improvements in salaries and support for constituency service were obtained, the coalitions for change sometimes increased in size. Most important, the members of these coalitions eventually turned their attention to "capacity building" within the legislature, particularly the development of the committee system, the cornerstone of the modern legislature and essential for performing the core functions of the legislature.

Other efforts included the transformation of the role of the chief presiding officer (e.g., the Speaker), a pivotal actor who was usually an agent of the executive during the era of neopatrimonial rule and often continued in this role during the first decade following the return of multiparty politics. Rather than leading the effort to rejuvenate the legislature, the Speakers in some legislatures including Kenya and Tanzania sought to limit the pace of reform. In Uganda and Ghana, as discussed in Chapters 3 and 5, different Speakers advanced and retarded the development of the legislature. In these cases, and in South Africa, the Speaker periodically shielded the executive from legislative scrutiny (February 2005).

Still other efforts included the professionalization of the legislature's staff, especially the strengthening of committee and research staff and the establishment of a parliamentary budget office. Coalitions for change also passed constitutional amendments and other enabling legislation (including changes in the legislature's internal rules of procedure) to shift power from the executive to the legislature. To summarize, while the specific package of reforms advocated by coalitions for change varied from one country to the next, the overall thrust of these efforts was clear—to increase the power and autonomy of the legislature, generally and especially vis-à-vis the executive branch, and to build the capacity of the legislature to the point where it could perform all four of its core functions, especially those performed on a collective basis.

Although the contributors to this volume argue that the extent and presence of a coalition for change is what explains the level of development in the six legislatures considered in this study, it should be acknowledged that this argument was arrived at post hoc. It was *not* the starting hypothesis that guided our inquiries in the field for the simple reason that the initial round of in-country research was an open-ended exploration to determine what African legislatures looked like a decade after the return to multiparty politics (or, in the case of Uganda, nonpartisan competitive politics). In the absence of a significant literature on African legislatures, save for a small handful of isolated studies noted above, there was little knowledge about how African legislatures were performing in the multiparty era prior to the research for this study. Put simply, the contributors to this volume started nearly "from scratch." This hypothesis, however, and especially the role played by "reformers," was considered more systematically in follow-up research in Ghana and Kenya and during the research in Nigeria, South Africa, and Uganda. The principal argument nevertheless remains a hypothesis that requires further testing through additional research in more countries.

One limitation of this inquiry is its case study approach. Although the "thick descriptions" of legislative practice in the six countries have provided a level of understanding unmatched by previous explorations of the subject, our main argument, and the evidence on which it is based, rests on more variables than cases. This is the classic dilemma inherent in the comparative case study method. While it yields a rich narrative of the dependent variable—the development of African legislatures after the return of multiparty politics—it does not permit a rigorous multivariate analysis of the independent variables identified in the narrative. Such an exercise, including quantitative measures of the dependent and independent variables, was beyond the scope and resources of the studies reported in this volume. The formulation of an appropriate research design for such a study, however, is impossible without a prior descriptive understanding of what the phenomenon to be researched and explained entails. The research reported in the chapters that follow should be viewed as laying the necessary groundwork for more ambitious efforts, a discussion of which concludes this volume.

The Countries Considered in This Volume

Of the six countries considered in this volume, four—Benin, Ghana, Kenya, and South Africa—are usually viewed as among those that have advanced the farthest with respect to democratization in Africa. All four have experienced a change of government via elections regarded by international and domestic observers as "free and fair," though in the case of South Africa, this did not involve a change of the party in power. Three of the four, Benin, Ghana, and South Africa, regularly receive high marks from Freedom House, which annually assesses the level of democracy in all countries by assigning them scores on two indexes—one for political rights and the other for civil liberties. The three have consistently been coded 1 or 2 on both scales, while the fourth, Kenya, has received 3s.[7] However, the extent to which the legislatures in the four countries perform the core functions that define modern legislatures varies greatly. As discussed in Chapter 2, the Kenya National Assembly is arguably the most developed and powerful of the group with respect to the performance of these functions, while the national legislatures in Ghana and particularly Benin are comparatively weak.

The performance of the legislature has also been much better than expected in two countries included in this study that have made less progress toward democratization. Nigeria has struggled to maintain democratic rule, and its 2007 elections were deeply flawed. Elections in Uganda in 2001 and 2006 were also flawed, and President Museveni's mode of governance increasingly resembles Africa's neopatrimonial regimes of the 1980s. For these reasons, Nigeria and Uganda regularly score below Benin, Ghana, Kenya, and South Africa on the Freedom House scales. From 2003 through 2007, Nigeria received 4s on both scales, while Uganda received 5s on the political rights scale and 4s on the civil liberties scale. Both countries are classified as only "partly free."

Notwithstanding these assessments, the legislatures in both countries have asserted themselves, although at different points following the resumption of competitive politics and the end of military rule. In Uganda, the members of the legislature achieved some notable successes in transforming their institution into a semiautonomous basis of political authority, though that authority has declined in recent years. In Nigeria, the Senate asserted itself late in its term in 2006 by blocking former president Olusegun Obasanjo's attempt to amend the Nigerian constitution to permit him to run for a third term. Since then, both houses of the legislature have become increasingly engaged in their oversight of the executive branch.

As noted at the beginning of this introductory chapter, the relationship between the extent of democratization and the capacity and power of the legislature in the six countries is modest at best.[8] While the development of the legislature would be impossible without the return of elected government on the basis of multiparty politics or competitive politics on a nonpartisan basis, these developments alone do not explain the emergence of the legislature in African democracies.[9]

That said, the six countries included in our study range from those labeled as "semiauthoritarian" (Ottaway 2003) or "competitive authoritarian" (Levitsky and Way 2002; Schedler 2006) to those considered to be "liberal democracies" or on the cusp of democratic consolidation. Their Freedom House scores run from a low of 5 on the political rights scale and 4 on the civil liberties scale to highs of 1s and 2s. As a group, the six reflect the significant variation in the levels of democratization present in thirty-four of Africa's forty-eight countries—all except those that are either failed states or states mired in despotic rule, those scoring 6 and 7 on the Freedom House scales and classified as "not free." The full array of African regimes including our sample of six is presented in Table 1.1. No claim is made that our sample is randomly drawn. Indeed, four of the cases investigated for this study were purposely drawn from the most democratic states on the continent.[10] However, our inquiry to address the research questions posed earlier in this chapter considers the legislative experience across the full range of African polities within which the emergence of the legislature is likely to occur.

Method and Approach

Given the paucity of literature, it was determined that the best method of inquiry was to conduct a series of intensive interviews with key informants, both inside and outside the legislature. Two to three dozen members of the national legislature were therefore interviewed in each country, except Nigeria. While efforts were made to interview a representative sample of all members in respect to party affiliation, region, ethnicity, and gender, the sample always included the presiding officer, the chair of the finance committee (if there was one), as well as the chairs and members of at least three committees concerned with the delivery of social services (e.g., education and health) or agriculture. Members of the key oversight committees, such as the Public Accounts Committee or its equivalent, were also included in the sample. Interviews with members were supplemented by interviews with senior legislative staff including the Clerk or equivalent, and with the leaders of prominent civil society organizations and interest groups concerned with parliament. The organizations selected were usually those active in democracy promotion or in lobbying the legislature and the executive to further their agendas.

The interviews obtained for this study were structured yet "open-ended" conversations that covered a list of specified topics but did not involve the use of a questionnaire with a long series of "closed-ended" questions with precoded response categories. The choice of a qualitative and narrative approach was dictated by the exploratory nature of the study as well as past experience interviewing political elites across Africa. Most interviews took between an hour and an hour and a half to complete.

The interviews in each country were conducted mainly by the contributors to this volume, supplemented in some cases by interviews conducted by

Table 1.1 Classification of African Regimes, 2008

Liberal Democracy	Aspiring Democracy	Ambiguous	Competitive Authoritarian	Electoral Authoritarian	Politically Closed
Benin (2,2)	Kenya (4,3)	Comoros (4,4)	Burkina Faso (5,3)	Angola (6,5)	Chad (7,6)
Botswana (2,2)	Lesotho (2,3)	Guinea-Bissau (4,4)	Burundi (4,5)	Cameroon (6,6)	Equatorial Guinea (7,7)
Cape Verde (1,1)	Liberia (3,4)	Malawi (4,4)	Central African Republic (5,5)	Congo, Democratic Republic (6,6)	Eritrea (7,6)
Ghana (1,2)	Madagascar (4,3)	Nigeria (5,4)	Djibouti (5,5)	Congo, People's Republic (6,5)	Somalia (7,7)
Mauritius (1,2)	Mali (2,3)		Ethiopia (5,5)	Côte d'Ivoire (6,5)	Sudan (7,7)
Namibia (2,2)	Mozambique (3,3)		Gabon (6,4)	Guinea (7,5)	Zimbabwe (7,6)
São Tomé and Príncipe (2,2)	Niger (3,4)		Gambia (5,4)	Mauritania (6,4)	
South Africa (2,2)	Senegal (3,3)		Togo (5,5)	Rwanda (6,5)	
	Seychelles (3,3)		Uganda (5,4)	Swaziland (7,5)	
	Sierra Leone (3,3)				
	Tanzania (4,3)				
	Zambia (3,3)				

Source: Freedom House, *Freedom in the World 2009.* This table updates one originally constructed by Larry Diamond in 2005.

Note: The numbers within parentheses are the political rights (PR) score and the civil liberties (CL) score for each country. The first number is the country's PR score; the second is its CL score. Scales run from 7 to 1, where countries scored as 1 are the most democratic, and countries scored as 7 are the least democratic.

knowledgeable local research associates engaged for this purpose, including three of the coauthors. The interviews were supplemented by the collection of a variety of relevant documents. These included the constitutions of the countries included in the study, the Standing Orders or equivalent rules of procedure specifying the internal organization and operations of the legislature, plus other legislation that facilitated or impacted the development of the institution. This included special enabling legislation to enhance the power and capacity of the legislature, for example, the establishment of a parliamentary service commission or parliamentary budget office. Field research in each country usually took between two and four months to complete.

While the interviews conducted in each country were with members of the current legislature at the time the interviews took place, each case study embraces the entire period beginning with the return of multiparty politics, or, in the case of Uganda, since the return of competitive politics to the present— from the early 1990s through 2007. During this period, each of the six countries elected a succession of between two and four distinct "parliaments" to serve terms of four or five years each. MPs and other knowledgeable actors interviewed for each case study were therefore asked several questions about the evolution of the legislature in their country since the beginning of this period, and asked to compare the practice of the current parliament of which they were members to its predecessors. Thus, while the legislatures in each country are the unit of analysis for this inquiry, that unit is discussed in terms of the succession of several discrete "legislatures" that functioned differently because of the high turnover of members, and the changing politics in the six countries.

The need to discuss the development of each legislature over a succession of legislative terms, however, posed a problem of nomenclature. While we are interested in explaining the distinctions between the first and most recently elected legislature, not all of the countries included in this study officially numbered its legislature from the return of multiparty politics onward. Benin, Ghana, and Nigeria adopted this practice, but Kenya and Uganda continue to number their legislatures from independence in the 1960s. We therefore refer to each cohort of legislators who were elected at the same time by the official name of the legislature in their country followed by dates of that legislative term (e.g., Kenya's Ninth Parliament, 2003–2007). To help the reader understand the equivalent order of each of these legislatures across all six countries, we have listed the terms for each parliament in Table 1.2.

A second terminological issue is that of finding a set of equivalent names for the different types of committees that comprise the committee systems in the legislatures considered in this volume, because the names vary from one legislature to the next. We therefore use the term *standing, housekeeping,* or *procedural* to refer to those committees whose principal function is to facilitate the day-to-day business of the legislature. These would include committees that have a direct impact on the proceedings such as the House Business

Table 1.2 Nomenclature of Parliamentary Terms by Country

Sequence of Legislatures After Relegalization of Multiparty and/or Competitive Politics	Benin	Ghana	Kenya	Nigeria	South Africa	Uganda
1st	First Legislature (1991–1995)	First Parliament (1993–1996)	Seventh Parliament (1993–1997)	First Assembly (1999–2003)	First Parliament (1994–1999)	Sixth Parliament (1996–2001)
2nd	Second Legislature (1995–1999)	Second Parliament (1997–2000)	Eighth Parliament (1998–2002)	Second Assembly (2003–2007)	Second Parliament (1999–2004)	Seventh Parliament (2001–2006)
3rd	Third Legislature (1999–2003)	Third Parliament (2001–2004)	Ninth Parliament (2003–2007)	Third Assembly (2007–2011)	Third Parliament (2004–2009)	Eighth Parliament (2006–2011)
4th	Fourth Legislature (2003–2007)	Fourth Parliament (2005–2008)	Tenth Parliament (2008–2012)			

Official Constitutional Name of Legislative Term

Committee, or the Committee on Standing Orders, or the Committee on Committees. These would also include committees that have an indirect impact on proceedings, such as the catering committee, library committee, and so on. The distinctive feature of these committees is that the specific issues with which they deal affect all members of the legislature.

By contrast, *departmental* or *portfolio* committees are those committees whose work is restricted to some set of substantively defined issues, and which are also expected to shadow the corresponding ministry or department in the executive branch. Departmental and portfolio committees facilitate a division of labor amongst members and are essential if the legislature is to perform its core functions well. A third type of committee is the *oversight* committee, which deals explicitly with scrutinizing the operations of the executive branch, for example, the Public Accounts Committee in former British colonies. Oversight committees are specifically charged with the task of determining whether funds allocated for a particular purpose were spent as intended. Departmental or portfolio committees also engage in oversight periodically, but do so mainly for the purpose of crafting new legislation or amending existing laws.

Cutting across the varying functions different types of committees perform is the distinction of whether a committee is a *permanent, sessional,* or *select* committee. Permanent committees are exactly what the name implies: they are appointed at the beginning of the parliamentary term, and last over a period of years until a new legislature is elected at the next election. Permanent committees are also reappointed when the legislature is reorganized at the beginning of a new legislative term. By contrast, sessional committees are committees whose members serve for only one session of the legislature, usually for one year, after which the committee is reappointed with a new membership. Select committees are committees that are created for some special purpose, usually to investigate a single issue, and which continue to function for a limited time until the committee tenders its report on how the issue in question might be resolved. Select committees may function for part of or more than one session of the legislature.

The contributors to this volume were asked to address a common set of topics and questions when writing their chapters, recognizing from the outset that not all of the six cases are alike. We therefore explore the political and constitutional context within which each legislature has evolved, beginning in the period immediately before the return of multiparty politics in the early 1990s, or, in the case of Uganda, in the period prior to the return of competitive politics. We then discuss the internal operations of the legislature, to assess the extent to which each one performs the four core functions that define the legislative process, particularly those functions that are performed on a collective basis, and how and why individual MPs devote varying effort to each. The varying pressures on MPs to devote time to constituency service and how they respond to these pressures is also discussed.

Because the establishment of a system of departmental and oversight committees supported by competent staff is essential if the legislature is to perform its core functions, each chapter devotes some space to this important aspect of capacity building and seeks to explain why the process unfolded as it did. The consideration of important legislation by some committees is also examined where it illustrates a broader point about the legislative process. The structure and impact of political parties is considered, though it should be noted that none of our contributors was able to conduct roll-call analyses to assess the extent of party cohesion, because few records, if any, are kept on the vote of members from different parties on proposed legislation. Finally, we assess the nature and agenda of a "coalition for change" or relevant group of "reformers," where such exists, and explain how and why the group came into being.

Because only two of the six countries, Nigeria and South Africa, have a bicameral legislature, the analyses presented in this volume are limited mainly to a discussion of the national assembly or to the lower house. The exception to this rule is Nigeria, where both chambers, the House of Representatives and the Senate, wield equal power and have sought to expand their authority in recent years. Beyond these broad guidelines, each contributor was free to pursue his or her case study as he or she deemed appropriate. No standardized template was imposed.

The Order of Analysis

Because the Kenya National Assembly is arguably the most developed legislature of the six considered in this volume, Joel D. Barkan and Fred Matiangi begin the discussion with a consideration of the Kenya case. Their examination chronicles the tortuous process of legislative development in that country, starting with how former president Daniel arap Moi tried to block the emergence of parliament during the first years of multiparty politics, but lost control over the process seven years later. The Kenyan case illustrates how and under what conditions a well-led and motivated coalition for change can emerge to alter the balance of power between the executive and legislative branch and jump-start the development of the latter.

Chapter 3, coauthored by Nelson Kasfir and Stephen Hippo Twebaze, considers the unique yet highly informative experience of Uganda. The literature on the development of legislatures in the West typically argues that legislative development is a function of the emergence of well-defined and disciplined issue-based political parties (e.g., Loewenberg and Patterson 1979, 125–140; Olson 1994, chapter 3). Kasfir and Twebaze challenge this conventional wisdom by demonstrating that the Uganda National Assembly developed the most during the period when Uganda was constitutionally a no-party state than when it became a multiparty system. Indeed, they argue that the absence of parties was an important factor in the success of the coalition for change in the Ugandan parliament. The pace of legislative development "ebbed" once the country formally relegalized multiparty politics and the boundaries between government and opposition were more firmly drawn.

Chapters 4 on Benin coauthored by Ladipo Ademolekun and Mouftaou Laleye and Chapter 5 on Ghana coauthored by Staffan I. Lindberg and Yongmei Zhou consider two cases, one Francophone and one Anglophone, where the pace and extent of legislative development has lagged behind the extent of democratization overall. Although both countries have experienced a double alternation of power through the ballot box, and although the balance of power between government and opposition has at times been nearly equal, neither has given rise to a robust coalition for change within its respective legislature. The reasons for this appear to be starkly different in the two countries. In Benin, the failure of the National Assembly to incubate a coalition for change appears to be a function of the fact that the party system in that country is highly fragmented and weak—the opposite of the Ugandan experience. In Ghana, the near parity in the number of seats held by the governing party and the opposition in the legislature resulted in President John Kufuor resisting any meaningful attempt to cede power to the legislature or encourage its development. In a manner similar to Museveni in Uganda, Kufuor fell back on the use of patronage to thwart the development of the legislature as the lines between government and opposition became more sharply drawn.

Chapter 6 authored by Peter M. Lewis considers an important but nonetheless relative latecomer among African legislatures—the Nigerian House of Representatives and the Senate. In a country still dominated by neopatrimonial politics and the scramble for rents financed by oil, Nigeria's record at democratization is arguably the weakest—together with Uganda—of our group of six countries. Similarly, its legislature, like those of its counterparts, made little effort to build capacity during the first four-year term of democratic rule, nor during the early period of its second elected term following the restoration of democracy between 2003 and 2007. That situation changed, however, when the Senate blocked former president Olusegun Obasanjo's bid for a third term. Since then, and especially after the 2007 elections, the pattern of legislative development found in Kenya, and to a lesser extent in Uganda, appears to be taking hold in Nigeria. A group of reformers serious about transforming the legislature supplemented by opportunists out for their own gain has begun to emerge in that country.

Our series of case studies closes with Joel D. Barkan's discussion in Chapter 7 of South Africa, which is a unique case, yet one that illustrates many of the patterns found elsewhere on the continent. The South African National Assembly is the best resourced legislature in Africa, yet its development is retarded by a combination of three factors—the overwhelming dominance of the legislature by the African National Congress (ANC), which held 72 percent of the seats in the Third Parliament; the political culture of the ANC, which has given rise to a party that is arguably more disciplined than any other in Africa; and the fact that the legislature is elected by party-list PR. A small but significant group of reformers seeks to strengthen the National Assembly vis-à-vis the executive, but until at least one of these three factors is changed, it is doubtful that they will succeed.

As readers consider these six cases, they should keep in mind the theme and variations suggested in this introductory discussion: that the development of African legislatures and their ability to perform the core functions of all legislatures turns on the structure of incentives facing the individual members of these bodies. These incentives can be altered when a group of reformers supplemented by others emerges to change their terms of service and engagement. Whether or not such a coalition for change emerges in any given legislature and how successful it is in pursuing its mission is a function of local conditions, including the formal and informal rules that structure the political process, the response by the executive, the quality of leadership within the legislature, the nature of the party system, and other factors. We shall revisit this theme and variations at the end of this volume to extract what generalizations we can as well as lessons learned from the cases that follow. We shall at that point shift gears and assess what our findings suggest for practitioners seeking to raise the performance of African legislatures and legislatures in emerging democracies generally.

Notes

1. Different analysts of the legislative process describe the core functions common to all legislatures in somewhat different but overlapping ways. For example, Gerhard Loewenberg and Samuel Patterson identify the core functions of the legislature as "linkage," "recruitment" of legislative and executive leaders, and "conflict management" (Loewenberg and Patterson 1979, 43–67), but their discussion of linkage includes representation and constituency service, while their discussion of conflict management includes lawmaking and legislating in the broad sense. Strangely, oversight of the executive is omitted from their three principal functions but is then discussed at length later in their book. Similarly, David Olson, in his discussion of the attributes of legislatures (Olson 1994, chapter 1), lists "policy-making" and "representativeness," that legislatures are collectivities of many members with equal powers, who must balance constituency service against considerations of policy.

2. Following colloquial practice, we shall, throughout this volume, refer to members of the legislature as "members" or "MPs" whether or not their formal title is member of Parliament, member of the National Assembly, deputy, representative, or senator, and so on.

3. There is an informal expectation in African countries that use PR (e.g., Mozambique, Namibia, and South Africa) that MPs must devote some attention to interests that are defined by shared geographical residence. Indeed, as discussed in Chapter 7, South African MPs are provided with an official stipend to regularly visit a geographically

defined "district" in addition to representing that segment of the electorate that voted for the political party on whose list they were elected to the National Assembly.

4. I am indebted to Shaheen Mozaffar for this insight.

5. Michael Bratton and Nicolas van de Walle used the prefix "neo" to extend Max Weber's ideal type of patrimonial rule to late-twentieth-century Africa (Bratton and van de Walle 1997).

6. When amending their constitutions to relegalize multiparty politics in the early 1990s, three-fifths of all African countries enacted amendments limiting the number of presidential terms any one individual could serve to two. Incumbent authoritarian rulers including Daniel arap Moi in Kenya and Jerry Rawlings in Ghana used such amendments to hang onto power for two additional terms in the multiparty era, because the amendments did not come into force until the holding of the first multiparty election. A similar clause was written into the 1995 Constitution in Uganda where elections were held on a nonpartisan basis, but it did not come into force until after President Yoweri Museveni had been in office for nine years. In other countries, including Zambia, Tanzania, and Nigeria, term limits were first applied to presidents who were elected in the first and subsequent rounds of multiparty elections held in their countries.

7. The Freedom House scales run from 7 to 1, where countries scored as 1 are the most democratic, and countries scored as 7 are the least democratic. This counterintuitive scoring system means that the lower the score, the higher the level of democracy in the country so ranked.

8. Because our study is limited to only six countries it is impossible to conduct a statistically valid correlation between the level of democratization and the capacity and power of the legislature. Such a test would also require the development of a valid quantitative measure of legislative power, the components for which are suggested by this study.

9. It is also important to remember that the early development of legislatures historically, especially in Europe, was not a function of democratization, but rather the result of monarchs needing to accommodate nobles on whom they depended for revenues and defense.

10. The initial field investigations for this study were limited to countries that scored high on the Freedom House scales on the hypothesis that there was a direct relationship between a country's level of democratization and the extent to which its legislature had developed into an autonomous institution of countervailing power. Once that hypothesis proved false, the extension of the study was altered to include countries where the record at democratization was low, but not so low as to include states scoring 6 and 7 on the Freedom House scales.

2

Kenya's Tortuous Path to Successful Legislative Development

Joel D. Barkan and Fred Matiangi

Kenya's National Assembly or "Parliament" (or House) is arguably one of the two most significant national legislatures on the African continent. It is the most independent in terms of the degree of formal and real autonomy it enjoys from the executive branch. It is also a popular body. In a survey conducted by the Gallup organization in June 2008, 67 percent of Kenyans approved of the operations of the House (Gallup 2008). Since 1997 when the former ruling party, the Kenya African National Union (KANU), nominally controlled the legislature with a narrow majority of only four seats, the National Assembly has evolved into an institution of genuine, albeit modest, countervailing power to the executive branch. Kenyan presidents can no longer assume, as they once did, that the National Assembly will automatically pass their bills into law. Nor can they assume that the legislature will refrain from vigorous oversight of the executive. With the possibility of a new constitution that will permanently change Kenya's political system from a presidential system to a system where executive power is shared between a directly elected president and the leader of the largest parliamentary party, or to a parliamentary system, executive power is today more dependent on the balance of power within the legislative branch than ever before.

Kenya's National Assembly, together with the South Africa National Assembly, is also the most active legislature in Africa with respect to the deliberation and amendment of legislation. Since 1998, the assembly has become increasingly engaged in the policymaking process on a number of fronts, including the crafting of legislation, oversight of the executive branch, and representation of Kenya's diverse interests at the center of the political system. The National Assembly has also become more engaged in the budgetary process, though such involvement remains at an early stage. And although Kenyan MPs, like their counterparts across Africa, are under intense pressure to devote substantial time and personal resources to constituency service, a significant and increasing proportion of Kenyan MPs—perhaps now a majority—devote significantly more time than previously to the three core functions of the legislature that are performed collectively within the institution. Even more important is the existence within the legislature of a group of reformers, which together with members who support reform because it serves their individual self-interests, has formed a "coalition for change" that has been effective at building the capacity of the National Assembly to the point that it can perform the core functions that define legislatures worldwide.

Though hard to measure with precision, this "coalition for change" is probably the largest and most robust of its type on the continent. In no other legislature considered in this volume has such a coalition emerged that has sustained both itself and the process of legislative development over a period of more than a decade (i.e., over two or more legislative terms). Although a similar coalition emerged within the Uganda National Assembly in the late 1990s and early 2000s, its impact has since "ebbed" as discussed in Chapter 3. Similar coalitions have either failed to emerge (e.g., in Benin) or been thwarted (e.g., in Ghana and South Africa) or have only been in existence for one legislative term (e.g., Nigeria), as discussed in Chapter 6. Though their successes have been less than the achievements of the coalition in Kenya, a comparison of the composition, efforts, and context within which these "coalitions for change" operate tells us much about why some of these legislatures have progressed more than others since the relegalization of competitive politics in the early 1990s.

The net impact of the coalition for change in Kenya is that the National Assembly is a very different institution today from what it was a decade ago. The emergence of the coalition and the reforms that it has brought about are partly a reflection of Kenya's tortuous transition to democracy, yet cannot be explained by the transition alone. Indeed, the Kenyan experience illustrates how the development of the national legislature is both driven by and a contributor to the process of democratization. As emphasized in Chapter 1, it is both the dependent and the independent variable. How did this dual process of democratization and legislative development proceed in the Kenyan context? What has driven the process in its early and later stages?

Legislative Development and Democratization in Kenya, 1963–1992

Consistent with the experience elsewhere in Africa, the process of legislative development in Kenya did not gain traction until after the country's second multiparty election in 1997. Kenya's transition to democracy—a transition that has been substantial yet still incomplete—has been long and difficult and typical of African countries that did not succumb to military rule. When Kenya became independent in 1963, it inherited a parliamentary system established in the country during the waning days of colonial rule (Slade 1969). With few exceptions, the parameters of that system conformed to the description of the British legislative legacy discussed in Chapter 1: Independence occurred after a series of elections held prior to independence in 1957, 1958, 1961, and 1963. These elections transformed the Legislative Council (LEGCO) from a deliberative body appointed by the colonial governor into a directly elected parliament from which the government of the day was formed.

Kenya's LEGCO evolved over a much longer period than most African legislatures and arguably left a greater mark on Kenyan politics than its counterparts in other former British colonies. Because Kenya, like Zimbabwe and South Africa, was a colony with substantial European settlement, the British established the LEGCO in 1906, one of the first in Africa.[1] Kenya's legislature has thus existed on an uninterrupted basis and within the British tradition for more than 100 years. However, like nearly every other African country that remained under civilian rule from the 1960s until the late 1990s, Kenya's political system was dominated by a powerful presidency at the expense of the legislative branch.

Within a year after independence in 1964, Kenya adopted a presidential form of government that continued uninterrupted until early 2008. Under Jomo Kenyatta, the leader of Kenya's nationalist movement and Kenya's first president, the political system quickly evolved into a system of benign authoritarian rule. When Kenya became independent in 1963, its politics were dominated by two coalitions of ethnic-based political parties. The largest of these coalitions was the Kenya African National Union. It was headed by Kenyatta and was the party of the largest, most-educated, and relatively prosperous ethnic groups, including the Kikuyu, Embu, Meru, and the Luo. Taken together these groups accounted for roughly 42 percent of Kenya's population. KANU was also the most politically cohesive of the two coalitions in that it traced its roots back to the beginning of Kenya's nationalist movement in the 1920s. The second coalition was the Kenya African Democratic Union (KADU) headed by Daniel arap Moi. It was composed of Kenya's smaller, less-educated, and less-prosperous groups. Although KADU was supported by the Kalejin and Luhya peoples in the central Rift Valley and western Kenya, the coalition also drew support from many of Kenya's most sparsely populated and underdeveloped regions across the north.

During the run-up to independence, the British banned the formation of political parties on a nationwide basis. In the first two elections for the LEGCO held in 1957 and 1958, parties could only form and campaign at the district level. The result was that from the outset of electoral politics, parties mobilized voters within areas that were usually homogeneous in terms of their ethnic composition. When these local parties came together to form KANU and KADU in 1960, the die was cast. From that point onward until the present, Kenya's politics has been marked by an ever-shifting series of ethnic coalitions that form and reform prior to each election. These coalitions are loosely held together by promises of jobs and patronage made by political leaders to each other and to their respective ethnic clienteles. One result is that ethnicity and patronage have been "the stuff" of Kenyan politics for more than fifty years. Although the saliency of these factors has begun to wane as a younger and emerging generation of political leaders seeks to mobilize the electorate (especially Kenya's growing urban population) on issues that cut across ethnic lines, identity politics remains the bedrock of Kenyan politics.

Given this reality, Kenyatta, like his counterparts across Africa, brought a swift end to the initial period of multiparty politics. In 1964, one year after independence, KANU swallowed KADU after Kenyatta lured Moi and the other leaders of KADU to abandon their party in return for positions in an expanded government. Moi became Kenya's vice president and Kenyatta's eventual successor, a key part of the deal.

Although the National Assembly sat regularly and parliamentary elections were held every five years, the legislature soon became a very different institution from what the British had envisioned at the end of the colonial period. Instead of an institution of intense debate between "government" and "opposition," the principal fault line was between the government and backbenchers of the ruling party. The quality of debate was lively during the early years, but it eventually subsided as MPs learned that the key to obtaining resources for their constituencies, in the form of schools, health clinics, and roads, was to toe the government line. Promotion from the backbench to the front was likewise dependent on supporting the government. The period did produce a handful of tenacious legislators such as John Marie Seroney and J. M. Karuiki who made the full use of the weekly question period to interrogate government ministers, and who sometimes submitted private member's bills for consideration by the House. However, over time, Parliament was slowly reduced to a near, if not complete, rubber stamp.

The development of the National Assembly during the Kenyatta presidency (1964–1978) was not only retarded by Kenya's transformation into a patron-client one-party state, but by the British parliamentary legacy. Just as MPs in Britain were poorly paid during the 1950s and 1960s, so did the British apparently believe that the members of the legislatures in their soon-to-be-independent colonies did not require high or above-average salaries to sustain themselves during their terms in office. Service in Parliament was to be a noble yet semi-amateur profession, not a well-compensated one. The result was that Kenyan MPs, and their counterparts across Anglophone Africa, were poorly paid compared to senior civil servants of comparable rank (e.g., district commissioners and assistant district commissioners). Similarly, and again as in Britain at the time, the new legislatures were not established with a full complement of departmental or "portfolio" committees responsible for specific areas of public policy, but rather with a small number of standing or "housekeeping" committees. Although the British House of Commons later established a committee system similar to that of the US Congress and other legislatures in established democracies, it had not done so at the time Britain's African colonies became independent between 1957 and 1968.[2]

Because the committee system was rudimentary, there was also no perceived need for or provision for professional committee staff and the expertise and institutional memory afforded by such staff. Indeed, staff assigned to the National Assembly were assigned by the Public Service Commission, the authority responsible for staffing the civil service as a whole. The annual budget for the legislature was also set by the Ministry of Finance. The result was that the National Assembly neither controlled its budget nor the recruitment and assignment of its own personnel, but was dependent for both on the executive branch. Not surprisingly, the executive limited the resources it granted the legislature. For example, from the early period following independence until 2008—a period of nearly fifty years, the Kenya National Assembly did not have its own legal draftsperson to assist MPs in the drafting of bills. Instead, all private member's bills were referred to the Office of the Attorney-General for drafting with the result that few ever made it to the House floor.

The fortunes of the National Assembly declined further during the presidency of Daniel arap Moi, who succeeded Kenyatta in 1978, and who continued in office through 2002, a reign of twenty-four years. Under Moi, Kenya evolved into a classic neopatrimonial state. By the end of the 1980s, it increasingly relied on repression in addition to patronage to maintain its leader in power. Whereas Kenyatta had presided over a system that both permitted and encouraged competitive politics at the parliamentary level so long as his presidency was never challenged, Moi demanded complete loyalty, indeed sycophancy, from the members of the National Assembly. Under Kenyatta, parliamentary elections were intraparty contests within the ruling party KANU, but they were largely free and fair contests with as many as ten candidates vying for each seat. Voters were encouraged to evaluate candidates, particularly incumbents seeking reelection, on how well they had serviced their constituencies by promoting local development in the form of schools, health clinics, feeder roads, water systems, and so on. Although this diverted incumbents away from performing three of the four core functions of the legislature to the point that they devoted most of their time to constituency service, the emphasis on constituency service was regarded as legitimate and demanded by the public.

Under Moi, voters were also encouraged to vote for candidates considered "loyal" by the president. Where they did not, the outcome was often manipulated with the predictable results—voter turnout dropped sharply and both the regime and Parliament lost legitimacy in the eyes of the public. This was particularly true during the run-up to the 1988 elections when the rules were changed to require the procedure of "open queue voting." Under this procedure, voters cast their "ballots" by lining up in public behind the representatives of their respective parliamentary candidates at each polling station. It was arguably the lowest point in Kenya's long decline into authoritarian rule. It also marked the beginning of the end of the Moi regime, as corruption grew and the economy faltered. By the second half of the 1980s, per capita income declined in Kenya for the first time since independence.

By 1990, many Kenyans had had enough. A handful of senior leaders both within and outside government, including senior members of the clergy and leaders of civil society organizations, began to speak out in opposition to Moi by demanding a return to multiparty politics, democracy, and the need for economic reform. None of these demands included calls for strengthening the National Assembly, but the need for a reinvigorated legislature as part of the transition from authoritarian to democratic rule became clear—first implicitly and then explicitly—as time passed.

Legislative Development Since the Resumption of Multiparty Politics, 1992–2008

Although the beginning of Kenya's transition to democracy started a year after the resumption of multiparty politics and elections in Benin, Ghana, and Zambia, Kenya was among the first group of African countries to break with the one-party era at the end of the Cold War. As noted in Chapter 1, the impetus for democratization was mainly internal although those demanding reform were cognizant of parallel demands across Africa.

One notable exception to this pattern was the pressure for reform mounted by the international donor community after the end of the Cold War. Freed from the constraints of that conflict, the Western donors pushed forcefully for democratic and macroeconomic reforms. These pressures were particularly forceful on Kenya.[3] In November 1991, the international donor community announced that it would suspend US$250 million in much-needed assistance to Kenya until the Moi government took real steps to implement basic macroeconomic reforms, reduce corruption, and end human rights abuse. The donors did not condition future aid on a return to multiparty politics, but the message was clear in light of the rising internal pressures for both political and economic reform.[4] Within a month, President Moi announced that his government would introduce a constitutional amendment to the National Assembly repealing Article 2a of the Kenya constitution that defined Kenya as a one-party state. This set the stage for Kenya's first multiparty elections in twenty-six years that were held a year later on December 29, 1992. Three rounds of multiparty elections have been held since—in 1997, 2002, and 2007—for president, for members of the National Assembly, and for the members of local government councils.

Members of the National Assembly are elected from 210 single-member districts that vary greatly in size and population from 3,600 registered voters to over 301,000 (Barkan, Densham, and Rushton 2006). Twelve additional "nominated MPs" are appointed by the president for a total of 222.[5]

Despite widespread opposition to Moi and KANU, both were returned to office in 1992 and again in 1997 with between 30 and 40 percent of the vote, because the opposition failed to unite behind a single presidential candidate and a single slate of candidates for the National Assembly.[6] KANU's victory was facilitated by the fact that Kenya's electoral system emulates the British practice of "first past the post" (i.e., that the winning candidate need only obtain a plurality of the vote). Its parliamentary majority also reflected the fact that the party swept nearly all of the seats in the most sparsely populated areas where the average number of voters per constituency is far below the national average. In 1992, KANU won 58 percent of the seats in the National Assembly. In 1997, following the appointment of the twelve nominated members under new rules, KANU's share dropped to 51 percent, a majority of only four seats.

Prior to 1997, President Moi had a free hand in appointing the twelve nominated members to the National Assembly. However, in the run-up to that year's elections, the opposition threatened to boycott the elections if Moi did not agree to a constitutional amendment requiring the president to appoint the twelve on a proportional basis according to the percentage of seats each party won in the parliamentary poll. As the boycott would have delegitimized Moi's reelection and probably resulted in another suspension of foreign assistance by the donor community, the president caved. The amendment was the first substantial, albeit small, step toward redressing the imbalance of power between the presidency and the National Assembly. It also marked a symbolic beginning of efforts by reformers within and outside the assembly to enhance the power and autonomy of the institution. From that point onward, the balance of power between the executive and the legislature slowly began to shift through a series of small but important incremental changes that transformed the National Assembly and brought it to the position it occupies today. Like the proverbial shifting grains of sands, the legislative landscape changed dramatically thereafter.

The Seventh Parliament (1993–1997)

Although Kenya's Seventh Parliament elected in December 1992 held out the promise of a reinvigorated legislature, it soon became clear that the holding of multiparty elections and the presence of opposition representatives in Parliament would not assure the emergence of the legislative branch. Notwithstanding the fact that Moi and his party did not command an electoral majority, the president sought to govern in the same manner as he had before the election. Little changed in respect to the capacity of the National Assembly to perform its core functions, or the extent of its power vis-à-vis the executive. Multiparty politics would be tolerated, but the modus operandi of neopatrimonial politics by the president vis-à-vis the legislature would remain the same: Opposition members and other critics within the National Assembly would be excluded from the decisionmaking process and become the targets of periodic harassment, while a combination of poor salaries, cash handouts for constituency service, and the prospect of patronage positions would maintain discipline amongst the ruling party's MPs. To this end, roughly 70 percent of KANU MPs and one-third of the entire House were appointed to positions of minister or assistant minister. The enlargement of the cabinet and co-optation of MPs may have accelerated with the resumption of multiparty politics—a practice that has continued to the present, and which is also apparent in other countries considered in this volume, especially Ghana.[7] KANU MPs were also under heavy pressure not to establish cross-party alliances of any kind, especially coalitions to empower the National Assembly.

Another mechanism used by Moi to maintain control over the assembly, and one used by other African presidents, was to control the appointment and approach of its chief presiding officer, the Speaker. Although the Speaker of the National Assembly is elected by his/her fellow MPs as at Westminster, it was clear from the outset of the Seventh Parliament that Francis ole Kaparo, the Speaker and a KANU loyalist well versed in the rules of parliamentary procedure, served at Moi's pleasure, and was the president's agent in the House. The Speakers in Ghana and South Africa have assumed similar roles as discussed in Chapters 5 and 7. In both countries the Speaker has periodically contained the independence of the legislature and/or blocked reforms or investigations that would enhance the power of the legislature at the expense of the executive branch. The Speaker in Tanzania likewise slowed the pace of reform following the resumption of multiparty politics in that country between 1995 and 2005. Both he and Kaparo were eventually ousted from their posts following national elections that brought a younger and more aggressive group of MPs into the legislature. In sum, the chief presiding officer plays a pivotal role in facilitating, modifying, or blocking reforms designed to enable the legislature to perform its core tasks.

The role expected by Moi of the head Clerk during the Seventh Parliament was the same. As the chief administrative officer for the National Assembly, the Clerk was nominally in charge of the recruitment, development, and assignment of assembly staff. Rather than build capacity, he took a passive stance and did little to increase the amount or quality of staff support provided to members. Indeed, several observers knowledgeable of assembly operations during this period allege that the then Clerk had close links to Kenya's intelligence services, and that he reported on the activities of MPs seeking to enhance the power of Parliament or otherwise challenge the president.

This combination of factors meant that while the day-to-day debates of the Seventh Parliament were far more lively and critical of the Moi government than those of the last one-party parliament—that is, the Sixth Parliament (1988–1992)—the National Assembly remained a weak and ineffectual body in terms of the performance of its core functions. Donor agencies, including the US Agency of International Development (USAID), also learned that any attempt on their part to strengthen the legislature would be sidetracked by the Speaker and the Clerk. The Speaker was quite explicit about what he (and Moi) regarded as "donor meddling in Kenya's internal affairs." The Speaker thus welcomed donor-financed study tours for MPs to the United States, Canada, and Europe, because he could dole out slots on such tours as rewards to compliant MPs. At the same time, he often took a "go slow" approach to any proposed reforms within Parliament and donor efforts to support them. Not surprisingly, MPs desirous of transforming the legislature were frustrated by the lock the chief presiding officer and the chief administrative officer had over House operations. However, at this stage of Kenya's transition, most reformers and leading members of the opposition seemed more inclined to confront the Moi government through speeches in plenary sessions than by seeking to transform the legislature into an institution of countervailing power. They had not yet focused on the reality that their ability to exert real power on the executive turned on restructuring the way the legislature functioned, especially the need for both MPs and staff to build sufficient institutional capacity to carry out its defining functions. Unfortunately, recognition of this reality by MPs would not manifest itself until after the election of the Eighth Parliament in 1997.

The result is that the Seventh Parliament accomplished very little in terms of crafting legislation or exercising oversight of the executive. It was nonetheless an important learning experience for some MPs regarding what they had to do to enhance the capacity and power of the institution to which they nominally belonged. The first legislative term following the resumption of multiparty elections was thus an interregnum during which time MPs came to appreciate Terry Karl's prescient observation that "elections alone do not a democracy make" (Karl 1986). A small group of MPs, mostly younger members of opposition parties, slowly realized that the operations of the assembly were unlikely to change until they seized the initiative to force needed reforms.

The full emergence of this group did not occur until after the election of the Eighth Parliament (1998–2002) and provides evidence for the argument presented in Chapter 1: First, that the development of the legislature is both facilitated by and a contributor to the process of democratization overall; it is both the dependent and independent variable. Second, that legislative development is the product of the presence of a "coalition for change" among members of the body itself. Third, that the development of the legislature will not occur until such a coalition identifies the steps to be taken to enhance the capacity of the legislature to perform its core functions, why those steps need to be taken, and how to persuade a majority of their fellow MPs to support these reforms. This in turn requires reformers to address the structure of incentives MPs face that maintains the status quo. While the Seventh Parliament differed little from the Sixth in terms of performance, a significant minority of its members appear to have appreciated these lessons by the end of its term.

The failure of the Seventh Parliament to accomplish more during its term may also have been a function of the cohort of MPs elected in 1992. Roughly 80 percent had one or more (though not necessarily consecutive) terms in previous one-party parliaments. Put simply, they were holdovers from the neopatrimonial system entrenched during the one-party era. Most, whether members of KANU or the opposition,[8] had narrow agendas of simply getting back into office rather than building the National Assembly into an institution of countervailing power. The average age of members of the Sixth Parliament was also surprisingly high at fifty-nine. And while there was a small group of somewhat younger newcomers who were genuinely committed to Kenya's transition to democratic rule (e.g., Paul Muite, Peter Anyang Nyongo), they had not yet reflected extensively on what was required to transform the House into an institution that contributed to the transition and helped consolidate the process. The result was that while the members of this group were very active in contributing to the rejuvenated debates, they were short on analysis of what was needed to remake the institution. Given all these factors—from Moi's approach to governance to the composition of the assembly—one can better appreciate with hindsight why the development of the Kenyan legislature did not commence until several years after the resumption of multiparty politics. It is a pattern replicated in nearly all of the other cases considered in this volume where the legislature eventually succeeded in enhancing its capacity and power.

The Eighth Parliament (1998–2002)

The move to transform the National Assembly began in 1998, three months after the election of the Eighth Parliament. As noted in the previous section, Moi and KANU were returned to power, but with a very narrow majority that emboldened the opposition to maintain pressure on the president. Having forced him to relinquish the power to name all twelve of the nominated MPs, those demanding reform realized that they were no longer powerless when it came to confronting him.

The impact of civil society. The efforts to transform the National Assembly began with a series of workshops organized by two Kenyan nongovernmental organizations (NGOs)—the Institute for Economic Affairs (IEA) and the Centre for Governance and Development (CGD)—during the first quarter of 1998. The two groups were and continue to be part of an indigenous community of more than two dozen civil society organizations that established itself immediately before and after the return to multiparty politics in the early and mid-1990s. The specific agendas of each group are different, but their overall objective was to open up political space, especially between elections, and to pressure the Moi government for greater transparency and accountability. Many of these groups received modest grants from USAID and/or from other bilateral donors on the theory that democratization is nurtured by the development of a robust civil society.[9] As might be expected, this gave rise to a small "cottage industry" of donor-supported NGOs, and several of these organizations fell by the wayside as the decade progressed. Others, such as IEA, CGD, the local chapter of Transparency International, and the Institute for Education and Democracy (which focused on election monitoring), continue to operate a decade and a half later and have survived one or more turnovers in their leadership. Today, Kenyan civil society also includes several prominent professional and business organizations such as the Kenya Law Society, the Institute of Certified Public Accountants of Kenya (ICPAK), and the Kenya Private Sector Alliance. It is the largest civil society community on the continent outside of South Africa and possibly Nigeria.

It is also a civil society community with a "rural reach." Although the leaders and headquarters of these organizations are all in Nairobi, an increasing number of these groups seek to represent constituencies that exist beyond the capital city. One reason for this "rural reach" is that from the late 1980s onward, during the initial demands for an end to authoritarian rule, an early and significant component of Kenyan civil society was the Christian churches, particularly the Catholic and Anglican hierarchies and other mainline Protestant denominations with their thousands of congregations across rural Kenya. These organizations, which had long approached social issues via their umbrella organizations, the Peace and Justice Commission of the Episcopal (i.e., Catholic) Church, and the National Council of Churches in Kenya, now turned to politics. Other organizations such as CGD began advocacy efforts on behalf of coffee, tea, and sugar farmers and for pastoralists by seeking to inform MPs about the challenges facing these rural constituencies. For all these reasons, Kenyan civil society has had a significant impact on both the process of democratization generally and on the emergence of the National Assembly. Civil society in Kenya has demanded more from the legislature than its counterparts in other African countries, and key members of the assembly responded to its calls.

In respect to the limited capacity of Parliament to perform its core functions, the Institute for Economic Affairs was the first to address the problem by calling attention to the inability of most MPs to understand the budgetary process. Beginning in the early years of the Eighth Parliament, the IEA mounted an annual workshop for MPs immediately after the minister of finance presented the government's budget for the next fiscal year in his budget speech before Parliament in June. The purpose of the workshop has been to explain the meaning and impact of the budget and of proposed changes in the tax code with the hope that such information would improve the annual budget debate. Other civil society organizations, including the Institute of Certified Public Accountants and several local think tanks, have since joined this exercise to raise the level of economic literacy among MPs, and to lay the groundwork for the time when Parliament might partner with the executive in formulating the budget. As noted in Chapter 1, the constitutional legacy bequeathed by the British did not provide the legislature with a significant role in the budgetary process. Parliament was supposed to debate and then approve the annual estimates presented by the government, but not to formulate or modify them. However, if Parliament is to play a role in the crafting of legislation, it will inevitably be drawn into budgetary issues. MPs seemed to grasp this reality, but in the early years of the Eighth Parliament, few had any concrete ideas on what such involvement would entail. Indeed as discussed below, it is a question that would not be addressed until the Ninth Parliament (2003–2007) and the Tenth Parliament (2008–2012).

Before assuming a greater role in the budgetary process, MPs needed to acquire greater economic literacy about both the process and the hard choices the Kenya government faced with respect to macroeconomic policy. More fundamentally, Parliament needed to first develop the capacity to perform its core functions. Toward this end, the workshops organized by the CGD beginning in the first quarter of 1998 were the catalyst for what became a decade of incremental steps, each building on the one before it, to transform the National Assembly.

The workshops organized by the CGD brought together approximately 25 to 30 MPs at each meeting who were identified as interested in pushing a reform agenda in the House. Nearly 100 eventually attended these and other similar meetings. Most were younger, more highly educated, and more likely to be professionals than the average MP. Not surprisingly, most were also members of the opposition who sought a more powerful legislature to exert greater influence over how Kenya was governed. Within this larger group was a core group of roughly 30 to 45 reformers. Their leader from the outset was Peter Oloo Aringo, an unlikely member of the group because he was an older (then fifty-seven) former minister in the Moi government who had once been one of Moi's most vociferous supporters.[10] He had since parted with the president, however, and had become convinced that Moi's neopatrimonial regime was responsible for most of Kenya's woes. He viewed a reinvigorated National Assembly as the counterweight to the imperial presidency created by Moi, and the key to future democratic governance. He now defined his political career in these terms.

The workshops convened by CGD operated at two levels. At a general level, the purpose of these gatherings was to formulate a reform agenda for strengthening the National Assembly and for containing executive power. At a policy level, workshops were held to address the specific problems affecting key constituencies—farmers of coffee and tea, Kenya's two principal export crops; pastoralists living on arid and semiarid lands; and residents along the Indian Ocean coast, an area important to Kenya's tourist industry and where its Muslim community is concentrated. Together they signaled the beginning of a series of changes in the relationship between the legislature and the executive branch and in how the National Assembly would conduct its day-to-day business.

Removing constraints. With respect to the reform agenda, the participants identified four critical changes to build capacity and improve the operations of the House. First, to remove the ambiguity in Kenya's constitution that blurred the lines between the executive (especially the office of the president) and the legislature with the result that the president dominated the legislature. Second, to make the Speaker more accountable to the members of parliament who elect him rather than to the executive. Third, the need for Parliament to control the recruitment, assignment, and terms of service of parliamentary staff. Fourth, the need for Parliament to control its own budget, especially the determination of salaries for its members and staff.

With respect to the first, the participants agreed to pass a constitutional amendment that would formally delink the National Assembly from the executive. Although the powers of the National Assembly are set forth in Chapter III of the Constitution of Kenya (Kenya 1998), the document is silent on whether Parliament can set its own budget, including the salaries of its members and staff. When coupled with the explicit restriction stated in Article 48 that Parliament may not impose any charge on the Consolidated Fund unless it reduces expenditures, it was clear that the autonomy of the assembly, as in other former British colonies, was not guaranteed by Kenya's basic law. Article 48 also bars the National Assembly from imposing taxes or altering the tax code unless it reduces taxes, a constraint that for all practical purposes blocks the assembly from initiating legislation in many areas of public policy, particularly the provision of social welfare services. The autonomy of the legislature was further constrained by Article 45, which stated that the Clerk and parliamentary staff are members of the public service, which is part of the executive branch. While the legislature can pass bills that the president refuses to sign after a second vote in which 65 percent or more of all members support the legislation (Kenya 1998, Article 46), Parliament is also at the mercy of the president because the latter can prorogue (i.e., suspend) or dissolve Parliament at any time (Kenya 1998, Articles 58 and 59).

In 2000, two years after the CGD workshops, the National Assembly amended Article 45 to formally delink Parliament and its operations from the executive branch. The amendment, which was passed over the objections of the Moi government, created the Parliamentary Service consisting of the Clerk and all staff working in the offices of the Clerk (Kenya 2000a, Article 45a). The amendment also created the Parliamentary Service Commission (PSC) (Kenya 2000a, Article 45b) and gave the commission the power to appoint, supervise, and exercise disciplinary control over all officers of the Parliamentary Service (Kenya 2000a, Article 45b.5). Articles 58 and 59 remain, but the constitution now explicitly recognizes the legislature as an independent branch of government that exercises its powers independent of, or together with, the executive branch. This was important for the future of Kenyan politics, because the amendment marked a modest but real shift of power from the presidency to the National Assembly. It is particularly significant because the passage of the amendment required the votes of 65 percent or more of *all* MPs, of whom more than half were members of the ruling party. Passage was secured through the coming together of a coalition of change composed of opposition MPs and most KANU backbenchers.

The passage of the constitutional amendment was matched by the passage of enabling legislation, the Parliamentary Service Act (Kenya 2000b) that was required to bring both the PSC and the Parliamentary Service into being. The PSC has ten members including the Speaker who chairs the commission, the Leader of Government Business who is a senior member of the government appointed by the president, and the Leader of the Official Opposition. Seven other members are elected by their fellow MPs. The first chair was thus Francis Ole Kaparo, but its vice chair was the reformer Peter Oloo Aringo.

Although Kaparo chaired the commission, the establishment of the new body diluted the power of the Speaker, who, for all practical purposes, had previously run the legislature by himself with the assistance of the Clerk. Indeed, Aringo and his fellow reformers had proposed the creation of the PSC with this goal in mind. Their only disappointment was that in order to secure passage of the constitutional amendment and PSC Act, they had to accept the Speaker as the chair of the new body, and thus share power with him. However, Kaparo had to share power with the reformers. Not surprisingly, it was a contentious relationship that had its ups and downs. Aringo nonetheless viewed the outcome with satisfaction. Ever the pragmatist, and an optimist, he was always willing to take "half a loaf" if it advanced his agenda, with the knowledge that he could (and would) return to the issue at some future date. It was a perspective that served the reformers well, and a trait shared by successful legislators everywhere.

The second major goal secured through the passage of the PSC Act is that it has enabled the legislature to recruit, assign, and set the terms of employment, including salaries, for all parliamentary staff by establishing the Parliamentary Service. Existing staff were required to join the new service and be answerable to the PSC rather than to the Public Service Commission if they wished to continue employment at the National Assembly. Most accepted the switch. It was a bold move that laid the legal groundwork for the eventual transformation of a 400-person staff of which only a handful could be considered professionals[11] to a staff that now has between three and four dozen members with university degrees in positions of assistant clerks or higher. Members of the PSC, especially the reformers, viewed the professionalization of staff as critical for increasing the capacity of the assembly to perform its core functions.

The need for raising the proportion and number of staff with professional training is particularly important if the National Assembly is to strengthen its system of portfolio and oversight committees, the heart of the modern legislature.

The "Blue Print" and the role of the donor community. Having established the PSC and the Parliamentary Service, the reformers turned next to making these mechanisms work. The first effort in this regard was formulation by the PSC of the "Blue Print," a twelve-year strategic plan that it produced at the end of 2000 (Kenya National Assembly 2001). The plan had three components to be addressed over the remaining years of the Eighth Parliament, and the entire periods of the Ninth (2003–2007) and the Tenth (2008–2012): (1) to develop and properly staff a complement of portfolio committees so that MPs could better perform the collective functions of the legislature; (2) to professionalize the members of the Parliamentary Service to better support MPs in their work—to this end, the existing staff was reorganized under four directorates; and (3) to provide adequate physical infrastructure for the assembly, including, but not limited to, office space for every member and meeting space for all committees.

The Blue Print established a formal agenda for strengthening Parliament for the first time. It also enabled the National Assembly, the PSC, the Speaker, and the Clerk to claim "ownership" of any changes that would follow. This was particularly important with respect to the relationship between the National Assembly and the donor community. Whereas the Speaker, Kaparo, had previously resisted donor initiatives, he was now more inclined, though still cautious, to accept donor support provided such support addressed the needs articulated in the Blue Print. The result was the signing, in 2001, of a memorandum of understanding between the National Assembly and the State University of New York at Albany (SUNY-Albany) for a USAID-funded program for technical assistance that is now in its eighth year of operation. Albeit US in origin and resources, the SUNY program is now led and entirely staffed by Kenyans and has become a model for how the donor community can contribute effectively to legislative development in an emerging democracy. Through a constant stream of workshops, retreats, and consultations for members over an extended period (2001 to the present), SUNY has run a "demand-driven" program that responds to specific requests from the PSC via the Speaker and the Clerk. During this time, it has strengthened several key committees, expanded Parliament's role in the budgetary process, and contributed (via an intern program) to the professionalization of parliamentary staff. SUNY also assisted the revision of the Standing Orders to modernize the operations of the assembly. The greatest advances in these areas came in the Ninth Parliament as discussed below. The success of the SUNY program turns on the fact that it is Kenyan run and "owned." Britain's Department for International Development (DfID) appreciated this reality and became a cofunder for the SUNY program in 2006. Other donors may do the same.

The Blue Print also addressed the constraint of limited infrastructure. Prior to that time, only a handful of MPs—the Speaker and the Deputy Speaker, the Leader of Government Business, and the Official Leader of the Opposition—were provided with offices at the National Assembly. The rest were expected to be on their own, a situation that made it very difficult for them to meet with constituents, representatives of civil society, or fellow MPs or to be on the premises to work on legislation. The number of rooms available for parliamentary committees was also limited though more plentiful than in several of the other legislatures considered in this volume (e.g., Benin and Ghana). During the Eighth Parliament, the Speaker, with the support of the PSC, acquired Country Hall and Continental House, two buildings immediately adjacent to the National Assembly in downtown Nairobi. Together they provided offices for the PSC, individual offices for all MPs, eight additional committee rooms, a library, a members-only health club, a restaurant, and extra parking. By the middle of the Ninth Parliament, the physical infrastructure of the Kenyan National Assembly equaled that of the South African National Assembly, by far the best in Africa.

It is important to note that the Speaker, Kaparo, slowly but surely shifted his position as the Eighth Parliament proceeded through its term. Although he remained close to President Moi, Kaparo realized that his future depended on acceding to at least some of the reformers' goals or he might be replaced. He thus accepted the formation of the PSC and became its chair. He also agreed to the USAID-SUNY program though wary of its long-term impact, and he moved vigorously to support MPs in their desire for offices and adequate facilities at the National Assembly. Indeed, like many opposed to or diffident about the need for reform, he embraced "bricks and mortar" as one of the achievements of his tenure as Speaker and earned MPs' appreciation for the improvements made.

Modernizing the committee system. It is widely recognized that the division of labor facilitated by a system of committees for different areas of public policy is the basis of the modern legislature. Without such a system, the legislature cannot fully perform its core functions and is at a marked disadvantage vis-à-vis the executive branch. With such a system, provided members perform their committee assignments and are supported by competent staff, the legislature can both scrutinize government operations and work with the executive to craft legislation.

However, as noted previously, the legislatures established by the British in Kenya and in their other colonies provided for only the most rudimentary set of "housekeeping" committees. While the Committee on Standing Orders established parliamentary procedures to facilitate the work of the House meeting in plenary session, there was no committee or body such as the Parliamentary Service Commission to chart the development of the legislature. Neither was there a system of departmental or portfolio committees to shadow the operations of individual ministries, departments, and agencies (MDAs), although the Standing Orders permitted such (Kenya National Assembly 1997, Article 151).[12] The National Assembly did have two committees to oversee the executive—the Public Accounts Committee (PAC) and the Public Investments Committee (PIC), but neither had real clout. The task for both PAC and PIC was to ensure that the government spent its funds in the manner specified in the annual budget. They did not scrutinize the policies or the day-to-day operations of MDAs. Both were also dependent on the annual audits performed by the Office of the Controller and Auditor General, but until the Ninth Parliament these audits ran between three and four years behind the time the expenditures were actually made. The result is that PAC and PIC were often referred to as the "post mortem committees." Neither had sufficient staff.

Although little changed during the Eighth Parliament, the reformers realized that the committee system as constituted did not serve them well. Both the PSC and the Blue Print recognized the need to strengthen and restructure the committee system. Eight departmental committees were therefore established for the first time. These were the Committee on Administration, National Security, and Local Authorities; the Committee on Finance Planning and Trade; the Committee on the Administration of Justice and Legal Affairs; the Committee on Defence and Foreign Affairs; the Committee on Agriculture, Lands, and Natural Resources; the Committee on Energy, Communications, and Public Works; the Committee on Education, Research, and Technology; and the Committee on Health, Housing, Labor, and Social Welfare. None of the committees was provided with adequate staff. Few performed as intended during the Eighth Parliament. However, the idea of a system of departmental committees was implanted, and substantial progress was made toward building the committee system in the Ninth Parliament.

The Constitution of Kenya Review Act (2000). Apart from the constitutional amendment to delink Parliament from the executive branch and the Parliamentary Services Act, little legislation of substance was passed by the Eighth Parliament. One reason for this lack of productivity was the ongoing struggle over a new constitution for Kenya. Space does not permit a detailed review of that struggle other than to note that reformers both inside and outside the National Assembly were determined to substantially amend Kenya's constitution or enact a new one that would be consistent with their aspirations for Kenya as a democratic state. The demand for a new constitution dates back to the beginning of Kenya's democratic transition in the early 1990s. Advocates of the transition argued that notwithstanding the repeal of Article 2a, Kenya remained a country where the preponderance of power was concentrated in an imperial presidency at the expense of the legislature and the judiciary. Neither were truly independent branches of government until the constitutional amendment of 1999 established the independence of the National Assembly, but the judiciary remained firmly under presidential control. There were few checks or balances, and the reformers were determined to change that. Not surprisingly, President Moi resisted their efforts.

The wrangles within Parliament over the Constitution of Kenya Review Act passed in 2000 reflect this struggle and consumed much time. The act established the Constitution of Kenya Review Commission plus an elaborate set of procedures that the commission and the country would follow to first draft and then enact a new basic law. The result was that although the commission produced a draft on the eve of the 2002 general elections, the draft was never ratified. Nor were two subsequent drafts ratified, of which one was defeated in a national referendum held in November 2005. With the exception of two significant amendments—the 2000 amendment establishing Parliament's independence from the executive, and the amendment passed in April 2008 establishing the position of executive prime minister—Kenya is still governed by the same constitution as in 1992 when the country resumed multiparty politics. Kenyan political leaders and civil society are still searching for a new basic law.

The Eighth Parliament thus ended with a mixed record. It established its formal independence from the executive to an extent unmatched elsewhere in Africa. It put into place new entities including the PSC, the Parliamentary Service, and a system of departmental committees that would become the basis for improved operations in the future. It drew up a strategic plan to guide its development, and it established viable and important relationships with both civil society and the international donor community. MPs also developed a better understanding of the budgetary process.

The long-term significance of these achievements given that they were the product of the ongoing struggle between democratic reformers and an executive still bent on authoritarian rule cannot be overstated. The emergence of a vocal and politically astute coalition for change was arguably the most significant accomplishment of all, because without this group the reforms adopted would not have been made. The immediate payoffs from these reforms, however, were modest when it came to changes in legislative performance. Apart from the enabling legislation discussed in this section, the number of landmark pieces of legislation passed were few. The record of the Eighth Parliament at oversight was similarly modest as it would be difficult to argue that either President Moi or the executive branch governed in a manner that was different from before the beginning of the reform process. Their power vis-à-vis the legislature, however, had eroded.

The Ninth Parliament (2003–2007)

The groundwork for the actual emergence of the legislature laid during the Eighth Parliament bore fruit in the Ninth and Tenth, confirming again that the development of a key democratic institution is a lengthy process. The broader political context within which the National Assembly functioned also changed dramatically in a direction that buttressed rather than frustrated reform.

A new president; new freedoms. On December 29, 2002, Mwai Kibaki was elected as Kenya's third president. It was the first time executive power had been transferred in the country by an election since independence, and it was the first time power had alternated between rival political parties. Barred by the constitution from seeking a third term in the multiparty era, Moi was forced to step down.[13] Kibaki, then seventy-three years old, had been a prominent political leader since independence when he was close to Kenyatta and served as Kenya's minister of finance. He became Moi's vice president in the 1980s but was eventually pushed aside. He emerged as the principal challenger to Moi in the presidential elections of 1992 and 1997 by coming in third and then second in the two polls. Had the opposition united behind a single candidate, it is very likely that he would have been elected president in 1997. Having learned that painful lesson, Kibaki reached out to Raila Odinga, a rival who had come in third in the 1997 election. Together they stitched together a broad panethnic coalition, the National Rainbow Coalition (NARC), and beat what remained of Moi's KANU by a margin of two to one. NARC also won 59 percent of the seats in the National Assembly to KANU's 30 percent.

Little, however, had changed with respect to the nature of Kenya's political parties. Both NARC and KANU were coalitions of ethnic blocs headed by local and regional bosses. NARC was in fact a coalition of coalitions that came together only eight weeks before the elections when Odinga joined Kibaki. There were few policy differences between the two parties, though NARC included the various constituencies that had opposed Moi and KANU and campaigned on the claim that NARC was the party of democratic reform.

During the 1990s, Kibaki had served as the Official Leader of the Opposition in the National Assembly but was never active in the coalition that brought about the reforms of the Eighth Parliament. He quietly supported these efforts but was a passive player, the quintessential "opportunist" in the reform process—willing to go along with, vote for, and benefit from the process, but unwilling to lead. Having personally experienced Kenya's decline under Moi, Kibaki was strongly committed to improving the quality of governance. But his commitment and perspective were mainly that of a technocrat rather than a democrat. He appreciated the downsides of neopatrimonial rule, and the need for greater transparency and accountability. But his solution to Kenya's problems lay in restoring the presidency and the public service to the level of managerial competence associated with Kenyatta's presidency, rather than via the building of institutions of countervailing power. Put differently, his focus was on improving the supply side rather than the demand side to achieve good governance.

Once in office, Kibaki governed as predicted. Although he was incapacitated for most of the first year and a half of his presidency,[14] his main goal was to restore Kenya's once vaunted public service to its former glory while embracing a more consistent approach to sound macroeconomic policy than Moi.[15] The results were not immediate. During the 1990s through 2002, Kenya's economy grew by 2 percent or less annually, while per capita income continued to fall. However, by 2004, the annual rate of economic growth had risen to 4 percent, its best in more than twenty years. It rose to 5 percent in 2005 and just under 7 percent in 2007, the final year of Kibaki's first presidential term. Foreign direct investment, which had all but dried up during the Moi era, began to flow back into the country, as did investments by Kenyans, many of whom brought money in from abroad. The periodic harassment of civil society and the press that marked the Moi years ended, as did harassment against members of the opposition. Although democratization per se was not Kibaki's principal goal, Kenyans began to enjoy more freedoms than at any time since independence. Kenya's scores on the annual Freedom House indexes began to rise, from 6 and 5 on the political rights and civil liberties scales respectively in 2001, to 3 and 3 from 2003 through 2006.[16]

Not surprisingly, Kenya's press, especially its investigatory press, civil society, and some MPs, began to flex their muscles by exploring the operations of the executive branch with greater vigor than in the past. One noteworthy example was the exposé of the Anglo-Leasing scandal beginning in 2004. The scam, which ultimately led to the dismissals of three cabinet ministers and the head of the central bank,[17] was a scheme to substantially overcharge the government for producing new passports and establishing a crime lab for the police. The overcharges were allegedly passed to confidants of Kibaki to finance his future political campaigns.

The Anglo-Leasing scandal was similar in magnitude or larger than the notorious Goldenberg scandal of the early 1990s, which cost the Kenya government $350 million. However, this time, the combination of a timely report by the auditor general, aggressive action by the Public Accounts Committee, and intense coverage by the press blew the whistle before the full loss occurred.[18] Though some observers, including representatives of the donor community, were appalled by the scandal because Kibaki had pledged "zero tolerance for corruption," others viewed the aggressive actions by Parliament and the press as a sign that genuine checks were finally in place to rein in the executive branch for the first time. Parliament's response to Anglo-Leasing clearly "raised the bar" for the future. Having become more aggressive in rooting out corruption, Parliament was now expected by the press and public to do more and did so early in the Tenth Parliament.

Continuity and change. The election of the Ninth Parliament in December 2002 resulted in a high turnover of MPs as it had in previous elections in Kenya. Because parties remained weak coalitions of local bosses that rarely distinguished themselves on the basis of policy or ideology, parliamentary contests remained referendums on incumbents' records at delivering the goods back to the constituency. The result is that more than half of the Eighth Parliament were not returned to the Ninth, and 53 percent of the incoming legislators were beginning their first term. The extent of both turnover and continuity is apparent from a review of Table 2.1, which summarizes the composition of the Ninth Parliament and the Tenth (2008–2012). About a quarter of the new parliament

Table 2.1 Composition of the Ninth Parliament and the Tenth Parliament (in percentages)

	Ninth (2003–2007)	Tenth (2008–2012)
Gender		
Male	92.0	91.8
Percent of female members who are nominated members	44.4	27.2
N =	(224)	(224)
Age		
Under 30	1.0	.4
30–39	12.0	10.0
40–49	27.8	37.1
50–59	35.4	34.6
60 and above	23.9	17.9
Average age	52.3	50.4
N =	(209)	(224)
Education		
Primary	4.0	.4
Secondary	1.3	.4
Postsecondary nonuniversity	29.9	14.3
University	42.4	61.6
Postgraduate	21.9	23.2
N =	(223)	(224)
Term serving in Parliament		
First	53.1	64.3
Second	23.2	18.8
Third	12.5	8.9
Fourth	5.4	4.9
Fifth	2.7	1.3
Sixth or more	3.0	1.8
N =	(224)	(224)

Source: SUNY Kenya. Data are for 210 directly elected members, 12 nominated members, and 2 ex officio members (the Speaker and the attorney general).

were elected to their second term, while 13 percent were elected to their third term. There was also a small band of 25 veterans, including Kibaki, who were elected or nominated to their fourth term or more. Together with some third termers who had not served consecutive terms, they were the holdovers from the period of single-party rule. The impact of the election on the assembly was thus one of high turnover tempered by a much smaller group of MPs who had seen the House evolve since the return of multiparty politics. With the exception of Aringo, few of this "old guard" were prominent in the coalition for reform.

The elections also reduced the ranks of the reformers. Whereas in the Eighth Parliament between 55 and 75 MPs could be included in this category, the number in the Ninth declined to between 30 and 35, a loss of nearly half of the original group. The most prominent loser was Peter Oloo Aringo, the vice chair of the PSC and the leader of the group. He had become so absorbed in advancing the reform agenda that he neglected his constituency and was punished at the polls. However, in recognition of his efforts during the Eighth Parliament, he was returned as a nominated MP.[19] It was to be his last term as he was unable to win his party's nomination five years later. Aringo's plight demonstrates the immense challenge reformers face. Given voters' high expectations for constituency service, MPs who do not address these expectations, even if engaged in serious work to strengthen the legislature, go down to defeat. While Aringo was a pragmatist with respect to advancing the reform agenda within the assembly, he lost touch with his constituents and paid the price.

Notwithstanding the high turnover, the Ninth Parliament was clearly an elite body that bore little resemblance to Kenyan society as a whole in terms of the background of its members. Whereas half of Kenya's population is under 18 years of age, the average age of all members was 52.3 years. As indicated in Table 2.1, only 1 percent were younger than 30, and only 12 percent of the House were under 40. Fifty-eight percent were between 40 and 59, while over a fifth were over 60.

MPs were also much better educated than the electorate. Only 5 percent had a secondary school education or less, while 42 percent were university graduates and 22 percent had postgraduate degrees—nearly two-thirds of the House. That MPs were older and significantly better educated than the population was no surprise, because this had been the pattern in previous Kenyan parliaments, and in other legislatures across the continent. In fact it would appear that over time, African legislatures and the Kenya National Assembly in particular have become progressively more "elitist" in terms of the social background of their members. This is in large part the result of the high value Kenyans—and Africans generally—place on education both for themselves and for those who represent them. When faced with the choice of voting for a college graduate and professional or for a candidate with less education, voters consistently opt for the former, reasoning that such individuals will be more effective in delivering the goods back home. Unless the candidate is a long-time legislator running on an established record of constituency service built over several terms, the less education, the less likely one will be elected. Running for Parliament in Kenya is also an increasingly expensive proposition that excludes most ordinary citizens. The evolution of the National Assembly into a progressively elitist institution continued with the election of the Tenth Parliament.

The National Assembly is also an overwhelmingly male institution. Of the 210 directly elected members in the Ninth Parliament, only 10, or less than 5 percent, were women. Eight of the 12 nominated members were women, bringing the overall percentage to 8 percent. This pattern is replicated in all of the other countries considered in this volume and elsewhere on the African continent where MPs are elected from single-member districts rather than by proportional representation as in Namibia and South Africa or by having a large number of seats reserved for women as in countries such as Uganda (see Table 3.1).

Changing the incentives for MPs: Better salaries. In Chapter 1, it was argued that the development of the legislature was dependent on the presence of a "coalition for change" within the body that altered the structure of incentives facing individual MPs. As explained in that chapter, the structure of incentives that prevailed from the mid-1960s through the 1980s and into the 1990s encouraged MPs to devote most of their time and resources to constituency service at the expense of the other core functions of the legislature.

The transformation of the legislature from a group of individual MPs looking outward to their constituencies to an institution of members engaged in collective action within required the breaking or partial breaking of the system of clientele relationships that perpetuated the emphasis on constituency service. The presence of reformers who recognized the need to break the constraints of neopatrimonialism was the first step. Devising a viable strategy for actually breaking such constraints was the second and more difficult challenge. It was basically a matter of connecting the proverbial dots. The workshops organized by the IEA, and especially by the CGD, launched the process. By bringing together MPs interested in enhancing Parliament's role in policymaking and oversight, civil society provided them with a venue to brainstorm about the future.

It was at these sessions that participants first homed in on several related issues of political finance. The first was salaries, which at the time of the workshops early in 1998 were a pitiful KSh10,000 or US$154 a month (see Table 2.2). MPs could not maintain themselves in Nairobi on this amount. Nor could they maintain a home in or make regular visits back to their constituencies, visits that were essential for their political survival. Although MPs received five other allowances for a total compensation package of KSh79,033 or US$1,220 per month, most MPs were still dependent on their personal wealth, contributions from their supporters, loans from the bank, a patronage appointment, or a

Table 2.2 History of MP Emoluments per Month, 1993–2008 (in Kenyan shillings)

Emoluments	1993–1997	January–June 1998	July 1998–September 1999	October 1999–2002	2003–2007	2008–Present
Basic salary (taxable)	10,000	10,000	10,000	10,000	200,000	200,000
Car maintenance allowance					75,000	n.a.
Transport allowance (tax free)	15,000	20,000	45,000	118,000	336,000	n.a.
Extraneous allowance	—	—	—	—	30,000	n.a.
Entertainment allowance	—	—	—	—	60,000	n.a.
Housing allowance (tax free)	33,333	33,333	33,333	33,333	70,000	n.a.
Sitting allowance (tax free)[a]	3,000	3,000	3,000	3,000	5,000	n.a.
Responsibility allowance (tax free)	7,500	7,500	7,500	7,500	n.a.	n.a.
Constituency allowance	5,200	5,200	5,200	5,200	50,000	n.a.
Grand total	74,033	79,033	104,033	177,033	485,000	851,000
Monthly total in US dollars[b]	1,140	1,220	1,600	2,720	7,460	13,090
Annual total in US dollars[b]	13,680	14,640	19,200	32,640	89,520	157,080

Notes: Notwithstanding the substantial increments in basic salary, most of the increases in the total package of compensation are in the form of increasing various allowances, which account for 76 percent of all compensation.

a. In addition to the sitting allowance for attending plenary sessions of the House, members of committees receive an additional committee sitting allowance of KSh5,000 per month.

b. The rate of exchange during the period included in the table ranged from 62 to 80 Kenyan shillings (KSh) to the dollar. The rate at the end of July 2008 was US$1 = KSh65.0. The dollar equivalents indicated in this table are calculated at that rate.

n.a. = not available.

cash handout from the president to survive economically and politically. Once the reformers grasped the relationship between their low emoluments, their vulnerability to the blandishments of the executive, and their inability to spend greater time legislating and on oversight, formulating the reform agenda was relatively easy. They began with the demand to significantly raise their salaries and other emoluments. The salary issue quickly became the rallying point around which the reform agenda as a whole fell into place. The constitutional amendment to delink the National Assembly from the executive and the creation of the PSC and the Parliamentary Service are best understood in this context. The demand for greater compensation soon attracted a much broader group of MPs, those we label "opportunists," to join the coalition for change.

From that point onward until the present, MPs have been engaged in a persistent quest to raise their salaries and other allowances, especially those for transport. As indicated in Table 2.2, their base salary remained unchanged at KSh10,000 through 2002, but the total package of emoluments was raised three times during the course of the Eighth Parliament. The most dramatic increments, however, occurred soon after the beginning of the Ninth Parliament in April 2003 when the House passed the National Assembly Remuneration (Amendment) Act of 2003. The act raised the basic monthly salary for MPs to KSh200,000 and the total package to KSh485,000, that is, US$7,460 a month and over US$89,000 per year. By 2008, at the beginning of the Tenth Parliament, the total package had risen to a whopping US$13,090 per month or US$157,080 per year—second only to Nigeria on the continent, and one of the highest in the world. In addition, MPs receive a car grant of KSh3.3 million ($50,769) to purchase a new vehicle to ensure visits to their constituencies, and an interest-free loan of KSh8 million (US$123,077) to purchase a home at the beginning of their term. When they leave the House, they also receive KSh300,000 ($4,615) in severance pay for each year served.

Not surprisingly, the Kenyan press and civil society blasted the most recent raises as excessive and greedy, while MPs defend them as necessary if they are to do their work. The truth lies somewhere in between. Without adequate salaries, MPs are vulnerable to the blandishments of presidential patronage that have crippled legislatures across the continent. Indeed, one can argue that the combination of adequate salaries and the enforcement of term limits is responsible for the emergence of the Kenyan National Assembly since 2002 as an independent institution that matters. Stated simply, MPs can no longer be bought in the manner that they were a decade ago. Research on legislatures elsewhere further suggests that without adequate salaries the development of a professional legislature where members define their careers in terms of long-term service is unlikely to occur (Squire 1992). The development of a modern committee system where members become specialists in different areas of public policy and where an institutional memory is established among both members and staff is likewise contingent on adequate pay. The appropriate question for Kenya is therefore not whether MPs should be well paid, but how highly paid. Similarly, a related issue is not whether the dramatic increases in salaries have resulted in a more powerful and independent legislature vis-à-vis the executive—because they have. Rather, the question is whether these increases have resulted in better efforts by MPs to perform the defining functions of the House.

Addressing the issue of political finance. Closely related to the issue of salaries is the issue of political finance. MPs in Kenya and other countries who are elected from single-member districts must run two campaigns. The first is the continuous campaign between elections that requires members to frequently visit their districts and to deliver government-financed projects for their constituents back home. The second is the campaign for reelection, which in Kenya occurs every five years. Both cost substantial amounts of money. Interviews conducted with MPs for this chapter suggest that MPs spend between US$500 and $1,000 each time they return to their districts. Since all but a handful visit their districts at least one a month, and some do so weekly or biweekly, the total spent on returning to the constituency can total between US$6,000 and $25,000 or more per year. It is one of the principal reasons why MPs have focused on raising their allowances, particularly for transport and for a new vehicle, as part of their total package of compensation. Viewed from their perspective, the allowances are essential for both performing the function of constituency service and establishing a record that will be rewarded at the time of the next election. Many legislatures in established democracies, including the US Congress, also provide their members with similar travel allowances to visit their districts.

The cost of running for Parliament in Kenya has also been rising, perhaps because MP salaries are now high. In 2002, the cost of running for a parliamentary seat typically ran between KSh3 million and KSh5 million (i.e., between US$46,000 and $77,000). By 2007, some candidates were spending up to KSh10 million, or over US$150,000.[20] Since Kenya has yet to establish a system of publically financed campaigns, MPs must raise these sums from their own savings and/or from wealthy supporters. Kenya's political parties provide some support, but the overall weakness of most parties and the fact that they are shifting coalitions means that they are similarly weak as electoral machines. Most MPs and their challengers are consequently on their own.

It is therefore not surprising that in addition to increasing their compensation, the most significant step Kenyan MPs took to address the issue of political finance in the Ninth Parliament was their passage of the Constituency Development Fund (CDF) Act in 2003. The act requires the government to distribute 2.5 percent of the annual budget directly to each of Kenya's 210 parliamentary constituencies for the purpose of financing local development. The amount allocated to each constituency is based on a formula that accounts for population and the level of poverty as determined by the Ministry of Planning. In 2004–2005, the first year of the CDF, the average annual disbursement per constituency was the equivalent of $378,000. By 2006–2007, the third year of the CDF, the growth of the Kenyan economy coupled with improvements in revenue collection by the Kenya Revenue Authority nearly doubled the disbursements as indicated in Table 2.3.

Passage of the CDF Act occurred over the strong objections of the Kibaki administration, which resisted the idea of the legislature earmarking a fixed percentage of the national budget for a purpose over which they would have little control. However, during its first three years of operation, the CDF has proven to be enormously popular with both citizens and MPs. Both like the guaranteed disbursements for the type of small-scale rural development projects for which MPs used to lobby central government ministries. Most constituencies

Table 2.3 The Constituency Development Fund

Year	Total Annual Disbursement in Kenyan Shillings	Average Disbursement per Constituency in Kenyan Shillings	Average Disbursement in US Dollars[a]
2004–2005	5.6 billion	24,600,000	378,460
2005–2006	7.2 billion	31,500,000	484,610
2006–2007	10.0 billion	42,000,000	646,150
2007–2008 (estimated)	10.0 billion	42,000,000	n.a.

Source: Muriuki Karui, chair of CDF Committee, Kenya National Assembly, from interview on May 30, 2007.

Note: a. The rate of exchange during the period included in the table ranged from 62 to 72 Kenyan shillings (KSh) to the dollar. The rate at the end of July 2008 was US$1 = KSh65.0. The dollar equivalents indicated in this table are calculated at that rate.

n.a. = not available.

have used the funds to rehabilitate school buildings and other infrastructure, provide drugs for local health clinics, and fund projects unique to each district. While the MP nominally chairs the constituency development committee that determines the projects on which the annual allocation will be spent, he or she is not directly involved in the day-to-day operation of the fund. The CDF Act was nonetheless amended in 2007 to ensure greater accountability and transparency in the manner in which monies are spent locally.

Together with the rural roads fund, a second mechanism for ensuring central government disbursements across rural Kenya, the CDF has reduced the power of the executive vis-à-vis the National Assembly, because it eliminated the need for individual MPs to beg the center for resources and be subservient in return. Like the legislation that permits the National Assembly to set its own budget, the act is another intrusion on the authority of the Ministry of Finance to set the annual budget by itself. Notwithstanding this shift in power, the establishment of the CDF did not increase the rate of reelection of incumbents in the 2007 parliamentary elections, the first since the enactment of the act. Indeed, the rate of reelection (33.8 percent) was one of the lowest in history, perhaps a backlash against the high salaries MPs also provided for themselves during the Ninth Parliament.

Strengthening the committee system. While the Eighth Parliament established the Parliamentary Service Commission and commenced operations of eight departmental committees for the first time, their performance left much to be desired. Participation by MPs assigned to the committees was uneven, and the committees themselves were not well supported by parliamentary staff.

During the course of the Ninth Parliament, the level of performance improved. Of the eleven committees that mattered most in respect to the passage of legislation and oversight of the executive branch—the eight departmental committees, the Liaison Committee,[21] and the two "watchdog" committees (i.e., PAC and PIC)—seven or more than half were regarded by members and senior staff as "active" and "competent" compared to less than a third in the Eighth Parliament. These seven—the committees on agriculture, education, finance, health, justice, the Liaison Committee, and the Public Accounts Committee—were all distinguished by having competent and energetic chairs. Indeed, the importance of a strong and committed chair was evident from the start. Stated simply, strong chair, strong committee; weak chair, weak committee. In addition to their energy and commitment, these chairs shared the following characteristics: All but one were serving in their second or third term in the house. In other words, they were not newcomers. All but one had established some measure of political gravitas prior to assuming their positions, that is, they were respected by their peers. Three of the chairs—the chairs of the agriculture, health, and justice committees—had a professional competence in the subject area of their committee. The chairs of the seven committees were also complemented by having at least one or two members who were as committed as they were, plus some adequate staff.

To be successful, a committee must thus have a "competent core" consisting of the chair plus one or two others who share his passion, a rather low bar given that the size of a typical committee in the Kenya National Assembly was ten or eleven members. Put differently, if a third of a committee's members devote sufficient time to the work of the committee, the committee can fulfill its expected role. This also suggests that a core group of only thirty-five to forty MPs can significantly raise the performance of the House as a whole. The significance of this fact, however, has both an upside and a downside. The upside is that a modest increase in the number of dedicated MPs that are appropriately assigned to all committees can have a visible impact on the institution. The downside is that at this stage of its development, and notwithstanding significant raises in their compensation, most MPs are not participating regularly, let alone actively, in committee work. Indeed, during the last year of the Ninth Parliament, the Speaker frequently observed that the level of absenteeism from committee meetings and plenary sessions of the House was unacceptably high.

The performance of the committee system also improved as a result of better support from parliamentary staff. By the end of the Ninth Parliament, all committees had at least one assistant clerk to provide clerical and other support. Roughly half of the committees were also assigned student interns from a pool of a dozen interns selected and trained by the State University of New York aid program. The intern program, which was started in 2003, is very popular with MPs, because the university students selected are among the brightest in Kenya and are often capable of providing a level of service to members that exceeds that provided by regular staff. Unfortunately, there are not enough interns to meet the demand.[22] The success of the program, however, underscores the importance of qualified staff for improving the committee system as a whole. Over time, better staff provides committees with both specialized assistance in the policy areas with which the committees are concerned, and an institutional memory that carries over from one parliamentary term to the next. Given the high turnover of MPs, the latter is particularly important for strengthening the committee system over the long term.

The committees also benefited from an ongoing series of workshops and multiday retreats organized and funded by SUNY on a range of topics at the request of the committee chairs. Until such time as the Parliamentary Service can provide committees with the expertise they require to conduct their work, the donor community, via the appropriate mechanism, can provide such support in a stop-gap measure. The need for an expansion of staff support is also underscored by the fact that the number of departmental committees was increased from eight to fourteen during the first year of the Tenth Parliament.

Finally, it should be noted that the performance of the Public Accounts Committee improved during the Ninth Parliament, because the auditor general was eventually able to bring the audits of annual expenditures up to date. This in turn enabled the committee to call attention to the Anglo-Leasing scandal and limit the damage caused by that scam. It also underscored the fact that in the case of the "watchdog committees," their ability to perform their function is not only dependent on the Parliamentary Service, but also on staff outside the National Assembly.

Major legislation, unfinished business, assessment. The Ninth Parliament also performed better than the Eighth with respect to the passage of major legislation. Space does not permit a discussion of these acts, but the range of topics addressed by the National Assembly can be appreciated from a review of Table 2.4. In addition to this legislation, several important bills did not secure passage in the Ninth Parliament but were subsequently passed during the first year of the Tenth (2008–2012). These include the major revisions to the Standing Orders, and the Fiscal Management Bill. Both increase the capacity and authority of the legislature vis-à-vis the executive.

A summary analysis of the bills introduced and passed by the Ninth Parliament (Table 2.5) reveals some familiar yet interesting patterns compared to other legislatures around the world. The first, as in most legislatures worldwide (Loewenberg and Patterson 1979, 60–62), is that the overwhelming preponderance of legislation (in this case, nearly 80 percent of all bills introduced) is proposed by the government. The percentage of government bills introduced and passed by the government is more than double that of those introduced and passed by individual members. However, closer scrutiny of the legislation introduced and passed by the government indicates that more than half are

Table 2.4 Major Legislation Passed by the Ninth Parliament

2003	The Anti-Corruption and Economic Crimes Bill
	Public Officer Ethics Bill
	National Commission and Gender Development Bill
	National Assembly Remuneration (Amendment) Bill
	Persons with Disabilities Bill
	Constituency Development Fund Bill
	Presidential Retirement Benefits Bill
	Public Audit Bill
2004	Government Financial Management Bill
	Investment Promotion Bill
2006	Cotton (Amendment) Bill (PM)
	National Museum and Heritage Bill
	Kenya Maritime Authority Bill
	Sexual Offenses Bill (PM)
	Statistics Bill
	Micro Finance Bill
2007	Political Parties Bill
	Supplies Practitioners Management Bill (PM)
	Nutritionists and Dieticians Bill (PM)
	Employment Bill
	Labour Institutions Bill
	Occupational Safety Bill
	Work Injury Benefits Bill
	Tobacco Control Bill
	Kenya Roads Board Bill

Note: Table excludes all finance and appropriations bills, and most amendment bills. PM = private member's bill.

appropriations bills or amendments to prior legislation. When one excludes these measures, the percentage of government bills that proposed new legislation and passed the House dropped to 30. While this figure must be treated with some caution, it is still clear that the National Assembly is no longer a rubber stamp. The output of the Ninth Parliament was also relatively modest: only fifty-one laws passed in five years, of which twenty-five were finance bills or amendments to prior legislation.

In sum, the Ninth Parliament was a significant continuation of what had become a decade-plus effort to build the legislature's capacity to perform its core functions and expand its authority vis-à-vis the executive branch. Building on its accomplishments in the Eighth Parliament, the coalition for change dramatically increased members' salaries and established the popular Constituency Development Fund—two moves that freed MPs from their prior dependence on presidential patronage. The reformers also made real progress in expanding the role and capacity of the committee system, especially the operations of the

Table 2.5 Summary Analysis of Bills Introduced and Passed by the Ninth Parliament

Total number of bills introduced	123
Number of government bills introduced	97
Number of private member's bills introduced	26
Percentage of all bills introduced that were government bills	78.9
Percentage of all bills introduced that were private member's bills	21.1
Total number of bills passed and signed into law	51
Percentage of all bills that were passed and became law	41.5
Number of government bills passed and signed into law	46
Percentage of government bills passed and signed into law	47.4
Number of private member's bills passed and signed into law	5
Percentage of private member's bills passed and signed into law	19.2
Number of government bills that were finance and appropriations bills	9
Number of government finance and appropriations bills passed into law	9
Percentage of all government bills *excluding* finance and appropriations bills that were passed and signed into law	42.0
Number of government bills that were amendment bills	15
Number of government amendment bills passed into law	15
Percentage of all government bills *excluding* finance, appropriations, and amendment bills passed into law	30.0

departmental or "portfolio" committees that shadow government ministries. Important initiatives such as the intern program were launched that enhanced the Parliamentary Service. The physical infrastructure of the House was vastly improved, though at great cost.

Notwithstanding these accomplishments and a radically improved structure of incentives they created for individual MPs, the volume of legislative output was modest, and absenteeism became a major problem toward the end of the parliamentary term. While this can be partly explained by the breakup of the NARC coalition government in November 2005, and by the run-up to national elections held in December 2007, it is clear that changing incentives did not motivate all MPs to devote more time to legislating and oversight. Many responded to the new incentives, but many did not. However, the experience of the Ninth Parliament demonstrates that when a small group of legislators becomes seriously engaged in the core functions of the legislature, the level of institutional performance improves.

The Tenth Parliament (2008–2012)

The presidential and parliamentary elections held on December 27, 2007, resulted in a political crisis that shook the confidence of Kenyans and their political establishment. Notwithstanding the enormous progress achieved during the first five years of the post-Moi era, Kenya became polarized along ethnic lines. Kibaki's NARC coalition split into two factions early in his term—one led by himself and his closest associates from the Kikuyu and Meru communities who reside in Central Province and parts of Eastern Province, the other led by Raila Odinga, a Luo from western Kenya who emerged as the head of a panethnic alliance opposed to what its members regarded as Kikuyu domination. By the end of 2005, Odinga organized the Orange Democratic Movement (ODM) to defeat a new constitution proposed by Kibaki in a national referendum held to adopt the document. In the aftermath of what was a stinging defeat, Kibaki dropped Odinga and his associates from the cabinet, while they began a campaign to defeat Kibaki in the next presidential election.

During the run-up to the 2007 presidential elections, Kenyans became sharply divided into two ethnic coalitions that were nearly equal in size and that rallied around their respective candidates. Kibaki campaigned for reelection as the leader of a new party, the Party of National Unity (PNU), while Odinga campaigned as the leader of the ODM. Public opinion surveys taken before the election indicated that the race would be very close, but Odinga led by large margins in the actual vote count forty-four hours after the polls closed.[23] However, three days after the elections and following a suspension in its reporting of the vote, the Electoral Commission of Kenya announced that Kibaki had won. Odinga and the ODM immediately claimed that the electoral commission, a body packed by Kibaki appointees, had stolen the election. Domestic and international observer organizations also questioned the results. In a spasm of spontaneous (but also organized) violence, ODM supporters attacked PNU supporters, especially Kikuyu, across Kenya. Within a week Kikuyu gangs retaliated by attacking supporters of the ODM, particularly Luos and Kalenjins. By mid-January 2008, Kenya was on the brink of civil war. An estimated 1,500 Kenyans lost their lives. More than 300,000 (mostly Kikuyu residing in the western third of the country) were chased from their homes and took refuge in special camps established by the Red Cross for internally displaced persons.

Peace was eventually restored on February 28 when both sides agreed to a power-sharing deal that recognized Kibaki as president, but forced him to accept Odinga as an executive prime minister with substantial authority for running the government. Known as "the Grand Coalition Government," the deal also resulted in a huge cabinet of forty ministers and fifty-four assistant ministers (42 percent of all MPs) to accommodate all factions on both sides.

While the elections resulted in ambiguous results at the presidential level, they produced a clear victory for the ODM in the National Assembly. The party won 99 seats compared to 43 for Kibaki's PNU, and 14 for what remained of KANU. A breakaway faction of ODM, ODM-K led by Kalonzo Musyoka who Kibaki appointed as his vice president before the power-sharing deal, won 16 seats with the remaining 38 scattered amongst minor parties. Following the allocation of the 12 nominated members, ODM had 105 of the 222-member assembly, while PNU had 46.

The impact of the ODM parliamentary victory was immediate. In a close contest for Speaker, Francis ole Kaparo, the long-time incumbent, was defeated for reelection by Kenneth Marende, a second-term ODM member, by one vote. The Clerk during the Eighth and Ninth Parliaments, Samuel Ndindiri, was also replaced. Subservient to Kaparo, he had become very ill during the final year of the Ninth Parliament and was on medical leave at the time of his death in April 2008. He was replaced by Patrick Gichohi, the Chief Deputy Clerk, who had been supportive of Aringo and the other reformers in the Ninth Parliament. Together, Marende and Gichohi bring new leadership that is likely to encourage rather than frustrate further efforts to build capacity in the National Assembly. Both are publically committed to reform. Both have a better rapport with the donor community than their predecessors.

They also face a new House as the 2007 elections produced a higher than average turnover of members than previous elections. Whereas slightly less than half of the members of the Eighth Parliament were reelected to the Ninth, only 33.8 percent of the Ninth were returned to the Tenth. The result is that 64.3 percent of the members of the Tenth are serving their first term (see Table 2.1). The membership of the Tenth is slightly younger than the Ninth and significantly better educated. Nearly 85 percent of all MPs are now college graduates, probably the highest in Africa. A new and better educated political generation is in the process of taking over the institution, the impact of which will not be known until the end of the parliamentary term.

The high turnover of the election followed by the appointment of an unusually large cabinet also means that few of the leading reformers in the Eighth and Ninth Parliaments, including Peter Oloo Aringo, Joseph Lagat, Paul Muite, or Peter Anyang Nyongo, remain in the House.[24] The record of Parliament during its first seven months in office, however, suggests that the members of the new legislature are as committed to enhancing and asserting the authority of their institution as were the members of the old. Several early indicators point in this direction.

First, in response to the formation of the "Grand Coalition Government," many MPs are worried that Kenya may be slipping back into a period of de facto one-party rule similar to what occurred after KANU and KADU merged in 1964. While this is unlikely, backbenchers from all parties have been in discussions to form a "Grand Coalition Opposition" to check what they see as the possibility of an unaccountable executive.

Second, and arguably more important, the Speaker and the members of the Tenth Parliament have moved to complete the unfinished business of the Ninth. This includes the revision of the Standing Orders and the passage of the Fiscal Management Bill. Under the power-sharing agreement of February 28, 2008, Parliament is also expected to play a major role in a renewed effort to draft a new constitution, a draft that will further expand the legislature's role in the governance of Kenya. Third, early indications suggest that the Tenth Parliament will be vigorous in fulfilling its oversight function.

Passed and pending legislation. The revision of the Standing Orders has long been an objective of the reformers that began in the Ninth Parliament to raise the performance of the House. Their demands for revision followed their realization that the establishment of the Parliamentary Service Commission alone would not result in a sustained effort to build capacity within the House. The then Speaker, Francis ole Kaparo, was not a strong supporter of the reform agenda and frustrated Peter Oloo Aringo in his role as chair of the commission. Indeed, the establishment of the Liaison Committee to facilitate the development of the committee system was a device to circumvent the Speaker. As discussed previously, the Speaker resisted early discussions about reform because of his close ties with then president Daniel arap Moi. He was also wary about strengthening the committee system, because the rise of committees would eventually erode his power over the House. By contrast, Kaparo sought, and in some ways succeeded in gaining, the support of the reformers and all members by providing the House with first-class infrastructure.

The revision of the Standing Orders was viewed by the reformers, particularly Aringo, as a way of transforming the role of the Speaker from a chief executive officer of the National Assembly as a whole to the regulator of parliamentary debates within the legislative chamber. The process of rewriting the Orders began in 2006 but was immediately stalled by Kaparo, who, in his capacity as chair of the Committee on Standing Orders, was not about to preside over his own demise. However, a special subcommittee of the Standing Orders Committee headed by the then Deputy Speaker, David Musila, was established to revise the Orders, another move to circumvent the Speaker. The subcommittee worked hard and eventually produced several drafts, but none were adopted by the House as a whole before the Ninth Parliament came to the end of its term.

Negotiations over the revisions of the Standing Orders were thus carried over to the Tenth where the new Speaker, Kenneth Marende, who had run against Kaparo as a reformer, supported the effort. A final draft was published in July 2008 and adopted by the Parliament in September. Its provisions will transform the operations of the House in several ways that enhance the capacity of the National Assembly and address some of its weaknesses, most notably rising absenteeism. A summary of the most important changes are as follows:

- There will be a prime minister's question time between 3:00 and 3:45 every Wednesday. All questions posed to the prime minister and other ministers must be answered. Failure to answer questions will incur sanctions as stipulated in the Standing Orders.
- The number of departmental or "portfolio" committees will be raised from eight to fourteen, thereby increasing the legislative division of labor amongst MPs. Committee proceedings will now be open to the public. Committees will be required to submit quarterly reports to the

House as a whole. Members of committees who miss four consecutive meetings of the committee will be removed. Put simply, committees that do not perform will be put in the public spotlight.
- The role of Parliament in the budget process has been radically transformed. All budget estimates submitted by the minister of finance to Parliament will henceforth be scrutinized by the departmental committees.
- The procedure for the introduction and consideration of private member's bills has been shortened and simplified, which should enhance the input by backbenchers.
- The discretionary powers of the House Business Committee—which is dominated by the Speaker and members of the executive—on scheduling debates has been reduced.
- The House as a whole will sit for an additional four hours per week and allow for parallel sittings by the plenary and individual committees.

In addition to these measures, the new Speaker and leadership of the House have obtained a commitment from USAID to install broadcasting facilities at Parliament. Radio broadcasts of plenary sessions were scheduled to begin by the end of 2008 with television to follow.

The Fiscal Management Act is the second major piece of legislation carried over from the Ninth to the Tenth Parliament. Its purpose is to provide a vastly expanded role for Parliament in the budgetary process, and it was originally submitted by Aringo as a private member's bill in 2007. Up to that time, responsibility for the annual budget rested solely with the executive, particularly the Ministry of Finance. But as noted earlier in this chapter, Parliament had begun to intrude on the ministry's authority with the passage of the Parliamentary Service Act in 2000 and the Constituency Development Fund Act in 2003. The response by the then minister of finance, Amos Kimunya, was predictable. Although he supported the expansion of Parliament's role in the budgetary process when he was a member of the opposition in the Eighth Parliament, he now resisted the proposal.

The act has four principal components. (1) A Budget Committee will be established in Parliament to monitor the budget and the budgetary process. (2) The minister of finance will henceforth follow a new set of procedures when formulating the annual budget estimates and presenting them to the House. Whereas previously the minister presented the budget estimates each June in the form of a budget bill that Parliament was expected to pass after a perfunctory debate, the new law required the minister to present a Budget Policy Statement (BPS) and a draft of the annual estimates no later than March 21. The purpose of the BPS is to lay out the government's budget strategy and macroeconomic policy while the draft estimates provide the details. A review of both documents will then be undertaken by Parliament coordinated by the Budget Committee. The review will begin by apportioning the relevant parts of the BPS and the estimates to each of the departmental committees. After reviewing these documents, the departmental committees will submit a series of reports to the Budget Committee. The Budget Committee will then harmonize the committee reports, including any recommended changes in expenditures, and forward Parliament's response back to the minister. The minister is then expected to prepare the final budget based on the review. These procedures are similar to those adopted by the Uganda National Assembly in 2001 and were in part inspired by that example. A discussion of the Uganda Budget Act follows in Chapter 3.

(3) The minister of finance will prepare a continuous series of quarterly compliance reports for the National Assembly that indicate the extent to which the objectives of the budget are being met. (4) Parliament will establish an Office of Fiscal Analysis, aka the Parliamentary Budget Office, whose mandate will be similar to the Congressional Budget Office of the US Congress. The Parliamentary Budget Office will assist MPs and various committees to understand the economic ramifications of the annual budget as well as the financial ramifications of any other legislation and proposed legislation before the House.

Although the Fiscal Management Act did not secure passage before the end of the Ninth Parliament, the National Assembly did establish the Office of Fiscal Analysis, its first step to build an internal analytic capacity to understand complex economic issues. Until now, the House has been dependent on input from civil society and think tanks such as the IEA, the Institute of Certified Public Accounts, and others. Moreover, parts of the act such as the requirement that the budget estimates be reviewed by the appropriate departmental committee have already been included in the new Standing Orders. The Fiscal Management Bill was passed by the National Assembly in December 2008, but President Kibaki had yet to formally assent to the act before the year ended. The president and the Ministry of Finance still wanted to limit Parliament's role in budget matters but realized that some form of legislation is inevitable. Once in force, the act will mark a sea change in the budgetary process.

Sustaining oversight. Just as the Public Accounts Committee flexed its muscles in uncovering the Anglo-Leasing scandal in 2004, the present committee has probed the irregular sale of the Grand Regency Hotel by the government in 2008. The hotel, which is a multimillion dollar facility in downtown Nairobi, was originally seized by the Kenya government as part of the assets owned by Kamlesh Pattni, a Kenyan businessman involved in the Goldenberg scandal of the early 1990s. The government stated that it would conduct a transparent sale of the hotel based on the required process of competitive bidding. However, the rapid sale to investors from Libya sparked a probe by the PAC, which concluded that the minister of finance had violated the rules. Minister Kimunya, a close associate of Kibaki, was then the subject of a vote of no-confidence in June 2008. Most ODM MPs voted for the measure, and Kimunya was eventually forced to resign. The entire affair was covered in depth by the Kenya press. As in the Anglo-Leasing case, the combination of the PAC and the press was effective in enabling the National Assembly to perform its oversight role.

A new constitution for Kenya? In the aftermath of the crisis that followed the 2007 elections, Parliament moved quickly to amend the constitution of Kenya to establish the office of executive prime minister as required by the agreement of February 28, 2008. The agreement also requires Kibaki and Odinga and their respective allies to agree on a new constitution, something that has eluded Kenya's political leadership since 1992. To this end, the National Assembly must amend the current Constitution of Kenya Review Act to jump-start the process, a revision that had not occurred by July 2009. Even more important is the emerging consensus on a series of provisions that are very likely to be included in the new basic law. These include the repeal or elimination of Articles 58 and 59 of the present constitution that permit the president to suspend or prorogue Parliament. Future parliaments will be elected for a fixed term of five years. The office of prime minister is also likely to be continued under any new document, raising the possibility that some measure of power-sharing between the president and the prime minister will become a permanent fixture of Kenyan political life. Parliament's role in the appointment of senior officials in the civil service, the military, and the diplomatic corps is likely to be expanded by requiring the legislature's confirmation of such appointments. The National Assembly is also likely to acquire the formal power to ratify all future loan agreements between the government of Kenya and organizations such as the World Bank and International Monetary Fund.

Conclusion

The Kenya National Assembly at the beginning of the Tenth Parliament was a very different institution than it was at the beginning of the Seventh Parliament, and its transformation suggests several generic lessons that are explored elsewhere in this volume. Having examined the long and tortuous process that has led the National Assembly to where it is today, four final comments are in order.

The first is that the experience of the Kenya National Assembly suggests that legislative development in the context of emerging African democracies is a process of continuous struggle. No African president, even those committed to democratic governance, wants to give up power to the legislative branch. The point is illustrated in one form or another in all of the remaining cases considered in this volume. Similarly, presiding officers who exercise considerable power within the legislature are usually less than enthusiastic about reforms, including the strengthening of the committee system, when such a development reduces their power. Reformers who seek to build the capacity of the legislature to enable it to perform all of its core functions do not have an easy time because their agenda takes power away from those who hold it when the legislature is weak. Indeed, this is the principal political challenge reformers face.

Second, because it is a political struggle, capacity-building in the legislature to the point that the institution can perform all of its core functions takes time. Reforms are conceived and put into place incrementally over periods of more than a decade, and only after democratic space has been opened and competitive politics returned. The initial results are also likely to be both significant and modest. In the case of Kenya, the reformers have achieved much in terms of building their institution and changing the structure of incentives facing MPs. However, in terms of actual legislative output, that is, major bills passed and signed into law, the full payoffs from the reform process have yet to be reaped. The development of the Kenya National Assembly is well advanced, but it is still a work in progress.

Third, the process of reform for the development of the legislature is usually led by a small core of highly motivated individuals who ultimately lose their seats because of their efforts. The most skilled reformers are often able to organize a broader coalition for change that embraces both themselves and opportunists who vote for reforms such as raises in pay, but who then retreat to the sidelines. There is good news and bad news in this mixed assessment. Only a small group of reformers, between 10 and 15 percent of the legislature, is needed to drive the process and achieve significant gains. And while it would appear that the attrition level among reformers is as high or higher than for the legislature as a whole, the group is reduced but partially replaced by each electoral cycle. However, as the legislature builds more capacity over time, the need is not for more reform, but how to persuade more legislators to take advantage of the opportunities created by the reforms that have been put into place.

Finally, although we have argued in Chapter 1 and in this chapter that the development of the legislature is most likely to occur when there is a coalition for change within the legislature, our examination so far has not yet addressed the question of why such coalitions emerge and succeed in some African democracies, but not in all. Our answer, in the form of a hypothesis drawn from the Kenyan experience, is that coalitions for change are most likely to emerge where civil society, including the press, is large and robust. As discussed earlier in this chapter, the relationship between the legislature and civil society in Kenya is symbiotic. The legislature is most likely to build capacity where civil society steps forward to both pressure and encourage MPs to develop their institution. However, the legislature is less likely to respond to civil society's exhortations unless civil society has real political clout, including the ability to mobilize followers in the countryside. That is why the Kenya National Assembly has arguably proceeded further at parliamentary reform than its counterpart in Uganda. Over the past quarter century, Kenya's large urban population and developed countryside have given rise to an expanded and diverse civil society that limits the practice of clientelist politics and especially neopatrimonial rule. Although it still tries, the ability of the executive to buy off the legislature and retard reform is much less than a decade ago. With the exception of South Africa, this is not, unfortunately, the situation in the other countries considered in this volume. We shall return to this hypothesis in Chapter 8.

Notes

1. At the height of its numbers just prior to 1963, there were 60,000 Europeans living in Kenya. European migration to Kenya began at the beginning of the twentieth century, but reached its peak in the period immediately after World War II. Until the late 1950s, Kenya's political, economic, and social structures resembled those of South Africa and Southern Rhodesia (i.e., Zimbabwe), a pattern very different from the practice in Britain's other major African colonies including Ghana and Nigeria.

2. With the exception of Southern Rhodesia, all of Britain's African colonies gained independence by 1968.

3. Democratization and democracy promotion became a key plank in the foreign policies of the United States, the United Kingdom, Canada, Germany, the Scandinavian countries, and the Netherlands. The effort in Kenya was led by the US and German ambassadors in an unusual campaign of public diplomacy.

4. The Consultative Group (CG) for Kenya and other countries consists of both bilateral and multilateral donors such as the World Bank that provide development assistance and is an informal forum to facilitate a common donor position. Because the World Bank is forbidden by its bylaws to condition assistance on political criteria, the decision to suspend aid was not explicitly conditioned on the relegalization of multiparty politics. However, the United States, the United Kingdom, Canada, and the Scandinavian countries all viewed this step followed by the holding of multiparty elections as the basis for the resumption of aid.

5. The Speaker and the attorney-general are also members, but serve on an ex officio (i.e., nonvoting) basis.

6. In 1992, President Moi won 36 percent of the popular vote, and in 1997 he won 40 percent. At the parliamentary level, KANU won 30 percent of the vote in 1992 and 38 percent in 1997.

7. We are unable to state with precision the extent to which the number of MPs appointed to executive positions has increased in all six of the countries considered in this book, but the number has certainly not diminished.

8. Although there were several prominent newcomers, most opposition MPs in the Seventh Parliament had been members of KANU during the one-party era.

9. Beginning with the 1992 multiparty election, USAID became highly involved in promoting Kenya's transition to democracy. Once the election was over, however, the agency realized that it needed to diversify its interventions beyond elections to sustain the process. USAID tried and failed to provide assistance to the Seventh Parliament, with the result that it turned increasingly to supporting an array of civil society organizations. Other Western bilateral donors that were committed to supporting the transition, especially Denmark, Sweden, and the Netherlands, did likewise, as did several foundations, including the Ford Foundation, the Friedrich Ebert Foundation, and the Friedrich Naumann Foundation.

10. During the 1980s, Aringo had gained some notoriety by addressing Moi at formal occasions as "Your Excellency, the Prince of Peace."

11. The clerk and deputy clerks, the sergeant-at-arms, accountants, and IT specialists.

12. The Standing Orders had been last revised in 1997 at the end of the Seventh Parliament and provided for the establishment of departmental committees. However, the assembly had yet to take advantage of this opportunity by actually constituting the committees.

13. Moi had been president for fourteen years and more than two elected terms when the constitution was amended in 1992 to allow for the resumption of multiparty politics. At that time, the constitution was also amended to require the direct election of the president for a maximum of two terms.

14. Kibaki was hospitalized as a result of an auto accident a month before the 2002 elections, and suffered a stroke, perhaps two, in the period immediately after his inauguration in January 2003.

15. Following the suspension of aid by Kenya's donors in November 1991, the country went through a decade of continuous ups and downs in its relationship with the donors. Aid was restored and suspended on three subsequent occasions as Moi never lived up to promises made to carry through on needed macroeconomic reforms and political reforms.

16. Kenya's score on the political rights scale dropped slightly to 4 for 2007 following the flawed election of that year.

17. The minister of finance, the minister of justice and constitutional affairs, and the minister of internal security in the Office of the President.

18. It is alleged that the Anglo-Leasing scandal could have cost the government as much as $800 million, but that the real loss was much lower, approximately $130 million.

19. Aringo was nominated by the Liberal Democratic Party, the partner party with Kibaki's coalition in the NARC coalition.

20. These estimates are based on MP responses to interviews conducted for this study. There was, however, considerable variance among the answers. MPs from urban constituencies or constituencies with high population densities located closer to Nairobi or in other relatively prosperous areas of the country reported spending the most, while MPs from remote areas, particularly across Kenya's north, reported spending as little as US$10,000 to $15,000. The trend of campaign expenditures, however, as in the United States has been steadily upward from one election to the next, especially after the resumption of multiparty politics.

21. The Liaison Committee is composed of the chairs of all the other committees and chaired by the Deputy Speaker. Its role is to coordinate and facilitate the work of the committee system as a whole.

22. The intern program was started with the hope that it would eventually provide a steady flow of new recruits into the Parliamentary Service. However, only about a third of those who have passed through the program have stayed on as employees at the National Assembly. Given their competence and energy, it is not surprising some members of the Parliamentary Service have resisted the idea that graduates of the intern program be given priority for future employment.

23. Odinga's lead at 2:00 P.M. on Saturday, December 29, as reported by all three television networks based on returns from the Electoral Commission of Kenya, was 380,000 votes, an insurmountable lead in the view of many knowledgeable observers.

24. Aringo who served as the vice chair of the Parliamentary Service Commission, Lagat who served as chair of the Finance Committee, and Muite who served as the chair of the Justice and Legal Affairs Committee all went down to defeat while Nyongo became minister of health services in the new government.

3

The Rise and Ebb of Uganda's No-Party Parliament

Nelson Kasfir and Stephen Hippo Twebaze

Uganda's unique approach to democratization through its short-lived no-party political system resulted in a surprisingly independent and frequently effective legislature. When Uganda returned to civilian rule in 1986 after two turbulent decades of authoritarian rule and civil war, the National Resistance Army (NRA), which had overthrown the previous military regime through a guerrilla insurgency, established a new political system by giving primacy to its National Resistance Movement (NRM). The Movement introduced democracy without parties, the "Movement system," to Uganda in order to avoid slipping back into the divisive and destructive politics of the country's two previous attempts at multiparty rule. NRM leaders, especially Uganda's new president, Yoweri K. Museveni, argued that a return to multiparty politics would again exacerbate the country's ethnic divisions and plunge Uganda back into turmoil. Thus, they proposed a political system without parties, but with free and competitive elections for president and Parliament, contested by individuals whom voters would judge on "individual merit."[1]

The expectations for the development of the legislature in this context were unclear. In 1986, the NRM simply appointed all legislators. In 1989, most legislators were elected indirectly. In 1994, delegates to a Constituent Assembly were directly elected to deliberate a draft of a new constitution for Uganda. The 1995 Constitution reaffirmed that Uganda would be a democratic state under the Movement system but provided for the possibility of changing to a conventional multiparty system. Elections for a new national legislature were held in 1996, Uganda's first directly elected legislature since the NRM assumed power. The elections of 1996 and 2001, and the Sixth and Seventh Parliaments they produced, operated under the Movement system of government. During the run-up to the elections of 2006, Uganda changed its system to conventional multiparty contestation.

A surprising number of academic inquiries have explored aspects of Uganda's parliament during the decade in which it operated under its new constitution and without parties. Useful studies have analyzed the introduction of stronger constitutional powers and the operation of the no-party system on parliament (Carbone 2008; Kazoora 2005; Kayunga 2001; Olum 2002). Valuable work has also considered candidate selection, electoral campaigns, relations with constituents, female MPs, and the effect of gender on relations among MPs (Carbone 2008; Kayunga 2001; Sabiti-Makara, Tukahebwa, and Byarugaba 2003; Tamale 1999; Tripp 2006). In addition, the report of the Constitutional Commission (Uganda Constitutional Commission 1993) provides rationales for many of the provisions of the 1995 Constitution.[2]

Substantive development of the legislature during the Sixth (1996–2001) and Seventh (2001–2006) Parliaments is surprising, because Uganda's post-independence history, marked by mass violence, coups d'etat, and war, would seem to favor executive dominance. In particular, the military victory that made Uganda's return to democracy possible gave the president extraordinary political influence. Patronage, always significant in Ugandan politics, further strengthened his hand, as it has every Ugandan president. The prohibition on participation by parties in the Movement system of governance also appeared to give a significant advantage to the executive.

Yet the legislature created by the 1995 Constitution confronted the executive frequently, created an impressive statutory basis for its autonomy, and played an active role in making law, shaping budgets, and overseeing executive action. Not only were the Sixth and Seventh Parliaments far more significant actors than all previous Ugandan legislatures, their assertions of autonomy and challenges to the executive compared favorably in several respects with assemblies in African countries with a less checkered past—including those discussed in this book.[3]

Nevertheless, the Ugandan Parliament's role changed during its first decade. The 1995 Constitution gave the Ugandan Parliament an independent role, more powerful in principle than any of its predecessors. While the two parliaments elected under this constitution took surprising initiatives, their institutional development was uneven and limited. From its high-profile initiatives, the Sixth Parliament, elected in 1996, emerged as a significant political actor, shaping legislation and holding the executive accountable, particularly for acts of corruption. But its actions aroused the anger of the executive, especially President Museveni, who actively intervened in parliamentary business and campaigned against many of its leading activists in the 2001 parliamentary elections, defeating some and chastening others.

The Seventh Parliament maintained a lower profile and made fewer efforts to curb the executive. Those who disagreed with the president were less successful in passing legislation than their counterparts in the Sixth. In particular, opponents of Museveni's plan to repeal the constitutional prohibition on a third presidential term were unable to stop him. Yet, a close examination of Parliament's handling of routine legislation and the budget, particularly in committees, shows that the Seventh persuaded the executive to modify many of its policies, even while Parliament conceded contentious issues to the president. Although far less noticed, legislative-executive cooperation on nonconfrontational policies, particularly during the committee stage, steadily became more firmly established. Both parliaments, despite their differences, demonstrated legislative autonomy and participation in governance unprecedented in Ugandan history.

How did Parliament manage to overcome, if only unevenly and to a limited degree, the tilt toward executive dominance that emerged from the fervent desire to avoid returning to Uganda's past violence, from Museveni's military victory, and from the irresistible attractions of political patronage? After reviewing the historical development of the forces that made executive dominance so powerful in the past, we provide a brief narrative of struggles in the Sixth and Seventh Parliaments to expand legislative powers and the executive's effort to constrain them. We then assess the impact of the reformers, their new constitutional opportunities, the infusion of new resources, the absence of parties, and the uses of patronage in a poor society on the development of the legislature by showing how they led to six institutional outcomes. Four of these outcomes help explain the rise of Parliament, and two suggest why it ebbed, although not to its former level of subordination.

First, the provision of constitutional powers and the willingness of reformers to deploy them immediately enabled Parliament to countervail the executive frequently and effectively. Second, the new constitutional powers led to a committee system that enabled reformers with the support of other MPs unconstrained by parties to expand Parliament's legislative independence and effectiveness significantly. Third, donor and government investments resulted in an expansion of institutional resources that enabled MPs to act more effectively in opposing the executive. Fourth, the absence of party discipline under the Movement system during the Sixth and Seventh Parliaments empowered reformers and other MPs to mobilize issue-based coalitions that challenged the executive effectively.

On the other hand, we argue that both the absence of party discipline and the far greater resources available to the executive eventually also enabled MPs supporting the government to build coalitions that weakened reformers committed to building legislative independence and autonomy. Lastly, the monetary burdens of electoral campaigns and constituency service made MPs vulnerable to patronage from the executive, which limited their willingness to maintain Parliament's independence. In exploring these outcomes, we call attention to the powerful and constant pull of patronage that limits the extent to which institutional change can expand legislative autonomy and effectiveness. We end this chapter by speculating how much of Parliament's independence will survive during the Eighth Parliament in which the restoration of multiparty competition resulted in a large majority of MPs supporting the president's party.

Patronage, the Democratic Opening, and Legislative Subordination

Since independence, rulers in Uganda, as in most other poor and predominantly agrarian African states, constructed patronage networks to maintain themselves in office. The more difficult it was for rulers to aggregate supporters on the basis of issues or ideologies, the more likely they were to rely on patronage as a central tool for governance. While states like Kenya, Benin, and Ghana were also governed through these networks, the pressures for patronage in Uganda were arguably greater. Uganda is one of the least urbanized African states, with only 12 percent of its population living in officially designated cities, municipalities, and towns (Uganda Bureau of Statistics 2002, 9). Its economy was largely constructed through state investment and control. Since the colonial period, its politics have depended on amalgamating highly fragmented local loyalties, usually through political notables.

Each Ugandan civilian regime began by attempting to assemble a broad voluntary alliance, but soon resorted to a mixture of patronage and coercion under a veneer of democratic rationales (Jorgensen 1981; Kasozi 1994). As governments failed to rule legitimately, trust among Ugandans steadily fell, leaving each successor government with a more daunting task (Kasfir 1999, 23–26). The economy grew weaker, shrinking the patronage base, which made it harder for rulers to maintain control over their clients. The result was increased violence, several state-orchestrated massacres, and two wars. When the NRA marched into Kampala in 1986, it found a failed state. No wonder the 1995 Constitution begins by "recalling our history which has been characterized by political and constitutional instability" (Uganda 1995, Preamble).

Uganda's democratic opening began with the NRA's military victory and the establishment of the NRM "no-party" regime. While the NRA/M had been committed to democracy throughout the guerrilla war, it took power with limited popular support in the parts of the country where it had not fought. In addition, it had no track record as a political organization. In a masterstroke, it used the enthusiasm for its victory to justify the nationwide adoption of the democratic local councils that it had invented during the guerrilla war to govern areas under NRA control. These councils became the basis for launching its no-party system.

To understand how independent Parliament became under the 1995 Constitution, it is useful to recognize how subordinate to the executive each predecessor legislature had been. Until Idi Amin's 1971 coup d'etat dissolved the

National Assembly, it had been organized on the Westminster model with the leader of the party or coalition holding a majority of seats serving as president (at independence, as prime minister). Despite the doctrine of parliamentary supremacy, no one could question the dominance of the executive—especially after Milton Obote, Uganda's first executive leader, summarily insisted in 1966 that MPs replace the independence constitution with a new one they had not even read.[4] As a current minister conceded, "Parliament was never the same again" (interview, July 1, 2005). The 1967 Constitution deepened legislative subordination by giving the president unrestrained authority to dissolve the National Assembly and make law when it was in recess (Uganda Constitutional Commission 1993, 289).

Following the overthrow of Idi Amin in 1979, an unelected National Consultative Council served as the legislature for a transitional period of almost two years. When the Uganda People's Congress won the flawed parliamentary elections in 1980,[5] its leader, Milton Obote, returned as president for a second time but was again removed by a coup in 1985. The National Assembly was an even more subordinate body during the second Obote period. An official serving then characterized it as simply "a department of government" (interview, July 6, 2005). Following its military victory in 1986, the NRA simply made the National Resistance Council (NRC), which had been its legislative organ during the guerrilla war, the national legislature. There was no separation of powers. It was an appointed "Parliament within the NRM, with the president as its chair" (interview, July 6, 2005). In 1989, it added more MPs through indirect, open-ballot no-party elections. By comparison with later parliaments, a minister who served in the NRC regarded it "as more homogeneous and less political. We'd discuss an issue in closed session for two or even three days until we resolved it" (interview, July 1, 2005).

The 1995 Constitution opened political space to participants from the old political parties and from the NRM. The overriding principle of its authors was to secure democracy by introducing safeguards to prevent another return to one-man rule. However, the NRM leadership also insisted on constitutional provisions that extended its control over government. Consequently, the 1995 Constitution contained somewhat contradictory features. It replaced the former parliamentary system with a hybrid presidential system based on the separation of powers and reinforced by several checks and balances that strengthened the authority of Parliament and the judiciary at the expense of the powers that had been available to the president in the 1967 Constitution. But it also introduced the Movement, or no-party, system that made it impossible for parties to contest for power. The commissioners' rationale for vastly increasing legislative powers was that "by constantly scrutinizing the plans, policies and performance of the executive, the legislature tries to make sure the executive serves the people effectively" (Uganda Constitutional Commission 1993, 285). The drafters intended a Parliament that could successfully challenge the president and his policies. But it would have to do so without relying on parties to organize its opposition—uncharted waters that brought both reward and peril.

The NRM's promise to restore democracy made during its guerrilla war heralded a fresh start but begged the central question: Could Ugandans design democratic institutions able to control the intersecting ethnic, religious, and regional cleavages that had caused unusual fragmentation in the past? In particular, could they create a legislature sufficiently insulated against the attractions of patronage that it would effectively challenge executive dominance? The task they faced was part of Uganda's basic political dilemma. All previous presidents had found it necessary to resort to patronage (and coercion) in order to govern. Yet, the more the legislature (and other institutions) countervailed the executive, the more difficult it would become for the president to build a patronage-based coalition to secure his rule.

Much of the struggle between Parliament and president during the decade following the adoption of the 1995 Constitution reflected this dilemma. MPs used their new and unprecedented constitutional powers to modify or reject government bills and to censure ministers, criticize policies of the executive, and hold the president accountable. In response, the president and the executive fought to build coalitions that would protect their policies, including attractive offers to co-opt legislative opponents. Since meeting their constituents' demands for patronage overstretched most MPs' resources, the temptations were hard to resist. These struggles had significant consequences for Parliament as an institution, for MPs' careers, and for the prospects of future legislative and oversight initiatives.

Struggles to Establish Independence and Autonomy in the Sixth and Seventh Parliaments

By briefly characterizing legislative-executive relations during the no-party period of the 1995 Constitution, we illustrate a few of the many efforts by MPs to build an independent and autonomous lawmaking body, capable of significant modifications in administration bills and of effective oversight—as well as efforts by the executive and its supporters in Parliament to defeat their initiatives. Our purposes are first to show that Parliament immediately became a significant political actor and then lost some of its clout, and second to provide illustrations supporting our explanations for the success, albeit limited, of those changes.

We characterize several struggles over legislation and oversight. To demonstrate how the legislative process worked, we present a case study of the passage of the Budget Act (2001). There were far fewer notable opposition victories over determined government resistance in the Seventh Parliament, but opposition coalition-building was sufficient to force the government to change course on a number of issues. We suggest some of the changes that made the Seventh Parliament progressively less aggressive and less successful in achieving independence and effectiveness than the Sixth. Nevertheless, fundamental reforms passed in the Sixth appear likely to maintain a significant, if smaller, countervailing role for Parliament as it enters the multiparty era.

The Sixth Parliament (1996–2001)

The spectacular confrontations with the executive that the first MPs elected under the new constitution engineered tended to overshadow their less noticed, but ultimately more sustainable, reforms. The two most important reforms were the Administration of Parliament Act 1997 (APA) and the Budget Act 2001 (BA) that expanded Parliament's capacity to counter the executive's initiatives (both acts are discussed below). These reforms succeeded because the no-party system provided the opportunity for supporters of the Movement to join with supporters of the old parties to defeat the government on several contentious issues. Supporters of the Movement had a large majority in the House (Carbone 2008, 157), but the absence of party discipline meant they frequently used it against the executive.

MPs used their new committees to change some of the executive's bills dramatically before sending them back to the plenary for passage. They aggressively pursued their responsibilities to oversee government expenditures. Reformers also made adroit and unprecedented use of private member's bills to lay the foundations for extending Parliament's autonomy and budget participation. The most convincing demonstrations of Parliament's bid for power approaching that of the president were its successful censures of two prominent ministers close to Museveni and effective threats forcing three others out of their positions. Corruption was an important thread running through many of the Sixth Parliament's deliberations in committee and plenary sessions. By attacking corruption, Parliament directly challenged the executive's ability to assemble the resources needed to use patronage as a tool for governance.

The struggles over privatization between the new Parliament and the executive provide one of many windows on the willingness of the MPs not only to rewrite bills, but to use the legislature as a platform to attack perceived corruption at high levels in the executive. Privatization put the president and Parliament on a collision course, because divestiture could be understood as either a legislative or an executive responsibility. MPs tried to prevent the sale of the Uganda Commercial Bank (UCB), the largest asset privatized in Uganda. The UCB's branches extended to each MP's constituency and, like many agencies serving small rural clienteles, regularly lost money. One MP spoke for many others in insisting "we cannot start selling before putting a rural banking policy in place" (*New Vision,* September 2, 1996). In 1996, soon after Parliament convened, the Sessional Committee on Finance and Economic Planning (FEP) sent a resolution to the floor opposing the sale of the UCB. Following the executive's concession that it would look into a rural banking alternative, the motion was withdrawn. Nevertheless, Parliament passed a private member's bill in May 1997 to keep the UCB in state hands.

Still, the government went ahead. The president met privately with certain MPs in May 1997 to persuade them to vote for the sale of the UCB (*New Vision,* May 27, 1997). MPs responded by passing a resolution that the government should hold 60 percent of the shares when the UCB was privatized in order to sell them later to Ugandans (*New Vision,* July 5, 1997). Instead, the government retained 51 percent. After revelations of fraud appeared, MPs demanded its cancellation (*New Vision,* November 17, 1998). They thwarted the government, but only temporarily. The UCB remained a public asset managed by the Bank of Uganda during the remainder of the Sixth Parliament.

The censures followed soon after. MPs wanted to show that "the constitution works" (interview, February 3, 2005). The support of those MPs who had declared for the Movement was critical in order to prevent the appearance of a partisan cleavage. As one journalist noticed, "the face of the censure was essentially Movement" (interview, February 5, 2005). Despite calling and addressing a meeting of the MPs in the Movement Caucus (MC), the president was unable to protect his ministers. His failure to hold his supporters became apparent when MPs identified with the Movement subsequently signed the censure petitions in unexpected numbers. For one MP, "this particular incident made me realize the power of individual merit" (interview, February 3, 2005). Quiet ministerial support for the motions also emboldened the supporters of censure (interview, February 5, 2005).

The fraudulent sale of the UCB set the stage. It led to the report of a select committee naming four cabinet ministers and calling on the minister of finance to take responsibility for failures in the privatization process (Uganda Parliament 1999, 8432). When 100 MPs, including Movement supporters, attended an informal caucus to draft a resolution to censure Matthew Rukikaire, the minister of state for privatization, he resigned (*New Vision,* December 10, 1998). The process picked up steam, reaching a minister related to the president by marriage and others who had long been members of the NRM. Ultimately, two ministers were censured, forcing a reluctant president to remove them from his cabinet, accept the resignation of two others, and remove his vice president from the Ministry of Agriculture to save her. Considering that ministers sit near the pinnacle of patronage networks, the censures were unparalleled in Africa. As one MP put it, "the executive got surprised by how much power Parliament had" (interview, July 4, 2005).

The Public Accounts Committee expanded Parliament's concern with corruption in the Sixth Parliament by aggressively pursuing questions raised in reports by the auditor general (AG). The PAC also broadened its oversight by inquiring into other dubious ministerial expenditures. However, when it began its work, it was bogged down by a five-year backlog of AG reports. In its first submission to Parliament, the PAC publicized many gross irregularities, including the payment of war debts incurred by the NRA and, in an area the AG had not audited, the procurement of building materials for the expansion of schools needed for universal primary education (Uganda Parliament 1999, 8650–8652).[6] It also confronted the government on its practice of classifying huge amounts of expenditures for reasons of national security, thus preventing their audit.

Parliamentary concern over corruption extended beyond the PAC. On the floor of the House, MPs alleged that over USh8 billion (US$4.6 million) in classified expenditures intended for antiterrorism measures were instead spent for patronage (interview, July 4, 2005). They succeeded in forcing Brigadier Henry Tumukunde, then director of military intelligence and a special interest MP representing the army, to make a statement to Parliament explaining the sources of his wealth (interview, August 1, 2005). Under pressure from PAC, the executive tabled the Public Finance and Accountability Bill (2000) that provided for auditing classified expenditures.[7] To reduce the burden carried by the PAC, the Sixth Parliament created a second committee, the Local Government Public Accounts Committee, which began work in the Seventh.

Making a Law in a No-Party Legislature: The Budget Act, 2001

The Budget Act is a characteristic example of high-profile legislation passed in the Sixth Parliament. It demonstrates how MPs built a nonpartisan coalition to pass a bill that government at first vehemently opposed, primarily because it dramatically expanded the influence of Parliament in the budgetary process.[8] Nothing as far-reaching occurred in the Seventh Parliament, nor will it in the coming multiparty regime, where the president has a majority unlikely to vote against his policy choices.

A delegation of twelve MPs asked the Ministry of Finance to bring a bill that would require it to submit its estimates for the next budget for comment to Parliament several months in advance of the annual budget speech by the minister of finance. This group then drafted a bill and asked the government to introduce it. But the executive continued its longstanding practice of keeping its budget secret until the day of the budget speech. When nothing happened, a minister told one of the proponents that the cabinet had refused to introduce the proposal. The proponent presumed members of the cabinet were deferring to a colleague, the minister of finance, who in turn was acquiescing to the intense opposition of his permanent secretary, Emanuel Mutebile-Tumusiime, and the principal secretary for finance, Keith Muhakanizi. These public servants were fearful that bringing Parliament into the budget process earlier would run the risk of determining priorities through popular rather than technocratic criteria.

A backbencher, Isaac Musumba, introduced the Budget Bill 2000 as a private member's motion on behalf of the Standing Committee on the National Economy that he chaired. He had been the lead counsel to the committee in the Constituent Assembly that drafted the finance section of the 1995 Constitution. Musumba and Beatrice Kiraso, a women's representative, and chair of the FEP, had worked in the Ministry of Finance. They had the expertise to write the bill and the credibility to persuade members of their respective committees. Both had recently attended a World Bank conference in Nairobi on the budget process.

Their bill provided specific dates for early submission of the executive's annual estimates of revenue and expenditure by ministry to Parliament's sessional committees. It gave committees explicit authority to call ministers, other officials, or private individuals to give evidence. The bill established a Parliamentary Budget Office and a Budget Committee within Parliament. Their strategy was twofold. They chose to introduce an "innocent bill," one restricted to timelines and resources for parliamentary analysis, to avoid mobilizing the executive against it. Amendments to limit government spending were deliberately withheld until the committee stage.

Musumba began to build a coalition by persuading the fifteen members of his committee to support the bill. He shared the bill with other MPs, including both proponents and opponents of the Movement. Kiraso and Musumba assembled approximately thirty supporters before Musumba introduced it. They felt that would give them the core they needed to overcome government opposition. They asked "What's wrong with Parliament being involved in making budget decisions when they represent the people? Now Parliament is only a rubber stamp!" Both felt their most telling argument was the opportunity the bill provided for all MPs to influence the budget for the benefit of their own constituencies. Musumba also circulated the bill to the Ministry of Finance, arguing that the executive should appreciate additional analysis of the budget and the chance to achieve greater harmony over its objectives. But the Ministry of Finance continued to fight against it. Frontbenchers spoke against the bill, but did no further lobbying. Musumba and Kiraso made no effort to alert the press. After the bill was introduced (but before the committee added amendments restricting the authority of the executive to change the budget), the executive decided not to oppose it.

As planned, the bill was submitted to Kiraso's committee on finance and economic planning.[9] This second committee was also supportive, and that gave the organizers an additional group of sixteen canvassers who persuaded more MPs to join their coalition. At this point, they introduced amendments to control the executive's access to supplementary funds beyond the budget already approved. The most important of these limited the executive to supplementary expenditures of no more than 3 percent of the total approved budget without prior approval by Parliament and required ministries to account to

Parliament for funds expended under supplementaries within four months of expenditure. These additions to the bill provided far more serious limitations on the executive than merely providing information on estimates a few months earlier than usual. In addition, the committee inserted a requirement that the Ministry of Finance provide an estimate of the financial implications of every bill introduced into Parliament.[10]

To build support, Kiraso invited MPs to attend her committee's hearings and arranged to have the bill discussed in other sessional committees before it was brought back to the floor. Despite the addition of the restrictive amendments, the government did not change its mind, perhaps because the bill seemed likely to pass. There was little opposition when the bill came back to the floor, and none from the minister of finance. The bill passed without additional amendments from the floor. For the first time, Parliament gained effective influence over expenditures for government programs.

The Seventh Parliament (2001–2006)

The president's decision to intervene personally, extensively, and forcefully in the campaigns for the 2001 parliamentary elections produced the noticeably greater restraint with which MPs opposed executive initiatives in the Seventh Parliament. Only 119 MPs (43 percent) returned to the Seventh Parliament. This level of turnover, however, is not unusual either in past Ugandan elections or in African elections with multiparty competition. Members of the president's inner circle quietly financed many newcomers (interview, February 5, 2005). Some MPs won despite opposition from the president. But those who succeeded were chastened and unable to mobilize their earlier enthusiasm for opposing executive initiatives, particularly when MPs discovered that those opponents who lost elections were blocked from all government appointments (interview, February 5, 2005). Partly for that reason, and partly because Parliament's rules of procedure were changed, all attempts to censure ministers in the Seventh Parliament failed.[11] The importance of protecting access to future patronage made MPs more cautious.

The atmosphere in the Seventh Parliament also changed as the prospect for the return to parties grew. This prospect strengthened the executive, mostly because MPs believed party discipline would affect their opportunities for patronage. An official with years of experience with Parliament noticed that "as political space opened up and MPs looked for political homes, Parliament started losing its cohesion" (interview, July 6, 2005). As one former MP regretted, "the tools [for opposing the executive] are there, but the motivation is not" (interview, July 6, 2005). The growth in partisanship resulted in a decline in the number of bills passed (*New Vision,* December 27, 2004). MPs made fewer concerted efforts to stop corruption. Zie Gariyo, the director of an anticorruption civil society organization, attacked the Seventh Parliament for its inaction in "checking graft" by comparison to its predecessor, "a vibrant crusader against corruption" (*New Vision,* October 21, 2004). Another civil society lobbyist felt that "people are concentrating more on making friends at the expense of their national obligations; now it is [based] more on if I need a water project in my constituency" (interview, May 18, 2005).

However, the contrast between the Sixth and Seventh Parliaments is not black and white. The Seventh engaged in spirited and sometimes successful battles to stop divestiture of the UCB, the Kinyara sugar works, and the Dairy Corporation. The district quota system for students entering Makerere University was a Seventh Parliament initiative unsuccessfully opposed by the executive (interview, August 19, 2002). Parliament also passed resolutions to declare northern Uganda a disaster area and to prevent moving the National Social Security Fund to the Ministry of Finance—both vigorously opposed (and ignored) by the executive. Even some of the constitutional amendments the president demanded were rejected by Parliament.

A marked degree of compromise in legislative-executive relations on many issues occurred in committees throughout the Seventh Parliament. Both MPs and ministries used sessional committees to try to harmonize their views on bills rather than bring their conflicts to the floor of the House. MPs often made significant changes to bills in committee. Ministers also frequently offered changes to their own bills, often leading committees to propose further modifications (interview, July 8, 2005). For example, the Access to Information Bill pitted the desire of many MPs for open government against the executive's interest in secrecy. For almost a decade, MPs had complained, particularly in light of PAC reports to Parliament, about the executive's failure to table a bill regulating disclosure of government records. In 2003, a private member introduced a bill that the executive took over in 2004 (interview, July 6, 2005). The Sessional Committee on Presidential and Foreign Affairs modified this bill by extending it to local government records, reducing the period that cabinet minutes could remain secret, and reducing the period during which requests for information had to be answered (Uganda Parliament 2004a, 6–9). In passing the act in May 2005, Parliament accepted the committee's main recommendations, and the president assented despite these modifications.

Political bills were an exception, however. In those cases, the president muscled through the policy he wanted. The Legal and Parliamentary Affairs Committee recommended changes in nineteen of twenty-nine clauses in the Political Parties and Organizations Bill 2001, arguing that restrictions on political parties were unconstitutional. The president refused to assent to the bill, because it expanded the rights of parties to organize at the district level rather than at the national level only. Parliament promptly reversed itself.[12] As a parliamentary official tartly commented, "many MPs are looking for the president's position in determining their vote" (interview, July 8, 2005). Later in the Seventh Parliament, Museveni decided to change the 1995 Constitution by repealing presidential term limits and strengthening executive powers. A two-thirds majority of Parliament was necessary. The president and his inner circle turned to patronage in creating this majority, most nakedly by paying USh5 million (US$2,775) to each of over 205 MPs who agreed to support the Movement's proposed changes in the constitution (*Monitor,* October 31, 2004). The Movement leadership also gained control over committees handling political bills, enabling it to cut deliberations short (interview, February 5, 2005).[13] It hurried the Movement Amendment Bill 2003 and the Constitutional Amendment Bill 2005 to the floor over protests that it was not allowing full discussion (interview, July 8, 2005). The executive's success in these hotly contested political issues gave the Seventh Parliament its somewhat misleading reputation as a rubber stamp.

The Seventh Parliament and the executive continued to clash over accountability for government expenses, particularly over classified accounts. MPs regarded classified expenditures as a significant source of patronage. One MP called this "the largest abuse. It is outside normal procurement. There is no advertising or prelisting of companies" (interview, July 4, 2005). Despite the delicacy of taking on the Ministry of Defense as well as other ministries, the PAC expressed its concern that this practice meant the AG could not audit billions of shillings worth of expenses and noted that Parliament never allocates money under a vote labeled classified expenditures (Uganda Parliament 2004b, 8774).[14] In addition, the PAC complained that some budgetary allocations to specific ministries were immediately transferred to the Ministry of Defense as classified expenditures (Uganda Parliament 2004b, 8774). Once Parliament passed the Public Finance and Accountability Act 2003, the AG gained the power to investigate classified expenditures. As a result, Parliament created an important instrument for reducing patronage.

The PAC took up other issues as well. In considering the AG's report for 1998, the PAC noted that government had paid USh37 billion (US$20.6 million) in domestic arrears (out of USh62.1 million owed by several ministries) outside Parliament's budgetary appropriations and thus illegally (Uganda Parliament 2004b, 8747). The PAC agreed with the AG that the maintenance of arrears amounted to public borrowing without paying interest and without parliamentary approval. In addition, the PAC recommended that the ministry ensure that no accounting officer committed a ministry to expenditures after exhausting its allocation. The House backed the PAC on both issues. A permanent secretary credited Parliament's attention to financial oversight with making accounting officers in the ministries more conscious of this responsibility and gave them support to resist inappropriate expenditures by their political superiors (interview, January 28, 2005).

After the new BA became operational in 2003, its procedures systematically involved MPs in committee discussions with ministry officials on preliminary budget estimates. For the first time, ministers had to justify their estimates to MPs before the budget was presented to Parliament. A parliamentary staff person involved in budget analysis said the government now "responds to committee recommendations in substantial ways," though it often disagrees (interview, July 1, 2005). In a significant sign of Parliament's growing power, several ministry officials came to the Budget Committee to urge it not to reduce their estimates. An MP remarked on ministers' performances before committees: "They are requested to give detailed explanations to justify their estimates, some are chased out of the committee for lack of sufficient information" (interview, May 25, 2005).

Success in doubling the percentage of the budget devoted to agriculture is a concrete indication of the influence of Parliament on the budget (interview, May 26, 2005; Uganda Parliament 2005a, 5). When the inspector general of government told a committee that his operational budget had been "slashed," it recommended an increase (interview, May 26, 2005). In several cases the Budget Committee persuaded the Ministry of Finance to change specific priorities in the budget (interviews, May 26, July 15, and December 21, 2005). Experience with the BA led to ongoing discussions to amend it by introducing a process in which ministers would consult with committees to set substantive ceilings on ministry expenditure (interview, July 4, 2005). Nevertheless, in a penetrating aside on the unyielding nature of patronage, a budget official who noted that "presidential pledges are a distortion of expenditure that should be rationalized," recognized that "no one can stop the president!" (interview, July 1, 2005; see also Uganda Parliament 2005b, 10). Despite government's control through its large party majority, MPs in the Eighth Parliament are likely to continue to assert Parliament's independence by scrutinizing legislation, ministerial spending, and budget estimates. They will not, however, challenge the executive as boldly as they did in the Sixth.

Parliament as an Institution

A substantial part of the explanation of the Sixth and Seventh Parliaments' expression of unprecedented independence and autonomy resulted from the expansion in their legislative authority granted by the 1995 Constitution and the accompanying Rules of Procedure (standing orders), newly drafted in 1996. Neither would have made any difference had MPs been unwilling to use them. In a patronage-driven society, no one could have been certain that MPs would have tried to countervail the executive. However, as the account above suggests, from the start several MPs aggressively used the legislative process to establish Parliament's autonomy and effectiveness. We call this group the "reformers," and identify thirty-six in the Sixth Parliament and twenty-seven in the Seventh.

Changes in Constitutional Powers and Rules of Procedure

While the separation of powers is always intended to make both the legislature and the executive significant actors in lawmaking and oversight, the specific distribution of authority varies widely among political systems (Squire and Hamm 2005, 39). Parliament remained a unicameral body, as had all previous Ugandan legislatures. For the first time, Parliament could, on a two-thirds vote, override the president's refusal to assent to legislation. Neither the Sixth Parliament nor the Seventh ever exercised this power. In another extraordinary departure from prior Ugandan executive-legislative relations, the constitution required the president to submit candidates for vice president, cabinet, and constitutionally established commissions to Parliament for approval.[15]

Also, for the first time, standing committees were entrenched in the constitution with the power to discuss bills, oversee government activities, and compel testimony from members of both the government and the public. The constitution gave committees and individual MPs the power to introduce legislation. No minister, nor the vice president, can serve on a committee. The executive must submit its annual budget to Parliament and make no expenditures until it is approved. The constitution prohibits delay by the president in convening the legislature. He must call newly elected Parliaments into session within a week after the prior Parliament's term has ended. The Speaker has the power to convene a session of Parliament and must do so within a year of the previous one. In addition, the president cannot dissolve Parliament until after the completion of its five-year term. Parliament has the power to remove the president from office during his term for abuse of office or incapacity. The constitution also gave Parliament the power to make its own rules of procedure and set its members' salaries. In addition, MPs elect their Speaker.

The 1995 Constitution also expanded Parliament by adding special interest constituencies for the representation of women, youth, workers, persons with disabilities, and the army to the conventional single-member seats intended to represent all interests in a constituency.[16] Special interest constituencies were introduced to assist marginalized groups to remove social barriers to full participation (Uganda Constitutional Commission 1993, 297).[17] In 1996, these MPs were elected by restricted electoral colleges rather than by universal franchise. The colleges varied from 200 to several thousand for the women's seats. In 2001, the electoral college was dropped in favor of the universal franchise for women's seats, but not for the others. About one-fifth of the MPs in the Sixth and more than a quarter in the Seventh Parliament filled special interest seats.[18] All MPs are formally equal, but the influence of the government in the associations providing the electoral colleges for special interest seats gave rise to accusations of greater presidential influence over many of these MPs, especially through patronage (interview, February 5, 2005; Tripp 2006, 193). To some extent, the special interest seats may have limited Parliament's attempts to exercise its legislative and oversight powers.

The Rules of Procedure were rewritten to take account of the constitutional changes. Reformers were vigilant to ensure these changes were followed. In many instances, the new rules simply repeated highly specific sections of the 1995 Constitution. The original rules added little to the constitutional expansion of legislative authority and thus do not independently account for the significant role played by this Parliament. When the Seventh Parliament took office, MPs who supported the president succeeded in modifying particular rules to reduce legislative assertion. While some changes were intended merely to clarify procedure, others insulated the president from attack; most notably those that made it harder to censure a high official (interview, February 3, 2005; compare Uganda Parliament 1996 and 2002, Rules 81–84).

However, the most important change in its Rules of Procedure after their revision in 1996 was Parliament's adoption in 2005 of open voting on all issues, originally to facilitate the passage of the constitutional amendments. Before then, committees and Parliament decided most issues by consensus, voting by division only if an issue were controversial. In a patronage system, like Uganda's, roll-call voting raises more difficult issues of accountability than it does in many other legislatures because it increases the president's power over MPs. While it makes MPs' votes transparent, open voting weakens the autonomy of Parliament by making it easier for the government to use patronage to gain a majority for its legislative initiatives.[19]

The Speaker made a decisive contribution to Parliament's unanticipated assertiveness during the first years of the Sixth Parliament. But later struggles over the choice of Speaker suggested that Parliament might not be able to sustain the full constitutional expansion of its authority. Both the principles of separation of power and of individual merit (discussed below) required the president to leave the election of the Speaker to the MPs. Nevertheless, Museveni intervened informally after discovering that he could not expect to get his own way automatically. The first Speaker, James Wapakhabulo, a prominent and longtime Movement member, unexpectedly turned out to have "a vision of Parliament" acting autonomously (interview, July 7, 2005). For example, he did not try to stop the censure petitions (interview, July 16, 2005). Museveni persuaded Wapakhabulo to become the national political commissar and then convinced members of the MC to support Francis Ayume, a long-serving minister without strong Movement credentials, as his replacement despite their widespread preference for Edward Ssekandi, his opponent (interview, February 5, 2005). MPs felt the president was "imposing a Speaker on Parliament" (interview, February 5, 2005). Nevertheless, when Museveni chose Ayume as his attorney general at the beginning of the Seventh Parliament, MPs elected Ssekandi their new Speaker.

The reformers consistently introduced and supported initiatives that strengthened Parliament's capacity to countervail the executive (interviews, January 17 and 18, February 3, 2005). They included Movement supporters and opponents. A few had been elected to special interest seats. They attended parliamentary sessions more regularly than others (interview, January 18, 2005). The reformers used the constitutional powers given to Parliament to deepen the separation of powers. Some of the reformers had served in the Constituent

Assembly, where they supported many of Parliament's new powers. They ensured that the Rules of Procedure in the Sixth Parliament reflected the new constitutional provisions—for example, the rules enabling committees to summon ministers, to exercise the powers of the High Court, and to demand documentation (interview, July 6, 2005). Reformers had to resist pressures from the president and ministers, most obviously in the censure debates.

Creation of the Committee System and the Basis for Parliament's Autonomy

An active committee system increases the capacity of a legislature to act independently by providing it the basis for developing its own sources of information and expertise (Krehbiel 1991, 5). The Sixth Parliament responded decisively to its new constitutional mandate by changing its mode of operation from a plenary-based to a committee-based legislature. In addition, reformers used their committee assignments to create legislation giving Parliament control of its own governance. The first change increased Parliament's effectiveness, the second its autonomy. The development of a committee system to consider legislation had begun in the NRC in the early 1990s. In response to "MPs who wanted to deal with everything on the floor," reformers argued that committees would streamline legislative business and enable MPs to specialize (interview, July 6, 2005). In addition to standing committees, the Sixth Parliament appointed sessional committees to consider and initiate legislative proposals as well as to oversee the performance of specific ministries. Parliament also appointed select committees to investigate problems. The number expanded from seventeen (seven standing and ten sessional committees) in the Sixth Parliament to twenty-two (twelve standing and ten sessional) in the Seventh. "Now the bulk of the work of Parliament is done in committees" (interview, July 6, 2005).

Committees leapt into life as soon as the Sixth Parliament was organized. Their members "went into depth on issues, visited sites throughout the country, called ministers to testify, invited stakeholders to public hearings, and not only went deeply into issues of oversight, like embezzlement, but followed through with the police. This was unheard of in the past" (interview, July 6, 2005). According to one MP, "the way we work in committees is we don't only call government officials, we also invite stakeholders to give their views. The procedure we use is bottom up" (interview, January 17, 2005). In the absence of party deliberations over programs, committees provided MPs with much of their information on policies.

For most of the Sixth and Seventh Parliaments, MPs were free to choose their committees. They often preferred committees that examined infrastructural projects so they could claim credit for those placed in their own constituencies (interview, September 22, 2005). Reformers joined committees that dealt with measures strengthening Parliament. Most of the MPs on the Legal and Parliamentary Affairs Committee were lawyers—until supporters of the president took it over to control the hearings for cabinet proposals to amend the constitution (interview, February 28, 2006). The executive often felt threatened by committees, "because they found out more than is usually known" (interview, July 6, 2005).

MPs rated the Legal and Parliamentary Affairs Committee, Social Services, Finance and Economic Development, National Economy, Budget, Equal Opportunities, the new HIV/AIDS, and both Public Accounts committees as the best performers (interviews, February 6, 9, 13, and 28, 2006). A seasoned observer estimated that not quite half the committees perform effectively (interview, January 9, 2006). In his view, the factors affecting performance include the presence of members with professional skills, the ability of the chair to steer the committee, and the experience of the committee's clerk. Lawyers and knowledgeable clerks often substantially improve the legislation that comes to their committees. Members of committees elected their chairs, but that did not mean the chair would be an active leader. "If the chair is active, the committee will also be active, if dormant, the committee also becomes dormant" (interview, February 5, 2005). Active committees sometimes took up issues ignored by their "natural" committees, resulting in "accusations of committees usurping each other's role" (interview, February 5, 2005). The importance of the policy to the government also affected the performance of committees. For example, the cabinet's emphasis on AIDS policy in coordination with the donors led to better performance by the HIV/AIDS Committee. Nevertheless, achieving quorums in committees was just as difficult as it was in the House. They were plagued by low attendance that sometimes resulted in decisions by only a few members (*New Vision,* January 7, 2005).

On its own initiative, the Sixth Parliament passed the Administration of Parliament Act 1997, and the Budget Act that provided the statutory framework for its independence from the executive and a larger role in the budgetary process. Both acts began as private member's bills and were developed in committees, demonstrating the significance of both innovations for expanding legislative autonomy. Both acts overcame initial opposition from the executive. The APA established that Parliament would administer itself by setting its own budget and employing its own staff. It gave Parliament the power to determine its expenditures, its officials, its security, its reporting service, and the allowances paid to MPs. It created a commission to govern Parliament and a Parliamentary Service responsible to it. In stressing the degree to which Parliament escaped control by the executive, a journalist insisted "the only formal influence the president has is the appointment of the Clerk to Parliament" (interview, February 5, 2005).[20]

The act carefully blends legislative and executive influence by including among the six members comprising the Parliamentary Commission three backbenchers in addition to the Speaker, who serves as chair, and the minister of finance and leader of government business (ordinarily the prime minister) to represent the cabinet. The APA also establishes the departments within the Parliamentary Service, including the Library, Research, and Documentation and Legislative Counsel. These facilities add significantly to Parliament's capacity. Once they were established in 1999, Parliament no longer depended exclusively on ministries and the attorney general for researching, drafting, and evaluating legislation. However, having authority over funds and getting them are not the same—despite the APA, the Treasury did not pay Parliament all the funds it had been authorized (interview, July 7, 2005). Nevertheless, the protection of the APA and the BA ensures that Parliament will continue to wield considerable influence despite the disappearance in the Seventh Parliament of its high-profile posture and the return of parties in the Eighth.

The role of reformers in these innovations was indispensable. They proposed and shaped the committee system. They used private member's bills to provoke the executive into taking them over for fear it would not be able to control the outcome. The APA, the BA, and the Access to Information Bill are examples. The reformers took the lead in passing these acts. They also participated in committee investigations of government fraud in privatization in the FEP and corruption in the PAC.

The Expansion of Institutional Resources

"Staff and facilities are linked to the ability of legislators to do their job" (Squire and Hamm 2005, 75). Or, in the words of a veteran parliamentary official, "you can't divorce the performance of Parliament from the performance of its staff" (interview, July 6, 2005). The relationship between resources and legislative emergence is complicated and hard to measure, however. Despite some evident successes, Parliament found it difficult to build the capacity to realize its formal powers.

Throughout the independence period, it had to share its own building with several ministries, only gaining use of most of it in 2000. In 2005, one wing was still occupied by the office of the president. Almost quadrupling the number of MPs since independence made it impossible to provide offices for all members. Chairs and vice chairs of committees and members of the Parliamentary Commission received individual offices, reflecting the new importance Parliament placed on those responsible for guiding its internal activity. Some other MPs had private offices, but most shared them.

Parliament's library, information technology, and budget offices remained small and poorly equipped, although their officials were reasonably well paid.[21] An official estimated that researchers, who often accompanied committees on field visits, produced approximately 170 reports a year (interview, May 31, 2005). MPs, on the other hand, complained of a lack of staff support (interview, May 18, 2005). Starting in 2003, the Budget Office did the analysis for the sessional and budget committees' recommendations to ministries for changes in the annual budget. Until the NRM era, there had been little continuity in parliamentary staff due to frequent political crises. Retention of staff continued to be a problem until the Seventh Parliament raised compensation of officials in the Parliamentary Service above that in the Public Service.[22]

One important criterion in establishing parliamentary capacity is the payment of adequate salaries that permit MPs to treat their legislative work as a full-time occupation (Squire and Hamm 2005, 79). To reduce public criticism, Ugandan MPs kept their salaries low and their allowances high. They were paid USh1.46 million (US$800) per month in 2005, but with allowances for travel and constituency expenses, their compensation could reach USh6 million (US$3,330) (interview, July 6, 2005). Their compensation was comparable to the most highly paid professionals and civil servants.

However, their expenses in their constituencies and election campaigns far exceeded this income—as the widespread indebtedness of MPs demonstrated. In 2005, MPs passed a constitutional amendment that gave them the power to pay themselves pensions in addition to their existing rights to gratuities (*New Vision,* July 9, 2006). They followed the constitutional change with the Parliamentary Pension Bill 2006 as their term ended, backdating their new pensions to 2001. The president refused to assent to sections of the bill, because of its impact on the budget. Overall, some observers argue that Parliament was underfunded, receiving an allocation of slightly less than 2 percent of the national budget—which the Treasury did not pay in full (interview, July 7, 2005). MPs in only a few African legislatures, most notably in Kenya and South Africa, receive greater compensation.

Adequate staffing is also essential to building legislative capacity. MPs receive office allowances that provide minuscule assistance, typically a clerk and sometimes a computer. At this stage, Ugandan MPs "are not autonomous," a newspaper columnist argued, because Parliament cannot provide them enough staff "to function effectively," unlike, "members of the American Congress" (interview, January 18, 2005). Instead, they must rely on their own businesses or ministry offices to manage their parliamentary work, if they are fortunate enough to have them. Toward the end of the Seventh Parliament, MPs began receiving annual constituency funds of USh10 million (US$5,500) that went some distance toward alleviating their personal expenses for constituency service.

The Movement System and Parliament

The Movement or no-party system of government had the unexpected consequences of first facilitating the reforms that supported Parliament's independence and efficacy and then restricting them. The 1995 Constitution required the Movement political system to be "broad based, inclusive and non-partisan" including, most pertinently for legislative behavior, "individual merit as a basis for election to political offices" (Uganda 1995, Article 70). The rationale for individuals rather than parties campaigning for office rested on the claim that choosing candidates for their personal qualities is more democratic than choosing them for their party labels. The essence of this claim is that the absence of partisan competition facilitates the mutual accommodation of different interests—precisely the argument Schumpeter attacked long ago as wishful thinking (Schumpeter 1950, 250–256). But in Uganda the experience of nonpartisan politics was positively regarded for several years after 1995, in part because of its contributions to effective legislative action.

Without parties there could be no party discipline. It was only a small logical step to assume that MPs should also be independent in making legislative decisions. Consequently, Uganda's legislative activity had to be organized on different and more informal bases than it is in legislatures in which MPs are expected to vote a party's position. Nonpartisan politics creates an inescapable ambiguity for legislative action. It allows MPs to act on their individual preferences while raising the transaction costs for winning coalitions. Since the government, and most lawmakers, will want to aggregate majorities in order to pass, modify, or prevent legislation, they will look for ways to organize reliable coalitions. Despite a belief in the principle of acting individually, some basis for organization will inevitably emerge (Michels 1962, 70–80).

While the ambiguity between the celebration of individual merit and the necessity of coalition formation greatly complicated legislative behavior, it provided unexpected opportunities for Parliament to countervail the executive. Reformers quickly discovered that the promotion of individual merit freed Movement supporters to join coalitions opposing the government without losing their Movement credentials—as long as these coalitions were sufficiently informal that no one could attack them as parties. But the consequences of individualism cut both ways. As one opposition MP put it, "the president knows that MPs are also not organized" (interview, May 18, 2005). In addition, the grounds for organizing coalitions changed over time. Speaking broadly, legislation was the product of coalitions formed on the basis of individual merit in the Sixth Parliament and shifted increasingly toward coalitions based on quasi-disciplined groups in the Seventh.

The two most important bases for organizing coalitions emerged from within Parliament—committees and caucuses. A parliamentary clerk observed, "committees substitute for parties in a partyless environment" (interview, July 7, 2005). "Committees are a place where like-minded members ally to change a bill" (interview, August 22, 2002). As the passage of the Budget Act demonstrated, committee members often became the core for mobilizing supporters. They usually defended the committee's position on the floor, although there were cases where MPs deserted their committees. An MP noticed the party-like role committees could play in a no-party legislature: "The chairs of the committees were tough on the executive, like an opposition to government" (interview, July 4, 2005). Another MP who had served in the multiparty legislature in the 1980s compared committees to internal party meetings where members' views would be incorporated into bills (interview, August 22, 2002).

Caucuses of all sorts flourished during the Sixth and Seventh Parliaments. Districts, ethnic and religious groups, newly arrived MPs, and of course the Movement served as the basis for competing and overlapping caucuses (Carbone 2008, 164–165; Kayunga 2001, 195).[23] "In the absence of organized opposition in Parliament, caucuses have played the role of an 'informal' opposition" (Kayunga 2001, 191). As organizations that could enforce discipline, they fell far short of parties. They took positions on shared interests rather than on programs across all issues as parties would. Members were free to join as many caucuses as they wanted. No caucus could bind its members to a position, even when they had voted for it.

Nevertheless, and even though their memberships overlapped, the largest caucuses in the Sixth Parliament, the Young Parliamentarians Association (YPA) and the Movement Caucus (MC), became active opponents in battles over reforms to strengthen Parliament or check the executive.[24] Only first-term MPs were supposed to be eligible to join the YPA (interview, February 3, 2005). Its members developed a considerable degree of social solidarity, including a joint savings scheme for political activities and fundraisers held in each other's constituencies (interview, January 18, 2005; Carbone 2008, 174–175). The YPA caucus provided a forum in which Movement and opposition MPs worked out shared positions that directly confronted the executive on parliamentary reform, privatization, and stopping corruption. While the YPA was an important vehicle for reform, many reformers were not members.

YPA MPs who returned to the Seventh Parliament formed its successor, the Parliamentary Advocacy Forum (PAFO). They intended to promote similar ideas about reform of Parliament, particularly addressing "discrepancies in governance issues" and strengthening the capacity of MPs "to initiate, critically analyze, and sustain major policy and legislative processes" (interview, February 3, 2005; PAFO 2002, 1). However, as the likelihood of a return to competitive parties became more evident, certain PAFO MPs committed the caucus to opposing the president and the Movement overtly rather than focusing on issues. That turned out to be a serious miscalculation. "The moment PAFO became partisan, it ceased to be effective in parliamentary affairs" (interview, January 18, 2005). Direct political opposition to national leaders made PAFO too dangerous for Movement MPs who would have pursued reform initiatives but were unwilling to cut their ties with the Movement. PAFO's political commitment identified an important constraint in the no-party system that weakened those building legislative coalitions from countervailing the executive successfully.

Similar problems affected the MC, although its official support for the executive gave it advantages that no other caucus had. Access to government resources made the MC the only caucus that could credibly threaten members who voted against its positions. Unlike PAFO, it could legitimately insist that its members vote its political positions. "Even though MPs don't have to follow a decision taken by the MC, failure to do so is seen as a betrayal" (interview, July 8, 2005). But Movement principles meant MC members' decisions were supposed to be made independently, like every other MP. Caucus members rejected "oaths of allegiance" and "codes of conduct" as inappropriate efforts to turn the caucus into a political party (Carbone 2008, 170). Since caucus membership was voluntary, MPs' compliance remained uncertain until late in the Seventh Parliament.

The government did what it could to get MC members to support its positions. President Museveni paid close attention to its deliberations and wielded great influence in their decisions (Carbone 2008, 167). In a statement hard to reconcile with any rationale for a no-party system, he insisted that "all Members of Parliament were elected either on a pro-Movement platform or a multipartyist one. Even if there are no parties in Uganda in the strict sense of the word, those Members of Parliament who came through the Movement ticket must remember that their primary loyalty is to the Movement and Parliament is secondary" (November 23, 1999, quoted in Kayunga 2001, 151).

The president intervened in the selection of MC leaders, making the position more attractive by promoting several to ministerial positions. He met frequently with the MC and often caused its members to reverse their positions, even on delicate issues involving internal parliamentary matters. On the other hand, the MC sometimes played an active role in legislative-executive relations. Sometimes it influenced the executive to modify its positions. "Yet the possibility was there . . . for members simply to disagree with the position expressed by the leadership" (MP quoted by Carbone 2008, 167). In a few cases, it persuaded the president to drop legislation that caucus members strongly opposed—for example, giving government the power to compulsorily acquire land and the president the power to dissolve Parliament (interview, March 29, 2005).

Over time, the government, and particularly the president, raised the stakes for MPs who attended the MC but voted against its positions. Both MPs supporting and opposing the government said that, as time passed, it consulted its members less and insisted they vote the government's position more (interviews, December 3, 4, and 10, 2003; May 25, 2005). Museveni's ability and willingness to use patronage to secure legislative support distinguished it from other caucuses. The president's threats and eventually electoral campaigns against Movement MPs who broke ranks increased the MC's capacity to insist members conform. The MC "solidified with elections to the Seventh" (interview, July 4, 2005). Even so, the leadership's incentives for imposing discipline remained limited (Carbone 2008, 184). Its transformation into a proto-party only became explicit in early 2005 when the National Resistance Movement–Organization

(NRM-O) was formed in anticipation of the return to multiparty competition for the 2006 elections. One indication of the impending multiparty era was the exclusion of prominent parliamentary reformers who had simultaneously been members of the MC and PAFO from the NRM-O (interview, July 4, 2005). But without party discipline, the fundamental problem remained. As a minister insisted, "the absence of a whip means you can't count on an MP's vote" (interview, June 27, 2005). The observation shows that patronage was not sufficient to eliminate the effect of independence created by the no-party system.

Freeing MPs from party discipline, even though it was far more uneven than the Movement's philosophy implied, made an essential contribution to the establishment of the autonomy and capacity of Parliament. Reformers could credibly appeal to other MPs to join them, despite executive or presidential opposition. Committees and caucuses provided instruments to build coalitions. Neither the APA nor the BA would have been passed if the government had been able to exercise tight party discipline. Nor would any of the censures or anticorruption initiatives have succeeded. A strong reforming impulse gripped the House throughout the period, although it was beaten back by the executive toward the end of the Seventh Parliament. Many MPs, especially the reformers, felt they were building a new democratic era in Uganda. Their freedom from party discipline made them effective at first, but eventually made them vulnerable to the president's capacity to instill relatively greater discipline among his supporters.

The Composition of Parliament

The demographic profile of MPs remained relatively constant between the Sixth and Seventh Parliaments. Comparison of MPs in the two Parliaments, set out in Table 3.1, suggests no significant differences in age, education, occupation, or incumbency. By themselves, these individual characteristics of MPs do not account for changes in legislative independence and effectiveness over the past decade. The absence of personal data from prior Ugandan legislatures makes a comparison across constitutions impossible.[25]

As in other African legislatures, Ugandan MPs were highly unrepresentative of the general population. They were mostly male, older, far better educated, and occupied higher paying jobs. Members of modal groups in both Parliaments were in their forties and in their first terms. They had postuniversity education and professional occupations. The completion of an "Advanced Level standard" of education is constitutionally mandated, so fluency in English was virtually universal. The youth of both assemblies may be their most surprising demographic characteristic. The mean age in both was only 45 years, younger than in the other legislatures considered in this book. Seventeen MPs

Table 3.1 Individual Characteristics of MPs, in Percentage (number in parentheses)

	Sixth (1996–2001)		Seventh (2001–2006)	
Seats		(280)		(305)
Seat type				
Men holding general interest seats	73.6	(206)	65.9	(201)
Men holding special interest seats	7.9	(22)	6.6	(20)
Women holding general interest seats	2.9	(8)	4.3	(13)
Women holding special interest seats	15.7	(44)	20.0	(61)
MPs ex officio (without vote)	1.4	(4)	3.3	(10)
Gender				
Male	81.4	(228)	75.4	(230)
Age				
Average	44.7 years		45.1 years	
39 and under	28.2	(79)	31.1	(95)
40–49	37.9	(106)	34.8	(106)
50–59	28.5	(80)	24.3	(74)
60–69	3.2	(9)	8.5	(26)
Not available	2.1	(6)	1.3	(4)
Education				
Secondary	1.8	(5)	2.0	(6)
University	43.2	(121)	38.0	(116)
Advanced	54.3	(152)	59.0	(180)
Not available	0.7	(2)	1.0	(3)
Occupation				
Intermediate civil servants	3.9	(11)	6.6	(20)
Senior civil servants	1.4	(4)	1.3	(4)
Business/managerial	24.3	(68)	22.3	(68)
Teachers	12.9	(36)	11.5	(35)
Professional	40.7	(114)	43.6	(133)
Politicians and others	15.4	(43)	14.1	(43)
Not available	1.4	(4)	0.7	(2)
Term in office				
First	49.6	(139)	50.5	(154)
Second	32.5	(91)	28.5	(87)
Third or fourth	17.1	(48)	20.7	(63)
Not available	0.7	(2)	0.3	(1)
Minister/minister of state	22.5	(63)	21.3	(65)

Source: Directories of Uganda's Sixth and Seventh Parliaments (omissions corrected).

in the Sixth Parliament and eighteen in the Seventh were under 30—including the five Youth representatives naturally. However, while only nine were 60 or over in the Sixth, twenty-six were in the Seventh. Men held most of the general interest (conventional) seats. The relatively large number of women in both parliaments was primarily due to the mandate of one woman's seat for each administrative district. The number of women winning seats from the general interest constituencies rose from eight in the Sixth to thirteen in the Seventh. However, the 20 percent rise in the number of female MPs was largely due to the increase in the number of districts, from thirty-nine to fifty-six, rather than to their defeat of male candidates.

The individual characteristics of Ugandan reformers are not distinctly different from those of all other MPs (see Table 3.2). Reformers, as mentioned above, were MPs who devoted significant effort to strengthening Parliament's capacity for autonomy, independence, and effectiveness. We identified 46 reformers, 36 in the Sixth (12.9 percent) and 27 in the Seventh (8.9 percent).[26] Reformers in the Seventh included 17 from the Sixth plus 10 newly elected MPs. We expected reformers to be younger, more educated, more likely to have emerged from the private sector and in their first term (Barkan et al. 2004, 235). Ugandan reformers bear out some of these predictions, although none of them conclusively. By comparison to all other MPs, Ugandan reformers were significantly better educated, but about the same age, although in the Sixth the youngest cohort of MPs was more highly represented. Reformers were most likely to be professionals, while teachers were conspicuous by their complete absence. Reformers were more experienced MPs, far more likely to be serving their second term as an MP in the Sixth and their third in the Seventh. They were also noticeably more male and much more likely, whether men or women, to hold general than special interest seats. The most striking difference between reformers and all other MPs was the presence of only one woman holding a special interest seat among reformers in either Parliament. This finding suggests that women in special interest seats may avoid engaging in reform because they feel particularly vulnerable to executive pressure.

We also divided both sets of reformers into Movement supporters and opponents.[27] In our judgment, 22 were Movement and 14 opposition in the Sixth, while the proportions were the opposite in the Seventh (7 and 20, respectively). This is a significant reversal, reflecting deepening cleavages over the president's policies. As Museveni raised the political stakes by bidding for a third term, it became increasingly difficult to separate the MP from the Movement. Those willing to fight for a stronger Parliament in the Seventh found it much harder to identify themselves credibly as supporters of the Movement.

The number of ministers and ministers of state (i.e., deputy ministers) in each Parliament amounted to more than a fifth of all members. The number rose slightly in the Seventh, but there also was considerable turnover. Of the 63 listed in the directory for the Sixth, only 34 held similar rank according to

Table 3.2 Individual Characteristics of Reformers as Opposed to All Other MPs, in Percentage (numbers in parentheses)

	Sixth (1996–2001)				Seventh (2001–2006)			
	Reformers		Other MPs		Reformers		Other MPs	
MPs	12.9	(36)	87.1	(244)	8.9	(27)	91.1	(278)
Gender and by type of seat								
Male	91.7	(33)	80.0	(195)	85.2	(23)	74.5	(207)
Men holding general interest seats	83.3	(30)	72.1	(176)	77.8	(21)	64.7	(180)
Men holding special interest seats	8.3	(3)	6.6	(16)	7.4	(2)	6.5	(18)
Women holding general interest seats	5.6	(2)	2.5	(6)	11.1	(3)	3.6	(10)
Women holding special interest seats	2.8	(1)	17.6	(43)	3.7	(1)	21.6	(60)
MPs without vote (ex officio)	0.0	(0)	1.2	(3)	0.0	(0)	3.6	(10)
Age								
Average	42.9 years		45.0 years		46.9 years		45.0 years	
39 and under	41.7	(15)	26.6	(65)	33.3	(9)	30.6	(85)
40–49	25.0	(9)	39.3	(96)	22.2	(6)	36.0	(100)
50–59	33.3	(12)	27.9	(68)	33.3	(9)	23.7	(66)
60–69	0.0	(0)	3.7	(9)	11.1	(3)	8.3	(23)
Not available	0.0	(0)	2.5	(6)	0.0	(0)	1.4	(4)
Education								
Secondary	0.0	(0)	2.0	(5)	0.0	(0)	2.2	(6)
University	33.3	(9)	45.9	(112)	11.1	(3)	40.6	(113)
Advanced	66.7	(27)	51.2	(125)	88.9	(24)	56.1	(156)
Not available	0.0	(0)	0.8	(2)	0.0	(0)	1.1	(3)

(*continues*)

Table 3.2 continued

	Sixth (1996–2001)		Seventh (2001–2006)	
	Reformers	Other MPs	Reformers	Other MPs
Occupation				
Intermediate civil servants	0.0 (0)	4.5 (11)	3.7 (1)	6.8 (19)
Senior civil servants	2.8 (1)	1.2 (3)	7.4 (2)	1.1 (3)
Business/managerial	27.8 (10)	23.8 (58)	25.9 (7)	21.9 (61)
Teachers	0.0 (0)	14.8 (36)	0.0 (0)	12.6 (35)
Professional	55.6 (20)	38.5 (94)	51.9 (14)	42.8 (119)
Politicians and others	13.9 (5)	15.6 (38)	11.1 (3)	0.7 (2)
Not available	0.0 (0)	1.6 (4)	0.0 (0)	
Term in office				
First	41.7 (15)	50.8 (124)	37.0 (10)	51.8 (144)
Second	44.4 (16)	30.7 (75)	29.6 (8)	28.4 (79)
Third or fourth	13.9 (5)	17.6 (43)	33.3 (9)	19.4 (54)
Not available	0.0 (0)	0.8 (2)	0.0 (0)	0.4 (1)
Reformers in Sixth who were so in Seventh			(17)	
Reformers in Seventh who did not serve in Sixth			(10)	
Ideology of reformers				
Movement	61.1 (22)		25.9 (7)	
Opposition	38.9 (14)		74.1 (20)	

Source: Directories of Uganda's Sixth and Seventh Parliaments (omissions corrected).

the directory for the Seventh. Only 28 (44.4 percent) were reelected to the Seventh Parliament—about the same percentage as returning MPs.[28] This is surprising since ministers have more resources to reward their constituents. Nevertheless, the appointments gave the president a built-in base for a coalition in support of his policies—an important consideration in a no-party legislature. Since ministerial appointments are also critical nodes in patronage networks, they not only create reliable supporters, but also serve to silence reformers (interview, July 4, 2005). For example, Musumba, one of the leading proponents of the Budget Act, was made a minister of state. Nevertheless, the performance of MPs in the Sixth Parliament, and for a time in the Seventh, demonstrates that co-opting MPs by making them ministers did not prevent the legislature from exerting its independence.

Constituency Service and Electoral Campaigns

The extraordinary financial costs MPs incur to win elections and meet constituent expectations in a poor and patronage-driven society pose an enormous challenge for developing Parliament into a significant political actor. A veteran journalist framed the problem this way: "The more MPs are indebted, the easier it is to compromise them" (interview, February 5, 2005). In 2004, six MPs were threatened with arrest for failure to pay their debts (*Monitor,* February 4, 2004). Indebtedness forced MPs to look for alternative sources of present or future income. In most meetings with the president, MPs asked him to pay their loans (interview, March 30, 2005). Many enrolled in professional courses in Uganda and abroad that took significant time away from legislative business, partly explaining the frequent difficulty in assembling a quorum for conducting business in the House and committees.

Voters regarded their MP first and foremost as a patron, a link in the chain of patronage that reaches to the president. Voters thought of representation in material terms.[29] Voting was largely a function of voters' expectations for improving their chances for receiving patronage—either personal or through constituency projects. MPs reinforced this conception. "To get elected, MPs tell voters it's their job to carry out development projects in their constituencies. So once elected, people expect them to build roads, health centers, and pay their medical bills" (interview, January 18, 2005).

Constituents also expected their representatives to contribute directly from their own funds to help them solve personal problems, such as paying school fees for their children, medical bills, weddings, and funerals (interview, January 17, 2005). Upon learning that his predecessor paid the school fees for many students from his constituency, an MP instituted his own scheme. He supported seventy students at a cost of Sh1.6 million (US$890) per school term. Like other MPs, he also contributed to churches, mosques, schools, and roads.

The services MPs felt obliged to provide to their constituents consumed inordinate amounts of time and money for MPs holding general interest seats and not much less for those in special interest seats with large constituencies, such as women holding district seats—at the expense of concentrating on legislative work. MPs returned to their constituencies often, once or twice a month and also for deaths or weddings in families of supporters (interview, June 30, 2005). A typical visit cost more than a million Uganda shillings (US$560)—one-sixth of an MP's monthly compensation.

MPs' financial problems were further complicated by the difficulties of raising funds in a no-party system. The absence of parties removed an important source of finance for campaigns and constituency service: "the weakness of individual merit is that you are alone" (interview, July 4, 2005). Since by definition there can be no party programs, an unanticipated consequence of the no-party system was greater emphasis on personal favors. As one MP put it, "individual merit means constituents think they can keep milking you" (interview, July 15, 2005). The individual merit system reinforced expectations that candidates must dispense patronage to attract voters.

Measured by Ugandan salaries, campaigns are extremely expensive, although the amounts seem small by comparison to US races. A journalist estimated that in rural constituencies a 2001 campaign cost up to USh200 million (US$111,000) and, surprisingly, half that in municipalities (interview, January 18, 2005). Others put the amounts even higher. MPs from poorer areas in the North estimated that they paid somewhat less. Without help from the state, these are extraordinary amounts for individuals to raise in a poor society. Even though the neutrality of the government was a premise of the no-party system, officials, most notably the president, openly supported their preferred candidates financially and in campaign appearances. Supporters of the president's policies received campaign funds from the Movement Secretariat (interview, December 1, 2003). Opposition MPs raised their funds from family, friends, and personal assets (interview, June 30, 2005). Many MPs regularly saved part of their monthly salaries to meet the costs of the next election (interviews, February 3 and June 30, 2005). In the Sixth Parliament, the YPA formed a joint savings scheme for the 2001 races. "For an MP, campaigns start the day you are elected. As an MP in the Sixth Parliament, I spent almost half my earnings constructing roads, building churches and schools" (interview, February 3, 2005).

To win support, a candidate had to invest personally in individual assistance and community projects. A candidate must be seen as caring and willing to sacrifice financially or personally (interview, June 30, 2005).[30] In the Kabale Municipality election for the Constituent Assembly in 1994 and for Parliament in 1996, 10 percent of all campaign expenditures was used to pay medical bills for supporters (author's observation). Voters also wanted churches, schools, roads, and women's and youth projects (interview, June 30, 2005). Candidates responded by providing assistance that could be seen to reach many potential voters, for example, by supplying iron sheets for schools or sports equipment for youth. Incumbent candidates also took credit for donor projects in their constituencies—even when they were members of the opposition.

Special interest seats also required expensive campaigns. One female MP estimated she spent USh60 million (US$33,300) to defeat the candidate the government had encouraged to run against her (interview, July 15, 2005). Candidates for other special interest seats had to campaign throughout the country, because their electoral colleges were national, even though their constituencies were regional. Nevertheless, a poor candidate sometimes won a special interest seat. One victor in a youth constituency had no job and no money, but won by making better presentations than his opponents (interview, July 15, 2005).[31] Nevertheless, poor MPs found it difficult to remain independent. As a former minister remarked, "Ninety percent of all MPs are needy and that is why their decisions are swayed by financial handouts like the recent Sh5 million that was given to them" (Richard Kaijuka, *Monitor*, August 15, 2005).

Conclusion

By the 2001 elections, the democratic rationale for the no-party system had become so threadbare that prominent members of the president's inner circle stated publicly that the time had come to return to multiparty competition. Museveni's response was to sack them from his cabinet. But, in retrospect, he had already begun preparations to restore party competition on his own terms. He had initiated a Constitutional Review Commission with a wide mandate before the election. In speaking to the Movement National Executive Committee in March 2003, he signaled the change and insisted on "other constitutional amendments I consider very necessary to ensure that we have effective government" (Museveni 2003, 18). After the Constitutional Review Commission reported, the cabinet submitted several bills to Parliament proposing more than 100 changes, many of which strengthened executive power. Among other amendments it adopted, Parliament voted to repeal the two-term limit for the presidency from the constitution and to restore multiparty competition. However, it successfully resisted other proposals, notably those giving the president the power to dissolve Parliament, shortening the years of legal practice necessary to qualify for judicial appointment, and providing the executive the power to seize land for investment.

The Eighth Parliament (2006–2011) contains 333 members, 28 more than the Seventh (*Monitor*, September 13, 2006). Of these, 215 were elected from general interest constituencies, while 105 (32.8 percent of voting MPs) represented special interest constituencies. The latter include 80 women's seats (reflecting the increase in districts) plus 5 seats each for youth, workers, and people with disabilities, and 10 for the Uganda Peoples' Defence Forces. There are also

13 ex officio seats for members of the cabinet who were not elected to Parliament and who cannot vote on legislation.

The 2006 multiparty elections returned the NRM as by far the largest party, with 214 seats (66.9 percent of voting members), plus at least 17 of the 40 independents who have formally agreed to vote with the party—over two-thirds of voting MPs in the Eighth Parliament.[32] The five successful opposition parties together won only 56 seats, 17.4 percent of the voting MPs (46 general interest and 10 women's constituencies). Now able to insist on party discipline, the NRM is likely to pass more of the executive's policies than Movement MPs managed previously. "Individual merit" can no longer protect MPs who might otherwise question government policies. Museveni predicted: "We shall pass all the amendments in Parliament we want. The period of beseeching is over" (*Monitor,* March 5, 2006). Consequently, the Eighth Parliament will find it far more difficult to act independently.

On the other hand, the statutory establishment of Parliament's autonomy and the harmonious working executive-legislative relationship that developed in committees and in budget deliberations during the Seventh suggest that the executive will continue to accept more involvement by Parliament than it ever had before 1996. The Eighth Parliament contains 173 incumbents, 54.1 percent of the 320 voting MPs in the new body. Many returning MPs have a decade's experience in parliamentary practice. Thus, the gains achieved in the Sixth and implemented in the Seventh are likely to give MPs in the Eighth a continuing and significant, although more modest, role in shaping legislation and overseeing the executive despite the overwhelming majority of the president's party.

A recent analysis based on the first half year of the Eighth Parliament supports our expectation that its committees will make effective contributions to bills and oversight. Not surprisingly, it predicts that "in the plenary the standard of debate will continue to be disappointing with the majority of the MPs reluctant to talk for fear of being whipped" ("Uganda in 2007," *New Vision,* January 25, 2007). Nevertheless, this journalist felt that committees chaired by both opposition and NRM MPs are performing effectively: "Some committees chaired by the NRM members have . . . done well" and "in 2007, the opposition MPs will continue to inject life into the otherwise dead accountability committees, namely Public Accounts, Local Government Accounts and Commissions and State Enterprises."

Indicating that it still can effectively exercise its powers of oversight, the PAC, led by an opposition MP, succeeded in forcing a minister to repay an advance from a radio station to avoid criminal proceedings (*New Vision,* January 3, 2007). The conflict early in 2007 between the executive and Parliament over MPs' demands for their new vehicle scheme demonstrates that MPs in the Eighth were insisting on the autonomy they had established in the Administration of Parliament Act to determine their own emoluments (*New Vision,*

December 29, 2006; January 15, 2007). MPs rejected the minister of defense's request to suspend the rules in order to rush through the deployment of Ugandan troops to Somalia because opposition MPs were not present (*Monitor,* February 1, 2007). Nevertheless, it is still too early to tell how much of Parliament's influence accumulated in the no-party period will survive the potent combination of party discipline in a party led by the president and controlling more than two-thirds of the seats.

Both the Sixth and Seventh Parliaments demonstrated far greater independence, autonomy, and effectiveness than their predecessors—the Sixth effectively, if only momentarily, countervailing the executive on significant issues; the Seventh losing ground, but by no means retreating to legislative submission. This chapter explains how these institutional outcomes were achieved despite the deeply embedded pressures supporting executive dominance. These pressures include the political dominance of Museveni, whom many continue to regard as their best protection against a return to Uganda's violent past. The continuing force of patronage as a tool of governance to overcome Uganda's divisive local loyalties and the precedent of prior legislative subordination also work against Parliament's independence.

The democratic opening following the NRA's victory in 1986 led to the new Parliament's unprecedented political significance. The 1995 Constitution, which had been enacted with widespread popular support, introduced an array of new powers intended to make Parliament the coequal of the executive. Soon after they were elected in 1996, a group of reform-minded MPs succeeded in mobilizing a majority of their colleagues not only to provide the framework for Parliament's autonomy and effectiveness, but also to confront the executive and the president directly by rejecting some of its initiatives and censuring some cabinet ministers. No one had anticipated the reformers' success. It happened because the no-party system, intended to protect the president from the old parties, made it possible for reformers to mobilize Movement supporters for measures that strengthened Parliament's independence. In addition, donors' and the government's provision of institutional resources reinforced the ability of reformers to take Parliament down unexpected paths.

However, patronage, which in Uganda has always been controlled by its presidents, worked to undercut Parliament's capacity to countervail the executive. The high costs of election campaigns and constituency service forced many MPs into debt, making them deeply vulnerable to attractive offers from the president. In addition, the president singled out some of the reformers and campaigned against them in the 2001 elections. As a result, the Seventh Parliament was less vigorous in its opposition to the president, particularly for political and constitutional legislation in which the president was determined to get his own way.

But it would be a great mistake to think that Parliament has become as subordinate as its predecessors. The development of the committee system and the passage of the APA and BA gave it an institutional base through which MPs have continued to modify legislation and budgets and oversee the expenditure of ministries. The first signs from the Eighth Parliament elected in 2006 indicate that this less dramatic level of independence and autonomy will continue—despite the return to multiparty competition and party discipline. So far, the massive majority enjoyed by the NRM, the president's party, has not meant that the executive can do whatever it wants. Parliament continues to play an important role, although not one that is coequal to the executive.

Notes

We thank John M. Carey, Marc W. Cassidy, John B. Kazoora, Roger Tangri, Michelle M. Taylor-Robinson, and Richard F. Winters for their helpful criticisms of earlier drafts of this paper and Jennifer A. Gapinski for coding the social characteristics of members of the Sixth and Seventh Parliaments. The research for this chapter is based primarily on fifty-four interviews we conducted between 2002 and 2006 with twenty-five MPs and fifteen others, half with employees of Parliament, and the remainder with members of civil society or the executive.

1. Political party organizations, including the former parties of previous regimes, would be allowed to exist, and individual Ugandans could be members of these parties. But parties could not nominate candidates for office, nor could candidates campaign on party platforms or labels.

2. The government appointed a twenty-person Constitutional Commission chaired by a justice of the Supreme Court in 1988 to make proposals for a new constitution. It was followed by a Constituent Assembly whose delegates were the first to be elected on a universal franchise and a secret ballot during the NRM regime. The National Resistance Council continued to act as Uganda's legislature during the period of the Constituent Assembly's deliberations.

3. Parliament is the name given the legislature by the 1995 Constitution. At independence, it was called the National Assembly. Following the two periods of military rule, it was renamed the National Consultative Council (1979–1980) and then the National Resistance Council (1986–1995).

4. The 1966 Constitution made Obote president. An interim document, it was replaced by the 1967 Constitution after extensive debate in the National Assembly, reconstituted as a Constituent Assembly.

5. This was Uganda's first postindependence legislative election. Most Ugandans believe that the Democratic Party, the other prominent Ugandan party, won the election.

6. The actions of PAC gained credibility from its chair, Augustine Ruzindana, who had previously been the inspector general of government, where he had gained a reputation for investigating and pursuing cases of corruption by officials.

7. The bill was debated and passed in the Seventh Parliament.

8. The most powerful public servant in the government, Emanuel Mutebile-Tumusiime, then the permanent secretary in the Ministry of Finance, Planning, and Economic Development, was reputed to have insisted, "this bill will come over my dead body" (interview, July 15, 2005).

9. Only sessional committees can consider bills.

10. After the Budget Act was passed, the Ministry of Finance found the power to provide "certificates of financial implication," an extremely useful tool to fend off pressure for additional expenditures from other ministries.

11. Indeed, the two ministers censured in the Sixth were reappointed to the cabinet in the Seventh.

12. The Constitutional Court later declared the act unconstitutional (*New Vision*, March 22, 2003).

13. Their strategy was simple because the method of committee selection had been informal. MPs chose their committees at the beginning of each session by signing a posted list up to a maximum of twenty-five. In 2004, an NRM MP got to the lists first and signed up members the MC had designated (interview, July 8, 2005).

14. It wondered why the utility bills for the Internal and External Security Organizations and a large advance to the vice president's housekeeper had to be classified. In another case, almost 1 billion Uganda shillings (US$4.5 million) in the president's office that was supposed to be paid for utilities turned out to cover salaries and facilitation for expenses in reducing insecurity caused by cattle rustling in districts neighboring Karamoja (*Hansard*, 3rd session, 3rd meeting, March 4–April 15, 2004, 9302).

15. The president may look outside Parliament for members of his cabinet. If he chooses someone who has not been elected, that person becomes an MP ex officio without voting rights. But a norm may be developing in which losing an election to Parliament disqualifies candidates for ministerial appointment.

16. Formal representation of all interests as opposed to a special interest is the only principle that cleanly divides the old seats from the new ones. For that reason, we refer to "general interest" as opposed to "special interest" constituencies or seats.

17. The seats for the army, the Uganda Peoples' Defence Forces (UPDF), depended on a different rationale—the role of the NRA in overthrowing dictatorship. The ten UPDF representatives increased the president's support in Parliament, although they did not invariably support his initiatives.

18. An increase in seats for women MPs accounts for the rise in the proportion of special interest seats. Each district is entitled to a seat reserved for a woman. Several new districts were created after 1996. In July 2005, Parliament approved twenty new districts.

19. If voting had remained secret, it is widely believed that MPs would have voted to retain presidential term limits in the constitution, preventing the president from running for a third term (interview, November 14, 2003; personal communication from an MP, October 2006).

20. But he correctly added that "independence also depends on people's ability to exercise it; government has been able to get most of the MPs onto its side."

21. In 2005, the library had twenty-six computers for MPs; the budget office had six for its eleven members of staff.

22. In July 2005, the Parliamentary Service employed about 100 officers, including 22 clerks (one for each committee) out of a total staff of 289 (interview, July 7, 2005).

23. The first caucuses of elected representatives during the no-party politics period were organized in 1994 at the beginning of the Constituent Assembly (*Monitor*, July 15–19, 1994). Kayunga suggests that while social and political concerns formed the basis for most caucuses in the Constituent Assembly, the organizational cohesion for those in the Sixth Parliament rested on ethnic identities (Kayunga 2001, 194).

24. According to Sallie Kayunga, the MC contained 188 members, while the YPA had 151—amounting to more than the membership of the Sixth Parliament (2001, 195). Giovanni Carbone counts 211 in the MC and 93 in the YPA (2008, 164). They may have counted at different times. In a system where organization is informal, it is impossible to be sure how many MPs belong to a particular caucus.

25. Demographic data on MPs became publicly available only with the Sixth Parliament when the first directory was compiled.

26. We constructed our lists by asking several of our interviewees to name MPs who put high priority on making Parliament more effective. We added those who introduced and managed the acts that reformed Parliament, the APA and the BA; those who led committees into new roles, for example the chairs of PAC and LGPAC; and those deeply involved in preparing the new rules of procedure. We excluded active participants in Parliament who concentrated on substantive legislation rather than making Parliament stronger.

27. We classified reformers as Movement or Opposition according to whether they generally supported or opposed the president's policies. Thus, we identified some MPs as Movement in the Sixth and Opposition in the Seventh—for example, the leaders of PAFO. We acknowledge the difficulties of making such classifications in an officially nonpartisan political system.

28. Seven of the ministers who served for at least part of both Parliaments had been presidential nominees in the Seventh (that is, served ex officio). Three of them had also been ministers in the Sixth.

29. Only in Kampala did many voters take notice of national issues. The one significant exception was the restoration of domestic peace, which many voters, particularly those in rural areas, credited to President Museveni because of his leadership in the guerrilla struggle.

30. Northern politicians imprisoned by the government received overwhelming electoral support in succeeding elections.

31. As an MP, he became a reformer.

32. The NRM holds 141 or nearly two-thirds of the 215 general interest constituencies, 59 of the 80 district women's seats, and 14 of the 15 seats for workers, youth, and persons with disabilities. Most of the independents who vote with the NRM are members who lost in NRM primaries, but ran anyway and won. The NRM won about the same percentage of general and special interest seats.

4

Benin: Legislative Development in Africa's First Democratizer

Ladipo Adamolekun and Mouftaou Laleye

Political developments in Benin during the first three decades of independence (1960–1990) were characterized by a high degree of instability, with the country recording one of the highest number of coups d'etat. By the mid-1980s—during the second decade of a Marxist regime that lasted from 1972 through 1989—a significant proportion of the country's trained manpower had fled overseas, which further weakened the economy. By the end of the 1980s, the economy was on its knees. The ensuing virtual collapse of the state and the economy coincided with the rise of twin movements for a democratic political order and a market economy. In response to the internal governance crisis and changes in global norms, both political and economic, following the end of the Cold War, the incumbent government and opinion leaders in the country agreed to discuss Benin's future directions at a Sovereign National Conference held in February 1990. At the end of two weeks of open, frank, and critical discussions, a broad consensus was reached on the principles that would govern Benin's future political, economic, and social life. The conference adopted a national program of reforms aimed at firmly establishing Benin as a liberal democracy and a market economy.

The new orientation and reforms were enshrined in a new constitution adopted through a referendum held in December 1990 (Benin 1990). The democratic order is organized around a multiparty system, and the principle of a competitive choice of political leaders through free, fair, and transparent elections. The president serves a maximum of two five-year terms and is directly elected via a two-round process that guarantees an electoral majority.

The legislative power resides in a single chamber, the National Assembly. The number of members, called deputies, is fixed by law, and there are presently eighty-three, making it one of the smallest in Africa and the smallest legislature considered in this volume. Deputies serve four-year terms and may be reelected without limit. They are elected from twenty-four multimember districts on the basis of party list proportional representation. Since the return of multiparty politics in 1991, Benin has elected five legislatures whose terms have overlapped those of three presidents—the longest period of uninterrupted legislative experience since independence. The First Legislature elected in 1991 was succeeded by the Second in 1995, the Third in 1999, the Fourth in 2003, and the Fifth in 2007. Our discussion in this chapter is limited to the development of the institution during its first four terms.

The Evolution of Parliament in Benin

The 1990 Constitution adopted after the National Conference is the seventh in Benin. Each of its predecessors also provided for a national legislature, but none completed its four-year term—an indication of the political instability experienced by the country during the 1960s and 1970s. The National Revolutionary Assembly of the Marxist era had features inspired by the concept and practice of "democratic centralism" that were inconsistent with the post-1990 democratic order. The result was that members of the First Legislature following the adoption of the 1990 Constitution had no parliamentary experience within a competitive democratic system. The constitution carried over some provisions of the preceding constitutions, notably the separation of powers among the executive, legislative, and judicial branches; the concept of the deputy as a national representative; and provisions on three of the core functions of the legislature—representation, legislating in the broad sense, and control and oversight of the executive.

The Formal "Rules of the Game"

The provisions in the 1990 Constitution on "legislative powers" (Benin 1990, articles 79–113) constitute the formal rules for the organizational structure and functioning of the legislature. Some of the key provisions are as follows:

- Greater clarity is provided in the separation of powers among the executive, the legislature, and the judiciary than in previous constitutions.
- The core functions of the legislature are specified in a more-detailed manner than in previous constitutions.
- There are clear provisions on the relationships between the legislature and other state institutions, including the newly created Constitutional Court.

Three provisions strengthen the separation of powers between the executive and the legislature. The assembly cannot pass motions of censure on the government, which is a common legislative prerogative worldwide. Nor can the legislature impeach the president of the republic. For balance, the president cannot dissolve the National Assembly. These exclusions were deliberately established to avoid provisions that were among the causes of governmental instability during the pre-Marxist era.

However, one significant carryover from pre-1990 constitutions is the provision that requires deputies to consider themselves as national representatives (Benin 1990, article 80). The provision dates back to the priority that the nationalist leaders of the immediate postindependence period attached to "nation building." Given voter expectations that deputies devote both time and effort to constituency service, the provision introduces a measure of tension into the role of the deputy and how deputies should approach their duties. Each is pulled between their de facto orientation toward their constituents in their electoral districts and their de jure responsibilities to the nation as a whole.

The Internal Organization and Administration of the Legislature

The legislature is administered in accordance with rules and procedures set out in its Règlement Intérieur (internal rules), the equivalent of the Standing Orders in Anglophone countries.[1] The legislature has five main organs: the plenary, the executive, the permanent commissions (committees), the parliamentary groups (party caucuses), and the conference of presidents.

Legislative Plenary

The meeting of all deputies is called the Plenary, and there are specific legislative functions that must be conducted by the legislature as a whole, most notably the vote of the annual budget.

Legislative Bureau (Executive)

The Bureau is elected by members of the National Assembly at the beginning of each legislature, and it serves for four years until the end of the legislative term. The stability in the parliament's executive is expressly provided for in the constitution (Benin 1990, article 82). The aim of the constitution makers was to provide opportunity for effective leadership of the work of the National Assembly. The Bureau comprises the president of the National Assembly (the Speaker in Anglophone countries), two (first and second) vice presidents, two treasurers, and two secretaries. In the case of multiple holders, the first enjoys a precedent over the second. For example, the first vice president acts for the president in his absence. It is only in the absence of both the president and the first vice president that the second vice president acts as president. The Bureau meets weekly during parliamentary sessions and monthly when the assembly is not in session. Special meetings can be called by the president of the National Assembly or at the request of a simple majority of the members. It organizes the work of the legislature, including the agenda for each plenary session, and determines its duration and regulates legislative debates. The Bureau also organizes the work of the permanent commissions or committees.

Two important roles are assigned to the bureau by the constitution. First the president of the republic is required to consult it on the appointment of ministers (Benin 1990, article 54). Second, the Bureau appoints some of the members of three of the principal governance institutions established in the constitution: the Constitutional Court, the Economic and Social Council, and the High Authority for Audiovisual and Communication (Benin 1990, articles 115, 140, and 143). Successive presidents of the republic have generally respected the provision on consultation, but in this role the Bureau has no equivalent in the legislatures in Anglophone Africa.

Legislative Commissions (Committees)

There are five permanent commissions or departmental committees that shadow government ministries, departments, and agencies, each with at least thirteen members: The legislature can also establish special or temporary commissions to consider specific issues. The five permanent commissions are on law, administration, and human rights; finance and currency; plan, equipment, and production; education, culture, employment, and social affairs; and foreign affairs, development cooperation, defense, and security. In almost every case, a permanent commission covers the activities of two or more ministries or departments as indicated in Table 4.1. This situation limits the ability of the commissions and their members to develop a specialized expertise compared to their counterparts in other legislatures where the number of committees is much greater. This likewise limits their ability to scrutinize and exercise meaningful oversight over the ministries for which they are responsible.

A significant proportion of the legislative work is carried out in the commissions. Each commission has an executive comprising a president, a vice president, two rapporteurs, and a secretary. Like the parliamentary executive, the commission executives have a four-year tenure, a fact that provides an element of stability and acquired expertise for the committee system. The two busiest commissions are those of law and finance, because all ministries and departments deal with legal and financial issues in the course of formulating policy in their areas. When a ministry or department deals with multiple subjects, it also comes under the purview of more than one commission. For example, the Ministry of Interior, Security, and Decentralization comes under both the Law Commission and the Foreign Affairs Commission.

Table 4.1 Distribution of Ministries and Departments Among the Five Permanent Commissions, July 2006

Permanent Commissions	Distribution of Ministries and Departments
Law, Administration, and Human Rights	Ministries of Justice, Relations with Institutions, and Government Spokesperson; Administrative and Institutional Reforms; Security and Local Authorities; Civil Service and Labor
Finance and Currency	Ministries of Development, Economy, and Finance; Budget; Microfinance and Promotion of Small and Medium-Scale Enterprise; Industry and Commerce
Plan, Equipment, and Production	Ministries of Development, Economy, and Finance; Agriculture, Livestock, and Fisheries; Environment and Protection of Nature; Mines, Energy, and Water Resources; Industry and Commerce; Tourism and Craft; Transport, Public Works, and Urban Development
Education, Culture, Employment, and Social Affairs	Ministries of Higher, Technical, and Professional Education; Primary and Secondary Education; Family, Women, and Children; Culture, Sport, and Leisure; Communication and New Technology; Civil Service and Labor; Health
Foreign Affairs, Development Cooperation, Defense, and Security	Ministries of Foreign Affairs; Defense; Security and Local Communities; African Integration and Beninese Living Abroad

Leadership of the commissions is shared among deputies from both the government and opposition. In the Third Legislature (1999–2003), deputies who were members of the opposition were the presidents of the commissions on finance, law, foreign affairs, and education, while a deputy belonging to the party of the president of the republic led the Planning Commission (in the Fourth Legislature, up to the March 2006 presidential election, all the permanent commissions were presided over by MPs from the government's bench). The situation since the presidential election, when Thomas Yayi Boni, an independent, succeeded Mathieu Kérékou as president, has been fluid, as Boni is not identified with any one party group. Because the Finance Commission performs the combined roles of both the finance committee (budget formulation) and the public accounts committee (budget audit) in Anglophone Africa, its president is always a member of the majority party or majority coalition in parliament regardless of whether it is the opposition or the president's party.

Commissions can summon witnesses, including cabinet ministers and other officials, to make presentations before them. Article 34.7 of the constitution also requires that government officials can be summoned to appear before the Plenary. However, the internal rule is silent on what recourse the legislature has if witnesses refuse. Ministers can also request to make presentations before commissions. The regular contact between the commissions and the government is assured by a provision of the internal rules that requires every commission to send the agenda for meetings to the government 48 hours in advance. Meetings of commissions are not open to the public, but each commission issues a weekly press release on its activities. However, a group of parliamentary journalists interviewed for this study claimed that the commissions rarely gave them reports about their work.

Predictably, the effectiveness of a commission depends on the quality of its members, especially the quality of its president, the committee chair. Their educational background, professional and technical competence, and the relevance of their prior working experience all impact on their ability to be effective commission members. Several interviewees asserted that the Commissions on Law and Foreign Affairs in the First Legislature were effective for these reasons. There were a critical number of seasoned lawyers with hands-on experiences in both the public and private sectors in the former, and a good number of former ambassadors and high-profile intellectuals in the latter. And in both cases, ministers and deputies on the commissions collaborated to nurture a "win-win" relationship between the executive and the legislature. For example, a former minister of foreign affairs in the early 1990s stated that he instructed the ministry's staff to respond promptly to requests for information by deputies in the relevant commission. He also selected members of the Foreign Affairs Commission for trips abroad. He in turn benefited from unsolicited advice (including periodic analytical pieces) that complemented what he obtained from the career diplomats in the ministry.

The effectiveness of the commissions is also raised or lowered by the quality of technical and professional staff, adequate equipment, and office space. To date, very little has been achieved in this regard. Only one or two assistants (usually generalist administrators serving as clerks) are assigned to each commission. This situation could change for the better as soon as the capacity-building efforts provided by several international donors begin to bear fruit. One major effort is focused on strengthening the capacity of the Finance Commission. A second is focused on developing a broad analytical capacity in all policy areas that will benefit all the commissions. Ad hoc capacity-building assistance has been provided to the Law Commission and there could be more in the future. Commissions could also request their technical and professional support staff (as their number increases) to tap into available analytical studies produced in-country in the national universities and other research institutions. In contrast to these promising initiatives is the persistent and negative impact of intense partisanship among members of the assembly, and the incoherence and indiscipline within parties and parliamentary groups on the work of the commissions. Partisan conflict also undermines the effectiveness of plenary sessions. Such friction is likely to continue until parties mature and a more democratic culture is established among deputies.

Political Parties and Parliamentary Groups

A parliamentary group (PG) comprises deputies who belong to the same political party or coalition of parties. Each deputy can belong to only one PG. Deputies who choose not to belong to a PG are recognized as "independents." A parliamentary group must have at least nine members to be formally recognized in the assembly. There were three parliamentary groups in the First Legislature, five in the Second, and six, including independents, in the Third. And in 2005, midway through the Fourth Legislature, the number of parliamentary groups had increased to eight, indicating a progressive fragmentation and weakening of the party system both inside and outside of the legislature. However, following the election of the Fifth Legislature in March 2007, the number of parties holding seats in the National Assembly dropped to three, albeit nearly a quarter of the members were elected as independents, continuing the fluid situation that existed prior to the election.

This fragmentation of the party system within the assembly during the Fourth Legislature reflected an even greater fragmentation of electoral parties outside the legislature. Following the adoption of the independence constitution in 1960, only three parties contested the legislative elections, while two contested in 1963. However, under the system of proportional representation adopted in 1990, the number of parties contesting elections since the beginning of the democratic renewal has increased with each election. Twenty-four parties contested the 1991 elections; thirty-one did so in 1995; thirty-five in 1999; and more than eighty in 2003! The number of parties that actually won seats has fluctuated between sixteen and eighteen. These are not only clustered into the eight PGs, but also into two broad and very loose coalitions—the Presidential Movement with fifty-two seats and the Opposition with thirty-one.

A PG seeking recognition at the beginning of a new legislature submits a "political declaration" stating its political orientation and policy priorities. However, an examination of these declarations reveals the absence of fundamental ideological or programmatic differences among the parties.[2] Indeed, the most striking feature of the declarations is the common commitment of every PG to the national consensus reached at the 1990 National Conference. The lack of ideological or programmatic differences may partly explain the increase in the number of parliamentary groups, as there is no "philosophic glue" to stabilize the membership of these organs.

Parliamentary groups nominate members to serve in the various legislative organs, including the legislative bureau and commissions. The groups normally take positions on proposed legislation submitted to the assembly by the executive and determine the positions that their members should take in the commissions. In practical terms, the groups empower a deputy to have a voice within a larger group while obliging him or her to toe the PG line, especially in plenary sessions. Most PGs, however, do not really function as coherent groups, largely because of indiscipline and incoherence within their constituent political parties. The result is that deputies often refuse to adhere to the official position of their PG in plenary sessions.

Although the existence of PGs helps to structure the deputy's relationship with the party system within the legislature, the fissiparous pattern of party competition has made the deputy's relationship with his or her party a difficult one. Three factors shape this relationship: First, the electoral method encourages the bundling together (in party lists) of candidates to maximize their prospects for election, but with little or no thought for shared ideas and ideals amongst members of the group. The result is that the deputies in the different PGs are most often strange bedfellows. Second, party leaders focus attention more on legislative activities that could enhance their chances in the next presidential elections or in the next cabinet reshuffle than on how they and the members of their PGs might become effective and influential legislators in terms of making public policy. Third, the fact that there are no clear ideological or philosophical differences among parties makes it easy for deputies to "migrate" from one party to the other. These factors combine to produce a high degree of indiscipline among the parties, and a high level of partisan politicization in parliament. While the party leaders are busy scheming for the next presidential elections,[3] each deputy is busy calculating the steps he or she needs to take (including switching parties or PG) to enhance one's prospects for re-election. The weaknesses of the party system have contributed significantly to the slow pace of strengthening the legislature in Benin.

Notwithstanding the weakness of PGs, their presidents have specific functions and prerogatives: They can request an open vote, recommend a deputy's suspension from a PG, and request the creation of a special (i.e., ad hoc) commission. In 2002, the National Assembly initiated and passed a law on the formal recognition of an official opposition whose leader has specific duties and privileges. Although President Kérékou promulgated the law a year later, the regulations required for implementing it have yet to be established. When the law becomes operational, the emergence of an official opposition is likely to significantly change the role of PGs that may have consequences for the behavior of deputies. But whether parties will become more coherent, and whether the pending law will change the prevailing reluctance among deputies to be a member of the opposition and promote an "opposition culture," only time will tell.[4]

Conference of Presidents

The Conference of Presidents is an informal group, having been denied formal recognition by the Constitutional Court in 1991. However, successive legislatures have found it worthwhile to maintain it as a coordinating body. It is chaired by the President of the Assembly and comprises the other members of the legislative bureau, the presidents of permanent commissions, and the presidents of the parliamentary groups.

The Legislative Calendar

The legislature holds two regular sessions per year, each for a maximum of three months: the first begins in early April, and the second during the second half of October. Special sessions can be held at the discretion of its president or at the request of the president of the republic. A special session can also be held at the request of a majority of deputies. A special session cannot exceed fifteen days. Legislative debates are public, and full texts of the debates are published.

Parliamentary Staff

The Administrative Secretary General (the equivalent of the chief clerk in Anglophone parliaments) is the leader of the parliamentary staff that provides administrative support to the legislature. The present incumbent is assisted by 167 staff members organized within two departments; one that is responsible for legislative services, and the other for finance and administration. The Department of Legislative Services provides administrative and secretarial support to plenary sessions (including the recording of the proceedings), the commissions, the Bureau, and the conference of presidents, but not to the parliamentary groups. The department is also responsible for documentation and archives and for communication. The Department of Finance and Administration is responsible for finance; accounts, materials, building, supplies, and maintenance; personnel and health services; restaurant and lodging; and protocol service. The president of the assembly has his own personal staff.

Only 51 (including the Administrative Secretary General), or less than one-third, of the 167 staff belong to the senior management cadre of the public service. They are managed under a special statute, the statute of parliamentary staff adopted in 1999, which is similar to the legislation specifying the terms of employment for civil servants. Because of the small number of professional and technical staff, the support provided to the legislative commissions is weak, especially in respect to analytical and research support. Only secretarial and administrative support is adequate. The Service Division responsible for documentation and archives has only two professional staff, who struggle to provide rudimentary services. Their information technology capacity and equipment (i.e., hardware, software, Internet access) are grossly inadequate, even by the prevailing standards in sister parliaments across Francophone Africa (e.g., Burkina Faso, Mali, and Senegal).[5]

Several international donors have tried to build capacity in the Office of the Administrative Secretary General. Three recent initiatives that have had some impact are a budget office focused on analysis, control, and evaluation (Unité d'Analyse, de Contrôle, et d'Evaluation du Budget) supported by the UN Development Program (UNDP 2000a); a policy analysis unit (Cellule d'Analyse des Politiques de Développement de l'Assemblee Nationale) financed by the Africa Capacity Building Foundation (ACBF 2001) and the US Agency for International Development (USAID); and a program to strengthen the assembly's capacity to draft legislation supported by USAID. Between 2001 and 2006 the donor community supported these and other initiatives in the amount of roughly US$4.1 million.

Another deficiency is the inadequacy of office space. There is an urgent need for office space for the new staff. Some of the persons interviewed for the study (including a few deputies) mentioned the need to avoid the politicization of the parliamentary staff and to strictly observe the provisions in the statute of parliamentary staff.

Relationships with the Executive

Since 1991, successive presidents of Benin have created a cabinet position to manage relations with the National Assembly. The minister considers his duties vis-à-vis the assembly as the executive's priority. He is represented in Porto Novo, the seat of the assembly, by a special assistant who manages the day-to-day business with the assembly, including its commissions. In all four legislatures since 1991, successive executives have had to deal with what Adrien Houngbedji, the president of the First Legislature (1991–1995) and Third Legislature (1999–2003), famously called "a majority with geometrical variability," that is to say, unstable majorities. The fragmented nature of the party system within and outside the legislature no doubt exacerbates this tendency. This absence of a stable majority that supports or opposes the executive complicates executive-legislative relations. In all four legislatures, deputies have periodically united across parliamentary groups to defend institutional and personal interests. In 1992–1993, deputies in the First Legislature united to prevent the executive from reducing their salaries, and in 2001–2002, deputies of the Third Legislature demanded and obtained considerable increases in salary despite cuts in the assembly's budget by the executive in the government's budget that was adopted that year by presidential decree.

Relationships with Other National Institutions

The 1990 Constitution provides that the legislature shall be involved in appointments to the following national institutions: the Constitutional Court, the Supreme Court, the High Court of Justice, the Economic and Social Council, the Superior Council of the Magistracy, and the High Authority for Audiovisual and Communication (i.e., broadcasting). Either the appointing authority is required to consult the leadership of the legislature or the assembly's bureau actually appoints specified members of some institutions. The assembly also initiates the work of the High Court of Justice, which tries the president of the republic and cabinet ministers for treason, and appoints half its membership.

The legislature must also collaborate with one or more of the other institutions in the course of performing its functions. For example, in performing its lawmaking function, it interfaces with both the Supreme Court and the Constitutional Court and it interfaces with the Chamber of Accounts of the Supreme Court in carrying out a posteriori control (i.e., audits) of public accounts. The constitution also requires that legislation passed by the assembly be signed by the president of the republic before it becomes law. However, if promulgation is unduly delayed, the president of the assembly may declare the law operational after consultation with the Constitutional Court.

To date, only two laws initiated by the legislature had to be re-presented to the Constitutional Court before their conformity with the constitution was confirmed. First, the assembly adopted the law on its Règlement Intérieur in June 1991, but it was not "cleared" by the Constitutional Court for three years because of disagreements between the court and the assembly on several provisions in the law. Agreement was eventually reached and the law was adopted in 1995. The second example concerned legislation creating the Superior Court of the Magistracy that the court returned three times to the assembly before agreement was reached on its provisions. This interdependence of the principal democratic institutions (of the executive, legislative, and judicial branches) that the 1990 Constitution requires is one of the critical factors for nurturing democratic culture in post-1990 Benin.

The Third Legislature, 1999–2003

The demographic profile of deputies in the Third Legislature was typical of legislatures across Africa. Most members were in their forties and fifties and thus much older than the average citizen. Most were also professionals or managers while more than half were serving in their first legislative term, reflecting a high turnover of MPs from the Second Legislature to the Third. As with their counterparts in the other legislatures discussed in this volume, most deputies were under intense pressure to service their constituencies.

Demographic Profile of Membership

There are six women in the eighty-three-member assembly, only 7 percent of the membership and one of the lowest worldwide.[6] However, two of the six parliamentary groups are led by women, of which one is the largest in the assembly. Fifty-four deputies (65 percent) were serving their first term, twenty-five

(30 percent) were in their second, and only four served in all three legislatures. As with the other legislatures considered in this volume, the turnover rate in Benin is rather high. The significance and power of incumbency, however, may be rising. Twenty-four of the twenty-five deputies who served a second term during the Third Legislature had also been members of the Second. By contrast, only sixteen members of the Second Legislature had been members in the First.

As noted in Chapter 1, the rate of turnover and experience directly affect the development and professionalization of the legislatures. Members who serve two and especially three or more terms provide an institutional memory. It is also important to mention that eight deputies (10 percent) of the assembly had served as cabinet ministers, including one prime minister. This indicates the presence of significant executive-branch experience inside the assembly.

The average age of deputies is 53. The oldest is 70 and the youngest is 35. An overwhelming proportion of deputies, roughly 76 percent, are in the 40–60 age bracket. It is striking that only two deputies are under 39, compared to eighteen who are over 60. Not surprisingly, the deputies who dominate debates and the work in commissions are thus middle-aged men, drawn from the 40–60 year olds, and usually in their second or third terms. Every deputy who had served in a cabinet position is among the active ("dominant") group in parliament. One is the president of the assembly, two are chairs of commissions. The average age of the parliamentary executive is 54, and the average for the leaders of the parliamentary groups is 58—both somewhat higher than the average of total membership. Perhaps this is a reflection of the deference to elders in most African cultures. The decrease in the number of young deputies under 39 (only two in the Third Legislature, compared to six and eight in the First and the Second Legislatures) and the significant increase in the number of elderly deputies 60 and over (eight in the Third compared to seven each in the First and Second) suggest that there are few "Young Turks" waiting in the wings. But it is also not a gerontocracy.

Besides age, a critical factor that determines level of participation in the National Assembly is proficiency in French. Several of the deputies interviewed for this study estimated that about one-fifth of the membership are not fluent in French, with obvious negative consequences for their participation in plenary debates and discussions in the commissions. The internal rules prohibit the use of any other language, but since literacy in French is not a criterion for election, voters continue to elect persons who are not fully literate in the official language. One obvious solution to this language problem would be a revision of the internal rules to allow for simultaneous translation into relevant languages—as was the case in the "Revolutionary National Assembly" before the "democratic renewal."

The breakdown by occupation of the twenty-four deputies interviewed is as follows: there are twelve in the liberal professions (lawyers, medical doctors, a veterinary doctor, engineers); five administrators/managers in the public sector;

five in teaching; and two others, one of whom is a leading business operator. These categorizations need to be qualified as there are several cases of multiple "professions," while about half also described themselves as professional politicians.

Social Responsibility and Constituency Service

All the deputies interviewed said that they tried hard to spend time with their constituents, though a significant number admitted having time and resource constraints doing so. The most common activity carried out during visits to constituencies is the provision of social assistance to individual constituents. A few deputies were able to finance or attract funds for financing local self-help community development projects. The expectations on the part of the citizenry and the deputies' descriptions of how they engage in constituency service are consistent with the findings in all of the other countries considered in this volume with the possible exception of South Africa. Where members are elected from single-member districts, or via PR in multimember districts that are relatively small in size, as is the practice in Benin and Senegal, the expectations for constituency service are especially high.

There is strong agreement between deputies and the public on this aspect of the deputies' role. Eighty percent of the deputies interviewed for this study mentioned their social assistance role. One of them put it graphically as follows: "I am a social security cash box." Another made much larger claims: "I am the social security for my village. . . . I must build the school and the rural road." Most deputies try to be helpful and responsive to their constituents' demands in proportion to their own personal resources and their lobbying skills at obtaining additional assistance from the business sector and from the state.

In return for the salaries and other material advantages that put deputies among the ruling elite of the country, they are also expected to lead exemplary lives, both within and outside the legislature. And their social responsibility requires them to remain close to their constituents throughout their legislative mandates. Given these norms and expectations amongst the public, parliamentary elections are mainly referendums on deputies' records at providing for and being in proximity to their constituents. These expectations also pose a fundamental dilemma for deputies. Do they devote most, or a significant portion, of their time to constituency service? Or do they concentrate on performing the core internal functions of the legislature, making laws and exercising oversight over the executive branch?

Incentive Structure Facing Deputies

The structure of incentives facing deputies was also typical of that facing the memberships of the other legislatures considered in this volume with the exception of Kenya and Nigeria. Deputies were modestly paid, but received substantial allowances to cover living costs and other expenses. Deputies were also provided substantial symbolic incentives.

Financial Incentives

The salaries paid deputies (about 800,000 CFA or US$1,500 per month, or US$18,000 a year) put them among the highest paid 5 percent of the population. The basic salary is fixed by law at the highest pay scale for public servants (including the military). Deputies are also entitled to the following allowances in addition to their salaries:

- Free utilities (i.e., water, electricity, and telephone)
- Cost of running a private parliamentary office in their constituencies
- Duty allowances for those in leadership positions
- Housing allowance (since 1997)
- Transport allowance (for constituency work and some specified parliamentary meetings)
- Family allowance (based on the same criteria as those applicable in the public service)
- Supplementary pay for work carried out in the legislative commissions (paid once at the end of each legislative session)

The legislature also guarantees interest-free loans for the purchase of a vehicle; this "credit auto" is worth 4 million CFA (US$7,430). Repayment is deducted from each deputy's monthly pay and calculated to ensure full reimbursement by the end of the deputy's four-year term. At the beginning of the Fourth Legislature, these loans were greatly improved to enable all deputies to purchase a strong new vehicle of their choice. The basic pay and allowances of the president of the National Assembly are higher than those of the other deputies. Indeed, he is now among the six highest paid public servants in Benin, after the president of the republic.

Symbolic Incentives

Deputies are entitled to a badge and a crest that would make them and their vehicle recognizable whenever they are on official trips or in public assemblies. Deputies can also wear scarves in the national color across their shoulders at formal public meetings. Deputies are entitled to diplomatic passports during their tenure, and the constitution confers parliamentary immunity on them (Benin 1990, article 90). Although each deputy is entitled to a working space, only parliamentary leaders (members of the Bureau, presidents of commissions, and presidents of parliamentary groups—about one-quarter of the assembly) have been provided with office space. Other deputies manage as best they can, using work spaces assigned to commissions when they are not in session. The deputies in leadership positions also have more benefits. For example, the president of the assembly and the two treasurers have official residences in Porto Novo. They and other members of the Bureau as well as the presidents of commissions are also provided with official vehicles.

Deputies' Views on Development Issues, Campaign Finance, and Declaration of Assets

When asked to discuss their views on development issues facing Benin, the deputies interviewed for this study focused on two interrelated areas of concern. The first was promoting development at the local level, most notably through support for the implementation of decentralization. The second was contributing to poverty reduction by channeling more resources to the rural poor. Several gave examples of what they were doing personally to promote local development in their constituencies, including using their own NGOs (i.e., hometown associations) to support poverty reduction efforts, working with community development associations, and lobbying relevant government ministries for services to their areas.

Regarding the problem of campaign finance, every deputy interviewed was critical of the centrality of money in politics, and all condemned the high cost of campaigns. However, a significant minority asserted that they spent very little on their own campaigns in 1999. Typically, they claimed that their reelection was due to their track record either during a previous legislative term or in the activities they carried out before becoming deputies. For example, the youngest interviewed (thirty-six years old) asserted, "My campaign was easy. It cost me nothing." This same deputy stated that he "entered politics reluctantly. . . . I was the coordinator of development associations in [my] districts. . . . I have excellent relations with my constituents because I am one of the most regular [deputies] on the ground. I visit my constituency every fortnight. I do not spend a single weekend in Cotonou." His response emphasizes the importance of constituency service and is consistent with the findings in all of the other countries discussed in this volume with the exception of South Africa where MPs are elected via PR. However, it also begs the question of how much this deputy and other deputies spend on visiting their constituencies. The cost of transport and serving as a "social cash box" is high, and deputies are, in essence, required to run a perpetual campaign in between elections.

The deputies made several suggestions for campaign finance reform, including a reduction in the number of political parties, the prevention of parties being hijacked by rich people, and the development of a "contribution culture" (i.e., the payment of party membership dues to ensure transparency about the source of party finance and management). Deputies also called for an urgent review of the role of the regulatory bodies charged with overseeing the electoral process to ensure adequate campaign funding and a more effective control of campaign expenses.

Given the estimates of running for office—at least 5 million CFA (US$9,640), the present reimbursement by the state is grossly inadequate. For the 1995 legislative elections, the minimum reimbursement for successful candidates was 800,000 CFA (US$1,540). This rose to an estimated 1.6 million CFA (US$3,080) in 1999.[7] Not surprisingly, these rising costs are the basis of requests by deputies for increasing state support of election campaigns. But the process needs to be more transparent. The few deputies who mentioned the desirability of membership dues did not address the fundamental problem regarding the absence of genuine party membership arising from the high number of deputies who constantly migrate from one party to another. Given such behavior, party members are unlikely to contribute to party coffers. And the best-designed civic education is not likely to make a difference until the deputies themselves set good examples.

Declaration of assets by all public leaders is arguably an effective way of providing a spotlight on some of the secret relationships among money, politics, and corruption. It is therefore not surprising that the deputies were divided on the need for such declarations at their level. Several asserted that deputies do not manage public funds and that the declarations should be limited to the president and treasurers of the National Assembly. However, a significant minority would support the declaration of assets by all deputies because of its potential to help reduce corruption. Many would also support stronger enforcement of assets declaration by the president of the republic and cabinet ministers, and by senior civil servants. But only a few supported public access to the actual documentation of assets declared. However, a few deputies were totally against assets declaration, arguing that the practice was ineffective and in conflict with tradition: chiefs and leaders do not declare assets; it could open them to ridicule.

Deputies were thus divided between supporters and opponents of the declaration of assets, with the former in a slight majority. And because individual assets are often inseparable from those of other family members (e.g., wife or parents with respect to land), declarations may not promote accountability.

Continuity and Change During the Fourth Legislature (2003–2007)

The Fourth Legislative elections held in March 2003 were contested by twelve party lists—six alliances of parties and six "stand-alone" parties. The elections were considered free and fair by both domestic and international observers. For the first time since the democratic renewal in 1991, the coalition of the winning presidential candidate (Kérékou) won a decisive parliamentary majority: 31 of 83 seats for the Union pour le Bénin du Futur, the president's PG, plus 23 seats for their allies, for a total of 54 seats, nearly two-thirds of the assembly. At the inauguration of the first legislative session, they were joined by another party that won 11 seats to make a total of 65 seats or 78 percent of all members.

The composition of the Fourth Legislature was somewhat more youthful than the Third. Only 16 percent were 60 or older compared with 21 in the Third Legislature, while 30 percent were under 50 compared to 27 percent in the Third. On the other hand, the first two legislatures were more youthful than the Third or the Fourth with 59 percent of the members under 50 years in the First, and 51 percent under 50 in the Second. This changing age structure most likely reflects the power of incumbency, as a higher portion of each legislature has been reelected with each successive election. This hypothesis is confirmed by examining the turnover rates, that is, the percentage of members serving their first term, in the Second through the Fourth Legislature. The rate has dropped with each election. The turnover rate among members of the Second Legislature was 81 percent. It dropped to 65 percent for the Third and again to 51 percent in the Fourth. The increasing percentage of incumbents being reelected in Benin is consistent with similar patterns in other Third Wave legislatures, but whether this can also be interpreted as evidence of the professionalization of the National Assembly (i.e., that deputies are increasingly viewing their service as a career) is unclear. With respect to gender, the Fourth Legislature also had only six women and the same percentage of members (7 percent) as the Third.

As in the previous legislatures, the deputies are divided into parliamentary groups. From seven at the beginning of the Fourth Legislature in 2003, the number increased to eight in early 2005. A few months later, the number was tactically reduced to four to ensure a fair distribution of seats in the National Electoral Commission. While these groups are the structures for partisan activities within the assembly, the deliberation and crafting of legislation are carried out mainly within the parliamentary commissions, whose number and functioning remain unchanged.

The experiences of the Fourth Legislature illustrate both continuity and change within the National Assembly:

- There was a significant improvement in information technology capacity with the provision of computers and Internet facilities to deputies under a UNDP-financed project. The assembly also used its own budget to provide every deputy with a laptop.
- Like the Third Legislature, the Fourth had a difficult relationship with the Constitutional Court with the former asserting that it had greater

legitimacy as an elected body compared to the latter whose members are only appointed.
- In 2005, the assembly passed laws on 1999 and 2000 public accounts, due in part, to pressure from development partners. Lessons learned from voting the 1998 law on public accounts proved useful. However, the audits remained five years behind schedule.

Surprisingly, the overwhelming majority enjoyed by the presidential coalition and its allies in the assembly was not very helpful to President Kérékou. The Fourth Legislature made more use of the control mechanisms provided in the constitution than any of its predecessors (seen later in Table 4.7). The table shows that of the five listed methods of control, the Fourth Legislature surpassed the record with respect to written questions, equaled the record with respect to the number of commissions of inquiry, and equaled or surpassed the number of oral questions and questions on current affairs. Only in regard to queries to president and ministers was its performance uncertain. The legislature also passed two laws on public accounts compared to the first ever passed by the Third Legislature.

Core Functions: Representation and Legislating

Like their counterparts in other African parliaments and elsewhere, the members of the National Assembly perform three core functions on a collective basis—representation, legislating in the broad sense, and oversight of the executive. These tasks are in addition to constituency service, which is performed on an individual basis but which is an aspect of representation.

Representation: "Nation" vs. Constituency

As noted earlier in this chapter, Benin's constitution requires that deputies consider themselves exclusively as representatives of the nation. There is also formal prohibition of any mandate that is not national. However, in practice, the prohibition is a fiction, indeed "political hypocrisy" in the words of one deputy. As noted by another deputy: "No deputy has ever visited another constituency [other than his own] to interact with the citizens and monitor their problems." One deputy provided this clincher: "If you forget that you are from a locality, you will not return to the assembly." Occasionally, when a deputy makes a passionate plea for his constituents, he is jokingly reminded that he is supposed to focus on national interests. The rare occasions when all deputies claim to defend national interests are when they question executive members on acts of omission and commission. All the deputies interviewed (except the

President of the Assembly) see themselves as representatives of specific geographic or communal constituencies and take seriously their role as defenders of the interests of their constituents. Like MPs across the continent, most deputies therefore spend considerable time visiting their constituencies and on constituency service as described earlier in this chapter. A deputy who is regarded as a champion of local interests by his constituents attracts the attention of his party and is likely to win a place near the top of the party's list for the relevant electoral district for the next elections. Indeed, almost every deputy serving a third term is a "patron," each with his own local fiefdom—a confirmation of the patron-client relationships within the political parties.

The methods used by established and aspiring patrons are very similar. They include the following:

- Regular visits to the constituency
- Lobbying the executive (including the president) for the inclusion of their communities as beneficiaries of development activities financed by the state
- Using personal resources to finance development microprojects
- Supporting local self-help development projects
- Providing financial assistance to local notables (e.g., traditional chiefs) who can deliver votes
- Searching for jobs for the youth and political appointments for allies and associates

It is on occasions when queries (interpellations) are posed to the president of the republic or to cabinet ministers, or when reports of commissions of inquiry are debated in plenary, that deputies assert loudly that they are custodians of "the national interest." One early example was the debate on the privatization of the Benin Brewery in 1992. The query to the president was signed by thirty-four deputies and the debates that commenced in a regular session were continued in two special sessions. The verbatim report ran into over 110 pages, and all the parliamentary groups as well as three-quarters of the membership spoke on the subject. Other occasions when deputies waxed strong as national representatives were the recurring conflicts over the budgets of 1994, 1996, 2000, and 2002. The minority of deputies who sought to defend the executive on such occasions also claimed that they did so in the national interest.

Considerations of representing one's constituency not only trump representing "the nation," they also take precedence over representing interests such as the business community, labor, or teachers that are defined by policy area rather than by geography. The result, as the descriptions above make clear, is that deputies are more likely to devote time on individual efforts on behalf of their local community than on the core *collective* functions of the legislature.

Lawmaking and Policymaking

As discussed in Chapter 1, lawmaking and policymaking are not the same, because a distinction must be made between the mere passage of laws and the making of public policy on which laws are based. Article 105 of the 1990 Constitution states that "the initiative for laws belongs concurrently to the President of the Republic and the National Assembly." However, both the deputies interviewed for this study and their constituents agree that the executive dominates the lawmaking function, because it initiates the legislative process by introducing legislation based on its policy agenda. Available statistics on the number of laws initiated by the executive and the legislature since 1991 confirm this perception, as indicated in Tables 4.2 and 4.3. This is also the pattern found in France, where 80 percent of all laws are initiated by the executive (Djerekpo, Laleye, and Tevoedjre 1998, 118), as well as the pattern in other established democracies.

The explanations for this imbalance include the need for the executive to initiate laws for running the country (including laws linked to regional, subregional, and international conventions).[8] More fundamentally, it reflects the need for increasingly complex and specialized legislation combined with the vastly superior resources of the executive compared to those of the legislature in terms of the number and quality of technical and professional staff. As discussed earlier in the section on legislative commissions, it is unlikely that the assembly's contribution to lawmaking will improve until the technical capacity of its commissions is strengthened. This is especially true for the Law Commission. That said, a few notable member's bills were passed into the law between 1991 and 2002. These include the Electoral Code by the First Legislature and the University Professors Retirement Law by the Third.

Whether a bill is initiated by the executive or the legislature, it must be promulgated by the president of the republic before it becomes law (Benin 1990, article 57). The president of the assembly must send bills passed by the body to the president of the republic within 48 hours. The latter is then required to sign the law within 15 days. If the president of the republic does not

Table 4.2 Laws Initiated by the President and Parliament, 1991–2006

Legislatures	By Executive	By Legislature
First (1991–1995)	74	13
Second (1995–1999)	110	6
Third (1999–2003)	98	9
Fourth (2003–2006)[a]	100	7

Note: a. As of August 2, 2006 (the legislature ended in March 2007).

Table 4.3 Typology of Laws Passed

Legislature	Ordinary Laws Passed – Initiated by Government	Ordinary Laws Passed – Initiated by National Assembly	Total	Ratification Authorizations[a]	Laws Passed After Constitutional Court Review[b]	Total[c]
First Legislature	32	13	45	42	1	88
Second Legislature	32	6	38	78	1	117
Third Legislature	27	9	36	71	20	127
Fourth Legislature[d]	30	7	37	70	13	120

Source: National Assembly of Benin, Administrative General Secretariat, Legislative Services Directorate (September 2006).

Notes: a. Also initiated by president.

b. These figures do not normally increase the total number of laws passed by the NA; they had been passed and then revisited to adjust them to the provisions of the constitution after court injunction.

c. This total includes the laws reviewed with a view to adjusting them to the constitution for the purpose of revealing totality of the work achieved by each legislature.

d. As of August 2, 2006.

sign, the President of the Assembly can make a request to the Constitutional Court to declare the law enforceable. The court normally grants such requests, unless it discovers an unconstitutional provision. Successive presidents of the assembly have used this procedure.

Another measure of deputies' contribution to the legislative process is the quality of the amendments they make to the bills submitted by the executive. The First Legislature scored highly in this regard by several informants. The "laws were always amended in a qualitative manner because of the quality of the deputies." It might be the case that the members of the Law Commission in the Second and Third Legislatures did not have the same expertise and dedication as those in the First. And it has already been mentioned that technical capacity to support the work of all the commissions has remained rudimentary.

Oversight and Control of the Executive

The assembly exercises both an a priori and a posteriori control of the executive's management of public finances. The former is through the voting of the annual budget and supplementary budget (if there is one),[9] and the latter is through the passage of the law on public accounts[10] following the audit of the annual public accounts by the supreme audit institution, the Accounts Section (Chambre des Comptes) of the Supreme Court. It is also important to mention that the Finance Commission can control the execution of the budget during the financial year. However, no Finance Commission has exercised this type of control. This failure of successive Finance Commissions to control the budget during the execution phase is only partly due to the limited amount of technical support available to the commission. Rather, it is mainly due to a general weakness of legislative control of public finances at all stages of budget management—preparation, execution, and auditing. This point is examined in greater detail below.

Voting for the Budget (Budget Authorization)

The role of the assembly in authorizing the budget is regarded by both deputies and outside observers as one of the distinctive features of the legislative process since the advent of Democratic Renewal in 1991. It has attracted attention because of the efforts by deputies to amend the budget, thus asserting legislative autonomy. The executive under two different presidents (Nicéphore Soglo and Kérékou) has consistently maintained that some amendments introduced by the deputies were inconsistent with the constitution. The result is that on four occasions (1994, 1996, 2000, and 2002), the executive-legislative disagreement over the budget ended by the executive unilaterally authorizing the budget by presidential decree (*ordonnance*). Since 2003, the budgets have been passed by the assembly and agreed to by the president.

The constitution provides two rationales for the president to authorize budgets by decree. Article 110 allows the president to adopt the budget by presidential decree if the legislature fails to pass it by December 31. Article 68 also permits the president to adopt the budget by decree without recourse to the Constitutional Court if he thinks that there is a national crisis that warrants the exceptional measure. Of the four presidential decrees made between 1991 and 2002, one invoked Article 110 and the three others invoked Article 68.

When the conflict first arose in 1994, the President of the Assembly challenged the decision of the president of the republic to invoke Article 68 before the Constitutional Court. However, the court's interpretation of the constitutional provisions on the powers of parliament in budgetary matters broadly favored the executive.

- Parliament's own budget must be submitted to the executive for inclusion in the government's budget.
- The principle of a balanced budget must be respected by parliament, that is, parliament cannot reduce public revenues or create or increase public spending unless the amendments include proposals for increasing revenues or generating savings in the equivalent amount.
- Parliament must respect the international financial commitments of the government as spelled out in the draft budget law.

The deputies interpreted these conflicts in terms of the struggle for autonomy of the assembly vis-à-vis the executive. They believe that members of the assembly must determine their own budget and that it be integrated into the national budget without change. They also believe that the legislature should have the opportunity to amend a draft budget law in respect of provisions that it considers to be in the national interest. With the exception of the successful rejection of a World Bank credit for road construction in the 1992 budget, which the government agreed to withdraw for renegotiation, no significant amendments have been made to the annual budgets since 1991. With regard to the parliament's own budget, the executive has prevailed in imposing significant reductions whenever there has been a disagreement between the estimates passed by the assembly and what the government has considered affordable or politically expedient.

The most drastic reduction of a budget was in 2002 when the budget was adopted by presidential decree following a reduction of more than 50 percent as indicated by Table 4.4. About 75 percent of the deputies of the Third Legislature interviewed for this study regarded the adoption of the 2002 budget by presidential decree as one of the landmark events in the Third Legislature.

The majority of deputies interviewed complained bitterly about the adoption of the 2002 budget in this manner. The President of the Assembly reflected the frustrations of his colleagues when he cried out in a press release that "[b]y invoking Article 68, the government is undermining democracy, good governance,

Table 4.4 Parliamentary Budgets, 1995–2005 (in CFA)

Year	Estimates	Actually Disbursed
1995	1,324,114,871	1,320,525,000
1999	2,119,545,115	2,069,545,115
2000	2,769,089,953	2,769,089,953
2001	2,990,589,859	2,990,589,859
2002	3,136,444,055	3,399,597,412[a]
2003	3,984,881,000	3,531,880,939[a]
2004	4,752,051,384	n.a.
2005	5,721,944,784	n.a.

Notes: Average exchange rate for 1995 to 2002: US$1 = 700 CFA; average exchange rate for 2003 to 2005: US$1 = 500 CFA.

n.a. = not available.

a. This figure is yet to be validated by the Finance Committee of the National Assembly.

and the correct functioning of the institutions. I call on all Beninois, men and women, to be vigilant to safeguard the gains of the National Conference" (*Le Républicain,* February 4, 2002).

The crux of the problem appears to be the noninvolvement of the legislature in developing the framework for the annual estimates of revenues and spending. Three remedies could be considered. First, parliament could be involved within the context of the recently adopted public expenditure management process and integrated with the Poverty Reduction Strategy Paper produced for the international donor community, particularly the World Bank. The second remedy is for the legislature to devise creative and less confrontational ways of pursuing its autonomy struggles, because these are sure to be countered by the executive. Third, the executive could stop invoking Article 68, which was intended for dealing with real crises facing the nation. Article 68 is a copy of Article 16 of France's 1958 Constitution, which has been invoked only once since its adoption in that country. Continued invocation of Article 68 to pass the annual budget, especially when bundled with one or more draft laws on hotly contested policies pending before the assembly, could distort the checks and balances enshrined in the constitution. For example, a contested bill to privatize the post office also became law through presidential decree on the adoption of the 2002 budget. This may in turn undermine the consolidation of democracy in Benin.

Voting the Law on Public Accounts

No parliament in Benin had ever voted a law on public accounts until the Third Legislature (1999–2003). This was because the public accounts were never audited until 1998, although the failure to perform such audits violated provisions in successive constitutions. The Chamber of Accounts attempted to conduct an audit following the Democratic Renewal in 1991, but found the task daunting as it faced a backlog of more than three decades of material to review. The chamber did, however, issue an interim report based on a "rapid" auditing of accounts from 1991 through 1994. Thereafter, nothing happened as a result of poor training and small staff until 1998 when the donors, including the World Bank, reached an agreement with the government on strengthening the capacity of the chamber. The process started in earnest in September 1999 when the government sent the audited public accounts for 1998 to the chamber, which completed its report in November 1999. As required by the Finance Law, the report included a declaration that the accounts were in conformity with the law—*le declaration générale de conformité*. However, the process dragged on until 2002, 31 months from the time the report was first sent to the chamber to the adoption of the law adopting the audit by the National Assembly. Table 4.5 presents the details of what is a five-stage process for the Public Accounts Laws for 1998 and 1999.

In adopting the law of public accounts for 1998, the National Assembly strongly recommended that the government implement remedial measures for expediting future audits based on recommendations previously made by the chamber and accepted by the government. One measure was a review of the

Table 4.5 Overview of Steps for the Adoption of the Law on Public Accounts, 1998 and 1999

Step Number	Action	Financial Years 1998	Financial Years 1999
1	Audited Public Accounts submission to Chamber of Accounts	September 27, 1999	August 21, 2001
2	Adoption of the Report on Public Accounts by the Chamber	November 5, 1999	December 20, 2001
3	Transmittal of the Report on Public Accounts to Minister for Finance	n.a.	April 4, 2002
4	Transmittal of the Draft Law on Public Accounts to National Assembly	December 28, 1999	August 7, 2002
5	Adoption of the Law	July 11, 2002	December 2005, along with the accounts for 2000

Note: n.a. = not available.

terms of service of public accountants. A second was the urgent need to review and update the Finance Law. The assembly also called for closer coordination among the three parties concerned with the audit process—the Ministry of Finance, the Chamber of Accounts, and the National Assembly.[11] Finally, the assembly requested the government and the chamber to introduce a draft bill on clearing the backlog of public accounts for the years 1960–1990 before the adoption of the 2003 budget.

The repeated delays in voting on a budget law are also a result of limited capacity of the assembly itself. Most deputies are inexperienced in dealing with audit reports. The assembly also lacks sufficient in-house technical and professional staff to assist deputies. Nor has it been able to contract external expertise in a timely manner. The obvious point to stress here is the need for urgent strengthening of the assembly's capacity in all aspects of public financial management—budget preparation, budget implementation, and the scrutiny of public accounts.

Oversight of the Executive

Regarding the extent of the assembly's control of the executive, the frank responses of deputies varied from "zero" to "modest." No deputy claimed that the legislative oversight has been "very effective." It is remarkable that this self-assessment is similar to those of the other actors interviewed for this study. Article 113 of the constitution lists four methods of legislative control:

- Interpellation (queries) to the president of the republic and his ministers[12]
- Written questions
- Oral questions, with or without debate, but not to be followed by a vote
- Parliamentary commissions of inquiry

The conditions governing the use of these different methods are set out in the assembly's internal rules. The frequency of the four types of questions as well as the number of commissions of inquiry established to probe into operations of the executive branch are given in Table 4.6.

Oral questions constitute a highly visible instrument of legislative control, and there is a fixed time period during parliamentary sessions (every Thursday afternoon) set aside for this purpose. The sessions are open to the public and the media. However, the manner in which the session is conducted and the ways in which the executive provides responses make the exercise ineffective. A minister's answers are often followed by rambling debates with no conclusions drawn by either side. Moreover, no sanctions have ever been taken against officials in the executive branch whose mismanagement has been exposed through the questions posed. Ministers and deputies play to the gallery under the glare of publicity, including live TV and radio coverage. There is also the

Table 4.6 Some Illustrations of Parliament's Oversight Function, 1991–2005

	Written Questions	Oral Questions	Questions on Current Affairs	Queries to President and Ministers	Commissions of Inquiry
1991–1995	1	100	1	2	2
1995–1999	55	43	15	0	5
1999–2003	7	55	43	1	6
2003–2005	88	55	22	0	6

Source: National Assembly of Benin, Administrative General Secretariat, Legislative Services Directorate (September 2006).

habit of the executive to use the occasion of the media briefing on weekly cabinet meetings to provide responses to issues raised during parliamentary debates—a clear abuse of the question procedure.

Deputies also expressed frustration at the lack of follow-up and the absence of sanctions regarding acts of omission and commission that have been uncovered through the queries posed to the president of the republic and cabinet ministers in successive legislatures since 1991. Two presidents were queried regarding two scandals: President Soglo on the "Brewery Privatization Scandal" in 1992, and President Kérékou on the "Cotonou Port Scandal" in 1997. The long debates on both occasions had no practical effects on how the government eventually tackled both problems. The commissions include investigations of the Cotonou Port Authority (1996), the renovation of the General Hospital in Porto Novo (1997), the organization of the 6th Francophone Summit (1998), the implementation of the Project on Health and Population (1999), the construction of social housing, *logements sociaux* (2000), and the implementation of the Privatization and Commercialiation Programme since 1990 (2001).

Four factors have limited the effectiveness of legislative control: (1) the incoherence and indiscipline of the parties in parliament, (2) the inadequacies of the internal rules, (3) the deputies' limited access to information, and (4) the executive's resistance to legislative control. As suggested above, the party system is unlikely to be strengthened until there is increased maturity on the part of party leaders. For example, a few party leaders could emerge who would take the work of the assembly more seriously rather than devoting most of their energy to enhancing their prospects for joining the cabinet, or running in the next presidential elections. As noted above, it is significant that the legislature in Benin cannot censure the government, a widespread method of control used by legislatures in many parts of the world.

With regard to obtaining greater access to information, three ministers interviewed for this study noted that the public service is the gatekeeper of information, and its officials decide the timing and amount of information to share with ministers, deputies, or the public. They added that if ministers complain, the deputies are likely to be in a worse situation. Civil society representatives interviewed, especially representatives of the media, also complained about the difficulty of accessing official information.

The fourth and most fundamental factor is the habit of successive executives since 1991 to put obstacles in the way of the legislature. No sooner is a legislative commission of inquiry established to probe a case of maladministration or corruption than the same matter is taken to court by the executive. The legislative effort has to be abandoned, for reason of being sub judice. And in one or two cases when a legislative inquiry was established, the inadequacy of funds ensured its premature termination—the executive did not provide the extra funds needed to complete the inquiry.

Internal Control:
Deputies' Oversight of the Parliamentary Executive

Article 84 of the Benin constitution requires the president of the National Assembly to present a report on the running of parliament's affairs to a plenary session. Article 21 of the internal rules likewise states that at the beginning of each parliamentary session, the President of the Assembly shall "present a report on his activities and management [during the preceding session]." Deputies are expected to critically examine the report and make observations. The internal rules also state that individual deputies can pose written or oral questions to the president of the assembly and that deputies can examine his/her stewardship through a commission of inquiry. A damaging report could lead to the president's removal provided two-thirds of deputies demand such action. In actuality, the reports are followed by rowdy debates, but no serious probing takes place. Worse, financial accountability is rarely scrutinized, because the legislature's treasurers rarely submit a financial report.

Many deputies claim that internal oversight function is not taken seriously. Put differently, there is no "control culture." When a panel of inquiry was set up on the management of the assembly's finances during the Third Legislature, the report was never tabled for debate. Some deputies interviewed said that there is a need to improve the management of the parliamentary staff with particular attention to staff discipline. A significant number of the Third Legislature deputies interviewed expressed dissatisfaction with the inadequate attention hitherto paid to staff discipline. They would like the internal rules revised to stress the need for timely and thorough accountability, including provisions for sanctions and their enforcement. Increased attention to internal oversight is likely to go pari passu with significant improvement in legislative control of the executive. Taking legislative control seriously, however, will require greater leadership on the part of the president and the other officers of the assembly.

The Assembly as Seen by Others

The views of the National Assembly by the public and leaders outside parliament were obtained through a series of interviews that are summarized in this section.[13] There is substantial overlap in the perceptions of these groups, largely because those questioned had belonged to two or more of these groups at various stages of their careers.

National Political and Administrative Leaders

Government leaders, both ministers and senior civil servants, are evenhanded in their views of the assembly in that they see both its strengths and weaknesses and acknowledge that it has some real constraints. For example, one minister observed that the problem of access to information that he experiences within his own ministry is worse for a deputy seeking to obtain information from the ministry. One secretary general (the equivalent of the permanent secretary or director general in Anglophone Africa) of a ministry explained that executive-legislative competition is largely at a rhetorical level, with each side playing to the gallery. On the other hand, when a ministry prepares its papers well and goes to the assembly with adequate copies and engages in "individual [and informal] relations," deputies cooperate and the system works. It appears that this collaborative approach is most typical of the technical ministries such as environment and works. Even the Ministry of Justice, which is responsible for introducing a large number of bills, admitted that the legislature delivers in respect to processing laws. Government leaders also feel that the assembly functions better at the level of the permanent commissions than at the plenary level. This is not surprising since informal relations often prove more effective in a commission than in the plenary, and because the commissions focus on a specific policy area.

Ministers who had served in previous legislatures, however, judged the Third Legislature as less effective than its predecessors.[14] They stressed the lack of discipline within political parties in the assembly and the lack of respect for punctuality that causes some ministers to fail to appear before the assembly. They also felt that senior civil servants did not pay enough attention to the critical role of the legislature in the policy process. For example, senior officials in the Ministry of Finance saw nothing wrong in the noninvolvement of the legislature in the preparation of the Poverty Reduction Strategy Paper, the government's strategy for economic development that is the basis for its requests for assistance from the World Bank and other donor agencies. "It will be sent to them [i.e., the deputies] when it is ready." This attitude suggests the need to educate career senior civil servants about the role and functions of the legislature in the policy process lest they risk interference or blockage by the assembly at some point in the future.

Local Political and Administrative Leaders

This group of actors, comprising district administrators (prefects or subprefects), other civil servants, and community and opinion leaders, has a very varied perception of the National Assembly across Benin. These variations depend on the regions and the individual deputies who represent them in the assembly. Local leaders tend to assess their representatives from two perspectives: their work in the assembly and their relationship with their constituents.

The general view is that the deputies fail the country. Criticisms are very severe about the inability of the National Assembly to vote for the budget (a reference to the frequency of budgets adopted by presidential decrees) and about members paying greater attention to their salaries and personal comforts than to the country's problems. There was also criticism of what most local officials regard as excessive partisanship and frivolous or self-serving interpretations of provisions of the constitution and the assembly's internal rules. The deputies were viewed as costing too much to taxpayers. There was a widespread view of a gradual decline of the level of performance within the Third Legislature. It was ranked as being the least effective legislature since the Democratic Renewal in 1991. The opposition within the assembly was viewed as being obstructive and disruptive, rather than constructive for nation-building and development. While those interviewed acknowledged the necessary role of opposition, they condemned the trend toward what they described as opposition for opposition's sake. They felt that deputies need to adopt a more discerning attitude lest they risk penalizing their constituency. A consistent theme was that while deputies are free to support their party's positions on various issues, these positions should not adversely affect the interests of their constituents. The role of the deputy is to lobby to bring the "goodies"—that is, "pork" (schools, health clinics, rural roads, etc.)—back to his people, and constituents do not really care how deputies fulfill these expectations or what concessions they might make in respect to personal or party positions. Here again, deputies are expected to be providers of constituency service first, and members of the legislature second.

With regard to constituency relationships, deputies were also criticized for being removed from the people, and for only showing up in the constituency when seeking votes prior to elections. There is a striking difference of perspective here between this criticism and the almost unanimous claim by deputies that they paid regular visits to their districts. This may be due to the fact that when deputies return to their constituencies, they give priority to meeting party members instead of making efforts to meet all sections of the population. Some opinion leaders alleged that political parties use the party-list voting system to force on the population candidates that are not popular. This observation appears to have foundation, because electoral constituencies lump together many communities and localities. Given a voting pattern where localities and ethnic groups divide their votes, the elected deputy always ends up as a community or ethnic group champion and the other communities in the same constituency feel that they do not have a deputy in the legislature.

The relationships between deputies and administrative officials are generally uneasy or superficially cordial, at best. In regions that were controlled by opposition deputies, the relations between deputies and administration officials were tense. Administrators accused deputies of instigating or actively supporting a number of social crises and unrest that the administrators had to manage. There were cases where deputies were said to look down on local administrators and preferred to deal with their ministers in Cotonou. On the positive side, government administrators acknowledged the contributions that deputies make to local development.

The Business Community

Members of the business community interviewed for this study were very outspoken about their disappointment with the performance of the assembly and the inconsistencies among members of the political class as demonstrated by the "migration" of deputies from one party to another. Business leaders were also very critical of the failure of the legislature to initiate laws that would create a more business-friendly environment conducive to the creation of more private enterprises and employment. According to one businessman, members of the National Assembly were not sensitive to strategic economic issues as evidenced by their poor handling of privatization programs.

Predictably, business operators use business criteria to assess the performance of the assembly, and their verdict is not surprising: In their view, the assembly is not cost-effective; deputies lack seriousness and do not speak the truth; and there is need for punctuality and regular attendance. Notwithstanding this perspective, they agree with the proposition that the "National Assembly is absolutely necessary for a democracy."

Members of the business community also take the view that the law on the declaration of assets by public officials should be strictly enforced in respect to ministers and senior public servants (including the police and the army), and that the public should have access to this information. Given these strong views and the remedies proposed, the quality of the assembly might be improved if more members of the business community sought election to the assembly or lobbied the legislature to adopt these reforms.

Civil Society

Representatives of civil society organizations were the constituency most critical of the National Assembly. Their stance appears to be based on their view of what good public management and good governance should be. It is also important to note that the NGOs have emerged as recruitment grounds for future deputies and ministers. Some deputies who became popular in their NGOs were wooed by their political parties. In some cases, the respect and popularity enjoyed by NGO leaders literally forced party leaders to adopt them as candidates on their party lists.

Notwithstanding their criticism, civil society representatives commended the "open-door" policy of deputies and the president of the assembly. They had little difficulty in gaining access to their deputies to lay out their positions on matters but complained that there is rarely any follow-up to the discussions that occur. They contend that the incoherence of political parties in the assembly hinders collaboration with their organizations. They were also critical of the weakness of legislative control of the executive with respect to corruption scandals that had been exposed in the media. They recommended electoral reforms that would include the abandonment of the existing centralized party-list system and the acceptance of independent candidates, but how this would address the problem is unclear. They would like all parties to increase the number of women deputies. They ranked the performance of both the Second and Third Legislatures as modest, compared to the good performance of the First.

The Media

Media practitioners as a group agreed that the assembly is playing an important role in democratic consolidation in Benin. Journalists expressed several concerns about the electoral system, the relevance of deputies' activities to the problems of the public, the performance of the legislature, and the imbalance in the executive-legislature relationship. Regarding the electoral system, journalists felt that its weaknesses were the result of the overwhelming role of political parties in candidate selection, the fact that primaries are not held to pick the candidates, and the growing role of money in political campaigns. They confirmed that the deputies do not have a good image in the eyes of the public as people regret having elected most of them. Deputies are viewed as being unaccountable and unresponsive. They suggested that many deputies would fail in their reelection bids because they had failed to deliver the "goods," yet as noted previously the rate of incumbents being reelected to the assembly has actually risen in recent years. Journalists acknowledged that deputies' representation function may have been negatively affected by the inherent tension between the concept of national representation and the demands of the public for greater constituency service. They also said that the assembly has made some contributions in respect to the core functions of the legislature, especially lawmaking during the Third Legislature.

International Aid Agencies

There is a consensus among Benin's development partners on the need to strengthen the capacity of the assembly. The case for support was made in a USAID report published in 1999: "A strategy of funding only institutions that provide appropriate incentives to carry out their constitutionally assigned role should be followed. The legislature and, to some extent, the courts have shown capacity for independence and integrity . . . and thus should be supported" (USAID 1999). It appears that other donors share this view, as the National Assembly ranks high among African legislatures that have received substantial financial and technical assistance from several development partners. These programs, however, appear to have had limited impact, as donors cite the same indicators of poor performance by the assembly as cited by the other groups reviewed in this section. These include the dominance of the executive in the legislative process, the failure to vote for the annual budget and the resort to budgets by presidential decree, and the low level of accountability by deputies to the governed. That said, donors are still committed to increasing the capacity of the assembly to be a more effective player in the budgetary process and in the analysis and drafting of legislation. Whether donor support can in fact build such capacity in the absence of better leadership from within the assembly, however, seems questionable.

Achievements and Constraints

Notwithstanding its limitations, the National Assembly can claim four notable achievements since the Democratic Renewal of 1991. The first is the uninterrupted functioning of the legislature through four elected terms, a major achievement when compared to the frequent interruptions of the first three decades of independence.

A second important achievement cited by both the deputies and other stakeholders is the contribution that the assembly is making to democratic consolidation. It is widely recognized as one of the principal institutions of the Democratic Renewal era. The fact that the president of the assembly is the number two personality in the state, after the president of the republic, confirms the prominent position of the legislature in the state institutional architecture. Parliament's assertion of autonomy vis-à-vis the executive and the growing strength of both political parties and civil society groups concerned with political issues are evidence of an emerging pluralistic democracy.

Third, the few successes in its scorecard in respect to lawmaking and oversight of the executive are not negligible. Certainly, these successes are more significant than those recorded by *all* previous legislatures combined in terms of their contribution to the building of a democratic society. Finally, the assembly deserves some credit for the tangible progress in social and economic development recorded from the early 1990s to date. A collapsing economy and a failing state were turned around by the joint efforts of the institutions of the republic that created a new environment conducive to development.[15] These achievements, however, are nonetheless modest when considered with respect to how well the National Assembly performs the four core and defining functions of the legislature, for here the accomplishments are partial at best.

Three main constraints to improved performance by the legislature have been identified in this study. First, the Benin legislature does not have adequate resources, neither financial nor infrastructural, to carry out its work. Deputies are poorly paid, making it difficult for them to meet voters' demands for constituency service while at the same time devoting a sufficient portion of their time to legislating and oversight. Members of the executive and the legislature also agree on the need for a new building with a larger chamber and adequate office space for both deputies and legislative staff. There is an urgent need for both branches to collaborate to construct a new office block within the shortest time possible. A second major constraint is the inadequacies of the current parliamentary staff, both in quantity and quality. As discussed earlier in this volume and this chapter, without an adequate provision of professional staff to the commissions (departmental committees) of the assembly, this system of committees will not function at the level intended.

Third, and arguably the most serious constraint, is attitudinal. Whether self-imposed by the deputies themselves, or by the executive, the attitudes of deputies and the leadership of the assembly must change if the body is to fully perform its assigned roles. Self-imposed constraints include, among others, the internal rules that hinder effective debate and require urgent review. Such a review was launched in late 2005, but one might ask why it took so long to address the problem. The same might be asked about the failure to provide resources for appropriate physical infrastructure, and especially for capacity building among legislative staff. Similarly, the two most critical constraints imposed by the executive are the lack of openness and frankness of most cabinet ministers in their relations with the assembly, and the reluctance of civil servants to grant access to information to deputies. Their attitudes must also change for the assembly to emerge as a stronger player in the political process. Put differently, and consistent with the experience elsewhere in Africa, the leadership of the assembly and deputies must assert themselves if the institution is to overcome its current problems and be respected by the executive. There must be a demand for reform from within, but whether this will manifest itself anytime soon is problematic so long as parties are weak and the leadership of the assembly remains fragmented.

Future Directions

If reform is to occur and the assembly strengthened, our findings suggest that the following actions should be taken:

- The assembly should complete the review of its internal rules and make appropriate changes to improve the quality and effectiveness of parliamentary debates. These would include the enforcement of sanctions against absenteeism and poor resource management; better time management; the implementation of a better strategy to communicate with the public; and effective participation by all deputies through the provision of simultaneous translation into Benin's various languages, as needed.
- The assembly (and the executive via the annual budget) should provide increased resources for capacity building for legislative staff. Alternatively, it must both seek and better utilize support from the donor community for this urgent task.
- Deputies need to achieve a better balance between their loyalty to their party and/or parliamentary group and their commitment to the National Assembly as an institution in a manner that ensures the coherence of the former and enhances the performance of the latter. This will require that deputies, and especially aspirants for higher political office, exercise a measure of self-restraint when it comes to asserting the interests of party groups.
- Cabinet ministers need to accept that the executive needs to work in partnership with the legislature, with due attention to openness, frankness, and mutual respect. In the absence of such a cooperative approach, executive-legislative relations are likely to be adversarial and unproductive. Each side must recognize that it has its respective role to play in the policymaking process.
- The government should issue guidelines to civil servants, and especially senior civil servants, on the critical role of the legislature in the policy process, with emphasis on its role in policy formulation. Civil servants also need to be directed to grant access to information to deputies (and the public as a whole) within the limits of the law.
- The legislature and executive should jointly begin to initiate the revision of certain provisions of the constitution as well as comprehensive revision of some laws whose inadequacies have been revealed during the first years of Democratic Renewal. Two priority areas are (1) enhancing

the autonomy and effectiveness of the Chamber of Accounts by constituting it into an independent Court of Accounts as required by a directive of the Economic Community of West African States (ECOWAS), which the government is already formally committed to, and (2) revising and updating the Finance Law (1986).
- The executive and the legislature should jointly organize orientation seminars at the beginning of every new legislature.
- Development partners should provide ample information about their respective programs and their procedures to the National Assembly in order to improve the deputies' understanding and evaluation of these programs and their implementation.

The likelihood of any of these reforms turns, in the final analysis, on political will. It is therefore significant that by the end of the Fourth Legislature there was an increasing awareness within both the executive and the legislature, and among the educated citizenry, that the National Assembly plays a critical role in nurturing a democratic culture and democratic consolidation in Benin. Thus, for example, the 2006 budget was adopted by the assembly before December 31 as required by the constitution, and the need for strengthening the legislature was highlighted in the campaign platforms of the major candidates involved in the presidential elections held in March 2006. The strengthening of the National Assembly and its emergence as an autonomous player will likely occur incrementally over an extended period. What is promising today is that the basis for such development is greater now than at any other time since the founding of the republic.

Notes

The authors would like to acknowledge the assistance of Mathias Hounkpe, policy analyst, Development Policy Analysis Unit of the National Assembly, Porto Novo, Republic of Benin, for assistance in updating an initial study completed in 2002 on which this chapter is based. We would also like to thank the many people who assisted us in Benin's two capitals (Cotonou and Porto Novo) and in the four parliamentary constituencies visited in different parts of the country. The views expressed by Mouftaou Laleye are his own and not necessarily shared by his current or former employer.

1. The current Règlement Intérieur were adopted by the legislature in 1995 and amended in 2002 (Benin 1995a and 2002a).

2. For examples of these declarations for the Third Legislature, see Maforikan 1999, 119–135.

3. Sixteen candidates contested the 2001 presidential elections, including the incumbent president of the National Assembly and two other deputies. The president of the National Assembly and two other deputies were candidates in the 2006 presidential elections.

4. The president of the assembly's observation on this point is noteworthy: "We do not have a culture of opposition. Instead, we have a culture of enjoying power. This

makes us ill at ease in opposition. . . . In reality, opposition is for the long haul. . . . It is a choice. Here [in the National Assembly], people are in opposition against their will" (interview, August 2, 2002).

5. With the possible exception of Ghana, the information technology capacity of parliaments of countries in the Economic Community of West African States compares unfavorably to the adequate to strong capacity in the parliaments of countries in the Southern African Development Community.

6. This low female representation contrasts with the huge success of Benin women in business. They constitute a significant proportion of the wealthy "Nana Benz" of the West African coast.

7. Regrettably, we were unable to provide comparable figures for 2003 and 2007.

8. For example, the conventions relating to a common framework for public financial management reform in all member states of the Union Economique et Monétaire Ouest Africain (UEMOA) adopted in 1997 and 1998 resulted in six laws initiated by the executive.

9. These are, respectively, *la loi des finances* and *la loi des finances rectificative*.

10. *La loi de règlement.*

11. For example, the Ministry of Finance has, on occasion, slowed the work of the Finance Commission of the National Assembly by taking a long time to respond to questions by the commission.

12. A query (unlike an individual deputy's oral or written question) is adopted in plenary by the National Assembly and sent to the president and/or his ministers. Upon receipt of response from the president or minister, the National Assembly may recommend necessary actions to the government. However, successive governments rarely have implemented these recommendations.

13. This section is based on interviews conducted with respect to the Third Legislature.

14. No interviews were conducted with deputies in the Fourth Legislature, so we are unable to present their judgments about the performance of the assembly during this period.

15. According to a UN Conference on Trade and Development report (2003), poverty in Benin (measured as proportion of population living on less than one dollar per day) is less severe than in six other UEMOA member states. Only Côte d'Ivoire and Senegal recorded lower levels of poverty.

5

Co-optation Despite Democratization in Ghana

Staffan I. Lindberg with Yongmei Zhou

Ghana's democratization is one of the political success stories in Africa (e.g., Gyimah-Boadi 2001; Jeffries 1998; Ninsin 1998; Nugent 2001) with a current record of five successive multiparty elections since 1992, of which the last three were judged "free and fair" and accepted by all major parties.[1] The third election, in December 2000, also led to an alternation in power when the incumbent president and old authoritarian ruler Jerry J. Rawlings of the National Democratic Congress (NDC) stepped down after two terms in office and conceded defeat to his party's main opponent, John A. Kufuor, the leader of the National Patriotic Party (NPP). The fourth successive democratic elections, which elected the Fourth Parliament (2005–2008) of the Fourth Republic, were held in December 2004, and in these the NPP strengthened their parliamentary majority and John A. Kufuor won a second term in office. The most recent parliamentary and presidential elections, held in December 2008 and January 2009, led to a second alternation of power after the NDC managed to regain a slim parliamentary majority and its presidential aspirant, John Atta-Mills, won the second-round runoff with 50.2 percent of valid votes against Nana Akuffo-Addo's 49.8 percent.[2]

The Ghanaian media is flourishing with numerous new newspapers, an increasing readership, and a strong growth of independent radio stations discussing policy and scrutinizing politicians. Freedom House's ratings of Ghana have soared from a low of 6 on both political rights and civil liberties in 1991 to a high of 1 on the political rights scale and 2 on the civil liberties scale in 2007 and 2008 (see Table 5.1). The Afrobarometer findings testify that 90 percent of Ghanaians categorically want to continue choosing their leaders through regular, honest, and open elections, and 70 percent are increasingly satisfied with the way democracy works, while the corresponding figure for a country such as Nigeria has plummeted to a mere 26 percent (Afrobarometer 2006).

The first few studies of voting behavior also suggest that citizens in Ghana tend to behave as "mature" democratic actors and have relatively stable preferences (Aryee 1998, 2001; Lindberg and Morrison 2008). By all indications, then, Ghana seems to have come a long way in developing a democracy with a mass-based support. Indeed, this trajectory places Ghana in a group of African countries whose transitions seem to be relatively secure (Lindberg 2006), a consolidated democracy

How do we then explain that one of its core institutions of democracy, the Parliament of Ghana, does not seem to flourish in the same way as democracy in general? This chapter analyzes the autonomy and performance of the Ghanaian legislature in terms of legislative and oversight functions and finds that these were strengthened during its first two terms following the return to multiparty politics in 1992 (i.e., from 1992 to 1996 and from 1997 to 2000) but has declined significantly since. This coincides with an alternation in power when the former opposition party NPP took control over the house and won the presidency in 2000. Why did this happen? The analysis suggests that limited resources for the legislature, weak capacity of the parliamentary service, a high turnover among MPs, and demands for constituency service all play a part in the explanation. Nevertheless, the most important explanation is to be found in the quest for survival of the new government of President Kufuor under conditions of high political competition, leading to co-optation of the legislature by the executive. The primary means for co-optation have been found in the hybrid constitution of Ghana making it possible for MPs to become ministers; in government's control over resources for constituency service; and in the creation of seats on procurement boards for ministries, departments, and agencies (MDAs) distributed as perks for loyal MPs. As in Uganda, the liberal dispensation of patronage by the executive to vulnerable MPs rolled back the progress that members had made to strengthen their institution. The ability of the NPP to enforce discipline within its ranks was another contributing factor, suggesting, as Kasfir and Twebaze argue in Chapter 3, that strong and coherent political parties can weaken, rather than contribute to, legislative development.

The Constitutional Legacy

When Ghana was ushered into multiparty politics by the general elections of 1992, it did so from a checkered history of periodic democratic and military rule since its independence in 1957. After three military regimes, two parliamentary, and one presidential regime had failed badly, Flight Lieutenant Jerry J. Rawlings seized power in a coup on December 31, 1981. Under his civilian-cum-military Provincial National Defense Council (PNDC), Ghana soon became a showcase of the World Bank and International Monetary Fund of structural adjustment with an annual gross domestic product (GDP) growth rate at around 5 percent over almost a decade. The PNDC also made Ghana a no-party electoral regime, with elections to local assemblies held in 1987, but strong internal as well as external pressure led to the inauguration of a multiparty democracy in January 1993. A constitution-making body (the Constitutional Commission) had taken over a year to deliberate, holding hearings all over the country, and in the end sought to find a constitutional hybrid between a parliamentary and presidential system as a remedy against the failures of the past. The result was a new constitution for the Fourth Republic since independence.

The essentially two-party composition of the legislature has changed dramatically over these past fifteen years (see Table 5.1). When Rawlings heading his NDC was declared the winner of the first presidential elections held in October 1992, the main opposition parties decided to boycott the following parliamentary elections in November. The NDC accordingly captured 189 out of the 200 seats, and the remaining few seats were won by largely sympathetic support parties and independents. The Second Parliament (1997–2000) was more balanced, with a sizable minority consisting mainly of the NPP's 61 seats. This was a period of vigorous activity and dynamism in the Ghanaian legislature.

The third consecutive elections held in 2000 brought an alternation in power, giving the NPP a slim majority in the legislature and ushering in its candidate John A. Kufuor, as president of the republic. A new Speaker was also elected, Pete Ala Djetey, who had an agenda to strengthen the legislature. This was a period of near parity and intense competition between the NPP and the NDC in the legislature as the former was trying to consolidate its control over the government while the NDC was striving to regroup. In the Fourth Parliament

Table 5.1 Number of Seats and Seat Shares by Parties in Parliament

		First Parliament (1993–1996)	Second Parliament (1997–2000)	Third Parliament (2001–2004)	Fourth Parliament (2005–2008)
NDC		94.5%	66.5%	46%	41%
	N	189	133	92	94
NPP		0.0%	30.5%	50%	55.5%
	N	—	61	100	128
Other Parties and Independents		5.5%	3%	4%	3.5%
	N	11	6	8	8
Total Seats	N	200	200	200	230
Average Freedom House Score, Political Rights		4.3	2.8	2.0	1.8

(2005–2008), the NPP increased its legislative majority to 128 out of (now) 230 seats, while the NDC gained only 94. How has the legislature fared under these conditions?

Performance and Impact of Parliament of Ghana

The impact of Parliament on politics and policy comes in many forms, translating into a multifaceted dependent variable. Not all of these are easily quantified or comparable. We need nonetheless to proceed with what is possible in a pioneering study such as this one. In this chapter, four main dimensions of how the legislature matters are analyzed utilizing several indicators for each dimension (see Figure 5.1). Taken together, they measure the levels of both formal and actual influence at any point in time, while the time series data establishes the trends (variation on the dependent variable) to be explained. These measures also assess the performance of Parliament with respect to two of the core functions of the legislature—legislating in the broad sense and oversight of the executive branch.

One set of indicators regards impact on *legislation,* from impact on policy initiatives to the number of bills introduced, passed, amended, or withdrawn. Second, a special case of legislation regards the *budgetary process,* including as a particular issue the budget and disbursements for the parliamentary service. Third, Parliament can matter in terms of exercising *oversight* of the executive. Finally, the legislature can have an impact on politics by influencing *appointments* for important positions such as ministers and senior judges.

Legislative and Policy Impact

The formal status and power of the Parliament of Ghana concerning policy and legislation are delineated in the Constitution of the Fourth Republic and the Standing Orders of Parliament. The Parliament of Ghana is a unicameral legislature consisting of 230 members (200 before January 2005) elected by plurality vote in single-member constituencies. Under Article 93 of the constitution, no other person or body has the power to pass any measure with the force of law other than Parliament. While most bills are expected to come from the executive, MPs can initiate legislation through so-called private member's bills. Parliament also determines its own agenda. The president cannot force the legislature to vote on a bill, nor can he or she amend laws unilaterally, dissolve the legislature, or rule by decree. The legislature in Ghana ultimately also has the right to pass a resolution to remove the president, vice president, or Speaker of the House under special circumstances (Article 69, and Standing Orders, part 16).

Figure 5.1 Measuring If the Legislature Matters—Dimensions and Indicators

Dependent Variable: Legislature's Impact

Dimensions	Legislation/Policy	Appointments	Budget	Oversight
Legal Provisions	• Exclusive lawmaking power • Sets its own agenda	• Exclusive power to approve nominations for ministers and Supreme Court Justices and members of Council of State	• Exclusive power to authorize public expenditures, taxes, and loans • Legislature's expenditures autonomous	• Minimum of 11 standing and 16 select committees with rights of High Court • Public Accounts Committee right to review audits • Follow implementation • Right to remove president
Indicators of Impact	• Statements • Substantive amendments of bills • Taking independent legislative initiatives • Bills withdrawn or rejected	• Nominations withdrawn or rejected	• Changes in budget estimates • Changes/rejections of taxes or loans	• Questions on the floor of the House • Public Accounts Committee achieving change • Investigations conducted on implementation

In reality, most of the impact on policy initiatives comes in the form of informal consultations between MPs and ministers. Statements on the floor of the House may also impact on policy formulation at various points, but it is hard to tell which comes first: the MPs making a statement on the floor leading to legislative action by the executive, or the executive starting work on an area leading to the MP making a statement. But in terms of legislation, we know the number of bills introduced to the Parliament and how many were subsequently enacted or withdrawn (Table 5.2). So far, none of the bills have been initiated from within the legislature by MPs, even though a few interest groups have received donor support to develop draft bills. For example, the initiative for a Freedom of Information Bill (1998) and a Domestic Violence Bill (2000) went through a consultation process and the sponsors identified bipartisan supporters in Parliament, but no MP has taken the initiative to introduce the bills in Parliament. Most parliamentarians are unaware of the two draft bills, but the draft Freedom of Information Bill found its way into the attorney general's office, and it has been rumored that it will be promoted as a government bill. As of 2008, however, the government had still not reintroduced the bill. Apart from this, all legislative initiatives have come from the executive and the legislature has limited itself to making amendments.

There are no statistics on the number of bills amended by the legislature in Ghana, and the compilation of such data would require a review of the daily parliamentary records. However, clerks assigned to the committees report in our interviews that roughly 60 percent of all bills are amended to some extent. Most such amendments are relatively insignificant, however, pertaining to matters of wording and minor adjustments. The clerks as well as most MPs also report that the First and Second Parliaments (1993–1996 and 1997–2000)

Table 5.2 Some Indicators of Impact on Legislation and Nominations

	First Parliament (1993–1996)	Second Parliament (1997–2000)	Third Parliament (2001–2004)	Fourth Parliament (2005–July 2008)
Bills enacted	80	64	92	70
Bills expired[a] or withdrawn	4	14	2	0
Withdrawn ministerial nominations	6	7	0	0

Note: a. There are two types of expired bills. The first type of expiration occurs when a committee purposely leaves the bill to "die" at the end of the year as a polite way of rejecting it. Such instances are included in the table. A second type, when the legislature genuinely cannot finish its work on a proposed bill and it therefore expires but is reintroduced the next year, is not included because it is not equivalent to rejection of a bill.

were more active in making more amendments that were substantial than the Third (2001–2004) and the Fourth (2005–2008). Even in the "rubber-stamp" First Parliament, the discussions were reportedly often heated and MPs had a significant impact on many of the bills introduced by President Rawlings' government.

In the Second Parliament, when opposition parties gained a third of the seats, intense debates flourished in the chamber, but a collaborative atmosphere characterized the committees' work, where a lot of substantive changes were made to many bills according to clerks, MPs from both the majority and the opposition, and the author's observations during this period. By all indications, this was the most assertive and vigorous of the four Parliaments, with a large group of highly competent opposition NPP MPs keeping everyone on their toes and a new cadre of MPs from the NDC taking their work as MPs seriously. In contrast, after the former opposition party NPP came to power in 2001, the legislature's independent impact in this regard started to decline. Fewer bills have been substantially altered, and debates both in the chamber and in the committees have been more muted.

Another and more tangible indicator of the impact of the legislature is the number of expired or withdrawn bills. Bills introduced in Parliament are not rejected outright as an act of courtesy, but rather the executive is advised to withdraw the bill. If such advice is not taken and the legislature is still unwilling to pass it, a bill is left in the filing cabinet of the committee to "die a natural death" at expiration of the parliamentary year on December 31. Despite being essentially a one-party Parliament, the First Parliament nevertheless managed to have four out of eighty-four bills withdrawn by the executive (Table 5.2). In the Second Parliament, the influence over legislation was further pronounced with fourteen bills out of a total of seventy-eight (18 percent) being withdrawn or purposely expired. The interviewees also list numerous bills that were significantly revised by committees during this period. However, in the Third Parliament, ninety-four bills were enacted, and only two bills (2.1 percent) were withdrawn and a fraction (four bills, 4.3 percent) were reported as changed significantly by Parliament: the civil aviation, labor, national reconciliation, and public procurement bills.

A review of the amendments of these four bills reveals that some significant changes indeed were introduced by the committees. In the Civil Aviation Bill (2004, Act 678), for example, Parliament deleted the executive's control over several functions in exchange for legislative control (e.g., clause 36). In the Labour Bill (2003, Act 651), Parliament amended clause 80 to the effect that trade unions and employment organizations shall not be directed, controlled financially, or materially aided by any political party, and also inserted the right of trade unions to appeal decisions by the executive to the National Labour Commission. In the Public Procurement Bill (2003), Parliament made a series of changes in the composition of tender boards (schedule 1) to the effect of removing executive dominance and placing MPs on the boards to increase Parliament's oversight function. In effect, the legislature on these occasions played an important role in reducing the influence and power of the executive, protecting civil society organizations from political pressure, and increasing Parliament's oversight and control functions. But the small number of bills that were subjected to significant changes suggests that Parliament's influence in this later period declined compared to the Second Parliament. President Kufuor also refused to assent to two bills after amendments were passed by the Parliament, something that never happened during the two terms of former president Rawlings. On these two occasions, the legislature did not use its constitutional power to override the president, further indicating the executive dominance in Ghanaian politics. During the Fourth Parliament, the executive did not withdraw any bills. Thus, these indicators show a legislature that over its first eight years showed increasing strength, whereafter its capacity and willingness to do so have declined.

Little Influence on the Budget

Enacting the annual Appropriations Bill is a special case of legislation, since it formally determines the allocations and expenditures of government for the coming year. Parliament holds the power of the purse for the nation, and its formal powers enshrined in the constitution in this regard are strong: Only Parliament can authorize public expenditures (Article 178), impose and waive taxes (Article 174), and authorize granting or receiving loans (Article 181). With regard to the legislature's impact on the budget in real terms, however, it is weak and it has not changed much during the period of the first four legislatures. Although Parliament follows the appropriation process as defined in the constitution, it has not become an effective forum for negotiations and compromises on allocation of national resources. Part of the reason is that Parliament does not have a budget office to assist MPs in dealing with the budget. The issue has been discussed informally a number of times, but neither of the main parties has pushed to make this one of their top priorities.

Typically, the annual estimates for MDAs are compiled by the Ministry of Finance and sent to Parliament by November 30. On the face of it, the executive has satisfied the constitutional requirement of introducing next year's budget in Parliament one month before the start of the fiscal year. But between November 30 and mid-February when the minister of finance formally presents the budget statement to Parliament, so many changes are made on the estimates that the ones Parliament receives by November 30 are not even distributed to members. The budget statement is debated from mid-February to early March, after which consideration of annual estimates of MDAs takes place by "shadow" committees. But rather than scrutinizing these, committees typically become advocates for their MDA, calling for increased allocations from the Ministry of Finance. No committee, in fact no MP, argues for reductions of any MDA budget and even reallocations within an MDA's budget are very rarely suggested. Tradeoffs between various MDAs are typically not discussed when considering the Appropriations Bill because every year the Appropriations Bill is presented after budget estimates of all MDAs have been approved, and it is considered a consolidated document of items that have all been individually approved. The process in 2002 was typical, and on March 18, the Appropriations Bill sailed through all the stages of first reading, consideration, and report by the Finance Committee, second reading, third reading, and final approval in less than four hours.

Parliament's own budget is a special case. The financial autonomy of the legislature is guaranteed by Article 179(2) of the constitution and Act 460 of 1993 providing that administrative and operational expenses of the Parliamentary Service are neither subject to budgetary review or control by the Ministry of Finance, nor to be voted on but only laid before Parliament for the information of members. Parliament's recurrent expenditures therefore are formally not to be subjected to any influence by the executive, but this autonomy has been compromised except in 2003 and 2004; the legislature submits budget estimates to the Ministry of Finance, which regularly makes substantive changes in the estimates.

In the fall of 2002, however, the new Speaker, Pete Ala Djetey, demanded that Parliament's constitutionally guaranteed financial autonomy be upheld and refused to submit estimates to the Ministry of Finance. After a heated argument that was partly held in public, President Kufuor had to back down and accept the new Speaker's stance. This was one of the main reasons why Kufuor decided two years later not to renominate Ala Djetey as Speaker for the Fourth Parliament. The new Speaker from 2004 and onward agreed to revert to the earlier practice of subjecting budget estimates to revisions by the Ministry of Finance. This is another indication of the declining power of the Ghanaian legislature. Following this move, the Ministry of Finance proceeded to slash Parliament's allocation from US$5.4 million in the estimates in November 2004 to a mere US$1.2 million in the final budget in March 2005, leaving Parliament with only 22 percent of its original allocation. By this time, that sum had already been spent in the first quarter, with the result that the Parliament was at the mercy of the ministry for its monthly disbursements in excess of the final budget for the remainder of 2005. In effect, every legislative or oversight activity that the legislature wanted to undertake had to be submitted to the executive for approval before funds were disbursed, thus undermining the autonomy of the legislature. In the following years, the budget and the actual disbursement to Parliament increased, but under strict guidance from the executive. Expenses that could substantially improve the capabilities of Parliament were generally not funded. A case in point was the construction of a new office building started during Ala Djetey's tenure as Speaker. The building would have provided appropriate infrastructure and space for clerks and committees to carry out their work. However, work on the building was halted throughout the Fourth Parliament.

Weakening Oversight Performance

In a formal sense, the oversight functions of the Ghanaian legislature are up to standard. The Standing Orders (part 20) requires Parliament to have a minimum of eleven standing committees, the most significant among them being the Public Accounts Committee (PAC), the Business Committee, the Committee on Government Assurances, and the Finance Committee. The powerful Business Committee consists of the majority and minority leaders in the House, their deputies, whips, and additional members. It determines the agenda for the House for each following week at their Friday meetings and can direct much of the legislative activities, timetables for bills, as well as reporting on oversight and questioning of ministers. It is the de facto gatekeeper of parliamentary business, and it is through this committee that the majority leader exercises much of his power. Along with the PAC discussed further below, the Appointments Committee, the Finance Committee, and the Committee on Government Assurances are important instruments for Parliament's oversight function, but their effectiveness is highly dependent on the will of the majority leader and the Speaker, who, as we shall see, have impeded their work in recent years.

The Standing Orders also require the legislature to have fourteen select (equivalent to departmental) committees with the rights and privileges of the High Court, meant to shadow ministries and inquire into activities of MDAs as needed (Article 103), exercising oversight of the executive. Members get the chance to indicate their preferences at the beginning of each year and are thereafter appointed to both standing and select committees as desired by the Committee of Selection chaired by the Speaker. After appointment during the first session, members typically serve on the same committees throughout the four-year life span of each Parliament, but changes do take place, and in particular, nonconformist members of the ruling party have been punished by removal from important committees.

All committee meetings are officially closed to the public and the media and the minutes are not made publicly available except in special cases, and this has probably contributed to the relatively collaborative atmosphere of most of the meetings. Most committees also have to meet in the lobby areas since the Parliament lacks sufficient meeting rooms. Members often come and go in a relaxed way and sometimes listen in, but the media and private individuals stay away. Over the years, the committees have invited civil society and other organizations to an increasing extent to hear their positions on issues pertaining to their interests, so the openness of deliberations has increased. Bipartisan agreements were the rule rather than the exception during the First and

Second Parliaments, but since President Kufuor's first term when NPP members were increasingly whipped to toe the party line, the work in the committees changed. Knowing that in the chamber the party line would prevail, members of the NPP adhered to the party line on contentious issues in the committee work as well.

Each committee is served by an assistant clerk and most committees have had their own clerk since 2005. Prior to that, each clerk assisted three or even four committees, limiting the time they could devote to each. Some clerks have worked over several years with the same committee, but most of them have changed frequently, reducing the possibility for accumulation of expertise or institutional memory.

Besides working through the committees, MPs can also exercise their oversight function by filing questions in the House, to which ministers are required to provide an answer within three weeks. Finally, MPs can petition complaints at ministers' execution of their duties with the Speaker, who determines further proceedings of the matter in question. Furthermore, Article 187 of the constitution requires all public accounts be audited by the auditor general, and the reports shall be submitted to Parliament within six months after the end of the fiscal year. Parliament then debates the reports and appoints a committee when necessary to deal with any questions.

In reality, the Parliament of Ghana has a relatively modest record of accomplishments in its performance of executive oversight. Members rarely use the investigative powers of parliamentary committees to probe into the implementation of enacted bills or into matters of malfeasance. MPs seem not to consider the full range of options available to them and tend to use primarily the option of filing questions to ministers in exercising oversight. Questions typically concern constituency matters such as when a particular road will be completed, or what the minister has done to ensure that this or that village will get a new school building, rather than national policy. While important matters for local development, these question-and-answer sessions fail to fulfill the mandate of the legislature to require transparency and accountability from the executive on the implementation of major policy programs. While the MPs (many of them in good faith) purport they do what they can to be watchdogs, the executive is for the most part unconstrained by the legislature.

In overseeing budget implementation, Parliament neither receives nor demands systematic budget reports. In fact, after parliamentary approval of the Appropriations Bill at the end of March each year, Parliament is unlikely to hear about the budget again until next year's budget presentation. As the official opposition prior to 2000, the NPP strongly criticized this feature of the budgetary process, arguing it was only in theory that Parliament held the national purse. They suggested a system of liquidity management that would restore parliamentary control, including a proposal that the auditor general should prepare an appropriation report comparing budget estimates with actual disbursements.

These suggestions were taken up neither by the NDC government nor by the subsequent NPP government, which was headed by the very MPs who actively advocated for the change. However, one step toward increasing transparency was taken in 2001 when the minister of finance presented a mid-year review of the budget to Parliament.

Once the auditor general submits the report on all public accounts to Parliament in accordance with Article 187 of the constitution, it is referred to the PAC chaired by the opposition for deliberation. For example, the auditor general's report on the 1996 accounts of MDAs of central government was introduced before Parliament on October 21, 1997, and referred to the PAC for consideration and report. The committee held thirty-three sittings at which evidence was collected from ministers, directors, and accountants. The PAC reported on several recurring malfeasances—for example, misappropriation and misapplication of funds and fraud and corruption in procurement and supply of goods and services, wages and salary administration, award of contracts, recovery of loans and advances, management of the pension scheme, and transfer of funds into the Consolidated Fund—and made a series of strong recommendations. However, the PAC's recommendations have been mostly ignored by MDAs and malfeasances keep recurring, because although the PAC has the same investigative power as a High Court, it does not have a High Court's prosecution power and cannot enforce its recommendations. The then minority leader J. H. Mensah also pointed out that lack of financial independence weakened the oversight function of Parliament. The PAC can not even afford to hire a counsel to help study the auditor general's report on the judiciary service because the executive only gives Parliament a very small budget. As Mensah put it, "if the culprit can decide whether you can investigate him, then you have lost the game to start with . . . [and] which suspect will give you the resources to investigate him?" (author's interview). The chairman of PAC during the Fourth Parliament, the NDC minority leader Albin Bagbin, was in full agreement with the assessment by the previous minority leader, but when the NPP came to power and Mensah became a senior minister, he did nothing about this.

Declining Influence on Presidential Appointments

The fourth and final dimension of the dependent variable also indicates the declining impact of the legislature after 2000 when Kufuor was elected president. The constitution requires that the president's nominees for appointment as ministers, deputy ministers, justices of the Supreme Court, and members of the Council of State must be approved by the legislature. The First Parliament forced then president Rawlings to withdraw six of his ministerial nominations (Table 5.2) despite his reportedly strong leadership. At the beginning of the Second Parliament, another seven of Rawlings' ministerial nominations were rejected. While this could indicate a weak quality of nominees, it also indicates a strengthening of the legislature's assertion of power. When the new president Kufuor presented his nominations for an NPP government at the beginning of the Third Parliament, however, not a single nomination was rejected and none were withdrawn by the executive despite there being at least four nominees who were seriously questioned in their capability or trustworthiness. The same was true in 2005, when three of President Kufuor's nominees were under scrutiny for making false statements or engaging in corruption. According to several interviewees, the executive exerted considerable pressure on Parliament to approve the nominations despite questions raised and paid substantial sums to members of the Appointments Committee to get them passed. In conclusion, while the Parliament of Ghana had some success in shaping policy during its first two terms, it has since declined in autonomy and performance.

Parliament as an Institution

The above review of the constitutional provisions and standing orders of the legislature in Ghana shows that the Parliament is endowed with a number of instruments to assert its autonomy and power. Its formal authority in terms of legislation, policy direction, nominations, budgeting, improving the conditions of service, and providing oversight are relatively strong. In terms of "real" variance on our multifaceted dependent variable of legislative performance, the legislature in Ghana gradually and partially strengthened itself from its inception through the first half of the Third Parliament, roughly from 1993 to 2002. However, since then Parliament has not continued to develop its capacity to effectively perform its core functions. During its third term, Parliament lost political power, and the legislature has decreased in stature as a democratic institution in its own right.

The legislature's impact on legislation and nominations also decreased during this later period. While its influence on the budget and importance as an institution of oversight over the executive have always been relatively weak, the new NDC opposition made efforts to exercise stronger oversight in 2004 and 2005. Particularly disappointing, however, is that Parliament's attempt to exert its constitutional right to financial autonomy has been curbed by the NPP administration when one would have hoped that the turnover of power would signify the final departure from Ghana's authoritarian past. How can we explain this development? What are the contributing factors? We proceed by looking first at some structural issues such as financial conditions, structure and composition of the Parliament's membership and staff, constitutional and other constraints, and then to a number of issues relating to the importance of agency and leadership qualities.

Institutional Capacity

The financial strength and human resources of an institution are often thought to be two major sources of its capacity to function effectively. With more funds available, a legislature can invest in everything from motivating staff through better incentives such as salaries and office space, to enhancing activities related to passing legislation or oversight. The availability of money, however, is dependent on both the autonomy of the legislature to control its own budget, and its ability to ensure that resource allocations voted for the legislature are in fact provided by the Treasury. In the case of the Parliament of Ghana, it had the constitutional authority to provide for its own expenditures but could not sustain that authority vis-à-vis the Ministry of Finance. Table 5.3 compares the budget allocated for the Parliament with the actual disbursements.[3] Under Justice D. F. Annan, the Speaker from 1993 to 2000, the Parliament received modest increases in both allocations and disbursements. Following Annan's tenure, there was a substantial increase in the budgetary allocation during the Third Parliament when the new speaker, Pete Ala Djetey, insisted on respect for the constitutional and financial autonomy of the legislature. Parliament's budget was increased by 740 percent from 2001 to 2004.

The Ministry of Finance under the new Kufuor government, however, moved to limit the disbursements throughout the Third Parliament to undermine the newly asserted autonomy of Parliament. By 2004, only 43 percent of the budgeted allocations were released to the legislature. Actual expenditures nonetheless doubled during the Third Parliament, and tripled during the Fourth. This did not, however, result in an equivalent improvement in legislation, nominations, budget, and oversight functions. Rather, as we have seen, it led to a decline in the autonomous impact of the legislature. In a series of moves discussed later involving the co-optation of MPs and replacement of the leadership of Parliament, the executive managed to bring the legislature under its control despite its increased financial strength.

The quality of a legislature's professional staff is another major determinant of institutional capacity. Legislation, scrutinizing the government's budget proposals and nominations, and conducting oversight activities require highly educated and well-trained professional staff, especially the committee clerks, research officers, and library resources. Through its Parliamentary Service Board, the Parliament of Ghana controls the recruitment of staff. Under the chairmanship of Annan, the Speaker during the First and Second Parliaments, merit seems to have been the dominating factor in the board's hiring decisions. Few if any of the first few cohorts of key staff seem to have been engaged for other reasons. However, the last few years' expansion of support staff in particular has brought an increasing prevalence of nepotism and favoritism according to informants. Hence, the total number of lower administrative officers and other support staff (e.g., drivers, ushers, secretaries, and watchmen) has increased

Table 5.3 Budgeted and Actual Expenditures for the Parliament of Ghana (in US$ millions)

	First Parliament					Second Parliament					Third Parliament				Fourth Parliament			
	1993	1994	1995	1996	1997	1998	1999	2000	2001	2002	2003	2004	2005	2006	2007	2008
Budget	n.a.	n.a.	n.a.	n.a.	n.a.	n.a.	3.4	2.3	2.0	4.6	9.7	14.8	13.2	12.0	19.3	20.7
Actual expenditure	2.2	n.a.	n.a.	n.a.	n.a.	n.a.	4.2	2.8	3.0	2.9	6.5	6.3	14.8	12.0	19.3	n.a.

Notes: These figures are approximations based on figures provided by Parliament that were exclusive of personal emoluments, which according to the accounts department typically constitute 45–55 percent of total expenditure.
n.a. = not available.

eleven times since the First Parliament opened in 1993 until the beginning of 2005, while the number of professional staff, including clerks to the committees, research officers, and librarians, increased only threefold, reducing its share to 10 percent of total staff (see Table 5.4).

The number of key officers has increased in absolute numbers, but the increase has not been proportional to priorities that would have reflected the best interest for Parliament as an institution. For example, a few of the new hires to senior positions were rewards for personal affiliation to the Speaker. This has undermined the capacity of the legislature to offer appropriate support to MPs in their various roles. The problem is most obvious during February and March when all key staff are tied up with work on the budget proposals, thus bringing the legislature to a stop on other matters. A mitigating factor has been the low turnover among key staff. Of the first group of ten assistant clerks hired in 1992, nine are still in service. All but one of the next cohort are also still working at Parliament. The first librarian and the first two research officers are also still in their positions.

The clerks, research officers, and librarians are relatively young. Most were hired immediately upon graduating with their first degree from one of Ghana's universities. Since age tends to be very significant in determining status in Ghana, these young assistant clerks and even senior clerks in their forties who have been in service for more than ten years have limited possibilities of influencing the work of a committee chaired by a much older male MP, typically from a family of high social standing, who is also a minister[4] and who in any case considers himself a "big man." Members often simply do not allow clerks to take initiatives and guide the work of committees. With a high turnover among MPs, this practice has significantly reduced the impact of the Parliament, because the accumulated experience among staff is not being used. It has also led to the paradoxical situation that while the Parliament is understaffed with

Table 5.4 Number of Staff in the Parliament of Ghana

	First Parliament (1993–1996)	Second Parliament (1997–2000)	Third Parliament (2001–2004)	Fourth Parliament (2005–2008)
Clerks, library, and research staff[a]	16	33	45	45
Share of total staff	33%	18%	14%	10%
Other administrative and support staff[a]	33	149	273	377
Total number of staff	49	182	318	422

Note: a. These numbers are from the first year of the period.

clerks and research officers, most of the existing ones are more or less idle during recess periods, and many do not work full hours even during sessions, thus wasting scarce resources.

There are signs, however, that the current situation may be improving. In the fall of 2004, clerks were asked by the leadership of the legislature to draw up annual work plans and budgets for their committees for the first time. Our interviews indicate that clerks have now begun to play a more proactive role. They clearly appreciate their expanding role as well as the fact that their salaries have more than quadrupled since 2003 (see Table 5.5). This has in turn motivated them to work harder and improve the quality of their input. One indication of this is that the phrase of choice—"Parliament pretends to be paying us and we pretend to be working"—is no longer heard as frequently.

Salary increases for staff are a direct result of the assertion of financial autonomy by the Parliament of Ghana during the Third Parliament when the controversial Speaker Ala Djetey decided to improve the conditions of service. First salaries (in equivalent US dollars) were restored to the level of the mid-1990s and then trebled or quadrupled for most staff.

While higher salaries, accumulated experience, and a new, more proactive role of clerks laid the foundation for an improved work ethic and enhanced quality of work, several factors still undermine the efficiency of Parliament. The absence of a plan for human resource development for the Parliament is one such factor seriously impeding development of its capacity. While a senior human resource officer was eventually hired in 2004, he has yet to make significant changes due to the lack of support from the Speaker during the Fourth Parliament, Ebenezer S. Hughes. Some officers have received training, but there was no documentation on these efforts before the arrival of the human resource officer, and according to interviews there is no prior analysis of needs and no coherent process. The problem has also been that among the few who have received more training, several have subsequently left their jobs for better opportunities. The limited staff capacity of Parliament as an institution thus contributed to its weak performance but can hardly explain the full variation over time.

The Composition and Role of MPs

Another factor in the performance of Parliament is the composition and role of its members. While the First Parliament was dominated by the NDC and labeled a rubber-stamp institution, it was (as shown in Table 5.6) populated by relatively young members with an average age of 45 years. Thirty-two percent of the MPs were age 40 or younger, and their impact on legislation and appointments were noticeable. Since then, the composition of the legislature has changed in two regards: the average age has increased significantly and so has the share of MPs with a first- or second-degree college education.

Table 5.5 Monthly Gross Salary (including allowances) of Key Staff (in US dollars)

	First Parliament				Second Parliament				Third Parliament				Fourth Parliament			
	1993	1994	1995	1996	1997	1998	1999	2000	2001	2002	2003	2004	2005	2006	2007	2008
Clerk of Parliament	n.a.	n.a.	n.a.	437	n.a.	438	n.a.	150	317	407	459	1,188	1,182	1,695	2,144	2,144
Senior assistant clerks	n.a.	n.a.	n.a.	415	n.a.	319	n.a.	96	234	289	328	924	942	1,199	1,452	1,452
Clerical officer	n.a.	n.a.	n.a.	103	n.a.	124	n.a.	43	92	119	138	290	298	304	390	390

Note: n.a. = not available.

Table 5.6 Characteristics of MPs

	First Parliament (1993–1996)	Second Parliament (1997–2000)	Third Parliament (2001–2004)	Fourth Parliament (2005–2008)
Turnover				
Share of new MPs	100%	68%	42%	56%
Education				
MPs with first degree	47%	65%	57%	68%
MPs with master's degree	17%	19%	27%	27%
MPs with Ph.D.	5%	4%	n.a.	5%
Age				
MPs age 45 and below	58%	43%	n.a.	25%
MPs age 40 and below	32%	18%	n.a.	10%
Average age	45 years	48 years	49 years	51 years
Gender				
Share of MPs who are female	8%	9%	9%	11%

It is argued elsewhere in this book that the presence of a younger cohort of members with advanced levels of education promotes reform. We find that in Ghana, however, more highly educated but also older MPs are winning more of the seats in successive elections. The share of MPs in Ghana's legislature that are relatively young (i.e., 45 years or younger) has in fact decreased from 58 to 25 percent since the beginning of the First Parliament in 1993, while the average age of all MPs has increased from 45 to 51 years (Table 5.6). This decline coincides with a weakening of Parliament's autonomy and impact, but it is doubtful if this change in the composition of MPs has much explanatory power for the change in Parliament's performance. Indeed, it could be argued that the stature and impact of the legislature should increase with more senior and therefore more highly respected and experienced MPs, especially those with higher levels of education. Yet it has not.

More significant than age and the level of education, perhaps, is the rate of turnover, which has ranged from 42 to 68 percent at the last three elections. The accumulated effect of these numbers means that there is only a very small number of MPs with significant legislative experience accumulated over several terms on which their colleagues can draw, and many of these have been appointed ministers or deputy ministers in the government. The paucity of members serving a second or third term makes it easier for the executive to influence the behavior of the remaining MPs. Although it may not be the most important factor, it adds to the power of the executive in combination with other factors discussed below.

Compensation and Constituency Service

Another hypothesis explored in the other countries discussed in this book is that the conditions of service for MPs, in particular their salaries, is a determinant of the legislature's assertion of autonomy and political impact. The salaries and conditions of service for MPs in Ghana are to be determined by a special commission appointed by the president. This practice was followed during the first two Parliaments, but beginning in the Third Parliament, after Kufuor became president, the commission was not reestablished. It was only after the end of the Third Parliament that the members of the commission were chosen, thus delaying the determination of the terms of service for MPs until July 2005. The delay over setting the terms of service made MPs vulnerable and is another example of the executive exerting pressure on the legislature.

The conditions of service for MPs in Ghana are mediocre and far below those enjoyed by MPs in those legislatures that have exerted greater autonomy and influence than the Parliament of Ghana. As indicated in Table 5.7, salaries and allowances trebled during the term of the Third Parliament and doubled again during the term of the Fourth. Notwithstanding these increments, the terms of service for Ghanaian MPs remain among the lowest in Africa. As

Table 5.7 Monthly Gross Salary (including allowances) of MPs (in US dollars)

	First Parliament				Second Parliament				Third Parliament				Fourth Parliament			
	1993	1994	1995	1996	1997	1998	1999	2000	2001	2002	2003	2004	2005	2006	2007	2008
MPs (US$)	591	461	353	494	414	437	374	389	722	770	1,322	1,293	1,340	2,300	2,760	2,760

such, they do not provide a strong incentive for MPs to be more proactive with respect to carrying out the core functions of legislating in the broad sense and providing oversight. Indeed, just the opposite. The present salary structure provides MPs with strong incentives to toe the line and not challenge the executive in the hope of getting significantly higher compensation via a ministerial appointment or appointment to a procurement board. The physical infrastructure supporting MPs is also low. Apart from the leadership, members do not have offices provided by the legislature, and the only offices available are those attached to the various committees. The Parliament of Ghana does, however, provide each MP with a two-room apartment plus a car loan, which is to be repaid during the course of the legislator's term.

The increase in pay came alongside the general rise in parliamentary expenditures, including expenditures for staff that the former Speaker Ala Djetey instigated during the Third Parliament. It has improved the conditions for MPs given their obligations to fulfill high expectations for constituency service. MPs in Ghana typically travel "back home" to their districts at least every fortnight regardless of distance. On each visit, constituents will address them about a range of issues that often require a financial contribution. MPs are expected to provide private assistance for unpaid school, hospital, water, and electricity bills. Intervening in problems with formal as well as informal authorities, aid for funerals and weddings, youth clubs, and relief from unemployment are other requests expected by the MP in addition to community development such as roads, markets, toilets, and attraction of investment. Most MPs have offices in their constituency and a small staff to assist them. The pressures on incumbents to "take care" of "their people" are high, and failure to do so inevitably puts the MP at risk for not being reelected.

Constituency service is not cheap, especially for MPs with no other sources of income beyond their salaries. During the Second Parliament (1997–2000), a typical weekend visit cost the MP between $200 and $400. A decade later, the amount has doubled.[5] After the NPP government took over in 2001, an emerging trend was the push by constituents for their MP (in NPP constituencies) to get a ministerial appointment, knowing that being a minister increases the possibilities for an MP to bring "pork barrel"–type projects back home to the constituency. An incumbent that does not become at least a deputy minister is therefore perceived by voters as a failure, opening up the possibilities for a replacement at the next election. However, this trend provides the executive with additional leverage over individual MPs and the legislature generally as we shall see later in this chapter.

Another source of funding for MPs in Ghana to deliver "pork" is what is called the MPs' share of the Common Fund. The Common Fund consists of 7.5 percent of all state revenues, which is distributed to local governments in Ghana's 110 administrative districts. Districts typically enclose two or three parliamentary constituencies, and MPs have spending authority over 5 percent of the Common Fund for community development purposes in their constituency. Currently, MPs can use the equivalent of about US$34,000 annually from this source. In addition, when in the past few years Ghana was declared a Heavily Indebted Poor Country (HIPC), the same formula was applied, generating about another US$9,000 per year per MP for developmental projects in line with the HIPC guidelines. In contrast with the expectations placed on MPs by their constituents, and supporters in particular, these sums do not amount to much.

The Co-optation of the Legislature

Perhaps the most important factor reducing the clout of Ghana's legislature is the use of its hybrid constitution by the executive, in particular its exploitation by the Kufuor government. The constitution provides that while the president and MPs are elected by separate ballots, the president is required to recruit a majority of his ministers from Parliament. When the constitution was written in 1991 and 1992, this was viewed as a remedy against the kind of gridlock that contributed to the demise of the Third Republic in 1981. What was not foreseen was that the provision has come to be used to recruit the most competent MPs to join the government, thus depleting the legislature of some of its best talent, and for enforcing loyalty to the executive among those MPs left behind. The ministerial salary is not the most important factor in this equation, although it provides a 50 percent increment (inclusive of allowances and benefits) in total pay. Rather, MPs from the majority party are under intense pressure from their constituents to become ministers to provide more goods back home for their constituents. Accordingly, most approach the president for an office. Indeed, MPs who fail to be appointed as ministers are perceived by voters as useless for bringing resources back to the constituency.

The younger and new NPP members report that the price for the possibility of a ministerial appointment is made known to them immediately: compliance with the will of President Kufuor and the executive. The president is well aware what a ministerial office means to constituents, and in order to increase the likelihood of his reelection and that of his party's MPs, he has accommodated as many as possible. This has increased the number of MPs that are either ministers or deputy ministers from thirty-seven during Rawlings's time, to fifty-five in the Fourth Parliament (Table 5.8). At the same time, the president needs the best and most experienced politicians to be part of his government and those tend to be MPs. Like neopatrimonial leaders before him, he must ensure the loyalty of these MPs, since many are influential politicians with substantial followings in their own right. Table 5.8 presents a set of figures on how this co-option has increased over the period studied.

The number of MPs that are members of the cabinet has more than tripled since the First Parliament, while the total number of MPs being some kind of minister has almost doubled. As of 2005, 74 percent of the cabinet was made

Table 5.8 The Increasing Co-optation of MPs in Ghana

	First Parliament (1993–1996)	Second Parliament (1997–2000)	Third Parliament (2001–2004)	Fourth Parliament (2005–2008)
Number of MPs in the executive				
MPs made cabinet ministers	4	8	12	14
MPs made other ministers	16	11	15	13
MPs made deputy ministers	17	18	16	28
Total MPs made ministers or deputies	37	37	43	55
Share of MPs in the executive				
Share of MPs made minister or deputy	18%	19%	22%	24%
Share of majority party's MPs made minister or deputy	20%	29%	43%	43%
Share of the executive that are MPs				
Share of cabinet that are MPs	24%	42%	63%	74%
Share of ministers and deputies that are MPs	50%	50%	50%	63%
Competitiveness of legislature				
Majority party's share of total seats	95%	67%	51%	56%

up of MPs and over 63 percent of the total number of ministers were MPs, compared to 24 percent and 50 percent, respectively, during President Rawlings's first term in office. Rawlings also understood the significance of legislative support. When the NDC faced a stronger opposition in the Second Parliament, the share of MPs that were made ministers went up. An additional explanation of Kufuor's wider use of appointments as patronage is that Rawlings was more unchallenged within the NDC party than Kufuor is within his party. In addition, the NDC had close to a two-thirds majority even in the Second Parliament. Rawlings did not have to go as far as Kufuor to co-opt the legislature. Although both the size of the executive and the size of the legislature have increased, the share of the majority party's MPs that are ministers has increased from a low of 20 percent in the First Parliament to 43 percent at present. President Kufuor has made almost half of his NPP MPs ministers in an effort to ensure both the loyalty of the legislature and the reelection of these MPs in future contests. This effort at co-optation has increased with growing competitiveness in the legislature, with the Third Parliament providing hard lessons in this regard. The NPP had exactly 50 percent of the seats, and a few smaller parties and independents provided President Kufuor with a slim eight-seat majority. Because the Parliament has no provision to cancel out absentees during voting, even a few MPs on ministerial duties or on sick leave or constituency business threatened the government with defeat in the chamber. The new NPP administration quickly learned just how crucial it was to whip its MPs into line with government policy.

In short, increased competition within the legislature did not lead to a rise in the power of the legislature as one might have expected, and as was the experience in Kenya at the end of President Moi's reign. Instead of increasing the leverage of the Parliament vis-à-vis the executive, it gave Kufuor and his administration strong incentives to contain the legislature. One means of control was whipping members of the majority, including forcing them to openly show their ballot to colleagues during officially secret ballots to ensure that no one defied the leadership.

Another tool was cash handouts to MPs that by all indications increased during this period. On Fridays and in conjunction with controversial votes in the chamber, the infamous brown envelopes became more frequent and thicker to facilitate weekend visits home. Strapped for cash by their low salaries and in need to service their constituencies, MPs from within the ranks of the NPP and from its support parties were "rewarded" for good behavior. Service on tender boards became another creative way to ensure loyalty. There are currently 176 seats on various MDAs' tender boards for MPs, and each seat accrues between 3.5 million and 7.5 million Ghanian cedis (US$400 to $800) per month for the MP, or roughly a 30 to 60 percent increase of their income. The allocation of these patronage positions is another way MPs are made to toe the line. Younger and new MPs from the NPP and members from the supporting smaller parties also report that a constant pressure is exercised through allocations of state-provided pork in the form of improvements to roads, schools, health clinics, and the like for loyal MPs while independent behavior is punished. The MPs that are ministers simply act as "in-house" extensions of the executive, making the trade-offs between loyalty and defiance obvious to colleagues.

The effects of a large number of MPs doubling as ministers is also felt directly in the House as they come to spend less time in the legislature. Ministers report to spending about a third of their time in the legislature, and the rest is allocated to their executive duties. When one-quarter of the members reduce their input by two-thirds, that has effects on legislative performance.

Parliament's power to obstruct-cum-control the president's political agenda is also circumvented by Article 108 preventing Parliament from proceeding on any legislative initiative that would incur budget or tax increases unless such initiative comes from the executive. While it can be argued that this article is a necessary constraint to ensure fiscal discipline in emerging democracies, it also effectively curbs the power of the legislature.

The Manipulation of the Presiding Officer

Finally, although the nomination of the Speaker and the majority leader are formally vested with the legislature, President Kufuor asserted control over these appointments. The result, as discussed in Chapters 2 and 3 on Kenya and Uganda, is that the chief presiding officer has served the executive and retarded the pace of legislative reform. When the NPP took over in 2001, it installed Pete Ala Djetey as the new Speaker. He was an established lawyer, former party chairman, and known to be "his own man." Together with J. H. Mensah, the veteran politician and staunch liberal who was made majority leader, they formed a team that was difficult for Kufuor to direct from his presidential office. They insisted on Parliament's financial autonomy and its control over the agenda as well as independence of symbolic ceremonies like the annual opening of the House. Even more important, they demanded significant improvements in the terms of service for MPs and staff.

In response, the Kufuor administration removed Mensah from his position as majority leader and his influence within Parliament by making him the senior minister for long-term development. One of the president's closest affiliates, Felix Owusu-Adjapong, was then installed as majority leader. A rift soon opened between Speaker Ala Djetey and the new majority leader based on disagreements on a series of issues. For example, the new majority leader made it clear that he disapproved of Parliament's financial autonomy even though it was consistent with the constitution. He also publicly contested the constitutional provision of the Speaker as the leader of the House. Adjapong lost these two battles but ultimately orchestrated a change of Speaker at the beginning of the Fourth Parliament. In a controversial election held in January 2005, Ala Djetey was replaced by Ebenezer S. Hughes, a confidant of Kufuor and Adjapong. Though he was a member of the NPP, Ala Djetey was renominated for the speakership and supported by NDC members who appreciated his efforts to assert the independence of Parliament. Under extreme pressure from the executive, NPP MPs were forced to show their voting cards to the NPP parliamentary leadership before casting them in the ballot mandated by the Standing Orders to be secret. Not surprisingly, Ebenezer S. Hughes won the contest.

Many members of the ruling NPP felt the removal of Ala Djetey was an infringement on the autonomy of the legislature. Forced by the majority leader to show their ballot openly in the chamber, and under threat to lose appointments and other privileges, they did not vote against the president's wish. One effect was immediate: Parliament's financial autonomy was curbed when the legislature's budget was again placed firmly back in the hands of the Ministry of Finance. The organizational and human resource reform program has also stalled, to the frustration of many senior clerks and the detriment of the institution's capacity. Similarly, the construction of a new office building for MPs and parliamentary staff that would also have provided adequate meeting rooms for parliamentary committees ground to a halt. Each of these developments illustrates the importance of the Speaker and that person's relationship with the executive in facilitating or blocking reforms designed to strengthen the legislature.

A large proportion of NDC MPs express their increasing frustration with the strengthening grip of the executive. There is also a hidden and relatively widespread discontent with the state of affairs among NPP MPs, but the fear of being politically isolated, stripped of appointments, and denied resources for the constituency has proven stronger than any ethical convictions, and there is little to suggest that their calculations in that regard are likely to change in the near future. In contrast to Kenya, a coalition for change consisting of backbenchers of the ruling party and opposition members emerged in Ghana but could not be sustained.

Conclusion

It is disappointing that one of Africa's most successful cases of democratization has a legislature that is not as potent an institution as the country deserves given its achievements on other dimensions of democratization. It is not unique, however, that a young democracy experience periods of executive dominance. Executive branches of government after all generally seek to extend their influence beyond their bounds not only in emerging democracies but also in established ones. Known in Latin American politics as the lack of strong-enough horizontal accountability (O'Donnell 1998), this phenomenon is expressing itself in various ways in Africa, too.

Not that the situation in Ghana is extreme or life-threatening to its young democracy, but it still raises concerns. Ghana's hybrid constitution, while providing Parliament with some clout and largely supported by both main political traditions in the country, has given the executive leeway to undermine the strength of Parliament as an institution. Due to both other structural factors and the persons involved, the legislature has not made use of its constitutional powers versus the executive. The closeness of the outcome of the third elections leading to NPP's first coming to power did not help, but instead worked as an incentive for the executive to increase its leverage over the legislature. Whether this pattern will continue during the Fifth Parliament (2009–2012) as a result of the NDC winning back the presidency but with only a very slim parliamentary majority, or whether the new NDC government headed by John Atta-Mills will show a greater commitment to democratization than his predecessor by supporting the development of Parliament into an independent institution, remains to be seen. The tradition inherited from earlier experiences with electoral politics in Ghana has increased the constituent pressures on incumbent MPs to provide both local development and individual assistance. Intense political competition comes into play also in this area, spurring MPs and candidates alike to raise the stakes by offering higher rewards time after time. Given these realities, MPs remain vulnerable to blandishments by the executive.

The incentives facing MPs and Parliament are in some ways stacked against reform, but the NDC won the 2008 elections on a platform strongly emphasizing "fundamental change" (purporting as much closeness to Barack Obama in the United States as possible). The new president and his vice president, John Mahama, are also both known for their integrity and for being highly principled and honest. Left to them alone, one could expect the performance of the Parliament of Ghana to improve. But whether they will succeed in being captains navigating the ship and not just seamen trying to stay afloat, to paraphrase Robert Jackson and Carl Rosberg's (1982) famous expression, is unclear at this juncture.

Personalities do play a role. The changing aspirations of the Speakers—from Justice D. F. Annan, who successfully achieved incremental improvements during the first two Parliaments; to Pete Ala Djetey, who was aggressive on Parliament's behalf but removed from office; to Ebenezer S. Hughes, who seemed to play it safe along the wishes of the executive and his close friend the majority leader—do count. President Kufuor's strategy to manage all incentives the best way he could, to co-opt a large portion of MPs while making the rest hope for nothing but to also "be in," has been successful. With the financial control of Parliament once again effectively in the hands of the executive, no change in this situation was expected during the Fourth Parliament. In this context, moderate increases in salaries for MPs and improved resources of staff in combination with a rise in the quality of the MPs themselves have not been strong enough factors to alter the situation. The election of the highly respected former Supreme Court judge Joyce Bamford-Addo as the new Speaker following the inauguration of the Fifth Parliament suggests that the possibilities for strengthening Parliament may arise again.

Serious efforts at reform would include a constitutional revision leading to a clear separation of power between the executive and the legislature. During their years in the opposition (1992–2000), NPP leaders who later became cabinet ministers, as well as MPs, spoke with some emphasis on this issue and called for change. But at that time it was the NDC side that was in power and not willing to listen. Now that the roles have been reversed for two full terms of office, one can only hope that one effect of the recent second alternation of power will be that both the NDC and the NPP finally agree that their respective interests would be better served by balancing the power of the legislative and executive arms of government.

One sign that such a constitutional change could occur came on January 30, 2006, when the minister for regional cooperation and the New Partnership for Africa's Development, Kofi Konadu Apraku, announced that the NPP government was prepared to consider a constitutional revision on this issue. Another was former president Kufuor's farewell speech in Parliament on January 6,

2009, when he finally acknowledged that the constitutional "overlap" of the executive and the legislature should probably be revisited (after having abused this for eight years). Only the future will tell whether this and other similar expressions are mere lip service or a genuine emerging commitment among Ghana's political elites to strengthen the legislature and thus democracy in their country.

Notes

1. There has been some debate about the actual level of fraud in the 1992 and 1996 elections, but current evidence suggests that the irregularities could not have altered the outcome. For further details on these two elections, and the one in 2000, see Boahen 1995; Green 1998; Gyimah-Boadi 1999a, 1999b, 2001; Jeffries 1998; Lindberg 2003; Lyons 1997; Ninsin 1998; Nugent 2001; Oquaye 1995; Sandbrook and Oelbaum 1999.

2. NDC captured 114 against the NPP's 107 of the 228 elected seats, with the remaining seven seats won by People's National Convention (2), Convention People's Party (1), and independents (4).

3. Figures on the budget for Parliament could only be traced back to 1999. None of the figures on actual expenditures were readily available and had to be calculated by assistants in the accounts department, which took two weeks. The poor recordkeeping in the Parliament of Ghana is another indicator of institutional weakness.

4. Following Ghana's hybrid constitution, MPs who are ministers can still serve on all select and standing committees except the select committee for their own ministry and in principle can also chair a committee, although the latter has not occurred.

5. A separate but not unrelated issue pertains to the cost of campaigning. I have shown in earlier research (Lindberg 2003) that the cost of an MP's election campaign was typically the equivalent of one year's salary as an MP (US$7,000) in the 1992 race, and that that sum had doubled in 2000. According to my preliminary reading of a follow-up survey conducted in summer 2005, it seems that the typical cost of campaigning has since skyrocketed to between US$50,000 and $100,000 per MP. A vast majority of these funds come from the individual and his personal business, relatives, and friends. The parties in Ghana provide only a fraction of campaign resources for most candidates.

6

Rules and Rents in Nigeria's National Assembly

Peter M. Lewis

In May 2006, Nigeria's National Assembly killed a bill to amend the country's 1999 Constitution that would have extended presidential tenure limits from two to three terms.[1] For months, President Olusegun Obasanjo's "third term agenda" had been the central political controversy in the country. Although Obasanjo personally remained quiet on the topic of term extension, lieutenants in the president's office, the ruling party, and the legislature orchestrated a campaign for changes in the law. Enormous sums of cash were reportedly mobilized for this effort, as bidding for legislators' votes reached 50 million naira each (about US$400,000) and more than 100 payments were apparently disbursed (Dickson and Elendu 2006). The carrots were accompanied by sticks, including private threats about legislators' political futures and possible investigation by the government's anticorruption agency. The campaign was broadly unpopular, with opinion polls showing more than 80 percent of Nigerians opposed to extending the president's time in office (Afrobarometer 2006). The assembly's rejection of the third term was widely hailed as a victory for democracy and a narrow escape from national crisis. Many commentators credited the legislature with imposing restraint on domineering executive authority and opening the door to more-effective separation of powers in Nigeria's fledgling democracy.

Amid the relief and kudos, however, it was clear that many of the members played both sides of the issue and did not move to reject the amendment until the last moment, when they acceded to overwhelming pressure from constituents and critical public discussion. Further, it appeared that quite a number accepted the bribes offered by proextension operatives, but then took advantage of secret voting to reject the measure.[2] A decisive moment for Nigerian democracy was shadowed by self-dealing and opportunism.

This episode is emblematic of legislative politics in Nigeria's Fourth Republic. Since the transition to democracy in 1999, the National Assembly has displayed unprecedented independence, increasing ambition, and broader reach. Lawmakers have advanced the roles and capacities of their institution, asserted their constitutional prerogatives, and attempted to exercise greater oversight of the executive and related branches of government. Yet the arena of legislative affairs is permeated by clientelism, corruption, and struggles over patronage. Party discipline is weak, and factionalism undermines the development of coalitions or the emergence of long-term agendas. Consequently, legislators largely follow personal and parochial goals. The assembly has only sporadically addressed policy concerns, displaying uneven expertise and capacity. This is reflected in public attitudes toward the legislature, which show decreasing confidence and growing mistrust.

These crosscurrents have broad implications for the course of Nigeria's democratic reforms. To a greater degree than any previous moment in Nigeria's political history, the legislature is emerging as a credible institution with the capability to shape laws, bolster accountability, and balance other branches of government. The National Assembly has become a venue for initiating, debating, and amending legislation, rather than merely ratifying initiatives from the presidency. Legislators have frequently checked executive actions and have introduced mechanisms of supervision over public spending, administration, and economic policies. Contestation with the presidency is vigorous, sometimes acrimonious, and largely unrestrained by rules or traditions. Lawmakers have introduced at least two attempts to impeach the president and have participated in unseating five of their own legislative leaders. Further, the legislature has emerged as a crucible of debate on important public issues such as constitutional change, budget affairs, revenue allocation, foreign debt, public spending, privatization, corruption, and election administration, among the more prominent areas. The committee system in the National Assembly has increasingly served to develop specialized knowledge among legislators and staff, reflected in the increasing sophistication of oversight and debate under several committees.

Such trends suggest a nascent process of institutionalization as the rules, organization, and functions of the assembly become more regular and substantive. The legislature has lasted into a third civilian term, an unprecedented institutional tenure that could allow for the establishment of political careers and the formation of more stable coalitions of interest. An increasingly effective, activist legislature could become a vehicle for change, enabling lawmakers to influence policy reform, pursue oversight of government business, and challenge executive power. A number of individual legislators have pressed for reform, and tentative caucuses have formed around specific issues along with a general agenda of good governance. A more effective legislature also raises possibilities for improving representation and accountability. As lawmakers provide constituent services and seek to meet the needs of their districts, an essential linkage between voters and government performance is strengthened.

The Incessant Scramble for Rents

While recognizing the real achievements and enhanced potential of legislative politics, it is clear that the Nigerian political system remains characterized by clientelism, factionalism, polarization, and inertia. The episodic history of Nigeria's National Assembly furnishes weak institutional foundations. The establishment of rules and norms has been complicated by recurring military interventions, changes in the structure of the assembly, and the shifting party system. Most fundamentally, the political process is structured around distributional contention and the capture of rents rather than mechanisms of representation or accountability. Rents are garnered through many avenues, including perquisites, access to government contracts, business deals in members' districts, and lucrative appointments to state enterprises or ministries after leaving elective office.

Illicit payments and misappropriation of funds are also common. Since the late colonial period, the legislature has served as a central arena for constructing systems of patronage and incorporating political elites into clientelist networks. The assembly has also been an important arena of contention among ethnic and regional interests, whether organized into sectional parties or diffused among smaller factions. Legislative position has long been regarded as a lucrative point of access to state resources and sinecures, though the premium on political office was intensified with the advent of Nigeria's petroleum economy in the 1970s, which greatly expanded and concentrated the rents mediated through state channels. With privileged claims on salaries, perquisites, appropriations, contracts, regulations, and state employment, politicians have viewed the capture of public office as a critical avenue of status and personal enrichment.

Consequently, important features of legislative politics run contrary to the expectations associated with representative democracy. The executive branch, wielding levers of patronage and influence in party hierarchies, has substantially dominated the National Assembly in Nigeria's civilian regimes. Within the assembly, politics typically concentrates on factional struggles over access to rents rather than issues of public policy or lawmaking. Political cleavages revolve almost entirely around sectional blocs and personalities, rather than programmatic concerns or ideological divisions. The absence of an effective opposition undermines the power of the legislature and alienates voters from their representatives. The distance between voters and politicians is widened by persistent electoral fraud and manipulation, which removes the accountability of legislators to constituents, and binds them more firmly to political barons. In the practice of Nigerian politics, the legislature often appears as little more than a trading floor in which political elites bid on the distribution of spoils such as allowances and special funds, development allocations, government appointments, and opportunities for private business.

The tension between institutional development and distributional politics—between rules and rents—arises from separate tendencies, and indeed separate paths in Nigeria's weak democracy. One path offers a glimpse toward substantive change, as the legislature begins to take on the attributes of a representative and deliberative institution, furnishing an outlet for elements of reform. The other path, more clearly delineated in current realities, reinforces the pathologies of civilian politics in Nigeria in which an insular political class scrambles for influence and resources at the expense of voters, constituents, and public purpose. Both these tendencies are evident in Nigeria's political dynamics. Forceful influences of history and structure tend to reinforce clientelism and distributional contention. Yet a number of factors could spur change, including generational shifts, spreading norms of accountability, and greater activism on the part of voters and civic groups. Further, self-dealing and governance are not always antithetical: In the pursuit of power and rents, legislators may find it expedient to strengthen their institution, to reduce the discretion of executive power, and even to address constituents' demands. Legislative development in Nigeria is very much a contingent process, in which disparate forces contend on shifting ground.

In the analysis that follows, I consider political incentives and processes in Nigerian democratic regimes, and the competing pressures underlying legislative politics. The next section examines neopatrimonialism, distributional politics, and rent-seeking in the Nigerian context, along with possibilities for countervailing influences. This is followed by a brief historical review of the Nigerian legislature, with particular attention to institutional structure and the social foundations of politics. I then recount crucial episodes in the politics of the Fourth Republic, and the implications of these events for legislative efficacy. A subsequent section examines the broader setting of the legislature and political performance as reflected in public attitudes. The question of shifting coalitions, and the emergence of agents of change, is taken up next. I conclude with reflections on Nigeria's political trajectory and the potential for legislative autonomy.

Nigeria's Political Context

Legislative politics in Nigeria can best be understood within the overall context of the political system. Under both civilian and military regimes, Nigeria has reflected the characteristics of a neopatrimonial state. In neopatrimonial systems, formal institutions are eclipsed by informal relations based on kinship, communal identity, and personal alliances (Bratton and van de Walle 1997). Despite a semblance of administration and law, power and resources are not regulated by institutions, but rather mediated through networks of loyalty and exchange. The distinguishing feature of these systems is the relative strength of social relationships and the comparative weakness of institutional rules and norms. In these settings, patron-client relations form essential bonds that comprise larger webs of influence. Clientelist networks provide a basis for a general system of political control, as powerful patrons at the center are linked with an array of dependents and subordinates who, in turn, furnish inducements to popular sectors. Patronage is a crucial adhesive for the regime, and the rulers' discretion over public resources becomes essential to stabilizing the system.

In the Nigerian setting, neopatrimonial politics have taken on particular features. Nigeria represents a comparatively diffuse and unregulated form of neopatrimonialism. In many other countries, this type of system revolves around a strong central ruler who acts as the chief patron and attempts to manage clientelist networks. Regimes dominated by personal rulers often have long tenure, and the leader is able to contain, if not discipline, contention among factions and groups. In contrast, Nigeria reflects dispersed avenues of clientelism and fluid distributional politics. This arises from the country's social diversity and the instability of regimes since independence. Nigeria's size and diversity have made it difficult for leaders to effectively incorporate and assuage the demands of competing ethnoregional segments. Many Nigerian governments have adopted collegial approaches to rule, and nearly all have sought to appease claims from diverse groups in order to form support coalitions. In addition, cycles of civilian and military rule have generally offset tendencies toward personal supremacy, allowing a wider class of politicians and officers influence within the state.

Nigeria's political economy also shapes the contours of neopatrimonial rule. In the first decade of independence, Nigeria's economy centered on the export of agriculture and solid minerals, which were diversified among different regional governments with some independent control over revenues. With the advent of the oil boom in 1970, the economy was transformed rapidly into an export monoculture in which revenues from a single dominant commodity accrued directly to the federal government (Forrest 1995, 133). Oil gave rise to a rentier state, with natural resource rents furnishing the bulk of state revenues and foreign exchange. The central government had broad discretion over the use of these revenues, which were exponentially greater than the resources available before the windfall. Further, the oil boom launched a dramatic expansion of the state's economic role, venturing into production, investment, employment, credit, subsidies, and regulation. In response to this fiscal concentration and growth, the focus of patronage and distributional contention naturally shifted to the center. Capture of the federal government, or access to the center, became core motives in national politics.

In civilian regimes, the pursuit of public office is spurred by the desire to acquire rents and secure patronage resources. Nigeria's diffuse patron-client ties, and myriad claims on state resources, have been summarized as a "prebendal" system of politics (Joseph 1987). Officeholders view their positions as personal sinecures, and they seek to divert state influence and resources for individual, family, or communal gain. The factional nature of politics in Nigeria, and the comparative weakness of personal rule, distinguishes Nigerian politics from patterns found in many countries controlled by a long-standing dictator. Corruption and clientelism are essential features of Nigeria's politics, but they play out in a more dispersed and chaotic fashion than in systems ruled by a strong leader or party machine. With pervasive concerns that the system may collapse at any time, and limited authority to mediate competition, politicians also perceive very short time horizons. This increases the urgency of rent-seeking, prompting a frantic grab for resources.

This broad-brush depiction of Nigerian politics helps in understanding the institutional setting, the incentives for political actors, and the circumstances of political competition. With regard to legislative politics, two general observations can be emphasized. First, executive dominance of the political system regularly constrains the scope and role of the legislature. The Nigerian National Assembly has never been a simple extension of presidential power, as in many single-party systems in Africa. Constitutional provisions have allowed for considerable legislative autonomy, including fiscal authority, and a separation of powers. However, executive leaders have been able to manipulate or marginalize the legislature through their control over patronage and other advantages of incumbency. Second, legislators have focused chiefly on the capture of rents, not only for personal aggrandizement, but also to build clientelist networks that might ensure political survival. A structure of incentives shapes the recruitment of politicians and their behavior in office, strongly reinforcing patronage politics and indifference to institutional rules.

Yet these resilient features of Nigerian politics have not precluded significant change in the role and behavior of the legislature. In the Fourth Republic, the National Assembly has emerged as a fledgling counterweight to presidential authority within the constitutional separation of powers. Legislators have certainly chased perquisites and private side payments, but they have also guided legislation, debated laws and government performance, and increasingly sought to exercise oversight of public business. The following analysis examines the sources of changing legislative behavior and the prospects for future reform. What has shifted among the perspectives and strategies of Nigerian lawmakers? What are the sources of institutional development? Can the legislature assert an independent role and become an effective branch of government? These questions, so crucial for Nigeria's democratic prospect, inform the discussion that follows.

The Evolution of Legislative Politics

Nigeria has had three civilian governments with working legislatures since independence. During long periods of military rule, civilian institutions have been suspended, while each succeeding democratic regime has been founded on a new constitution. The First Republic (1960–1966), established at independence from Britain, governed somewhat longer than a single term, but was terminated by a military coup. Similarly, the Second Republic (1979–1983) was ushered in by military rulers and then usurped by the armed forces a few months after the regime's second election. The military ruler General Ibrahim Babangida laid the groundwork for a Third Republic, proceeding as far as elections for a civilian National Assembly and for the presidency. Election results were annulled in June 1993, however, and the transition was aborted by General Sani Abacha's palace coup shortly thereafter (Osaghae 1998). A new democratic regime was inaugurated once again by military leaders in May 1999 under a constitution issued shortly before the swearing-in. This is known as the Fourth Republic, although it is the third elected civilian regime to actually govern Nigeria. Each of Nigeria's democratic governments has reflected different institutions and political structures, based on constitutional design and changing party systems.

Nigeria's First Republic was a federal parliamentary system. In a typical transfer of institutions from the colonial power, Nigeria inherited the British Westminster model at independence, though with some aspects of the US system (Dudley 1982, 129). A lower House of Representatives was apportioned among the regions on the basis of population, and an upper house, the Senate, was distributed evenly across the units of the federation. Executive power was claimed by the majority party (or coalition) in Parliament. The federal structure was intended to accommodate the broad ethnic and regional divisions that made up the territory. Each of the then three regions reflected a dominant ethnic group: in the Northern Region, these were the Hausa-Fulani, an amalgam of two predominantly Muslim groups; in the Western Region, control was held by the Yoruba, roughly balanced among Muslims and Christians; and in the Eastern Region, the leading group was the Igbo, who were predominantly Christian. In a national context, each of these ethnolinguistic groups was a minority, but together they accounted for two-thirds of the Nigerian population, and they entered into a vigorous tripartite rivalry. Within each region, the dominant group easily eclipsed numerous smaller minorities, and each formed the basis for a major political party. The Northern People's Congress (NPC), with strong backing from Hausa-Fulani elites, held sway in the Northern Region. The National Council of Nigerian Citizens (NCNC), headed by Nnamdi Azikiwe, had the overwhelming allegiance of Igbo voters (Sklar 1963).[3] The Action Group (AG), led by Obafemi Awolowo, attracted a substantial following among the Yoruba. The federation was quickly polarized among three ethnically segmented regions ruled by dominant parties and leaders.

This structure of political contention proved corrosive for the new democracy (Diamond 1988). The regions were strong relative to the center, with substantial independent powers and control over local export revenues. Revenue allotments, along with inherited surpluses from the colonial-era commodity boards, enabled sectional elites to build patronage networks through the ruling parties and regional governments. Each leadership sought to consolidate dominance within their region and to fend off encroachment from other parties or factions. They also jockeyed for position at the federal level. The central government was controlled by the NPC, which held a commanding position in the Northern Region and benefited from a population advantage that gave the north a majority of seats in the legislature, as seen in Table 6.1. The federal NPC-led government attempted to divide and weaken the opposition by entering into an expedient though brittle alliance with the NCNC, and by undermining the power of the AG in the Western Region.

In the First Republic, the First Parliament was sharply divided among these sectional groups, and the various caucuses in the legislature generally represented communal and factional interests. Political parties exerted discipline through their parliamentary machinery. Ethnic identification, personal linkages to party leaders, and the inducements of regional patronage usually served to maintain party loyalties. Legislators' salaries (at least £1,000, or US$2,800, and about a third greater with allowances for housing, vehicles, and travel), were substantially higher than alternative compensation as teachers or civil servants (the background of many members of the First Parliament), and the desire to preserve their positions, or to supplement their incomes with opportunities from regional governments, provided strong incentive to comply with party hierarchies (Mackintosh 1966, 92). Where the draw of patronage was diminished, as in the divided Western Region and the weakened AG, party members defected in droves.

Within the Parliament, party factions clashed over issues ranging from procedural matters and personal emoluments to more salient concerns such as financial oversight, the national census, and electoral affairs. On the whole, however, legislative politics reflected few disputes over policies or political outlook. The

Table 6.1 Composition of the House of Representatives in the First Republic

Party/Coalition (No. of Seats for Leading Party in Coalition)	Number of Seats
Northern People's Congress (NPC = 134)	148
National Council of Nigeria and the Cameroons (NCNC = 81)	89
Action Group (AG = 73)	75
Total seats available in House of Representatives	312

Source: African Elections Database, http://africanelections.tripod.com/ng.html.

main arena of contention was the House of Representatives, which had the power to draft legislation, vote on money bills, and review legislation initiated in the Senate. The Senate had fewer prerogatives, being limited mainly to delaying legislation from the House or proposing bills to be forwarded to the lower chamber. The legislature had only three working committees, which largely served administrative and business roles. There was little expertise in specific policy areas. Overall, Parliament was an anemic political body, never sitting more than fifty-four days in any year. Both chambers were generally quiescent toward the executive and rarely initiated law (Mackintosh 1966, 113).

While the opposition could be vocal in debate, they exerted little substantive power. The ruling coalition effectively used the Standing Orders to control the parliamentary agenda and suppress debate or criticism. Given the leverage of the executive and the relative weakness of opposition, the Parliament had little capacity to veto or modify legislation. In a rare instance of executive retreat, the government withdrew a bill renewing the Anglo-Nigerian Defence Pact in the face of parliamentary opposition. Even in this case, observers have noted that stiff public opposition to the bill, rather than legislative resistance, was really a central factor in forcing the government's decision (Dudley 1982, 60). In 1962, when the Public Accounts Committee in the House raised questions about overspending by the federal government, the majority party dissolved the committee and appointed new members from the ruling coalition.

The NPC government was effective in fracturing the opposition by co-opting some elements in its coalition and by declaring a state of emergency in the turbulent Western Region, which badly undermined the Action Group and its leadership. Opposition power in the Parliament was further weakened by a steady stream of "carpet crossings" of members from weaker parties to the ruling coalition. By the end of the First Parliament, the AG faction had dwindled from a peak of seventy-five members to merely twenty-one representatives. This prompted the prime minister to deny the existence of an opposition altogether (Mackintosh 1966, 104).

Northern political dominance and regional polarization ultimately led to the demise of the First Republic. Disputes over the national census fractured the NPC's coalition with the NCNC, followed by a protracted crisis arising from the 1964 federal and regional elections (Diamond 1988). The growing sense of political crisis was accentuated by a rising trend of communal violence, which soon induced the military to step in. Two coups in 1966 culminated in ethnic violence and civil war. The military regime of General Yakubu Gowon prevaricated on a return to civilian rule, and he was ousted in 1975 by General Murtala Mohammed and his adjunct, General Olusegun Obasanjo. Obasanjo assumed power the following year after Mohammed's assassination in a failed coup attempt, and supervised the country's first transition from military rule to civilian democracy.

Legislative Dynamics in the Second Republic

Legislative politics in Nigeria's second civilian regime were shaped by new institutional and political settings. A presidential system was adopted in place of the Westminster system inherited at independence. The Constituent Assembly crafted a 1979 Constitution that was substantially modeled on US institutions (Akande 1982, v). This included a presidential executive and significant changes in the role and composition of the National Assembly. The assembly had greater prerogatives than the earlier Parliament, notably with regard to money bills, budget oversight, and committee authority, but could not form a government or topple the executive through a vote of no confidence. Laws might originate in either chamber of the assembly, and passage required the assent of both houses. A majority vote of two-thirds would override a presidential veto. The legislature retained its structure of representation, apportioned by state population in the House of Representatives and by uniform seats for each state in the Senate. Legislators were elected from single-member constituencies. The federal system was altered from the original three-region configuration to nineteen states at the time of the political transition. This was intended to dilute the large ethnoregional blocs and party dominance of the First Republic, as legislators would be elected to state constituencies with more discrete local concerns. The House was expanded from 312 seats in the First Parliament to 450 seats in the new civilian regime (Akande 1982, 44).

The party system also reflected new alignments and bases of appeal. The 1979 Constitution required a broad geographic spread of votes as a condition for election to the presidency (Akande 1982, 126). This encouraged the formation of parties that could reach beyond ethnoregional appeals to more diverse constituencies. The National Party of Nigeria (NPN), which was to dominate the Second Republic, proved successful in forging a coalition of elites for the purposes of electoral competition and the distribution of rents. Like its chief competitors, the NPN had a lineage from the first civilian regime, as its core leadership and backers had been associated with the NPC. This was echoed in the other leading parties, including the Unity Party of Nigeria (UPN), led by the veteran AG chief Awolowo, and anchored by its southwestern Yoruba base; and the Nigerian People's Party (NPP), headed by former NCNC leader Azikiwe, with strong electoral support in the Igbo-majority states of the southeast. The UPN and NPP were largely unable to surmount their sectional appeals, but the NPN proved adept at using tactical alliances and largesse to gain support in diverse parts of the country, including some of the "heartland" of their chief competitors (Joseph 1981). Two minor parties (the People's Redemption Party and the Greater Nigeria People's Party) also held significant positions in the states and the assembly. The distribution of parties is shown in Table 6.2.

Executive dominance was as prevalent in the Second Republic as in other regimes. During the entire four-year civilian term, only one bill was introduced

Table 6.2 Distribution of Parties in the National Assembly of the Second Republic

Party	Senate (95 Seats)	House of Representatives (449 Seats)
National Party of Nigeria (NPN)	36	168
Unity Party of Nigeria (UPN)	28	111
Nigerian People's Party (NPP)	16	78
Greater Nigerian People's Party (GNPP)	8	43
People's Redemption Party (PRP)	7	49

Source: African Elections Database, http://africanelections.tripod.com/ng.html.

and passed by the legislature (relating to a trivial expansion of facilities at the international airport), while all other legislation was initiated by the presidency. Although some bills were energetically debated, executive preferences shaped the agenda within the assembly. The notion of "agendas," however, applies only in the most generic sense of preferences by members of one branch or another. In practice, attention to legislation was episodic and fragmented, on the part of the presidency as well as within the assembly. Neither branch fostered clear targets or legislative plans. In consequence, much of the contention on the assembly floor consisted of procedural dickering with little relationship to a broader set of goals and concerns. The assembly did not exercise significant oversight of the executive or other government operations. Legislative maneuvers were often pursued as tactical efforts to gain advantage in the struggle for influence and access to state resources.

During the Second Republic, the oil windfall crested and then ebbed. Oil prices and production peaked in 1980, a year in which federal revenues were over US$25 billion. After 1981, rapidly declining prices yielded lower revenues and an eventual fiscal crisis. However, the atmosphere of bounty in the initial years of the civilian government created a frenetic scramble for state-mediated rents. Legislators could claim generous salaries and allowances, which totaled more than US$70,000 at the time (Falola and Ihonvbere 1985, 109).[4] In addition to their direct compensation, assembly members often had privileged access to government contracts, loans, land, appointments, and licenses, as well as influence over regulatory or bureaucratic rulings. Many secured these benefits personally, though just as frequently they acted as middlemen for notables and business interests who provided compensation for their assistance. Since influence over legislation or assembly procedures could be instrumental in procuring these benefits, legislative affairs were fractious and often paralyzed by haggling among competing interests. Politics in the assembly chamber functioned more as a trading floor among brokers than a deliberative body with oversight and legislative responsibilities. Enterprising legislators could obtain special allowances for travel and committee activities, sway allocations and projects for their districts (which typically allowed for kickbacks and inside access to contracts), or enter into private deals with other legislators and business cronies. They could also increase their salience for party "kingmakers," opening possibilities for other elective offices or senior appointments. Many debates and procedural tussles in the assembly had the quality of maneuvering for visibility.

While the National Assembly in Nigeria's Second Republic scarcely fulfilled its institutional roles, it did serve as a central arena for the mediation and distribution of rents. The assembly was not substantially engaged in the generation or passage of laws, and only sporadically addressed issues of public policy and performance. Factions in the legislature, often for partisan advantage, occasionally scrutinized government operations, but it cannot be said that the assembly exerted regular oversight of the executive branch, the bureaucracy, or the public enterprise sector. The most salient aspects of legislative politics were the distributional struggles among parties and factions. High revenues, and a proliferation of access points for state patronage, served to accentuate the "prebendal" features of Nigerian politics (Lewis 1994, 444). With short time horizons, legislators competed for favors and largesse, which could be disbursed by officials in the presidency, legislative leaders, and party hierarchies. Although a dominant party controlled government, and the leading opposition caucuses were fairly close-knit, there was actually little party discipline. As the ruling NPN consolidated its control of the electoral system and its scope of largesse, many opposition legislators crossed the carpet to affiliate with the ruling party. The lax enforcement of constitutional provisions over party affiliation facilitated such opportunistic behavior. Unstable alliances led to fragmentation and drift in the assembly. As with other institutions in the Second Republic, the degeneration of the legislature contributed to a rapid erosion of governance. Moreover, electoral contention became increasingly unruly and lawless (Diamond 1995, 438–439). The premium on political office led incumbents and challengers to employ violence, fraud, and corruption in electoral contests.

These circumstances prompted the military to step in once again, and the Second Republic was terminated at the end of 1983. General Ibrahim Buhari ruled for less than two years before his ouster by General Ibrahim Babangida, who professed a desire for a rapid return to civil rule. As it turned out, Babangida prolonged his transition program for several years, creating additional states and elaborating new rules for elections and political parties. He experimented with a mandatory two-party system based on ideological orientations as a way of further diluting ethnic appeals. Legislative elections were held in July 1992, though the new assembly was virtually powerless. The putative Third Republic was to be ushered in by a presidential election in June 1993, but

General Babangida annulled the election results, effectively ending the transition. Amid a political crisis, Babangida stepped aside and handed affairs to a caretaker civilian committee. They were shunted aside in a matter of weeks by the defense minister, Sani Abacha, who created a predatory authoritarian regime.

When Abacha died unexpectedly in 1998, the ruling military council quickly appointed General Abdulsalami Abubakar, who supervised a brisk program of transition to democracy. Abubakar's regime established the transition calendar, electoral rules, and constitutional design. Political party registration was reopened, though parties had to be qualified by the electoral commission. Certification for national elections required a geographic spread of votes, and a minimum threshold of votes in local government polls. Following these criteria, three parties eventually qualified for the general elections. Elections for state and national offices were held early in 1999. Although the polling was marred by disarray and widespread malpractices, a general desire for reform encouraged acceptance of the results. Through a hasty and chaotic process, the Fourth Republic was launched in May 1999 (Lewis 1999).

Legislative Foundations of the Fourth Republic

Only a week prior to the inauguration of the new regime, the military government released the 1999 Constitution. Modeled largely on the 1979 charter, the new document maintained the presidential system, though with an expanded federal structure of thirty-six states. The bicameral legislature was preserved, with single-member districts elected at four-year intervals, simultaneously with the president. Despite the proliferation of states, the House of Representatives, with 360 seats, was smaller than the previous civilian regime. The 1999 assembly, like its predecessor in the Second Republic, had constitutional authority over budgeting and spending by the federal government, substantial control over the legislative budget, and prerogatives for committee formation and oversight activities. By law, the legislature was required to sit at least 188 days a year, and the finances and qualifications of members were to be declared and vetted (Nigeria 1999). Both the rights and the obligations of the National Assembly were enhanced over preceding governments.

The party system in the Fourth Republic was fundamentally different from those under earlier civilian regimes (Lewis 2003, 134). Babangida's abortive experiment with nonsectional parties had a lasting impact on political coalitions in Nigeria by breaking up regional and ethnic party structures and channeling political groupings into multiethnic "national" entities. The People's Democratic Party (PDP), which quickly ascended to dominance of the Fourth Republic, was established by the Group of 34, a collection of notables from diverse areas of Nigeria, most of whom had been associated with the Social Democratic Party, Babangida's "center-left" creation. The PDP had a thin programmatic identity but was successful in bringing together diverse constituencies and fashioning an effective electoral machine across the country. The other large association, the All People's Party (APP), emerged from leaders of the National Republican Convention, which had been the "center-right" party established by the military regime.[5] Many of the founding APP members had also been close to the leading political party sponsored by General Abacha in his bid for civilian legitimacy. The APP reflected regional diversity, though its electoral appeal was strongest in the northern states. A third grouping, the Alliance for Democracy (AD), had a more pronounced regional identity, arising from the mainly Yoruba coalition of democratic activists who had opposed the 1993 election annulment and resisted the Abacha autocracy. Despite their geographic base, the AD was perhaps the most ideological of the parties, embodying a strong democratic and reformist orientation. The APP and the AD made a tactical alliance in the 1999 presidential election, though the disparities in the origins and political values among the party leaders made for a fragile coalition.

The degree of party dominance in the Fourth Republic surpassed that of any previous government in Nigeria. During the First Republic, the NPC had been able to govern the parliamentary system with a 47 percent plurality in the assembly. The NPN position in the Second Republic was even smaller, with just 38 percent of legislative seats. By contrast, as seen in Table 6.3, the PDP won a commanding majority of 57 percent of seats in the 1999 assembly, with nearly identical margins in both houses. This increased to 62 percent after the 2003 election, and a remarkable 73 percent in 2007. The fact that these outsized majorities were obtained through highly flawed electoral practices also colored legislative politics. The expanding hegemony of the PDP increasingly drew aspirants and voters toward the party as the greatest potential source of patronage. Yet the PDP, like its competitors, was a loosely constituted association of interests rather than a coherent organization for organizing votes or framing policies. Tenuous party discipline meant that legislators were not bound by a platform or guidance from the party hierarchy. This offered degrees of freedom to pursue self-aggrandizement, as well as opportunities for institutional or policy agendas. All these motives could be witnessed in the operations of the assembly.

The First Assembly, 1999–2003

Time and resources created formidable institutional deficits in the first National Assembly. The long interval between civilian regimes and the hurried pace of transition to the Fourth Republic were two important temporal factors. There was little institutional memory in the Fourth Republic. A limited number of legislators and party leaders had participated in civilian government under the presidential system. The average age of representatives in the first term was just fifty-one years, suggesting that few could have had significant experience

Table 6.3 Party Dominance in the National Assemblies of the Fourth Republic

Assembly/Parties	Senate (109 Seats)	House of Representatives (360 Seats)
1999		
People's Democratic Party (PDP)	59	206
All People's Party (APP/ANPP)	29	74
Alliance for Democracy (AD)	20	68
Other	1	12
2003		
People's Democratic Party (PDP)	76	223
All Nigeria People's Party (ANPP)	27	96
Alliance for Democracy (AD)	6	34
Other	—	7
2007		
People's Democratic Party (PDP)	87	263
All Nigeria People's Party (ANPP)	14	63
Action Congress (AC)	6	30
Other	2	4

Source: African Elections Database, http://africanelections.tripod.com/ng.html.

in the previous civilian regime, which ended sixteen years earlier. More than half the members in the House had never held elective office, and few would have served a full term in any government. Only 15 of the 360 new House members listed their prior occupation as a "politician," with the majority citing backgrounds in business, the professions, education, and agriculture.[6] Most politicians were neophytes who confronted a steep learning curve. The assembly building itself was newly constructed in Abuja, as the capital moved from Lagos in the late 1980s. The parlous state of public finances inherited from the military regime limited the funds available for staffing and equipping the legislature. Members in the first term operated with a skeletal staff and few documents, computers, or library resources.

Conditions of political recruitment also skewed the composition of the assembly. The compressed schedule of party registration, nominations, and political recruitment left the parties with few filters for attracting qualified or dedicated candidates. The short-term financial attractions of politics were heightened by a weak economy and by the uncertainties surrounding the durability of the transition. Consequently many of the candidates who flocked to the new parties were poorly prepared and tended to view public office primarily as a chance for quick personal gains. The free-spending ways of new legislators were subject to controversy from the beginning of the government, and financial improprieties in the assembly were extensively documented by an investigative panel in 2000 under Senator Idris Kuta. Upon taking office, legislators awarded themselves generous allowances for housing and furniture, amounting to tens of thousands of dollars per member, in addition to their substantial salaries and other perquisites. Although base salaries were relatively modest at US$8,000 annually, the total package after allowances totaled as much as US$75,000 (Ugbolue 2000). The Kuta investigations reported further large allowances taken by the Speaker of the House and the Senate President, in addition to misconduct by other members. Charges of venality and lack of integrity among legislators were kept in the forefront by a stream of revelations in the press and official bodies of inquiry. Public resentment was palpable, as when labor unions staged a protest over the exorbitant furniture allowances claimed by the assembly.[7]

The first term was marked by prominent struggles over leadership. Within a few months after inauguration, the leaders of both chambers were removed. In July 1999, the new Speaker of the House of Representatives, Alhaji Salisu Ibrahim Buhari, was the subject of a media exposé that revealed he had falsified age and educational qualifications in his personal documentation for the assembly. His resignation was followed by arrest and a court conviction for fraud. Similarly, in November, Senate President Evan Enwerem was impeached under charges of falsifying his age, education, and other qualifications on his official resume, as well as exhibiting "gross incompetence." Presidential appeals on behalf of the embattled senator were ineffectual. The second Senate President, Chuba Okadigbo, was at political loggerheads with Obasanjo, a rivalry that culminated with Okadigbo's impeachment on charges of corruption in August of 2000. In this instance, the presidency actively campaigned for the senator's removal, citing evidence of profligacy and misappropriation of funds.

If the spectacle of self-regarding behavior was dismaying, it was hardly surprising in light of previous Nigerian experience. Yet the tumult also revealed a new element of transparency arising from the media and the assembly itself. Investigations by the press brought down a House Speaker and maintained a public focus on integrity and financial affairs in the legislature. This was complemented by the Kuta panel and pressures for probity from within the assembly. The motives of critics were rarely unambiguous, as many used the leadership and financial scandals for political advantage. The maneuvers among rivals, however, were paralleled by a reformist impulse.

Notwithstanding this incessant rent-seeking, a small though significant group of new legislators, including a number in the ruling party, focused on issues of governance and public policy. This fostered tension among party elites, who were often mainly concerned with the control of voting and patronage, against a fledgling caucus of reformist lawmakers who pressed for the development of institutions and a stronger policy agenda. Perhaps two dozen members were seriously concerned with policy or institutional agendas, but they could periodically enlist others on particular issues and bills.

Executive-legislative tensions were prominent during the first term of Obasanjo's presidency. From the outset of the Fourth Republic, legislators seemed intent on asserting their prerogatives and resisting the arbitrary dominance of the president. Obasanjo, a strong personality with a military background, was visibly frustrated by the legislature's contentious stance (Adegbamigbe 1999). Yet the president was unable to prevail in a number of early disagreements, including the impeachment of Senate President Enwerem and the level of allowances and perquisites in the assembly. Among the 306 bills initiated by the first legislature, only a fifth originated with the executive, nearly all the rest being proposed by members of the House (National Assembly of Nigeria 2003). Further, a number of items close to the president's agenda were resisted or substantially modified by the legislature. Among these were the anticorruption bill, which some legislators challenged for the implied expense and open-ended powers of antigraft institutions.[8] A presidential veto was overridden in 1999 for the establishment of a Niger Delta Development Commission. The assembly also contended with the executive over the annual budget, resulting in regular delays of appropriations and incidents of provisional spending without legislative approval. In addition to contesting the scope and size of spending, fiscal affairs were embroiled in debates over proper constitutional authority. The president, seeking agreement with the International Monetary Fund (IMF) as a path toward debt relief, pushed for tight budgeting and rapid progress on privatization, especially in such critical sectors as refineries and electricity. The assembly tended to push for expansionary budgets (not least because of their own institutional costs) and to resist privatization measures (Ogbu 2000). The contestation between Obasanjo and the assembly created a stalemate on core reforms, and the IMF standby agreement signed in August 2000 was essentially stillborn.

A pivotal incident concerned the Electoral Bill, which was intended to reform the rules and administration of elections. On the eve of the 2001 holiday break for the legislature, President Obasanjo reportedly convened a late-night meeting with the two leaders of the assembly in which he passed along his preferred alterations to a bill that had just been approved by a legislative conference committee. When the ad hoc "amendments" came to light days later, the assembly clamored to reopen the debate and pass a new bill through normal, transparent legislative procedures. The presidential machinations were rebuffed, and a new bill passed the following year. The growing tensions between the president and the assembly culminated in a bid to impeach Obasanjo in August 2002 on a variety of charges, including misuse of funds, abuse of constitutional powers, and general disregard for the rule of law. Some 287 members of the House eventually signed the complaint, including 200 members of Obasanjo's own party, the PDP ("Obasanjo and the Survival Game" 2002). Obasanjo publicly apologized to the assembly for arrogance and impolitic behavior, and promised a more consultative and transparent approach to governing. Further negotiations brokered by two former heads of state (Yakubu Gowon and Shehu Shagari) led to agreements with both chambers, which withdrew their formal charges just weeks before the nominating convention for the 2003 elections (Aziken 2002).

In other respects, the National Assembly was hardly an engine of efficiency or enterprise. Although many bills were proposed, a little more than 10 percent of pending legislation was passed by the First Assembly. Among the bills for which a final determination was made, seventeen originated from the executive, and just six from the House of Representatives. Only a single bill proposed by the executive was actually voted down by the assembly (National Assembly of Nigeria 2003). Many important initiatives, notably the repeated efforts to pass amendments to the constitution, languished in debate, committee deliberations, and simple inaction.

The committee system was energetic despite the shortcomings in experience and technical capacity. The opportunities in the new democratic dispensation encouraged committee participation, along with the possibilities for allowances, travel, and heightened reputations. Each house maintained more than forty committees, averaging twelve members each in the Senate, and about twenty-five each within the House. Dozens of members served on multiple committees. Both chambers maintained committees on public accounts as well as finance, along with committees on defense, security, foreign affairs, economic affairs, environment, petroleum, privatization, the judiciary, anticorruption, women's affairs, and many other key issues. Legislative committees in the First Assembly took time to establish staff, create agendas, and develop expertise. Oversight and advisory functions were uneven and generally weak. Yet a process of institutional development was evident as the committees became increasingly vocal on electoral reform, debt management, public finance, corruption, and other areas.[9]

Nigeria's First Assembly in the Fourth Republic exhibited familiar elements of neopatrimonial politics, as struggles for patronage and personal aggrandizement occupied the attentions of many legislators. Members of the assembly, however, also made pronounced efforts to assert the constitutional separation of powers and build the capacity of the institution. Despite many shortcomings, the First Assembly revealed an unprecedented vigor in balancing the power of the executive and attempting to address some of the critical issues facing the country. The First Assembly of the Fourth Republic was not a mere replication of previous legislatures, which had been cowed by party leaders or seized by venal imperatives. While the new assembly exhibited mixed motives and equivocal behavior, members took steps to assert the roles and responsibilities of a legislature in a presidential federal democracy.

How do we account for this apparent shift? Several explanatory factors are relevant. First, a process of political learning has been evident, fostered by history as well as comparative experience. The Fourth Republic was inaugurated after three decades of nearly continuous military rule in Nigeria, shadowed by two unsuccessful civilian regimes. The risks of democratic failure have been evident to segments of the political class. The importance of an active legislature has also been demonstrated by several nascent democracies in Africa and in other regions. Further, the new generation of Nigerians that entered political life in 1999 has been more assertive in testing their prerogatives and the roles of their institution.

A second major factor is the changing nature of patronage and rent distribution in Nigeria. Weaker structures of clientelism in the new regime have allowed space for a wider array of interests and agendas. Under preceding military rulers, Nigeria's economy not only stagnated, but also experienced a degree of liberalization that dismantled many elements of the state-mediated economy. Privatization, deregulation, and the reduction of government employment substantially contracted outlets for supplying largesse. In consequence, patronage from the center has been less abundant or certain than in previous regimes. At the time of transition, the prospects of largesse were also limited by low oil prices and depleted state coffers. While many among the new political class entered politics in hopes of capturing benefits, the networks of patronage were often tenuous and indistinct. The loose affiliations within the new political parties differed from the sectional party elites that managed affairs under previous civilian governments. This created a more permissive setting for reform elements and political entrepreneurs. While the dominant motives of clientelist politics have been much in evidence, tenuous patronage structures allow for more diverse initiatives on the part of politicians.

Finally, personalities and sectional politics come into play. Olusegun Obasanjo was a familiar figure in Nigeria and his imperious style provoked reactions among many legislators. This was influenced by ethnic rivalries as well, since Obasanjo personified a negotiated "power shift" to the southwest of the country, though many politicians from the north and the east resented his role. Obasanjo could not exert broad authority in the PDP during his first term, lacking initial control of both appointments and patronage resources. Factional turbulence in the party was expressed in legislative affairs, and President Obasanjo was quickly confronted by an unruly assembly eager to challenge executive authority.

The Second Assembly, 2003–2007

Having weathered the storm of impeachment, Obasanjo secured the PDP nomination for a second term in 2003 and turned his attention to consolidating his authority over the party. With new party executives and changes in senior appointments, the incumbent president was less beholden to party oligarchs and better able to influence the electoral map. The nomination procedures within the parties were opaque, and in most parts of the country the 2003 elections were marked by fraud and misconduct. The resulting legislature reflected a turnover of about 80 percent of its members in both chambers. Candidates were rarely voted out of office; rather, they were replaced mainly through new nominations decided by party kingmakers. A number of opposition members were also shut out through electoral rigging. While party elites were better able to screen candidates and to weed out incumbents, the flawed elections aggravated problems of accountability, as officeholders had little connection to their constituents.

The turnover of legislators afforded opportunities for both the public-minded and the self-interested, accentuating contradictory orientations within the assembly. With the completion of a full term of civilian government, there was greater confidence in the continuation of an electoral regime, leading many able individuals who earlier avoided politics to enter public office. Legislators and analysts observed that the overall quality of the Second Assembly had improved, as better-educated and more experienced people entered politics.[10] Also, several reform-oriented candidates emerged from civic organizations and segments of the parties. Since the political transition, Nigeria's robust civil society was engaged with many issues of governance. Associations such as the Civil Liberties Organization and the Constitutional Rights Project gave particular attention to legislative performance and legal reform. Legislators also developed greater competence in policy areas through interaction with nongovernmental organizations, especially in such areas as economic literacy, anticorruption strategies, and approaches to electoral reform. By the second election, some civic activists had decided to enter electoral politics. These elements of change, however, were overshadowed by the larger structures of politics. The ruling party's hegemony reinforced the influence of a political oligarchy and sharpened the competition for rents among the political class.

Paradoxically, the assertion of executive influence through a dominant party did not produce a complaisant legislature. In the early period of the new administration, relations with the assembly were more cooperative, as a new cohort of legislators acclimated to their offices. The presidency gained support for important goals such as debt relief, which members supported through legislation and international lobbying (O'Regan 2005). After a modest honeymoon, however, legislators once again were inclined to contest presidential power and to assert their own agenda. Divisions within the ruling PDP, especially the growing antagonism between Obasanjo and his vice president, Atiku Abubakar, aggravated divisions within the assembly. The assembly continued to experience leadership problems, as the new Senate President, Adolphus Wabara, was enmeshed in a corruption inquiry and induced to resign in 2005. Opposition caucuses, though diminished in size, remained assertive. A modest, though significant group of reformist legislators emerged to offset executive power and encourage vigorous oversight roles. Several of the most visible reformers came from constituencies where elections had been relatively transparent and credible, including Lagos, Kano, and Cross River.

The committee system, organized along the same lines as in the first term, was vigorous in probing government affairs and exercising oversight functions such as "due process" reviews of public spending. Legislative committees conducted inquiries into the use of funds for debt alleviation, procurement, and financial management for the 2007 elections, and issues related to privatization, the petroleum sector, and the administration of the Federal Capital Territory (Abuja). Tensions between the president and the assembly were less prominent in the early years of the new term, though the budget process remained contentious and issues such as constitutional reform and anticorruption efforts were controversial. In the final year of the Second Assembly, legislators were more frankly assertive toward the executive, and key committees (including Finance and Public Expenditure) played a prominent role in challenging the administration.

The events of 2006 were pivotal in the evolution of executive-legislative relations. Since the 1999 political transition, opposition groups and civic activists had called for a "Sovereign National Conference" to address major questions of constitutional change and political accord. The Obasanjo government generally disregarded such calls, but in 2005 Obasanjo convened his own "Political Reform Conference" to consider central institutions and revenue-sharing arrangements. Supporters of the president introduced a proposal to eliminate or extend the two-term limit in the constitution, but the initiative was largely rejected by conference members ("Third Term Agenda" 2005). The following year, however, a package of constitutional amendments was put forward in the assembly. The proposed bill included 116 separate items, including a provision to extend presidential tenure to three terms. The "third term agenda," as it came to be known, was integrally related to the president's increasingly bitter feud with Vice President Atiku, who sought the PDP's presidential nomination for the 2007 election. Operatives in the presidency and the ruling party sought to disqualify Atiku (largely on the basis of corruption charges) while opening the possibility for Obasanjo to remain in office. Advocates of the extension argued that Obasanjo was making headway on essential economic and anticorruption reforms and needed more time to consolidate these gains. The argument made little impact on its merits, but the mixture of political threats and economic inducements wielded by figures close to the presidency began to build momentum behind the amendment.

The campaign for the third term galvanized resistance from diverse quarters in the assembly (Adedoja and Epia 2006). Opposition parties raised concern about the creation of a political oligarchy under the PDP, a party led by a former military ruler. Similar objections arose from within the PDP, especially the group arrayed around Vice President Atiku. In addition, the implicit bargain over the "power shift" to a southern president in 1999 entailed a rotation among different segments of the country. The northern political establishment, anticipating the return of the presidency to their region in 2007, feared that the third term was an effort to freeze them out of power. Political newcomers, including most members of the legislature, were apprehensive that incumbents would become entrenched and limit mobility. Moreover, members were aware of adamant opposition in most of their constituencies. Media discussions, text messaging, and civic activism amplified these sentiments. More than one representative noted that if he voted for the third term, he wouldn't be able to show his face in his home district.[11] Another prominent PDP member, Senate President Ken Nnamani, while remaining publically neutral on the issue, resisted efforts by third-term supporters to manipulate the assembly's procedures and intimidate senators into accepting the measure.

The controversy over term limits unfolded against a background of growing concern about the integrity of the 2007 elections. In view of the disarray and misconduct in preceding elections, voters (and many politicians) hoped that the upcoming polls could be conducted with greater transparency and better organization. Yet the electoral commission was evidently unprepared for a credible exercise, while the presidency and the ruling party elite seemed determined to secure the outcome. The PDP nominated a little-known governor, Umaru Yar'Adua of Katsina State, for the presidency, as Atiku decamped to a new party, the Action Congress. The PDP executive employed the nomination process once again to screen candidates for the assembly election. Within the assembly, the Elections Committee was fairly complacent about the administration of elections, though committees concerned with finance and expenditure scrutinized the operations of the electoral commission, uncovering serious malpractices in procurement and accounting.

Concerns about the 2007 elections proved well founded, as the April polls were judged by many to be the worst in Nigeria's history (Transition Monitoring Group 2007; National Democratic Institute 2007b). Massive evidence of fraud, misconduct, and corruption was reported by domestic and international observers, as well as the independent media. More than 200 people were killed in electoral violence. The PDP secured the presidency with an unprecedented margin of 70 percent, in addition to capturing nearly three-quarters of the seats in the assembly. These results varied dramatically from several preelection polls that showed diminished support for the ruling party.[12] Among many prominent critics, Senate President Nnamani condemned the conduct of elections and the ambition for political monopoly among leaders of his party, the PDP. In the wake of the badly flawed elections, disgruntled parties showed prudence in pursuing their complaints with the judicial election tribunals. More than ten gubernatorial elections were overturned, and dozens of assembly seats were transferred or submitted for new voting.[13]

The Third Assembly, 2007–2011

President Umaru Yar'Adua was inaugurated along with the new National Assembly in May 2007. Once again, fewer than 20 percent of the members returned from the preceding legislature, and fewer than two dozen House members had tenure dating back to the First Assembly. The president's office and the PDP hierarchy attempted to exercise greater control through the nominating process, and few incumbent legislators gained renomination. Many of the veteran members of both houses pursued reforms, particularly with regard to the electoral system, public expenditures, and constitutional change. While this group comprised perhaps two dozen members, several had the institutional experience to exercise leadership and to utilize the system in the pursuit of change. They also faced major challenges as a minority in a turbulent clientelist system rife with factions and self-dealing.

President Yar'Adua had an ascetic reclusive image that suggested a degree of integrity but also raised questions about his strength as an executive. Having attained power virtually through appointment by the ruling party, Yar'Adua had little electoral base or identification with any substantial constituency. Several weeks after his inauguration, he named a cabinet that included several Obasanjo loyalists, even as the former president sought to continue his own influence through a lifetime position as PDP executive. President Yar'Adua moved slowly to shape his administration, gain control of the party, and frame an agenda. He gave early signals of independence when he canceled several large contracts that had been awarded to reputed Obasanjo cronies, and he stayed clear of the electoral tribunals that overturned numerous PDP victories in the states and the legislature. Yar'Adua also supported an alternative PDP leadership that supplanted Obasanjo's favored group. The new president, however, waited more than a year after his election to reshuffle senior executive offices and top military posts and procrastinated several months longer on cabinet changes. In the policy realm, his administration took steps to reorganize the corrupt, dysfunctional national petroleum corporation, to revitalize the moribund power sector, and to address festering instability in the oil-producing Niger Delta. These initiatives were announced with fanfare but yielded few concrete improvements. For some observers, Yar'Adua's actions reflected deliberate caution, though for many others, they smacked of weakness and indecision.

The lack of dynamism in the executive branch clearly emboldened many in the new assembly. Both houses of the legislature expanded the number and scope of committees, mushrooming to eighty-four in the House of Representatives and fifty-four in the Senate. Committee activity was spurred partly by political ambition, but also by reaction to misconduct in numerous departments of government. The perquisites and payments for committee membership encouraged participation. Abundant revenues (a result of surging oil and gas proceeds and fiscal management) enabled the assembly to staff and expand their entities and offices. After two terms of civilian government, the assembly reflected an unmistakable strengthening of the institution, having advanced from the inexperienced and resource-poor legislature evident in 1999. The committee system provided the venue for numerous probes into the affairs of the executive as well as the legislature itself. The most assiduous and capable, about a dozen committees, were those focused on public finance and legislative affairs, including committees on the budget, fiscal affairs, external debt, and assembly rules and procedures. A few committees for such issues as HIV/AIDS, women's affairs, and the Millennium Development Goals were also quite active, with concerted assistance from donors. Another fifteen to twenty committees functioned adequately, pursuing inquiries or legislation regarding elections, the electricity system, transportation, and health. Many committees were thin on competence, and more than half met infrequently or not at all.

In 2007, only five months after the inauguration of the new assembly, yet another leader fell in disgrace when the new Speaker of the House, Patricia Olubunmi Etteh, was forced to resign after a probe into contracts through her office. The most notorious probe was conducted by the Power and Steel panel in the House, which detailed the Obasanjo government's allocations of some US$16 billion to the electricity sector, although electricity production declined and efficiency in the sector deteriorated (Nkwazema 2008). A sample of other probes, actively reported in the national media, covered safety funds in aviation, projects in transportation and public works, fertilizer distribution under the Agriculture Ministry, land and housing sales in the Federal Capital Territory, spending and projects under the Nigeria Delta Development Commission, the funding of prominent teaching hospitals, and the use of constituency project funds by legislators and governors. While the investigative activities were revealing, there was also a sense of ambivalence among many citizens who were saturated with revelations, and skeptical about political grandstanding.

Nonetheless, committee activities revealed a growing willingness and capacity to exercise legislative oversight of the presidency along with a degree of self-regulation. In other respects, however, the assembly was less effective or enterprising. The proliferating committee system, while an important source of information and pressure, was an uncertain mechanism of accountability, possessing limited enforcement capacities. This aspect of legislative activity also proved a drain on energies, as many members served on multiple panels. Few legislators in the first two terms had participated in more than two committees, but in the Third Assembly some members were involved in as many as a dozen committees. There was evidence that members sought committee assignments in order to bolster their influence or access to resources. An assessment of the committee system conducted under the new Speaker of the House, Dimeji Bankole, prompted him to dissolve all but three of the House committees, with a commitment to rationalize the system (Ameh 2008). Yet this exercise concluded three months later with the creation of an additional twelve committees. Bankole also noted that by mid-2008, the House had 65 bills before it, but only 11 had passed. During the entire year, the Senate considered 120 bills, while passing only 8 (Okanlawon et al. 2008). This rate of resolution was scarcely greater than the sluggish pace of the First Assembly, suggesting that business in the legislature remained mired in factional carping and immobilism.

The assembly's shortcomings as a legislative body were shadowed by regular reports of electoral disputes and reversals from the 2007 polls, and assorted scandals involving representatives and senators.

Notwithstanding this level of performance, members of the Third Assembly voted themselves three additional increments in compensation—in September 2007, in January 2008, and again in August 2008. While their base annual salary remained modest at US$16,000 per year, assorted allowances equivalent to thirteen times their salaries raised the total compensation to US$224,000 annually, the highest in Africa, and one of the highest in the world.

Given these proclivities, it is not surprising that the reputation of the assembly in the public eye is rather dim. Survey data clearly illustrate the deficit of legitimacy for the legislature in the Fourth Republic. As indicated in Table 6.4, Nigerians rarely contact their National Assembly member and hold limited

Table 6.4 Public Attitudes Toward the Legislature

Survey Question	2001	2007
Contacted member of the National Assembly (% within past year)	5	11
Degree of trust for the National Assembly (% Somewhat/Quite a lot/A lot)[a]	21	26
How many of the following people do you think are involved in corruption (members of the National Assembly)? (% Most/All of them)	44	54
Do you approve or disapprove of the way (your National Assembly representative) performed their job over the past year? (% Approve/Strongly Approve)	46	37
Which of the following is closest to your view: "The members of the National Assembly represent the people; therefore they should make laws for this country, even if the President does not agree." (% Agree/Strongly Agree)	n.a.	76
"Since the President represents all of us he should pass laws without worrying about what the National Assembly thinks." (% Agree/Strongly Agree)	n.a.	15

Source: Afrobarometer surveys, August 2001 ($n = 2,190$) and January-February 2007 ($n = 2,410$).

Notes: a. Responses changed among surveys. For 2001: "Quite a lot" and "A lot" were the top categories. For 2007, "Somewhat" and "A lot" were the top categories. In 2001, 29 percent said their level of trust for the assembly was "none." This increased to 33 percent in 2007.

n.a. = not available.

trust in the legislature as an institution. Nigerians increasingly perceive corruption as a major problem in the assembly, and they have declining confidence in the performance of their own elected representatives. At the same time, Nigerians overwhelmingly believe that the National Assembly, as a representative elected body, is the proper source of legislation, rather than the executive. Nigerians hold strong views about the appropriate role of the legislature in their democracy, even as they are increasingly discouraged by the actual performance of the assembly. Indeed, these public perceptions mirror the disparities in legislative politics that we have emphasized throughout this analysis. A number of politicians have a sense of the institutional roles of the legislature in a presidential, federal democracy, and a significant proportion of representatives have sought to shape the activities of Nigeria's National Assembly toward those objectives. Members of the assembly have developed the capacities of the institution, advanced legislation, extended oversight activities and attempted to provide constituent services. Many representatives have also used their positions to garner perquisites, solicit favors, peddle influence, siphon public funds, assemble business deals, and inflate their status. The tensions within the legislature between being a body of rules and being a trading floor for the distribution of rents remain central to Nigeria's struggle for a more durable, credible, and responsive democracy.

Conclusion: Paths of Change?

This chapter discusses legislative politics in Nigeria within the broader structures and dynamics of the nation's political life. Nigeria's civilian regimes (like their military counterparts) reflect patterns of neopatrimonial politics, marked by the influence of personal networks and distributional politics, and contrasted by the relative weakness of formal institutions. Clientelist relationships and the disbursal of patronage are dominant features of the system. In a state dominated by centralized petroleum revenues, struggles over the circulation of rents provide central goals in seeking and utilizing public office. Under these circumstances, legislative politics have often appeared more as a market for bargaining over spoils, rather than the deliberation of laws or the oversight of government.

The National Assembly in Nigeria's Fourth Republic has reflected contradictory directions. While misconduct and self-interest have been abundant, the legislature has increasingly challenged the executive in both legislative and administrative arenas. The National Assembly has shown unprecedented autonomy and drive in crafting and debating legislation, pressing for oversight of the presidency and other branches of government, and seeking greater transparency in government affairs. The larger question, raised in Chapter 1 and in other chapters of the book, is the degree to which a "coalition for change" is emerging in the Nigerian legislature. Have political incentives changed for politicians in the current regime? Does the legislature reflect greater capabilities than in preceding governments? Is the legislature a site of potential reform in Nigeria's political process?

The current legislature is unquestionably more autonomous and capable than its predecessors. Although motives are ambivalent, a critical mass of perhaps twenty legislators has emerged in each term to challenge executive prerogatives and press an institutional agenda. Contention with the presidency occurred during the Obasanjo administration, with a highly assertive executive, as well as in the Yar'Adua government, with a comparatively diffident executive. Two factors that appear to encourage the assertiveness of the legislature are weaknesses among the political parties and the persistence of the regime. Weak party discipline, the low salience of ideology, and high turnover have all created significant space for legislators to pursue individual agendas. Consequently, many members of the assembly have sought to contest presidential power or to press for change in various sectors and operations of government. Moreover, the persistence of the democratic system, after the landmark of two completed terms and three elections, has encouraged a few politicians to consider political careers, based in part on performance and a public profile. Several veteran members, often joined by tyros with a reform agenda, have pursued change in the legislative arena and through committee oversight. In each term, this core group has constituted perhaps 10 percent of the assembly, though their skills and experience have often enhanced their institutional weight. Over time, the capacity of the legislature has generally improved as changing incentives and opportunities have enhanced attention to laws, policies, and development of the institution.

The legislature in Nigeria has nonetheless been marked by turbulence, corruption, factionalism, and inertia in legislative affairs. Many of the assertive actions of legislative committees are motivated as much by opportunism and publicity-mongering as by serious efforts at oversight. Yet Nigeria's legislature has introduced an unmistakable element of transparency into the political process, as inquiries and debates regularly bring to light the operations of government and the use of public resources. Further, the National Assembly has emerged as a credible third branch of government, and a tentative countervailing authority to the presidency. While not possessing a decisive coalition for change, Nigeria's legislature has moved beyond the quiescent patronage politics of earlier regimes, to assert a new role as a potential locus of accountability. The contestation within Nigeria's legislature between efforts to establish a body of rules, and the much greater scramble for rents, reflects a crucial arena of contention for the country's democratic future.

Notes

Special thanks go to Uwa Airhiavbere for invaluable research assistance.

1. The provision on term limits was buried in a list of 116 proposed changes to the constitution.

2. In the last days of debate, when the amendment seemed in peril, supporters of the third term tried unsuccessfully to change the assembly voting rules to force a public roll call.

3. Originally named the National Council of Nigeria and the Cameroons, the party was renamed after independence to attract a wider appeal. Azikiwe became the first president of the new Nigerian Republic in 1963, although Prime Minister Tafawa Balewa retained executive authority.

4. The average salary for legislators was about US$16,000 (slightly less in the House of Representatives than in the Senate), but allowances for transport, accommodation, and travel were multiples of base pay.

5. The APP was later renamed the All Nigeria People's Party (ANPP) in a bid to heighten its profile as a "national" party.

6. Information about members of the House of Representatives can be found on the National Assembly website at www.nassnig.org.

7. The furniture allowance for home and office amounted to US$25,000–$35,000 per member, at a time when average income in Nigeria was estimated at less than US$300 (Ugbolue 1999).

8. Many of these objections were clearly contrived and disingenuous. See Uwugiaren and Ugbolue, 1999.

9. A review of press reports on committee activity in the First Assembly shows a steady increase in news over time, with a marked increase in committee initiatives from 2002 forward.

10. Confidential interview, Abuja, January 2004.

11. Darren Kew, personal communication, April 2006.

12. A poll by the Afrobarometer network conducted two months before the elections showed the PDP with no more than a third of support among eligible voters (Afrobarometer 2007).

13. In December 2008, the Supreme Court upheld the results of the 2007 presidential election, ruling against a petition for annulment brought by the leading opposition candidates.

7

South Africa: Emerging Legislature or Rubber Stamp?

Joel D. Barkan

We conclude our series of case studies with a discussion of the South African National Assembly because, at first glance, this body appears to be a creature of the South African experience and thus an "outlier" or "exception" that has limited utility for understanding the process of legislative development across sub-Saharan Africa. It is well known that the structural context of South African politics is markedly different from that in the rest of Africa in two important respects. First, its politics are still largely shaped by the legacy of the apartheid era when a government elected by only 11 percent of the population monopolized political and economic power. Since 1994 when the African National Congress (ANC) came to power on the basis of one person, one vote, the overriding political issue has been how to overcome the inequalities bequeathed by apartheid while keeping the country on a prudent course of macroeconomic policy that raised economic growth.[1] While this question has faced other postcolonial regimes in southern Africa, it is a salient issue in only four countries of the subcontinent.

Second, as the only industrial and urbanized society in Africa, South Africa's politics do not resemble those of the agrarian societies to its north.[2] With few exceptions, South Africa is not a country whose peoples are mobilized politically on the basis of their local community of residence or on the basis of their ethnic affinities (though ethnicity is a factor[3]), but rather on the basis of race and class. Patron-client structures are therefore not the dominant form of political organization that they are elsewhere on the continent. Clientelist relationships do exist, but the most important forms of political organization are those normally associated with the politics of other industrial and urban societies, that is, political parties with clear programmatic agendas and interest groups such as trade unions and professional and business organizations that are established to address the economic concerns of their respective members and are autonomous from the state. While different political parties certainly draw their supporters from different types of communities and neighborhoods—a clear reflection of residential patterns established during the apartheid era—geography per se is not an important basis of political cleavage. Whereas "left-right" politics are barely visible across the rest of the continent, they permeate South African politics.

However, one should not—as South African social scientists are prone to do—dwell excessively on these factors and assert that South Africa is an exception to the politics of the rest of the continent in most respects. Notwithstanding its unique history, South Africa is still in the midst of a transition from authoritarian to democratic rule. And like the other forty-five countries of the continent that returned to some measure of electoral democracy during the 1990s, the South African National Assembly faces several challenges that are similar to the challenges faced by legislatures to the north. Moreover, the independent variables that appear to advance or retard the development of legislatures across Africa, including the other countries considered in this volume, appear to have the same effects on the process in South Africa. It is therefore instructive to consider this case of legislative development in comparison with legislatures elsewhere on the continent precisely because the conditions in South Africa are so different. Examination of the South African case facilitates a comparison and a theoretical understanding of what drives the development of African legislatures and legislatures generally, because it provides us with a greater variance in respect to each of the key independent variables that shape the process.

Few systematic and comprehensive studies exist of the South African National Assembly though the assembly has been the subject of several analyses in recent years. In marked contrast to South Africa's constitution and electoral system, the national legislature has attracted limited scholarly attention. A review of the National Assembly during the First Parliament following the end of apartheid, between 1994 and 1999, was published by the Institute for Democracy in South Africa (Idasa) in 1999 (Calland 1999), and the institute's Parliamentary Monitoring Group continues to summarize the proceedings of both the National Assembly and the National Council of Provinces, the upper house of Parliament.[4] Christina Murray and Lia Nijzink (2002) have examined the constitutional powers for both houses and for South Africa's provincial legislatures, and others (Nijzink and Piombo 2005; February 2005; Hughes 2005; and Calland 2006, chapter 4) have also discussed the National Assembly in recent articles. However, none of these studies assesses or explains the assembly's performance in comparison with the performance of legislatures elsewhere in Africa or in other emerging democracies. Moreover, two of these studies are preoccupied with Parliament in its oversight role and neglect the other functions of the legislature.

Testing the Conventional Wisdom: A "Rubber Stamp" Legislature?

The conventional wisdom among students of South African politics is that the National Assembly is a weak legislature and little more than a rubber stamp for the ruling ANC. Though it has all the formal accoutrements of a modern legislature—detailed and published rules of procedure, an extensive committee system, a large professional staff, and an elaborate physical infrastructure, those who subscribe to this position argue that the National Assembly cannot be regarded as an autonomous branch of government and certainly not an institution of countervailing power capable of checking executive power and holding it to account.

A cursory review of the assembly and the political context within which it operates leads many observers to this conclusion. Indeed, a combination of six factors or tendencies provide evidence for this view: (1) South Africa's one-party-dominant political system; (2) the impact of South Africa's electoral system of proportional representation; (3) the increasing centralization of power within the ANC during Thabo Mbeki's tenure as president of both the ANC and of South Africa; (4) the policy objectives of the ruling party; (5) the role of the presiding officer in the National Assembly; and (6) the political culture of the ruling party.

A One-Party-Dominant System

South Africa is a one-party-dominant political system and has been such since the country's transition to majority rule in 1994. The number of effective electoral and parliamentary parties, as calculated by the Laakso-Taagepera index, is 1.81 (Laakso and Taagepera 1979).

The ANC won 62.5 percent of the vote in 1994, 66.4 percent in 1999, 69.7 percent in 2004, and 66.5 percent in 2009. Because members of the National Assembly are elected via proportional representation (PR), the party held a similar percentage of seats—279 out of a total membership of 400 in the Third Parliament (2004–2009). The ANC increased its percentage and number of seats to 73.3 and 293 in April 2005 after the initial round of "floor crossing," a controversial procedure passed by the previous Parliament. Under this procedure, members of the National Assembly were permitted to switch parties at the end of the first year of their five-year term. As the Third Parliament was elected in April 2004, floor crossing was permitted in April of the following year. The procedure was highly controversial because it violates one of the basic principles of PR, namely that voters are represented by the party of their choice because they vote for parties and not for individual candidates, and because party strength in the legislature is supposed to reflect their proportion of the vote. Opposition parties were especially aggrieved by the procedure, because the net effect of floor crossing was to erode the representation of the opposition and small parties in particular, thus undermining another feature of PR—that it assures the representation of minorities. Given these controversies, the procedure was repealed toward the end of the Third Parliament and will not be permitted in the Fourth (2009–2014).

The opposition, which was reduced from 121 to 107 seats after floor crossing, is also fragmented. In the election for the Third Parliament, the largest opposition party, the Democratic Alliance (DA), won only 12.5 percent of the vote and 50 seats, one-eighth of all MPs. The remaining 71 seats were divided among ten parties, of which only the Inkatha Freedom Party (IFP) won more than 5 percent of the vote.[5] The domination by the ANC is compounded by the fact that the DA draws most of its support from white and Coloured voters, while the ANC is supported mainly by African South Africans. Thus, in the elections for the Third Parliament, there was no credible alternative to the ANC that drew significant support from South Africa's majority racial group, and party alignments remained drawn along racial lines. This pattern is likely to continue during the Fourth Parliament as a result of the 2009 elections. Although a new African-led party, the Congress of the People (COPE), clearly took votes away from the ANC and reduced its majority, it did not dislodge the ANC from its commanding position as the dominant party in South Africa and in the National Assembly.

The Impact of Proportional Representation

Members of the National Assembly are elected via the Droop method of list PR, which is implemented at two tiers. At the national level, 200 members are elected from competing national party lists, while at the provincial level, 200 are elected from a series of nine sets of competing provincial lists. The number of members elected from each province varies in relation to the percentage of South Africa's population living in the province. Voters thus cast a single ballot for the party of their choice and do not have the option of indicating their candidate preference. The use of the "closed list" system in turn means that leaders of all parties, and especially ANC leaders, control the rank order of their candidates on both the national and provincial lists. This in turn means that ANC MPs are expected to be highly disciplined and toe the line when it comes to defending their party's positions in Parliament.

Failure to accept party discipline may result in a lowering of one's position on the ANC's list at the next election, denial of renomination, or one's immediate "redeployment" to another position deemed important to the party (i.e., sitting ANC MPs can be summarily dropped from Parliament in the middle of their elected term).[6] While the number redeployed during any one parliamentary session is relatively small (five or fewer per year), it is a weapon the leadership has not been reluctant to use. This was especially true after Thabo Mbeki became the ANC leader and president of South Africa in 1999, until he himself was "redeployed" and forced to resign from the state presidency in September 2008.[7] The threat of redeployment has had its intended effect, particularly on those ANC MPs who have few opportunities for employment in the private sector at salaries approaching those they receive as MPs. MPs with limited formal education—usually African members who owe their seats to their involvement in the armed struggle against apartheid—are most vulnerable to the threat of being redeployed. Highly educated MPs and professionals, a disproportionate number of whom are white, are less susceptible to this pressure.

Increasing Centralization of Power Within the ANC

The ANC is a highly centralized organization in which power became increasingly concentrated in the hands of President Mbeki and the party leadership after his ascension to the presidency in 1999 and especially after his reelection in 2004. As president of the ANC, Mbeki (and now his successor) chaired the party's two highest organs, the National Executive Committee and the National Working Committee. These committees make day-to-day policy, with the Working Committee setting the agenda for the cabinet of the South African government and the ruling party's agenda for Parliament.

Although the ANC has historically been a centralized organization similar to the soviet model, the ANC leadership was forced to grant considerable autonomy to local party cells and community groups during the 1980s when the fight against apartheid played out in South Africa's urban townships while the party's top leadership was in exile or jail. Nelson Mandela accepted such autonomy after becoming president of both the ANC and South Africa in 1994, but Mbeki reasserted central control following his ascension to the presidencies of both party and state after Mandela retired.

It is also important to appreciate that the ANC is very different from most political parties elsewhere in Africa. Unlike those parties, the ANC is *not* a patronage-based organization dominated by the head of government that comes to life solely at the time of national elections to mobilize rural voters. Rather it still views itself as a liberation movement and is a party with a clear ideology and program. Thus, it is also a party that maintains a significant organization vis-à-vis government and the public between elections although the organization has atrophied in recent years. Similarly, until his removal from office, Mbeki was not a neopatrimonial party leader in the manner of a Mobutu, Moi, or Robert Mugabe. Despite some scandals—most notably the recent allegations of bribery against Jacob Zuma, who became president of the ANC in December 2007 and president of South Africa following the elections of 2009—South Africa is relatively free of corruption. Most important, corruption and patronage are not the bases of the party's power and control.[8] However, Mbeki's centralization of power meant that he regarded Parliament as a subordinate branch of government—both to the executive and to the highest organs of the ANC. Whereas Parliament had been a vibrant center of political intellect and talent during Mandela's presidency (1994–1999), Mbeki and the ANC disinvested from the institution in the years that followed (Calland 2006, 94–104).

With respect to the Parliament, this means that the ANC leadership expects that it is the decisions of the National Working Committee sitting in Pretoria, not Cape Town (where the National Assembly is located), that calls the shots in terms of setting the parliamentary agenda and determining which legislation shall be passed. The Working Committee communicates this agenda via its Political Committee to the ANC parliamentary caucus, which meets weekly for up to three hours.[9] Following initial announcements, selected ministers take turns discussing the issues to be addressed by legislation that they will introduce or that will be read for the second time during the following week. Party whips are present and play a key role in enforcing discipline. Questions from the floor follow and the discussion is sometimes quite extensive, even spirited. But it is also clear who is in charge and what is expected of the rank and file. As one long-time participant described it to this author, "The process is democratic, but it is not 'bottom-up.'" He further observed that the relationship between ministers and the ANC rank and file, including chairs of portfolio committees, is mixed. Some ministers develop a very cooperative and symbiotic relationship with committees and their chairs, while others are prone to dictate.

Other parties also caucus weekly, thus emphasizing the importance of party for the manner in which the National Assembly transacts its business. In addition, each party maintains a caucus or "study group" for each portfolio committee. Given the ANC's large majority, it is within the ANC committee study groups that the details of most legislation are thrashed out. Meetings of portfolio committees are open to the public including the press, but meetings of the study groups are not. ANC committee study groups are thus viewed by the executive and by the Working Committee as the arenas within which the policy orientation of the party's leadership is implemented. This in turn means that while meetings of the entire committee exhibit considerable debate between parties, and while the same occurs on the floor of the National Assembly as a whole, the decisionmaking process occurs largely behind closed doors within ANC organs—in the National Working Committee, in the Political Committee, in the ANC parliamentary caucus, and in the ANC committee study groups prior to the meetings involving all parties. Not surprisingly, this frustrates some members of the opposition, though others contend that much genuine business, such as the deliberation and crafting of legislation, is also conducted in the multiparty forums.

The Working Committee further asserts its authority by appointing (via the Political Committee and in consultation with the party's chief whip) the chairs of all portfolio committees in the National Assembly as well as the chairs of the

Rules Committee, the Committee on Committees, the Speaker and the Deputy Speaker. The Working Committee (again, via the Political Committee in consultation with the chief whip) is also the dominant voice in committee assignments though MPs are given the opportunity to state their preferences. A key individual in this process is the ANC's chief whip. He is arguably the most powerful MP, as he makes recommendations on which ANC MPs will serve as committee chairs. He also determines who speaks for the ANC on issues of national importance, and for how long. Control of floor debate by the ANC whip increased throughout the Third Parliament.

During the First Parliament, which sat from 1994 to 1999, committee assignments were based more on MPs' preferences than they are today, while committee chairs were elected by the members of the committee. The control of assignments and chairships by the Working Committee and Political Committee is perhaps the main indicator of increased control by the ANC leadership since Mbeki became president. Yet another indicator was the decision by the ANC following the 2004 elections to name the chair of the Standing Committee on Public Accounts (SCOPA), a position historically chaired by a member of the opposition in Commonwealth countries.

The Policy Objectives of the ANC

The nature of "the ANC project" impacts greatly on the relations between the ANC and "the loyal opposition." The raison d'être of the ANC, since its inception in 1911, has been to reverse 300 years of racial domination by South African whites over African and other nonwhite citizens. As enshrined in the Freedom Charter of 1955 and in subsequent documents since 1994, the elimination of political, economic, and social inequality between the members of different classes and racial groups remains the guiding policy of the organization more than fifty years hence.[10] This in turn shapes the ANC's relations with other political parties and how especially it judges and interacts with the Democratic Alliance, the largest opposition party and the "official opposition" in the National Assembly.

Given its formal commitment to a "democratic South Africa," the government and the ruling party have, with few lapses, scrupulously respected the rights of the opposition.[11] But there is a clear tension between respecting the formal rights of the opposition and engaging the opposition, or to put it more accurately, letting the opposition engage the ANC. There is a significant philosophical and social distance between the ANC and the Democratic Alliance that is unlikely to be bridged in the near term. Indeed, the relationship borders on hostility. This in turn leads the ANC to keep the DA at arm's length and view the party with suspicion. Why this approach?

The answer lies in both the ANC's "project" and the manner in which the DA approaches its work. With respect to the first, the ANC is prepared to listen to and work with those opposition parties who accept the ANC's main agenda. In other words, those parties that may oppose the ANC yet provide useful criticism regarding how to best achieve true equality in South Africa by reversing the legacies of apartheid are treated with respect and engaged. Conversely, those parties that are perceived as opposing the project itself, and who are intent on "scoring points" by opposing the ANC on nearly every issue and every piece of proposed legislation for the purpose of "keeping the government on its toes," are loathed.

The relationship between government and opposition is also colored by style and tradition. On the one hand, the ANC regards itself as a "nonracial" party, one whose supporters are predominantly African in terms of race and culture, but a party that includes the members of all racial groups. By contrast, it perceives the DA as not only a "white" party, but one that is mired excessively in the traditions of the British House of Commons. The preponderance of DA MPs are English-speaking whites, and the style of many, especially the party's former leader, Tony Leon, is regarded as unnecessarily argumentative for argument's sake (i.e., that the DA emphasizes debate over substance and thus does not contribute to better legislation or, by extension, to a "better South Africa").

The ANC's relationship with other opposition parties is more cordial. ANC MPs frequently remark that, much to their initial surprise, they get on well with Afrikaans-speaking whites, regardless of their party and including those who are members of the Democratic Alliance. The reason given is that Afrikaans-speaking politicians, including those from the former ruling party of the apartheid era, understand "the ANC's project," because they once pursued a similar project on behalf of their community—the use of state power to uplift a subordinate group.

The Role of the Presiding Officer

A key individual in the development of the National Assembly during the first ten years of the postapartheid era was the Speaker, Frene Ginwala, who served in that capacity during the First and Second Parliaments. Regarded by many MPs as somewhat imperious and autocratic,[12] she was also highly respected for the commitment and professionalism she brought to the operations of the assembly. Having served as the head of the ANC's policy research office, Ginwala's charge following the 1994 elections was to "make the assembly work" in a manner that reflected the political transition. This meant that she had to take control over an operation and (largely Afrikaaner) staff inherited from the apartheid era; orient more than 300 MPs who had not previously served in any legislature to their new roles including an understanding of legislative procedures; coordinate with the ANC Working Group, committee chairs, and with the leaders of the opposition; and most important, pass an unusually large volume of legislation required to restructure the legal framework bequeathed by the apartheid state.[13]

The Speaker saw her role as that of transforming the National Assembly into a more representative and popular body reflecting the sea-change in the political system. This in turn meant that she pushed members in two directions that were sometimes viewed as contradictory to each other. On the one hand, she "nurtured" members, particularly ANC MPs, to learn the skills of being a legislator and was highly respected for such. On the other, she often kept members of her own party on a short leash, a practice that was resented by some committee chairs. This was particularly true with respect to legislative oversight of the executive, though she candidly acknowledged that a major challenge for the assembly was to exercise its oversight role more effectively, especially after most of the legal framework of the postapartheid era had been passed. Given her pivotal role and style, it is not surprising that many ANC MPs regarded her as an overdemanding taskmaster who could have presided with a lighter hand. At the same time, members of the opposition interviewed for this study regarded her as "tough" but "highly competent" and "fair."

Partly because of her style, but also because she represented an independent force, Ginwala was unceremoniously dumped as Speaker by Mbeki and the ANC leadership following the 2004 elections. She immediately retired from the National Assembly and was succeeded by Baleka Mbete, a younger and less strong-willed successor. Mbete served until September 2008, when she was promoted to the position of deputy president following Mbeki's resignation. Her stewardship is often described as "disorganized" and "undistinguished." One irony of these changes is that while Ginwala's successors have probably wielded less power vis-à-vis members and committee chairs than Ginwala, the National Assembly itself has lost stature. The subordination of the assembly—to the ANC's national leadership and to the executive branch—is also reflected by the increased power of the ANC's chief whip.

The Political Culture of the ANC

ANC MPs emphasize the unique political culture of their party and its impact on the way the party governs, including its approach to parliamentary practice. Several considerations are relevant here. The first, as its name clearly states, is that the ANC is a *congress* and hence a "big and diverse tent." Though it draws the preponderance of its supporters from the African population, it has never wavered from its commitment to nonracialism and includes a significant number (indeed a disproportionate number) of non-African minority members (i.e., whites, Coloureds, and Asians) within its leadership ranks. It is simultaneously the party of urban workers, intellectuals, nonwhite professionals, and the rural poor. It is also a party that operates in close association with the South African Communist Party and the Congress of South African Trade Unions.

Most fundamentally, and given its long-term objectives, many ANC leaders still regard the party as a "liberation movement" whose goal is to transform society rather than to govern society toward some narrower set of policy goals.

The tensions between key constituencies within the ANC are well known, and a perennial question in South Africa is, "How long will the movement remain intact?" Because it is "a big tent," its members cannot be expected to forever march in lockstep with the leadership or with each other. Thus, while the value of "democratic centralism" is still very much alive amongst ANC cadres, and while the practice of redeployment is accepted as a strategy for maintaining party discipline and utilizing the individual talents of its diverse membership, there is a strong sentiment among many MPs that the leadership should loosen the reins. Within the National Assembly, this sentiment is articulated most frequently by younger MPs (i.e., those in their thirties), by those who are better educated, and by a few "old timers." In their view, centralized control has been taken too far, because such control is no longer necessary for the ANC to successfully pursue its broad policy agenda. This in turn produces both a loyalty to the leadership, and an internal dynamic of debate that shapes the party's approach in the National Assembly.

Much More Than a Rubber Stamp?

The picture presented above appears to confirm the conventional wisdom that the National Assembly is a rubber stamp of the ruling party and therefore not an autonomous body or institution of countervailing power. The reality is both more complex and more hopeful if indeed an autonomous legislature is a hallmark of liberal democracy. The case for autonomy can be summarized in terms of six arguments: (1) The National Assembly is an active body that amends most legislation introduced by the executive. (2) There is a viable system of portfolio committees albeit of varying capacity and skill. (3) Civil society in South Africa is both pluralistic and strong. (4) There is a free press that reports on legislation pending before the National Assembly, and on executive-parliamentary relations. (5) The National Assembly receives substantial resources for individual members and for the institution. (6) Last, but not least, the era of ANC one-party dominance may be at the beginning of nearing its end.

The National Assembly Amends Most Legislation

The National Assembly is an active body that amends most legislation. Between 75 and 80 percent of legislation introduced by the executive is amended, often significantly, before the legislation becomes law.[14] This is particularly true of "major" legislation, that is, legislation that involves major changes in government policy and/or includes controversial proposals. Although the executive introduces all but a handful of bills, and private member's bills rarely become law, the final text of most legislation is crafted by the legislature.[15] Bills are first introduced in the National Assembly by the cabinet minister responsible for the policy in question. This is the "first reading" of the bill, after which it is referred to the appropriate portfolio committee for review and amendment. Bills reported out of committee for the "second reading" before the assembly as a whole are considered ready for passage and, if passed, are forwarded to the upper house, the National Council of Provinces, for its assent. Some bills are referred back to committee for further amendment before a formal vote, including amendments desired by the minister. In contrast to most Commonwealth legislatures, there are only two official readings, or considerations, of each bill instead of three. The process, however, is anything but swift, as it often takes up to two years before proposed legislation is refined and passed into law.

During the First Parliament following the assumption to power by the ANC in 1994, the National Assembly passed 494 bills—an unusually high volume driven by the party's desire to repeal or amend most laws passed during the apartheid era. The volume dropped significantly during the Second Parliament, which sat between 1999 and 2004, when the assembly passed roughly 300 pieces of legislation. The volume dropped further during the Third Parliament. Nevertheless, the sheer volume of legislation considered by the assembly coupled with the high percentage amended suggests that the National Assembly is a productive body compared to most other legislatures in Africa, and, for that matter, when compared to the legislatures of many established democracies. Short of coding each piece of legislation introduced to the assembly—an effort beyond the scope of this study—it is impossible to quantify with greater precision the actual autonomy and power of the National Assembly. Many amendments were no doubt minor, especially with respect to the overall policy of the legislation considered. The assembly did not reverse or significantly alter the thrust of the legislation intended by the ANC leadership. The impact of the assembly, however, was still impressive.[16]

The Emerging System of Portfolio Committees

Modern and autonomous legislatures that impact on the policymaking process are invariably legislatures with a well-developed system of portfolio or ministerial committees—committees that shadow the ministries, departments, and agencies (MDAs) that make up the executive branch. A feature of weak legislatures is that the committee system is either nonexistent or lacks any genuine capacity to participate in the crafting of legislation or oversight of the executive. Emerging legislatures in fledgling democracies fall somewhere in between—their committee systems are not fully established, but they have developed some observable capacity to contribute to the legislative process. South Africa falls within this middle category in a pattern that is very similar to emerging legislatures elsewhere on the continent, especially in Kenya—and, to a lesser extent, in Ghana and Uganda.

It is important to note that prior to 1994, before the postapartheid era, Parliament had only five committees, none of which were portfolio committees that shadowed government MDAs. Today, the National Assembly has twenty-six portfolio committees plus several standing committees, including the Rules Committee, the Committee on Committees, and SCOPA. Committees also have the power to summon any individual or institution to appear before them and give evidence under oath or to submit reports upon request. Committees may also receive petitions from any interested persons or institutions.

Most committees have roughly twenty to twenty-five members, of which fifteen to eighteen are ANC MPs. Given their large majority, ANC MPs serve on only one committee, while DA MPs usually serve on two to ensure the party's participation in all. MPs from smaller parties, however, must pick and choose. Not all parties are represented on all committees.

What does "capacity" consist of at the committee level? At its most basic level, capacity consists of a "critical mass" of a committee's membership that is capable of participating fully in the committee's work. This means that they understand the issues addressed in the legislation under consideration, that they have developed at least a layman's expertise on these issues, and that they are sufficiently motivated to devote the expected amount of time required for committee work (e.g., they attend all or nearly all committee meetings, they prepare for such meetings by reading all documents to be considered, they make an effort to learn about the general policy area and major issues that fall within the committee's responsibility, etc.).

Interviews with more than two dozen MPs, including members of the opposition, the chairs of six committees, and the former Speaker (Ginwala), suggest that a "critical mass" for a typical committee is from between one-third and one-half of its members. Yet when then asked how many committees have such a membership, the answer was consistently "only between one-quarter and one-third," that is, between six and eight of the portfolio committees. Indeed, there was little variance in the assessment of the committee system among those interviewed. Up to one-third of the committees were deemed as doing "an effective" or "very good" job, one-third were rated as average, and a third were rated as "not effective" or "below average." There was also a general agreement that a major challenge for the National Assembly was to increase the proportion of committees that could be rated as "effective" by upgrading and training their members.

That may be easier said than done, because a large number of ANC MPs, perhaps as many as 200 or 220, are individuals of limited educational background and/or professional experience. These are individuals who gained their seats on the basis of their historical commitment to the ANC, especially during the armed struggle prior to 1994. Indeed, the proportion of ANC MPs with professional experience was arguably less in the Second and Third Parliaments than in the First as a result of a high turnover of MPs following the elections of 1999 and 2004 (Calland 2006, 95).[17]

Committees that are regarded as having developed "capacity" also share several characteristics associated with effective committees in the other legislatures discussed in this volume. First, the committee is invariably chaired by a highly motivated and knowledgeable MP who is intent that his or her committee performs its expected role. In most, albeit not all, cases, such chairs have a professional knowledge of the policy area with which the committee is concerned, or they have committed themselves to learning the policy area in detail. Second, the chair is surrounded by between a half dozen to a dozen committee members who share his or her interest in the committee's work. Together they constitute a solid core that makes the committee work. Such members are more than likely to also have a professional or personal interest in the policy area of the committee. Whether or not a critical mass exists in a particular committee is also a function of the chair's ability to motivate his colleagues, and some are clearly more skilled at rallying the troops than others. Third, the committee has succeeded in recruiting a small staff, often no more than one or two individuals, who are knowledgeable about the subject matter before the committee and/or who can facilitate the administration of the committee. This includes, among other skills, the ability to reach out and consult with (and manage) key interest groups that weigh in on most legislation. Fourth, the committee has an adequate budget that enables it to recruit specialized staff and to pursue such investigations as it deems appropriate and necessary for fulfilling its role (e.g., it has a travel budget). Fifth, committees have assigned space where they can regularly meet as well as office space for their staff.

Sixth, and perhaps most important, the committee is respected by other legislators, by the presiding officers of the National Assembly, by the ANC's leadership, and by organizations outside the legislature that are concerned with the same area of public policy. This in turn results in the committee being lobbied periodically by these outside organizations, because they have concluded that the "committee matters." Committees that exhibit these features in the National Assembly are also committees that from time to time may generate tensions with the ANC leadership, including the cabinet minister whose ministry the committee shadows. When the minister and the portfolio committee disagree, especially when the committee chair does not support the minister's perspective, there are tensions.

Another factor that determines the quality and capacity of committees is the volume of important legislation directed to the committee. Committees such as justice, finance, trade and industry, local government, transport, and social development (and sometimes health) are consistently rated as among the best in part because they dealt effectively with a large flow of legislation dropped in their laps by the executive. This volume in turn meant that the ANC assigned some of its most-talented MPs to chair these committees, a critical factor in the development of the committees themselves. Put differently, some committees have failed to develop significant capacity because they have not had to—they could "coast" while others could not.

Finally, it is important to note that because the most-talented committee chairs are individuals with higher than average education and professional background, a disproportionate number of committees deemed "effective" are those chaired by white members of the ANC, or members of other racial minorities. Six of the seven committees mentioned in the previous paragraph fall within this category. Not surprisingly, this situation generates its own tensions within the ranks of the ruling party, though these tensions are rarely acknowledged in public.[18]

Civil Society

The National Assembly functions within a pluralistic society that has given rise to a well-organized civil society. If there is one aspect of South Africa's "exceptionalism" that is significant for the autonomy of its legislature, it is the fact that the country is a highly urbanized and informed society with a much larger civil society than that found elsewhere in Africa. Civil society across Africa is overwhelmingly an urban phenomenon organized mainly by professionals, though in some countries (as in South Africa) labor unions are an important component. Indeed, a major constraint on the democratization of many African countries is that their civil society is weak to nonexistent outside the major cities, that it has no "reach" into the rural areas. Civil society in South Africa does not suffer from this problem. It is also more likely than its counterparts elsewhere in Africa to organize itself around a series of specialized economic interests they wish to defend. Civil society organizations thus seek to lobby both the executive and the legislature about relatively narrow economic issues with which they are concerned. For example, in 2004, a national association of pharmacy proprietors were very vocal in their opposition to a government bill that sought to regulate the prices pharmacies could charge for prescription drugs.

Several hundred such organizations articulate their positions on legislation addressed to their interests. Many do so by contacting the appropriate portfolio committee. The committees have become a sounding board for civil society, with the result that the most proactive committees are those that seek to preempt criticism by inviting representatives of these organizations to testify before these committees. Such consultation in turn limits the options open to the executive on any one piece of proposed legislation. Put differently, the chairs and active members of the most-effective committees know that part of their duty is to canvass relevant civil society organizations before writing the final version of a bill. Such consultation might be viewed by some as a powerful constraint on the National Assembly, but the real constraint created by these organizations is on the executive, because it is via the deliberations of the legislature that bills that displease civil society are modified and adjusted to balance the desires of the government with the concerns of those most affected by the proposed legislation.

It should also be noted that relations between civil society and government are not necessarily adversarial. This is because the most-effective ANC chairs reach out to organizations with large African memberships and/or a presence in the townships or rural areas in order to balance lobbying by wealthier groups that are often fronts for established and white business interests. Civil society thus strengthens the role of Parliament vis-à-vis the executive.

The Existence of a Free Press

Although some observers argue that the South African press is less provocative today than during the final years of the apartheid era, and that the press has been "dumbed down" like the media worldwide, the press is free to print what it wants—and does. Though it is drawn to the sensational, such as the Arms Deal scandal of 1999–2000 and the "Travelgate" scandal of 2004, it covers the major stories emanating from the National Assembly. These include changes of key personnel such as the presiding officers and chairs of the most important committees, the progress of controversial legislation, statements by party leaders, and the investigations by SCOPA.

The press corps assigned to cover Parliament numbers approximately forty-five. Senior members contend that although meetings of the portfolio committees are open to the public, the assembly has become a more "opaque" institution since 1999. They state that during the First Parliament (1994–1999), relations between the press and key committee chairs were more informal than today. The press also had greater access, both on and off the record. Two reasons are given. The first is that under Mbeki, the ANC was less forthcoming to the press generally than under Mandela. There was a studied coolness toward the press, and younger African journalists are subject to quiet pressures to not be too aggressive in their questions or investigations.[19] The second is the departure from Parliament of committee chairs and other "stars" who "got on well" with the press by making themselves accessible after hours, and so on. Still, the press is a force to be reckoned with. And given that its coverage of Parliament informs civil society, the press contributes to the mobilization of those organizations that lobby the National Assembly or seek to hold it to account. Conversely, when the press is highly critical of the performance of the National Assembly, as it was over the ANC's handling of the controversial Arms Deal in 1999–2000 (and especially the party's reining in of SCOPA), it may undermine public confidence in the institution. The long-term impact of the press on the evolution of the National Assembly is difficult to assess. Though the relationship is arguably less open today than it was prior to 1999, it is clearly far more open than during the apartheid era.

Institutional Resources

A major finding from earlier work on both African legislatures (Barkan et al. 2004) and the development of legislatures in other countries, including the United States (Squire 1992; Squire and Hamm 2005, 75), is that resources count. Legislatures that cannot acquire or otherwise generate adequate resources to support their members and operations are unlikely to become autonomous and powerful bodies. The level of salaries is especially important, particularly where MPs are elected from single-member districts and thus confronted by a series of incentives to devote more time to constituency service than to the collective functions of the legislature. While this pressure does not exist in South Africa to the extent that it does elsewhere in Africa, salaries and other personal emoluments as well as staff and physical infrastructure together form a critical package of resources without which the legislature cannot develop. That said, resources alone, do not a legislature make.

Both the National Assembly and the National Council of Provinces are very well endowed compared to most African legislatures. Only in Kenya and Nigeria does an African legislature provide resources for its members on a level that approaches that of South Africa. South African MPs are well endowed in three important respects. First, MPs receive a basic salary of R30,000 or nearly US$4,700 per month. This translates to a monthly take-home pay after taxes and other deductions of US$3,000. In addition, MPs receive health and pension benefits, a daily per diem while Parliament is sitting in Cape Town, and travel allowances, including air fares, back to their places of residence when Parliament is in recess.

Second, *all* MPs are provided with a personal assistant, as well as a private office with Internet access. Indeed, the physical complex of buildings for both houses of Parliament is impressive by any standard. In addition to the chambers for each house and individual offices, there are meeting rooms for parliamentary committees, larger offices for the presiding officers, office space for staff, plus an attractive and modern visitor center.[20] The entire complex is information-technology friendly and dotted with flat-screen televisions announcing scheduled committee meetings and other events or broadcasting the proceedings of the House. Giant banners outside the main parliamentary buildings trumpet the role of Parliament in South Africa's democracy. The surrounding grounds are impeccably kept—a quiet city park adjacent to the center of Cape Town's business district. Apart from supporting MPs, these facilities project an image of parliamentary importance and power that is greater than what it actually is. Put differently, "the rhetorical and visual image" of the National Assembly exceeds its actual "political clout" while at the same time nurturing such clout.

Third, beginning in the Second Parliament (1999–2004), MPs have been provided R5,000 (US$780) a month to support "constituency service." Although MPs are elected via PR with the result that there are no formal parliamentary constituencies in South Africa, the ANC initiated a practice of defining geographic constituencies for each of its members and assigning MPs to these areas. ANC MPs are expected to visit these "constituencies" whenever Parliament is in recess, hold public meetings there, meet with individual constituents to help them with their problems (e.g., obtaining pension payments), and to hire and keep in frequent contact with a personal representative in the constituency when they are not there. ANC MPs are also graded by the party on constituency work, a rating that is supposedly considered when the party determines their positions on the party's list for the next election.

To facilitate and encourage constituency service, "constituency allowances" are paid to each party based on their number of MPs in the National Assemblies, but not to the MPs themselves. Smaller parties not only receive far less, they have far fewer MPs to cover all of South Africa. As a result, only the DA and IFP maintain serious constituency efforts, but they do not cover the entire territory of the country. The overall impact of constituency work is also difficult to assess and beyond the scope of this study. Interviews with ANC members suggest that the party views constituency service as an important aspect of each MP's job, and that such work enables the party to better understand the particular needs of different types of communities and interests. For example, one informant noted that regular visits to a canning factory in his "constituency" taught him how pending legislation on labor relations would play out in that facility, the largest employer in the area. Notwithstanding this support, Robert Mattes reports that compared to African countries that elect their legislatures via single-member-district systems, the percentage of South Africans that have ever met their MP is among the lowest at 0.2 percent (Mattes 2002).

In addition to the resources provided to individual MPs, Parliament has an extensive and qualified staff to facilitate the operations of both the National Assembly and the National Council of Provinces. Several key members, including the secretary to the National Assembly and the unit manager of legislation and procedures, are holdovers from the apartheid era. Both are Afrikaaners and stated that the assembly is a far livelier and important institution today than it was prior to 1994 when the executive kept the legislature on a tight leash and the committee system was very weak.

By contrast there are now approximately ninety staff assigned to facilitate the work of the committees alone. A major constraint, however, is the absence of specialized staff who can provide individual MPs or the committees as a whole with adequate research support. Committee chairs were particularly vocal on the need for better research support even though Parliament maintains a unit for this purpose. Committee chairs and the leaders of the opposition parties desire control over the research done on their behalf. They want staff dedicated to their needs and their committees rather than sharing a pool of researchers. They argue that dedicated research staffs would nurture greater expertise among both staff and members on the policy areas with which each committee is concerned. The institutional memory of the committee would also be enhanced.

Considerations of party also undermine the work of the present research staff. The ANC relies heavily on its party headquarters in Johannesburg for policy research. The DA also hires its own research assistants. Most MPs interviewed for this study did not regard the present practice of outsourcing of research as satisfactory, because the research is not produced on time or is of poor quality. However, most did not seem eager to utilize the research produced by parliamentary staff because it must be shared across party lines.

Conclusions

This review of the South African National Assembly fifteen years after the end of apartheid presents a mixed yet fascinating picture of the evolution of this legislature. It also provides an additional data point from which to obtain a comparative understanding about the development of emerging legislatures in emerging Third Wave democracies generally, and particularly in Africa. Our conclusions can be summarized as follows.

First, in respect to our initial question of whether the National Assembly is a rubber stamp or an autonomous and significant body, the answer is ambiguous. The National Assembly is the proverbial glass of water that is either "half full" or "half empty" depending on one's perspective. Because it is nearly impossible to quantify or otherwise measure the degree of legislative autonomy or power, we are left to rely on "thick description" that suggests the National Assembly falls somewhere in between. At the same time, there is a consensus that, compared to the former parliament of the apartheid era, the legislature today is far more powerful than the one it displaced. During the previous regime the legislature *was* a rubber stamp.

One might also ask whether the South African National Assembly would have produced different outcomes in terms of its legislative record during its first fifteen years as a popularly elected body had it been granted greater autonomy by the formal rules of South Africa's constitution and had the ruling party and the assembly as a whole not been subject to the leadership style of President Mbeki. The answer to both questions is most likely "no."

Had either of these situations been the case, four specific outcomes probably would have occurred: (1) The National Assembly and especially its strongest committees probably would have taken greater initiative with respect to the introduction of legislation. (2) Had MPs been elected from single-member districts or small multimember districts instead of by party list PR, MPs from all parties would have devoted more time to constituency service at the expense of the collective activities of the legislature. In other words, the behavior of South African

MPs would have more closely resembled that of legislators in the other countries considered in this study. (3) The presence of racial minorities and women within the assembly would have undoubtedly been less than it is under PR. (4) In the absence of the combination of PR and Mbeki, party discipline within the ANC would have been less. This in turn might have resulted in greater independence of the Standing Committee on Public Accounts to investigate instances of malfeasance within the executive branch. The portfolio committee on health might also have been more assertive in resisting the government's policy on HIV/AIDS. On the other hand, an electoral system based on single-member districts would have produced an even greater ANC majority in the National Assembly than the party has obtained under PR (Barkan et al. 2006), with the result that the overall dominance of the executive would have been similar.

Notwithstanding these variations, the nature of the legislation passed in terms of the policy thrust of that legislation—to overturn the legal framework inherited from the apartheid era and to begin to reverse the social inequities bequeathed from that period—*would have been substantially the same.* Moreover, the volume of legislation passed to realize these goals was greatest during the First Parliament (1994–1999) when Mbeki was *not* president.

Would the committee system have functioned differently? The answer here is more complicated. Committee chairs would have exercised greater autonomy and been elected by committee members as was the practice during the First Parliament. Committees would also have been subject to fewer constraints imposed by the Speaker, but the overall functioning of the committee system in terms of approach (including the role of the ANC study groups) and legislation passed would have been similar. Whether the same or similar individuals would have emerged as the chairs of key committees is unclear, but the number of chairships held by highly educated (and older) minority members would probably have been less had MPs been elected from single-member districts because the overall election of educated racial minorities would have been less. This scenario would have produced a weaker system of portfolio committees than that which has evolved since 1994. In this instance, greater autonomy of individual MPs as a result of single-member districts would probably have resulted in less rather than more legislative power vis-à-vis the executive branch.

As for the impact of the former Speaker, had Frene Ginwala not been in charge, it is quite likely that the assembly would not have performed as well as it did. Despite her controlling tendencies, and those of the Working Committee, the bottom line is that debate within the portfolio committees and within the ANC study groups was often intense. Even more important, there was often true bargaining and compromise among members, and between committee members and the ministers responsible for legislation under consideration. At the same time, Ginwala, together with her professional staff, "made Parliament work."

If the National Assembly has a major weakness, it is in its capacity and modalities for performing its oversight role. It is still feeling its way, especially in the wake of the reining in of SCOPA's investigation of the Arms Deal in 1999–2000.[21] Many ANC MPs felt burned and/or intimidated by that exercise, while opposition MPs regarded it as an unambiguous failure of the National Assembly to fulfill its constitutional role. The former Speaker also acknowledged that the handling of this particular inquiry had complicated if not compromised the assembly's capacity in this area. Ginwala and several key ANC chairs also believe that now that most of the ANC's legislative program has been translated into law, there is a need for the National Assembly to expand its oversight role. Put simply, the agenda for ANC and thus for the National Assembly as an institution needs to shift from the passage of essential legislation to greater scrutiny and accountability over the implementation of this legislation.

One might add that given the dominance of the ANC, and the fact that it is now in the middle of its second decade in power (with accompanying tendencies toward corruption that occur when one party is in power a long time), the need for a more systematic and expanded effort at oversight is clear. It is also clear that neither SCOPA nor the individual portfolio committees will become more proactive in this task unless given the green light by the Working Committee. The same can be said for the role of the National Assembly in approving major appointments made by the executive such as the appointment of ministers, judges, heads of state-owned corporations, commissions of inquiry, and so on. So long as the president has the unfettered authority to make such appointments on his own, the power of the legislature is diminished.

Fulfilling its oversight role also involves the capacity and opportunity of the National Assembly to question executive policies. The government of South Africa's policy on HIV/AIDS is perhaps the biggest and most controversial issue in this regard. Many ANC MPs were extremely disappointed in the Mbeki government's approach and indeed have said so within the study group for the portfolio committee on health. Here again, when the ANC leadership is determined to clamp down on or contain "dissent," it is in a position to do so.[22] However, as Mbeki ultimately learned—at the ANC party congress in December 2007 when he was defeated for a third term as party president, and again in September 2008 when the Working Committee asked him to resign as South Africa's president—the willingness of MPs to accept centralized control is not unlimited.

By all accounts the National Assembly is also a marginal player with respect to the budgetary process. While the Finance Committee is highly respected, it does not have an impact on the budget because of the firm commitments the government and the minister of finance, Trevor Manuel, have made to pursue a prudent macroeconomic policy. They have thus also held firm to upholding the Commonwealth tradition of the executive setting the budget. While one sign of an independent legislature is its ability to both set its own budget and reallocate the budget prepared by the Ministry of Finance, such independence is unlikely in South Africa anytime soon. This is in marked contrast to Kenya and Uganda where the legislature has established a parliamentary budget office and expanded its role in the budgetary process, and in Tanzania where the idea of establishing such an office is gaining support among members of the backbench.

A final observation about the autonomy of the National Assembly regards the composition of the assembly itself, especially the ANC's delegation. When discussing the work of the assembly, with the chairs of the most successful committees, all of whom are ANC, it is clear that one of the greatest constraints in raising the capacity and effectiveness of the assembly is the quality of the ruling party's MPs. Not surprisingly, interviews with leading opposition MPs confirmed this assessment. The diversity of the ANC parliamentary caucus has already been discussed, and in this regard the basic dilemma is as follows. While the ANC is a nonracial party, it is also the party of the majority and thus of the African population of South Africa. Its most educated and experienced MPs, however, are either white or members of South Africa's other racial minorities (i.e., Indians and Coloureds). The leadership of the party in the assembly, the group that carries the load, are disproportionately non-African. This situation exists not only because African ANC MPs are generally of lower professional backgrounds, but also because the best African MPs have been creamed off and promoted to positions in the executive—to become ministers or deputy ministers. Others have left for the private sector to take advantage of the many opportunities that were previously nonexistent. What remains in Parliament is decidedly the "second team."

A challenge to both the assembly and to the ANC is therefore to nurture and recruit university-educated and talented Africans to become MPs. This may also mean that some existing members may be given lower rankings on future party lists or dropped altogether. This will be very difficult given the historical loyalties and the contributions of some in this group who sacrificed greatly during the fight against the former apartheid regime. But their departure is inevitable—either by design or by attrition. So long as the National Assembly remains a one-party dominant legislature—and it is not clear that it will—the greatest prospect for raising the capacity of the assembly lies with the evolution of the ANC cadre in the legislature. It is something that the party leadership may or may not want to hasten. Indeed, the present situation gives them greater control. The level of turnover between the First and the Second Parliaments and between the Second and the Third have been high—slightly less than half of all members in both cases. High turnover generally retards the development of legislatures, but in this context the reverse may be true.

Looking forward to subsequent Parliaments five to fifteen years in the future, we can also conclude that the capacity and autonomy of the National Assembly is likely to rise, albeit incrementally over time, for two reasons. First, the pool of potential African MPs with high or relatively high educational backgrounds—for the ANC and for the opposition—will surely rise. Indeed, it is already happening. Second, at some point a credible African-led opposition to the ANC will emerge that will reduce the dominance of the ANC or displace it as the ruling party. The emergence of COPE, a largely middle-class party that took votes away from the ANC in the 2009 elections, suggests that the potential for significant changes in the composition and dynamics of Parliament in the near term should not be dismissed. Once parity or near parity is achieved between the parties, it is very likely that the assembly will become a more open and less controlled branch of government—a pattern already apparent in other African countries.

Similarities with the Rest of Africa and Beyond

Returning briefly to the factors discussed in Chapter 1 that have contributed to the development of the legislature elsewhere in Africa, we find that notwithstanding the very different societal and political context within which the assembly functions, none of the explanatory variables relevant for the development of other African legislatures is questioned here. On the contrary, the findings drawn from the South African case are consistent with those drawn from our previous case studies. Put differently, if one holds the unique features of the South African example constant, the factors present in the other countries are present here as well. Conversely, to the extent that the South African case provides a very different value for a key independent variable than those found in other countries, the results are in the expected direction.

We therefore find the following: (1) The absence of the pressures of patron-client politics present in most other African countries coupled with the PR electoral system means that South African MPs are not diverted from performing the collective functions of the legislature by spending excessive amounts of time on constituency service. (2) The provisions of the South African Constitution and Procedures of the National Assembly are not unusually restrictive or permissive with respect to the scope of the legislature when compared to legislatures elsewhere. (3) The high level of resources available to the National Assembly, in the form of the level of MP salaries, and the level of collective resources (staff and infrastructure), contributes to the capacity of the institution. (4) Conversely, the absence of parity between government and opposition in combination with South Africa's form of electoral system contributes to the subordination of the National Assembly to the leadership of the ruling party. (5) Where the National Assembly falls with respect to the presence or absence of a coalition of reformers and/or opportunists seeking to expand the power of the legislature is less clear.

A core group of "reformers" certainly exists, but it consists of two distinctly different groups of MPs that are unlikely to join forces in the near term.

One group, consisting almost totally of proactive ANC MPs, certainly considers its mission to be one of reform, but the meaning of reform is largely limited to translating the "ANC's project" into law and reality. This group is itself divided between the chairs of the most active portfolio committees and the party's rank and file within the National Assembly. It is also divided between the chairs of the most active committees and the presiding officers (i.e., the Speaker and Deputy Speaker and the ANC chief whip) who often seek to limit the autonomy and initiatives of activist chairs. Reformers within the ANC are more inclined than either the rank and file or the leadership to decentralizing power to the portfolio committees within the National Assembly and to enhancing the assembly's oversight of the executive branch. Conversely, the inclinations of the presiding officers are to focus more on the passage of laws than on oversight, and they are less likely to challenge the executive. Indeed, were they to try otherwise, they would probably be removed from their posts.

A second and smaller group of "reformers" are those activists within the opposition who believe that accountable government and the future of South African democracy require a more powerful legislature. Their perspective of the executive, however, is inherently adversarial, because they seek to check its power rather than redirect it. In sum, and consistent with the situation elsewhere (e.g., Kenya), the evolution of the legislature into an institution with the potential for exercising countervailing power will most likely occur when there is a coalition for such that bridges the divide between the ruling and opposition parties. Such a coalition has yet to emerge in South Africa as a cohesive group. The basic elements are there, but when such a force will come together will be a function of the realignment of South Africa's political parties, the outcomes of future elections, and thus the changing composition of Parliament itself.

Notes

This chapter is based mainly on interviews conducted with thirty-six members and staff of the South African National Assembly between April 28 and June 7, 2004. Approximately one dozen knowledgeable observers, including several prominent journalists, civil society activists, and academics were also interviewed. A small number of the original sample were reinterviewed in December 2005, again in June 2007, and in November 2008 after Thabo Mbeki was replaced by Kgalema Motlanthe as president of South Africa to capture changes during the Third Parliament elected in April of 2004. This study is limited to a consideration of the National Assembly, the lower house of the Parliament.

1. This is actually a basket of overlapping sectoral issues (e.g., education, health, urban planning, land and agricultural policy, public works and infrastructure, trade and industry, macroeconomic policy, etc.), embracing nearly all aspects of South African life.

2. Nearly 60 percent of South Africa's population is now classified as urban.

3. Ethnicity has at times been the basis for political mobilization, especially in Kwazulu Natal where the Inkatha Freedom Party has made explicit appeals to Zulu culture and solidarity.

4. The Parliamentary Monitoring Group is a project of Idasa. Its purpose is to monitor the activities of Parliament and all key committees by disseminating periodic reports to subscribers seeking to track the progress of pending legislation. See www.pmg.org.za.

5. All other parties won 2 percent or less. The DA saw its own ranks reduced to 47 MPs by floor crossing, while the IFP was reduced to 23.

6. "Redeployment" can also mean a promotion out of the National Assembly to a cabinet position or to another high position in government, for example, an ambassadorship.

7. Mbeki was defeated in a bid for a third term as ANC president in December 2007 by Jacob Zuma, after which he became a lame-duck president of the country as a whole. The ANC eventually forced Mbeki's resignation after he sought to renew the prosecution of Zuma on alleged charges of corruption. The conflict between the two men ultimately split the party.

8. Indeed, Mbeki made this very distinction by firing Zuma from his post as South Africa's deputy president in July 2005 along with thirty ANC MPs who supported Zuma's retention. Zuma, who was the leader of government business in the National Assembly, continued in his position of deputy president of the ANC.

9. The Parliamentary Caucus meets every Thursday and consists of all ANC members of both the National Assembly (the lower house) and the National Council of Provinces. Over 300 members are usually present at the caucus. While the caucus is nominally chaired by an ordinary MP, it takes its marching orders from the Political Committee, a liaison body appointed by the National Working Committee and chaired by the ANC's deputy president.

10. In the run-up to its assumption of power in 1994, the ANC published its Reconstruction and Development Program (RDP) policy, which was intended as the blueprint for realizing the goals of the Freedom Charter within the context of the 1990s. However, the macroeconomic realities facing South Africa meant that RDP was soon replaced by the Growth, Employment, and Redistribution (GEAR) program, a less ambitious program of poverty reduction consistent with the Washington consensus. Not surprisingly, there is much debate within the ANC as to whether GEAR is in fact consistent with the historic goals of the ANC.

11. One such lapse was the decision by the ruling party to assume the chairship of the Standing Committee on Public Accounts (SCOPA).

12. In the words of one long-time ANC member and MP, "While I have no doubt that the Speaker is committed to democracy, the problem is that she has difficulty getting round to practicing it."

13. While the most onerous apartheid laws, such as the Race Classification Act, the Group Areas Act, and the Suppression of Communism Act, were all repealed in 1991, much of the technical legislation that buttressed the apartheid state remained. This was especially true in respect to legislation pertaining to labor and social welfare legislation, and to the structure and operations of local government. The justice system also had to be completely overhauled.

14. This estimate was provided by the senior unit staff member for managing legislation and procedures at the National Assembly.

15. Roughly a half-dozen private member's bills are introduced each year. Half are introduced by the opposition parties, particularly the DA, while the remainder are introduced by ANC MPs. Of the latter, most are introduced on behalf of the ANC caucus for a particular parliamentary committee as a mechanism for expediting the introduction of legislation that would otherwise be introduced by the relevant minister. Such bills are introduced with the knowledge and support of the ANC's National Working Committee, the Political Committee, and the ANC Parliamentary Caucus.

16. For a thorough discussion of the challenges in measuring legislative output, albeit in the US context, see (Clinton and Lapinski 2006).

17. A significant number of MPs with high or relatively high education and experience left Parliament. A large proportion of those who left were in fact promoted to senior governmental positions. Others left because they decided to seek more remunerative or interesting employment in the private sector. A few others were also dropped from the ANC list. Whatever the reason, the quality of the present ANC membership is regarded by many observers as less than it was during the First Parliament.

18. Privately, several of the African ANC MPs interviewed for this chapter noted that this is a problem. All, however, were also quick to acknowledge that those who held the chairships of key committees certainly deserved their posts, especially those who had "been through the struggle." Moreover, in some instances, the tensions noted were more the result of generational differences rather than differences of race—younger MPs felt that they should be given more opportunities for leadership.

19. Mbeki himself appeared before the National Assembly for questions only quarterly, whereas Mandela did so monthly.

20. The visitor center engages in an array of "outreach" activities, including several targeted to schoolchildren by providing them with opportunities to visit and observe the assembly when it is in session.

21. The Arms Deal was the biggest scandal involving allegations of corruption since the ANC took power in 1994. The allegations focused on the minister of defense, who supposedly received kickbacks for contracts to a German supplier of Corvettes to the South African Navy and a British aerospace firm for aircraft. At the recommendation of the auditor general, SCOPA aggressively pursued the matter, only to be shut down by the ANC Working Group with the assistance of the Speaker and the ANC chief whip. The leading ANC member of the committee was forced to drop off the committee and eventually left the National Assembly. The case is regarded as a major failure on the part of the ANC to respect the work of the assembly (February 2005).

22. Suppression of dissent or of the grassroots has its limits. At the National General Conference of the ANC held in June 2005, President Mbeki was booed for his sacking of Deputy President Jacob Zuma following formal allegations of corruption against Zuma. Similarly, in the Free State and the Western Cape, the provincial party organizations of the ANC voiced their displeasure with Mbeki's practice of appointing provincial premiers by electing different individuals to serve as provincial party chairpersons—a clear slap at the center.

8

Conclusion

Joel D. Barkan

We began this inquiry with two observations: First, that an established legislature is a defining attribute of *all* democracies. Second, that the legislature is beginning "to matter" in some of Africa's emerging democracies, but not all. It is beginning to matter institutionally, because for the first time some African legislatures have the capacity to perform the four core functions that distinguish this political institution from all others. It is beginning to matter politically, because by performing their core functions better than in the past, African legislatures are becoming more autonomous and more powerful "players" in the political process. They have "clout," and where they have clout, these legislatures contribute to the consolidation of democracy by raising the level of accountability by those who govern to those they rule.

To emerge as significant institutions, however, the members of these bodies must break a web of constraints that have historically crippled the legislature and blocked its development across Africa. As discussed in Chapter 1, these include the demographic features common to most African countries, the constitutional limits placed on African legislatures since independence (which were largely a legacy from the colonial period), and the structure of incentives facing individual MPs that resulted from the period of neopatrimonial rule. Taken together these constraints forced MPs to emphasize constituency service at the expense of the core functions of the legislature performed on a collective basis—representation, legislating in the broad sense (i.e., policymaking), and oversight of the executive branch.

Our generic argument or "story" is that legislative development occurs when a viable group of legislators that we call "a coalition for change" emerges to break out of these constraints to reshape the structure of incentives and the formal rules. Yet when compared as a group, the six legislatures considered in this volume vary greatly both in the extent to which such coalitions have emerged and the level of institutional development they have consequently achieved. This raises the questions of how and under what conditions these coalitions arise and what explains their varying success. We conclude with some provisional answers to these questions.

Explaining Legislative Development

A combination of two or more of the following six variables explain whether a viable coalition for change emerges in a particular legislature, and how successful it is in breaking the constraints that inhibit the development of that legislature. Not all of these variables are present in all six cases, but the direction of their impact, with the possible exception of political parties, is clear.

The Presence of "Reformers"

The presence or absence of a coalition for change in any given legislature depends first on the presence of a core group of committed "reformers." Reformers are MPs who understand the changes required if their legislature is to perform its defining functions, and who are willing to lead their fellow members to make those changes. The experiences of Kenya, Uganda, South Africa, and more recently Nigeria suggest that the number of reformers need not be large to be successful provided they can elicit the support of a larger group of MPs we identify as "opportunists"—members of the legislature who will not lead the process of breaking constraints, but who realize that it is in their personal interest to join those that do. Together "reformers" and "opportunists" can periodically muster majorities within parliament to change the formal rules, and most important, improve the terms of service for members. They can also make important changes in the organizational structure of the legislature, such as the establishment of a system of portfolio committees, a separate parliamentary service, or an office of budget analysis. They can improve the quality of support provided to members and committees by improving the recruitment, training, and organization of parliamentary staff.

Although the number of reformers need not be large to be effective—as few as 10 percent, and sometimes less, of all MPs—the group faces a continuing dilemma: Because most MPs across Africa are reelected on the basis of their records of constituency service, those who devote substantial time to reforming the legislature are often defeated at the next election. Over time, the ranks of reformers dwindle and must be renewed. This is particularly true in Africa where the turnover of membership is already high—often 50 to 60 percent of all members, and sometimes more (e.g., Kenya in 2007) lose their seats.

Given this dilemma and other challenges, reformers are distinguished from their fellow MPs more by their attitudes and political orientation than by their backgrounds; that is to say, by what is in their heads. Reformers are invariably highly educated compared to the population of their country, but so too are the majority of opportunists and those opposed to reform. Reformers appear to be somewhat younger than the average age for all MPs. However, it is not their chronological age that sets them apart, but whether they consider themselves to be members of a "new political generation" that wants to change the way politics takes place in their country, especially within the legislature.

Reformers are more committed to democratization and the achievement of democracy than other MPs. They view the development of the legislature as a key element of this process. Reformers are also more outward looking in terms of where they take their normative cues. In marked contrast to their peers who are less involved in efforts to develop the legislature, reformers are Internet savvy. They are very much aware of political and economic practices beyond the borders of their own society, beyond Africa, and around the world. Put differently, reformers are more likely to subscribe to global norms and see themselves and the institutions to which they belong operating on these standards. Rather than resist the changes that come with globalization, they embrace them.

Given this outlook, it is not surprising that the legislatures with the greatest number of reformers are in countries with the largest urban populations, and in countries most engaged in the global economy—Kenya, Nigeria, South Africa. While the legislatures in Ghana and Uganda have incubated their own champions of reform, the numbers have been much smaller relative to the overall size of the legislature and the population at large. The MPs in these countries have also been more vulnerable to the blandishments of patronage proffered by presidents seeking to maintain the status quo than their counterparts in the other countries. Perhaps because its legislature is among the smallest in Africa with only eighty-three members and located in a small country, the National Assembly of Benin has yet to give rise to a group of deputies committed to the development of their institution.

Civil Society

A major driver for democratic reform both within and outside the legislature is the presence of a large and talent-laden civil society, especially one whose networks stretch beyond the capital city into the countryside. Just as civil society was a prime mover in the early protests that demanded democratization across Africa in the early 1990s (Bratton and van de Walle 1997), so too has civil society been an important impetus for the development of the legislature. In the years following the first, and especially the second and third, rounds of multiparty elections since the end of one-party or military rule, civil society organizations began to engage the legislature at two levels. At the institutional level, selected civil society organizations in some (but not all) African countries sought to improve the performance of the legislature as part of their programs to advance democratization in those countries. Kenya, South Africa, and to a lesser extent Uganda are examples of this pattern. At the interest-group level, other civil society organizations including business and professional organizations approached the legislature to obtain support for their own agendas. Such approaches were at first highly tentative, as these organizations had previously sought favors only from the president and agencies of the executive branch. In countries where a system of portfolio committees was established within the legislature, civil society began to target those committees relevant to their interests. South Africa and, more recently, Kenya are examples of such lobbying, though the frequency of such lobbying in the latter remains modest.

It is at the institutional level where civil society organizations have had their greatest impact by assisting legislatures build capacity to perform their core tasks. By holding workshops, retreats, and other forums to inform selected MPs, civil society organizations planted key ideas of what a reformed legislature might look like and how to achieve such reform. The stronger the civil society and the greater its engagement with the legislature for the purpose of building capacity in these bodies, the greater the likelihood that a group of reformers, and ultimately a broader coalition for change, emerges in the legislature. It should also be noted that several bilateral aid agencies and foundations, most notably USAID and the German party foundations, have at times supported these civil society initiatives to strengthen the legislature.

Lingering Neopatrimonialism

When legislatures increase their capacity to perform their core functions and enhance their power, however, they invariably do so at the expense of the executive branch. As discussed in Chapter 1, the period prior to the relegalization of multiparty politics was marked by presidential dominance entrenched through neopatrimonial rule. African presidents bought off members of the opposition and used the disbursement of patronage to undermine the independence of the legislative branch. Over time, the legislature and its members were stripped of resources and forced to become rubber stamps.

With the return of competitive politics and multiparty politics in the early 1990s, the legislature in some countries became an arena of struggle between the executive and those seeking to make the executive more accountable and transparent to the general public. Reformers, civil society, and the bilateral international assistance agencies wanted to build up the capacity of African legislatures so that they could better perform their core functions, especially legislating in the broad sense and oversight of the executive branch. The performance of these functions would translate into greater transparency and accountability, both horizontal and vertical, by the executive to the public, a critical ingredient of democracy between elections.

The prospect of enhanced legislative power, however, has meant the reduction of executive power. Not surprisingly, most African presidents, including those installed after the return of competitive politics, such as Mbeki in South Africa, Kufuor in Ghana, and Obasanjo in Nigeria, viewed this prospect as a zero-sum game. So too did holdovers from the era of authoritarian rule, for example, Rawlings in Ghana, Moi in Kenya, and Kérékou in Benin. The process of legislative development thus became one of contested terrain, with reformers seeking to accelerate the process and most African presidents trying to block it. Where coalitions for change have emerged, the history of legislative development in Africa over the past decade has been largely a struggle between such coalitions pressing their agendas versus executives pushing back to maintain the status quo. Executive resistance has usually taken the form of reverting to the old playbook that worked well during the era of authoritarian rule—the appointment of large numbers of MPs to positions in an expanded cabinet and cash buyouts. While this has worked in some cases, for example, Ghana and Uganda, it no longer does in others such as Kenya and Nigeria where coalitions for change have raised MP salaries to such a high level that members cannot be bought as easily as in the past.

The Chief Presiding Officer and Chief Administrative Officer

Because the development of the legislature and the expansion of its power comes at the expense of the executive, presidents in several countries have historically sought agents within the legislature to stall reform. The chief presiding officer and the chief administrative officer, that is, the Speaker and the Clerk in Anglophone countries and the President of the legislature in Francophone Africa, have often been targeted for this role. This was especially true during the era of authoritarian rule, but has carried over to the competitive era. Ghana, Kenya, and South Africa are all examples where presidents have leaned heavily on the Speaker to contain reformers, though the specific reasons for doing so vary from case to case. In Ghana, President Kufuor wanted to limit the level of financial resources available to Parliament. In Kenya, former president Daniel arap Moi wanted to maintain his control over the National Assembly after failing to win a majority of the vote in the first multiparty election. In South Africa, Thabo Mbeki wanted to end an investigation by the Standing Committee on Public Accounts into alleged corruption over a controversial arms deal.

The presiding officer might himself resist the demands of reformers when his own power is threatened, as recently occurred during the struggle over the revision of the Standing Orders in Kenya. However, the Kenya case also suggests that presiding officers who resist coalitions of change must sometimes accommodate their demands if they want to keep their jobs. Even then, they may be swept aside when the opportunity presents itself—for example, when the new

Speaker is elected at the beginning of a new legislative term, as in South Africa in 2004, Tanzania in 2005, and Kenya in 2008.

The approach taken by the former Speaker in Ghana and the election of new Speakers in Nigeria in 2007 and Kenya in 2008 also illustrate how the chief presiding officer can be a force for reform. The Speaker of the Ghanaian Parliament insisted on the financial autonomy of his institution, though this eventually led to his replacement in 2004. The Speaker in the Nigerian National Assembly took steps to reform a dysfunctional committee system by reducing the number of committees from seventy-two in the House of Representatives and fifty-four in the Senate to thirty each. The Speaker in Kenya facilitated the passage of a much-needed revision of the Standing Orders that had been stalled by his predecessor.

Whether utilized to promote or retard the development of the legislature, the position of the chief presiding officer is a pivotal role. The administrator responsible for the day-to-day deployment of parliamentary staff also plays a pivotal role that facilitates or retards the development of the institution. While the Speaker and MPs determine whether or not the capacity of the legislature will be enhanced, it is the Clerk who implements such decisions on a day-to-day basis through the recruitment and assignment of key legislative staff. The assignment of staff to legislative committees would be one example.

Political Parties

One of the most interesting and controversial findings emerging from this study is the varying impact of political parties on legislative development. As Nelson Kasfir and Stephen Twebaze note in their chapter on Uganda, the conventional wisdom derived from the literature on legislative development in the West is that the presence of strong legislative parties is necessary for the process. However, with few exceptions, political parties across Africa are weak, because they are loose coalitions of ethnoregional constituencies that can rarely be distinguished from each other on policy grounds.

Considered in this context, two arguments are made. First, that legislatures are weak because political parties within these legislatures are weak. This explains why African MPs have historically spent minimal time legislating or on oversight compared to constituency service. Because few programmatic differences exist between parties and party discipline is weak, why bother? The policy outcomes will be the same. Moreover, if an MP votes against his or her party's leadership, there are few sanctions for doing so. It is only when there are real issues at stake between legislative parties that the legislature matters.

The counterargument advanced by Kasfir and Twebaze and considered less directly in the other chapters is that weak parties, or more important, no parties, are best for legislative development. They demonstrate that the greatest advances in the development of Uganda's Parliament occurred during the period between 1996 and 2006 when the country operated under the Movement system of government, especially during the Seventh Parliament. Political parties were permitted to exist during this period, but parliamentary elections were conducted on the basis of candidates' "individual merit," thus blurring the lines between government and opposition within the legislature. "Reformers" in Parliament were thus able to establish a coalition for change consisting of backbenchers that raised MPs' salaries and strengthened the committee system. The coalition also greatly enlarged Parliament's role in the budgetary process. However, once reformers within the legislature became vociferous advocates of multiparty politics, the lines between government and opposition became sharply drawn, at which point President Museveni moved to crush those who had been the leaders of the coalition to strengthen Parliament. In this case, stronger parties meant the end of the effort to build capacity within the legislature, albeit Parliament retained some of its previously won gains.

The experiences of the other five countries considered in this volume yield a more ambiguous picture. On the one hand, the weakness of political parties and the absence of programmatic distinctions certainly facilitated the formation of the coalition for change in the Kenya National Assembly where a coalition of opposition MPs and backbenchers from the ruling party came together to pass needed reforms. The weakness of parties, especially the ruling PDP in Nigeria, has resulted in similar reforms.

Conversely, the experience of the one African country with a "strong" party system, South Africa, suggests that strong parties do not enhance the ability of MPs to perform their core functions, but if anything weaken the legislature. One must be careful, however, in drawing conclusions from the South African case. Has the South African National Assembly in fact been weakened by the presence of well-defined political parties, or is this situation the result of other factors? The overwhelming parliamentary majority enjoyed by the ANC in combination with an unusual degree of party discipline resulting from the party's internal culture and the use of party-list proportional representation to elect the National Assembly may be the real factors weakening the legislature. Finally, the experience of Benin and Ghana suggest that weak parties do not guarantee that a coalition for change will emerge in the legislature that enhances its capacity to perform the core functions of the legislature. The question of how parties impact the development of African legislatures requires further investigation.

The Electoral System

The choice of electoral system, the procedure for translating votes into seats, impacts the legislative process in two ways—the number of parties represented in the legislature and the relationship between the executive and the legislative branch. Given that the voting patterns for parties in most African countries exhibit a high geographic concentration of the vote, the choice of electoral system does not determine the number of parties represented in the legislature to the extent that it does in countries where the geographic pattern of party voting is more dispersed (Barkan, Densham, and Rushton 2006). In the context of agrarian and plural societies, the number of parties are more likely to be determined by these factors than by electoral system design.

Whether or not members are elected from small single-member or multi-member districts or by party-list PR does have an impact on how MPs spend their time. The choice of electoral system also affects the relationship between the executive and the legislature. A comparison of the South African case with the other five cases considered in this volume indicates that MPs who are elected by PR, as in South Africa and Namibia, devote considerably more time to legislating than to constituency service. Conversely, MPs elected from geographic districts, as in the other five cases, spend more time on constituency service than MPs elected by PR. This comparison suggests that the use of PR may have a more positive impact on the internal operations of the legislature than election from single-member districts. Yet PR also forces a high level of party discipline on its members that inhibits cross-party alliances for reform. For example, where a ruling party elected by PR has an overwhelming majority in the legislature as the ANC does in South Africa, the combination weakens the legislature vis-à-vis the executive branch. This is particularly true with respect to the ability of MPs to perform their oversight function.

Another aspect of the electoral system is whether it reserves some number of seats for special constituencies such as women, youth, the disabled, or racial minorities. In South Africa, where party-list PR is employed, the major parties use the party list to ensure that talented members of racial minorities and women are elected to the National Assembly. In Uganda, where a system of single-member districts is employed, roughly one-fifth of the national legislature is elected from a series of special-interest constituencies. In both cases, these mechanisms have enhanced the power of the ruling party and consequently the executive at the expense of the legislature, because the MPs elected by these mechanisms owe their seats to their party's leadership.

Changing the Incentive Structure

Having reviewed the variables that give rise to or inhibit "coalitions of change," we turn next to a summary of what these coalitions have achieved to break the constraints that have historically retarded legislative development across Africa.

Formal Rules, Legislative Powers, and Internal Rules

As discussed in Chapter 1 and in the case studies that followed, the constitutions inherited by African states at independence and especially at the beginning of the 1990s favored the executive at the expense of the legislature. These legislatures were limited in terms of the type of legislation they could write and played almost no role in the budgetary process. Their internal rules of procedure also limited the ability of these legislatures to perform their core functions. Most power within the legislature was concentrated in the hands of the presiding officer, whose job it was to maintain the status quo rather than to raise the capacity of the institution. The committee structure was rudimentary and did not provide for a system of portfolio committees to shadow the ministries and departments of the executive branch. Legislative staff were part of the public service and thus part of the executive.

The experience of Kenya, and to a lesser extent Uganda, demonstrates that these rules can be rewritten—by amending the constitution and/or the internal rules of procedure, and through ordinary legislation. In Kenya, MPs amended the constitution to permit the establishment of the Parliamentary Service. They also revised the Standing Orders in 1998 and again in 2008 to first establish and then expand the system of portfolio committees. In Uganda, the passage of the Budget Act of 2001 provided MPs with a significantly larger role in the budgetary process. Although African politics, including legislative politics, is permeated by informal relationships and clientelist ties, formal rules still matter *and* can be changed by members of the legislature.

Last, but not least, it should be remembered that the legislatures in all six countries enacted constitutional amendments in the 1990s limiting the presidents of their countries to two elected terms.[1] The importance of term limits as a mechanism for containing the executive power vis-à-vis the legislature in Africa cannot be overstated. The inclination by African presidents to entrench themselves in power through neopatrimonial means emasculated legislatures prior to the return of multiparty politics. Most African presidents continue to resort to patronage when challenged by the legislature. The examples of Moi in Kenya and more recently Kufuor in Ghana, Museveni in Uganda, and Obasanjo in Nigeria are cases in point. But term limits literally wipe such leaders from the scene before they can accumulate sufficient resources to buy off all who oppose them. Only in Uganda has the legislature amended the constitution to repeal term limits, a country where the incumbent president had already been in office for eighteen years and accumulated the means to continue through patrimonial means. The "ebb" of the Uganda legislature since 2004 and the election of the Eighth Parliament in 2006 coincide with this change.

MP Emoluments

The importance of providing appropriate salaries and other emoluments to MPs so that members can be less vulnerable to the blandishments of presidential patronage while meeting their obligations for constituency service was discussed at length in Chapter 1. Because constituency service is essential for their political survival, most legislators will not devote sufficient time to legislating and oversight until they are provided with the means to address their primary need.

MPs' success in addressing this fact of political life varies greatly across the six legislatures. Since the late 1990s, the legislatures in Kenya and Nigeria have raised members' total compensation package by very large amounts, especially allowances, while compensation in South Africa was already high. Compensation in Ghana and Uganda has also risen in recent years, but remains low as is compensation in Benin as indicated in Table 8.1.

While the level of members' compensation cannot "explain" legislative performance by itself, these figures are highly suggestive. Where members are more highly paid, members are arguably performing all four core functions of their institution better than in the past, with the result that the legislature has emerged as a political force. Conversely, where the level of compensation remains low, as in Benin and Ghana, the legislature remains a weak institution. Put simply, there is a clear, albeit rough correlation between legislators' pay and legislative performance as observed previously in non-African legislatures (Squire 1992). Indeed, the relationship between members' pay and institutional performance may be applicable to all legislatures.

Notwithstanding this finding, the huge disparity in compensation—between Benin and Ghana on the one side and Kenya and Nigeria on the other—raises two obvious questions: How much compensation is enough? How much is excess—indeed, greed? It is beyond the scope of this analysis to do more than raise these questions for two reasons. First, any answer is highly subjective and in the eye of the beholder. MPs in both Kenya and Nigeria have argued vociferously that they need such levels of compensation to do their jobs, while citizens and especially the press voice concern, indeed outrage, that their recent raises have gone too far. In anticipation, perhaps, of this reaction, it is noteworthy that in determining their own compensation, MPs in both Kenya

Table 8.1 Annual Compensation for Members of Parliament, 2008 (in US dollars)

	Benin	Ghana	Kenya	Nigeria	South Africa	Uganda
Base salary	18,000	n.a.	36,900	16,000	56,400	9,600
Other allowances	n.a.	n.a.	120,100	208,000	9,680[a]	30,360
Total	n.a.	33,120	157,000	224,000	66,080	39,960

Notes: a. South African MPs receive a significant allowance of 5,000 rands per month for travel to their designated "constituency." However, this sum (equal to roughly US$9,680 annually when the exchange rate was US$1 = R6.2) is paid to the MP's party rather than directly to the member.

n.a. = not available.

and Nigeria ascribed relatively modest proportions of their total emoluments to salary—23 percent in Kenya, only 7 percent in Nigeria. Most of the money is in the form of allowances, which are justified on the grounds that they enable MPs to perform their jobs. It is a distinction largely lost on the public, and it suggests a troubling cynicism by members.

Second, until appropriate measures of legislative performance are constructed and the relevant data for these indices collected, it is impossible to do more than estimate the levels of legislative performance in the six countries or others. For the same reason, it is also impossible to measure the causal relationship between pay and performance with precision.

Institutional Resources

The impact of providing more resources to legislatures at an institutional level is also both logical and clear. The legislatures in Kenya, Nigeria, South Africa, and Uganda provide office space for all MPs and appropriate meeting space for parliamentary committees. The legislatures in Benin and Ghana do not. Indeed barely a quarter of members in Benin and less than that in Ghana have offices at the National Assembly.

The lack of space is particularly serious in Ghana where parliamentary committees must meet in the public foyer of the legislature. The complement of parliamentary staff available to MPs is also much greater in Kenya and South Africa, especially the latter, than it is in the other four legislatures. The quality of staff in terms of professional expertise is arguably the highest in South Africa, where all MPs are provided with secretarial assistance, and parliamentary committees are supported by parliamentary staff. The South African National Assembly also has a research office to help members understand legislation. A similar office is in the process of being established in Kenya.

The National Assemblies in Kenya and South Africa are also the most advanced with respect to information technology. All MPs in both countries are provided with computers plus access to the Internet. While not all MPs actually utilize these services—probably no more than half— it is an important resource for those who do, because it increases the proportion of members who become aware of global practice on a wide range of issues. Notwithstanding the importance of these institutional resources, we are again unable to assess their impact on legislative performance with precision in the absence of better measures of legislative performance.

Legislative Performance Observed

The comparative case study method used in this volume has yielded a series of unique and rich descriptions about the nature of legislative practice in six

African countries. After comparing these narratives, we are able for the first time to reach several conclusions about what drives the process of legislative development, and what steps need to be taken to ensure that this development occurs. We are also able to observe and describe *at a narrative level* the approximate levels of performance of each of these legislatures and provide a general assessment of which are performing better than others with respect to their core functions.

As noted at the beginning of this volume, and because this study is of an exploratory nature, the authors of the six case studies embarked on their inquiries on an "open-ended" basis. They were not instructed to march in lockstep with each other but rather to ascertain "what is going on" (and not going on) in the institution to which they were assigned. As these studies represent a first cut at the comparative analysis of African legislatures, no other instructions made sense. Indeed, seeking methodological rigor before basic understanding risked missing the proverbial forest for the trees. The limitations of this approach, however, must be acknowledged: Namely, that we are unable to measure with precision the relationships between our key dependent and independent variables. We can only suggest the nature and direction of these relationships, and emphasize the importance of our findings.

The narratives presented in the preceding chapters provide much information about how well MPs perform three of the four core functions of the legislature and the challenges they face. Ordinal estimates of the level of performance for each country are provided in Table 8.2.

In respect to *legislating in the broad sense,* that is to say, contributing to the crafting of legislation and the making of public policy, the country narratives suggest that all six legislatures are performing much better than during

Table 8.2 Comparative Performance of the Four Core Functions of the Legislature

	Benin	Ghana	Kenya	Nigeria	South Africa	Uganda
Legislating in the broad sense	Low	Low	Moderate	Moderate	High	Moderate
Oversight of the executive	Low	Low	Moderate and rising	High	Was high, now moderate	Was moderate, now falling
Representation	n.a.	n.a.	n.a.	n.a.	n.a.	n.a.
Constituency service	High	High	High	High	Low	High
Fish and Kroenig PPI[a]	.56	.47	.31	.47	.63	.44

Notes: a. PPI is the Parliamentary Powers Index (Fish and Kroenig 2009). Source of data is a communication from Steven Fish.

n.a. = not available.

the era of authoritarian rule, but that some are doing much better than others. In terms of the volume and importance of legislation passed, our assessment is that the legislatures in Kenya and South Africa are the best performers, followed by Uganda where the capacity of Parliament has slipped somewhat in recent years. In Nigeria, the performance of the legislature in terms of the number of bills passed has risen greatly. The proportion of bills passed, however, remains low, though this pattern is often present in established legislatures. Notwithstanding some successes, the legislatures in Benin and Ghana appear to be low performers when compared to the other four. They do not pass large volumes of legislation and their ability to deliberate such legislation is severely limited because their respective systems of parliamentary committees, especially their departmental or portfolio committees, are weak and underresourced. The failure by the National Assembly in Benin to pass the annual budget on several occasions is an example of its limitations.

A similar assessment can be made about which legislatures perform better than others with respect to *oversight of the executive*. The picture here is more volatile and consequently more ambiguous. Neither the Benin nor the Ghanaian legislature appears to have been very active with respect to oversight in comparison to the other four, and the records of the latter have changed in recent years. Until the Eighth Parliament (1998–2002), the oversight record of the Kenya National Assembly was also poor due largely to the fact that the reports by the country's auditor general were several years in arrears. However, in recent years, the Public Accounts Committee has become more active, indeed at times aggressive, in investigating cases of suspected malfeasance in the executive branch. The same pattern is present in the Nigerian legislature, though its aggressive performance at oversight is more recent and no doubt politically motivated, that is, MPs view oversight as a mechanism to bring down political opponents.

By contrast, the oversight records of both the South African and Uganda legislatures have declined in recent years from levels that were among the highest. In the case of South Africa, the ruling party, which holds a majority on the Public Accounts Committee, has discouraged aggressive oversight since the committee embarrassed the government in its probe of the Arms Deal in 2001. A similar pattern has unfolded in Uganda. During the Sixth and Seventh Parliaments, the Public Accounts Committee was quite active, including a probe of corruption by senior army officers in partnership with President Museveni's brother in the Congo that forced the president to establish a commission of inquiry on the matter. Parliament also censored and forced the resignation of two cabinet ministers after probing other irregularities. However, since the election of the Eighth Parliament in 2006, the legislature has become more quiescent as Museveni has strived to limit its independence.

Unfortunately, the narratives do not provide us with sufficient information to assess how well each of the six legislatures perform the function of *representation*. To the extent that African legislators are elected from single-member or small multimember districts, and most are, they cannot be indifferent to the demands of their constituents. Plenary sessions of the legislature in all countries except South Africa are often punctuated by MPs illustrating general arguments with examples from the constituencies they represent. How well they actually articulate these concerns and lobby effectively on their constituents' behalf, however, cannot be determined without closely scrutinizing their day-to-day activities in the legislature, including committee sessions, as well as their activities in relevant government departments of the executive branch. As this was beyond the scope and resources of this study, we cannot make a determination of the performance of this function.

Finally, upon asking MPs about their activities to provide *constituency service* and the expectations they face, the case studies confirm that for many (with the notable exception of members of the South African National Assembly, who are elected by PR) this function remains very important in terms of the time and resources they devote to the task. The level of performance by the members of five of the six legislatures considered is roughly the same—they all strive to be active in this area, especially through regular visits to their constituencies on weekends. But as stressed at the outset of this study, constituency service is a function performed individually, not collectively. Its performance, even if excellent, does not enhance the capacity and power of the legislature *as an institution*. Indeed, it probably detracts.

Measuring Legislative Performance

If this study, and the subfield of comparative legislative research, has one serious limitation, it is the paucity of appropriate measures of legislative performance and development. As discussed in the previous section, our case studies provide rich narratives of what is occurring in a sample of African legislatures that permit rough comparisons within the group. We are able to suggest which legislatures are performing better than others, and we are able to offer plausible explanations why this is so. But we cannot reach more definitive conclusions because we lack direct quantitative measures of legislative performance—our dependent variable and our independent variable.

Legislative performance, when defined in terms of the four core functions of the legislature, constitutes our dependent variable because it is the phenomenon to be both explained and improved. For the same reason, measures of legislative performance are indicators of legislative development—how far a given legislature has moved toward playing its unique role in the political system.

Legislative performance is also our independent variable with respect to the broader goal of democracy and democratization. If all established democracies have legislatures that perform their core functions well, then presumably there will be a high level of correlation between how a country scores on various measures of legislative performance over time and how it scores on summary measures of democratization such as the Freedom House scales. Put simply, the higher a country's score on one or more appropriate indexes of legislative performance, the higher it is likely to score on measures of democratization that do not include reference to the legislature. Without suitable measures of legislative performance, however, these relationships cannot be explored.

How might we address this problem, and what does this study suggest? First, measuring legislative performance and development is a highly complex exercise, which may explain why so few measures exist. One noteworthy attempt has been the pioneering work of Steven Fish and Mathew Kroenig (Fish 2006; Fish and Kroenig 2009). They have constructed a summary measure of the formal powers of legislatures that they call the Parliamentary Powers Index, or PPI. The PPI is constructed by first determining how many specific powers a legislature has from a list of thirty-two, and then computing the percentage of affirmative answers. Scores thus range from .00 to 1.00. The higher the score, the more powerful and autonomous the legislature. PPI scores for each of the six legislatures in this study are provided across the bottom of Table 8.2.

Although the PPI provides an excellent assessment of the formal rules shaping the legislative process, it contains few direct measures of legislative performance. For example, the PPI includes an assessment of whether the "legislature is regularly in session" but no assessment of the committee system—whether there is one, its size and structure, or its performance. Yet a viable committee system is essential for high legislative performance with respect to the functions of representation, legislating in the broad sense, and oversight. Indeed, our assessments of how well the six legislatures perform the legislating function and the oversight function are based in large part on a reading of the narratives of committee performance with respect to these tasks.

Some items included in the PPI may also be misleading—for example, whether "the country lacks a presidency entirely or there is a presidency, but the president is elected by the legislature." On this question, South Africa thus receives a higher score than the other five cases in our sample. However, on closer inspection, this "power" masks the reverse reality that in the context of South Africa's PR electoral system, it is the leader of the ruling party who has a much larger say in determining the party's list prior to an election and thus the composition of the legislature, than it is the legislature determining who becomes president. Other items, such as whether the legislature "controls the resources that finance its own internal operation and provide for the perquisites of its own members," provide important data.

The result is that while South Africa's score of moderately high on the PPI is consistent with our narrative and summary assessment of the South Africa National Assembly's performance of the four core functions, the scores for Kenya and Benin are not. Although we argue in Chapter 2 that the Kenya National Assembly is one of the best performers on the continent and the best performer of the six, it scores quite low on the PPI. Conversely, Benin, which is a weak performer, scores moderately high. These somewhat puzzling results demonstrate how hard it is to develop valid measures of legislative performance. Fish and Kroenig have broken new ground, but there is much work to be done.

In addition to assessing the formal powers, future efforts at measuring legislative performance need to assess actual behavior—of individual members and of constituent units and groups within the legislature such as committees and parliamentary staff. It is also desirable to construct specific measures for each of the four core functions legislatures perform, because, as noted throughout this study, these different functions exist in tension with each other. Legislatures and individual members that score high on one may not, indeed probably will not, score high on all four.

Developing such measures, however, requires the systematic collection of data that is not yet available on most legislatures.[2] Moreover, collecting such data will be difficult, time-consuming, and expensive. The challenge, however, goes beyond that of data collection alone. It is also a challenge of being able to accurately measure and meaningfully interpret the data that is obtained. For example, one seemingly simple measure of legislative performance is to count and assess the number of bills introduced and passed. Yet anyone who has contemplated or tried to conduct such an exercise knows that it quickly bogs down in a thicket of issues such as assessing and weighting the relative importance of bills, assessing the impact of bills passed, and so on. It is a potential quagmire from which there is no easy solution, as students of the US Congress, who have relatively easy access to data, appreciate well (Mayhew 1991; Clinton and Lapinski 2006).

Notwithstanding these challenges, the author in collaboration with two other scholars[3] has already embarked on a follow-on study that will assess and compare legislative performance in Africa more systematically than the present effort, but which utilizes the findings from this effort as its point of departure. Known as the African Legislatures Project (ALP), it seeks to overcome the limitations of this study in at least four ways. First, it addresses the limitation of more explanatory variables than cases by enlarging the sample of legislatures from six to eighteen. Second, having completed the exploratory examination of legislative development and performance reported in this volume, it pursues a more structured inquiry to yield more data for a common and comprehensive set of variables from all cases included in the study. Third, it addresses the need to develop better measures of both legislative performance and likely determinants of that performance, for example, the strength of the committee system and the configuration of political parties. Fourth, because ALP is being conducted in the same countries as the Afrobarometer surveys, it also measures public attitudes toward the legislature, an exercise that will enable comparisons between public perceptions and actual performance. Because ALP is an ambitious undertaking that will require data collection in eighteen countries, it is not expected to result in publishable findings until 2010. Early working papers are intended to be available from the project's website (www.africanlegislatures.org). Until then, the present volume will have to fill the void in the literature on African legislatures.

Implications for Democratization in Africa and the Policy Community

We close with a final commentary on what the present study suggests for the larger process of democratization in Africa, and for the policy community concerned with that endeavor. What lessons have we learned? Upon reflecting on our principal findings, at least six stand out.

First, institutional development, especially the development of institutions of countervailing power, which is what legislatures are, takes time—at least a decade and usually more—to carry out. Some of the legislatures considered in this volume have made progress during this time frame. Others have not. None has made significant progress in terms of raising its performance of the core functions in less time. It is also a complex and tortuous process that is interrupted by the high turnover of MPs at election time, with the result that the process must, to some extent, start over at the beginning of each legislative term. The development of the legislature also takes place in an adversarial environment that varies in the degree of hostility toward the process. Executive authority, particularly presidential authority, is rarely eager to see an expansion of the legislative branch and will usually seek, overtly or gently, to frustrate the process. The resort to neopatrimonialism is typical of the methods used.

Second, like democratization itself, the development of the legislature is fundamentally an internally driven process. Without the presence of reformers and ultimately a coalition for change *within* the legislature, the development of the institution will not occur. International donor agencies in particular need to keep this reality in mind before seeking to build capacity in these bodies. Without local partners, and without local ownership, any externally funded program to support legislative development in the context of Africa's emerging democracies is unlikely to succeed.

Third, there are a number of variables that have an impact on the development of the legislature that can be altered to accelerate its development, but there are also a number that cannot. For example, legislators, sometimes in partnership with donors and/or civil society, can revise the formal rules, increase salaries for MPs and staff, restructure the committee system, and provide a better physical infrastructure to improve performance by members. It is far more difficult, however, to alter the party or electoral system, or the executive, or especially the structure of civil society. Indeed, it is not wise to try.

Fourth, reformers in legislatures that have arguably achieved the most are those that have gone first for the "quick wins," such as raising the salaries for MPs, and then moved on to more challenging tasks such as changing the rules through the passage of enabling legislation and building new structures such as a system of portfolio committees. Quick wins facilitate the emergence of a larger coalition for change without which complex reforms are less likely to occur. Kenya, Nigeria, and Uganda are all examples of this sequence.

Fifth, as the case of Uganda, and to a lesser extent South Africa, makes clear, legislative development produces fragile gains. Whatever is achieved is vulnerable to being rolled back, especially when presidential authority is challenged directly.

Sixth and last, reformers need to cultivate allies outside the legislature, including civil society and the press, but especially interest groups that can advance their agendas through partnerships with the legislature. While the process of legislative development is internally driven, it must also be a process that is valued by those outside the institution if the institution is to flourish. Until such time as society makes continuous demands on the institution for specific legislation, oversight, and other collective outputs (in contrast to constituency service), its ability to emerge into a full player will be modest at best.

With these considerations in mind, we expect that the process of legislative development over the next ten years will be similar to, but slightly different from, the process during the preceding decade. The issue of raising salaries will probably be resolved in most of the remaining legislatures, where poor pay is still a problem. Members of these legislatures are well aware of what their counterparts earn in neighboring countries and will try hard to achieve a measure of parity. The challenge of building capacity, particularly of the committee systems, will continue to occupy all African legislatures, including those considered in this study, in the near term. Increasing the technical capacity of the legislature to engage the budgetary process effectively will likewise continue for the foreseeable future.

The common finding from our case studies is that legislative performance is highly uneven—across legislatures, but also within them. Even the best performers have much to improve. This is particularly true of the performances by individual MPs. While reformers lead and opportunists follow, many of the latter remain unengaged in the day-to-day work within the institution to which they nominally belong. The incentives have been changed and are more highly attractive in some legislatures than in the past. It is now time for MPs remaining on the sidelines to join the process. How that will occur is the next but unwritten chapter in the story.

Notes

1. In Uganda, the provision was enacted by a Constitutional Assembly in 1995, and not by Parliament, which did not come into being until the following year. However, the assembly was the legislative body at that time.

2. One useful, albeit partial, exception to the paucity of such data is the data on public perceptions of legislative performance collected by the Afrobarometer. However, the focus of this inquiry has been limited mainly to the function of representation and to an evaluation of constituency service in particular.

3. Robert Mattes, director of the Centre for Social Science Research at the University of Cape Town, and Shaheen Mozaffar, professor of political science at Bridgewater State College. The African Legislatures Project is based at the University of Cape Town.

Bibliography

ACBF (African Capacity Building Foundation). 2001. *Accord de don entre l'Assemblée nationale du Bénin et la Fondation pour le renforcement des capacités en Afrique.* Porto Novo and Harare: ACBF and Assemblée Nationale du Bénin.
Adedoja, Tokunbo, and Oke Epia. 2006. "Anti–3rd Term Lawmakers Meet Civil Society Groups." *This Day* (Lagos), April 21.
Adegbamigbe, Ademola. 1999. "Jitters in the House." *The News* (Lagos), August 2.
Afrobarometer. 2009. "Surveys." www.afrobarometer.org/surveys.html.
———. 2007. "Nigeria in 2007: Close Election as Allegiances Shift." Press Release No. 3, April 12. www.afrobarometer.org/NigeriaPR3.pdf.
———. 2006. "Term Limits, the Presidency, and the Electoral System: What Do Nigerians Want?" Afrobarometer Briefing Paper No. 35. www.afrobarometer.org/papers/AfrobriefNo35.pdf.
Ahmed, Syed Intiaz. 2006. "Civilian Supremacy in Democracies with 'Fault Lines': The Role of the Parliamentary Standing Committee on Defence in Bangladesh." *Democratization* 13 (2) (Summer): 283–302.
Akande, Jadesola O. 1982. *The Constitution of the Federal Republic of Nigeria 1979, with Annotations.* London: Sweet and Maxwell.
Alderfer, Philip W. 1997. *Institutional Development in a New Democracy: The Zambian National Assembly, 1994–1996.* Ph.D. diss., Department of Political Science, Michigan State University.
Ameh, John. 2008. "Bankole Sacks 69 Committee Chairmen, Deputies." *Punch* (Lagos), August 1.
Apter, David E. 1955. *The Gold Coast in Transition.* Princeton, NJ: Princeton University Press.
Aryee, Joseph R., ed. 2001. *Deepening Democracy in Ghana: Politics of the 2000 Elections.* Volume. 2. Accra: Freedom Publications.
———. 1998. *The 1996 General Elections and Democratic Consolidation in Ghana.* Legon: University of Ghana.
Assemblée Nationale du Bénin. 2008. Official website. http://assembleebenin.org.
Aziken, Emmanuel. 2002. "Intrigues Behind Obasanjo, Na'abba Rapproachment." *Vanguard* (Lagos), November 17.
Barkan, Joel D. 2008. "Legislatures on the Rise?" *Journal of Democracy* 19 (2) (April): 124–137.

———. 1984. "Legislators, Elections and Political Linkage." In Joel D. Barkan, ed., *Politics and Public Policy in Kenya and Tanzania,* revised ed. New York: Praeger, 71–101.

———. 1979. "Bringing Home the Pork: Legislator Behavior, Rural Development and Political Change in East Africa." In Lloyd Musolf and Joel Smith, eds., *Legislatures in Development.* Durham, NC: Duke University Press, 265–288.

Barkan, Joel D., Paul Densham, and Gerard Rushton. 2006. "Space Matters: Designing Better Electoral Systems for Emerging Democracies." *American Journal of Political Science* 50 (4) (October): 926–939.

Barkan, Joel D., with Ladipo Ademolekun, Yongmei Zhou, Mouftayou Laleye, and Njuguna Ng'ethe. 2004. "Emerging Legislatures: Institutions of Horizontal Accountability." In Sahr Kpundeh and Brian David Levy, eds., *Governance and Public Sector Management in Africa.* Washington, DC: World Bank, 211–256.

Bauer, Gretchen, and Hannah Evelyn Britton, eds. 2006. *Women in African Parliaments.* Boulder: Lynne Rienner.

Bayart, Jean-François. 1993. *The State in Africa: The Politics of the Belly.* London: Longman.

Benin, Republic of. 1998–2006. *Journal officiel de la République du Bénin.* Porto Novo: ONIP.

———. 1999–2004. *Le Conseil Economique et Social, Deuxième mandature.* Cotonou: Imprimerie Tunde. http://assembleebenin.org.

———. 2002a. *Règlement Intérieur. Assemblée Nationale du Bénin.* Porto Novo: Assemblée Nationale du Bénin.

———. 2002b. *Répertoire des lois votées de 1992 a 2002.* Porto Novo: Assemblée nationale du Bénin, Service de documentation et des archives.

———. 2002c. *Cour Suprême, Chambre des Comptes. Rapport sur exécution de la loi de finances pour année 1999.* Cotonou: ONIP.

———. 2001a. *Cour Constitutionnelle. L'élection présidentielle de 2001.* Cotonou: Published with the assistance of USAID.

———. 2001b. *Cour Suprême, Chambre des Comptes. Manuel a l'usage des responsables aux finances des partis politiques.* 2nd ed. Cotonou: Imprimerie Moderne la Solidarité.

———. 2001c. *Rapport général de l'élection présidentielles de mars 2001.* Cotonou: ONIP.

———. 2000a. *Cour Suprême, Chambre des Comptes. Rapport sur l'exécution de la loi de finances pour l'année 1998.* Cotonou: ONIP.

———. 2000b. *La contribution du Parlement au renforcement de la gouvernance au Bénin* (prepared by P. Badet, C. Djrekpo, and N. Kassa). Cotonou: Assemblée Nationale et Programme des Nations Unies pour le Développement (UNDP), mimeo.

———. 1997a. *L'Hémicycle Revue trimestrielle, Assemblée Nationale du Bénin.* Porto Novo: Assemblée Nationale du Bénin.

———. 1997b. *Cour Suprême, Chambre des Comptes. Rapport public.* Année 1994.

———. 1995a. *Règlement Intérieur. Assemblée Nationale du Bénin.* Porto Novo: Assemblée Nationale du Bénin.

———. 1995b. "A propos du vote du budget général de l'Etat par l'Assemblée Nationale." In *Les Finances du Renouveau,* Numéro spécial 1995 du Bulletin d'Informations. Cotonou: Ministère des Finances, 21–26, 31, 33–42.

———. 1991. *Constitution de la République du Bénin [1990].* Cotonou: Imprimerie Notre-Dame.

———. 1986. *Loi organique No 86-021 du 26 Septembre 1986 relative aux lois de finance.* Porto Novo: Imprimerie Nationale.

Boahen, Adu. 1995. "A Note on the Ghanaian Elections." *African Affairs* 94: 277–280.
Bratton, Michael. 1998. "Second Elections in Africa." *Journal of Democracy* 9 (3) (July): 51–66.
Bratton, Michael, and Nicolas van de Walle. 1997. *Democratic Experiments in Africa: Regime Transition in Comparative Perspective.* New York: Cambridge University Press.
Burnell, Peter. 2001. "Financial Indiscipline in Zambia's Third Republic." *Journal of Legislative Studies* 7 (3) (Fall): 34–64.
Calland, Richard. 2006. *Anatomy of South Africa: Who Holds Power.* Cape Town: Zebra Press.
———, ed. 1999. *The First 5 Years: A Review of South Africa's Democratic Parliament.* Cape Town: Idasa.
Carbone, Giovanni M. 2008. *No-Party Democracy? Uganda Politics in Comparative Perspective.* Boulder: Lynne Rienner.
Carothers, Thomas. 2002. "The End of the Transition Paradigm." *Journal of Democracy* 13 (1) (January): 5–21.
Clinton, Joshua D., and John S. Lapinski. 2006. "Measuring Legislative Accomplishment, 1877–1994." *American Journal of Political Science* 50 (1) (January): 232–249.
Dahl, Robert A. 1989. *Democracy and Its Critics.* New Haven, CT: Yale University Press.
Diamond, Larry. 1996. "Is the Third Wave Over?" *Journal of Democracy* 7 (3) (October): 20–37.
———. 1995. "Nigeria: The Uncivil Society and the Descent into Praetorianism." In Larry Diamond, J. Linz, and S. M. Lipset, eds., *Politics in Developing Countries: Comparing Experiences with Democracy,* 2nd ed. Boulder: Lynne Rienner.
———. 1988. *Class, Ethnicity, and Democracy in Nigeria: The Failure of the First Republic.* Syracuse: Syracuse University Press.
Dickson, Prince Charles, and Jonathan Elendu. 2006. "Third Term: Nigeria Saved from Blood Bath." www.elendureports.com/index.php?Itemid=1&id=226&option=com_content&task=view.
Djerekpo, C., F. Laleye, and E. Tevoedjre. 1998. *Le depute et le parlement Beninois.* Cotonou: Imprimerie Tunde.
Dudley, Billy. 1982. *An Introduction to Nigerian Government and Politics,* Bloomington: Indiana University Press.
Falola, Toyin, and Julius Ihonvbere. 1985. *The Rise and Fall of Nigeria's Second Republic, 1979–84.* London: Zed Books.
February, Judith. 2005. "More Than a Law-Making Production Line? Parliament and Its Oversight Role." In Sakhela Bhulungu et al., eds., *State of the Nation: South Africa 2004–2005,* 123–142. Pretoria: Human Sciences Research Council Press and East Lansing: Michigan State University Press.
Fish, M. Steven. 2006. "Stronger Legislatures: Stronger Democracies." *Journal of Democracy* 17 (1) (January): 5–20.
Fish, M. Steven, and Mathew Kroenig. 2009. *The Handbook of National Legislatures: A Global Survey.* New York: Cambridge University Press.
Fondation Friedrich Ebert. 1995. *Le Programme des partis politiques au Bénin.* Cotonou.
Fondation Friedrich Naumann. 1995. *Assemblée nationale du Bénin. Première et deuxième législatures (1991–1999).* Cotonou: ONEPI/La Nation.
Forrest, Tom. 1995. *Politics and Economic Development in Nigeria,* 2nd ed. Boulder: Westview Press.
Gallup. 2008. "Report of a Survey of Kenyans for the Gallup World Poll: A Power Point Presentation." Washington, DC: The Gallup Organization.

254   Bibliography

Gamm, Gerald, and John Huber. 2002. "Legislatures as Political Institutions: Beyond the Contemporary Congress." In Ira Katznelson and Helen V. Milner, eds., *Political Science: The State of the Discipline,* 313–341. Washington, DC: American Political Science Association and New York: Norton.

Ghana Attorney-General's Department. 2000. Parliamentary Service (Staff) Regulations 1995 (C.I. 11). February 28.

Ghana Minister of Finance. 2003. Public Procurement Bill (prepared by Yaw Osafo-Maafo). February 19.

Ghana Minister of Justice. 2005. Representation of the People (Amendment) Bill (prepared by J. Ayikoi Otoo). April 19.

———. 2001. National Reconciliation Commission Bill (prepared by Nana Akufo-Addo). July 6.

Ghana Minister of Roads and Transport. 2004. Civil Aviation Bill (prepared by Richard W. Anane). August 25.

Ghana Parliament. 2005–2008. Register (Preliminary) of Members of Parliament. Accra: Parliament of Ghana.

———. 2005. Appropriation Act No. 688. Assented April 5.

———. 1996–2000. Register of Members of Parliament. Accra: Parliament of Ghana.

———. 1998. *Summarized Report of the Second Session of the Second Parliament of the Fourth Republic of Ghana,* No. 6. Accra: Parliament of Ghana.

———. 1997. *Summarized Report of the First Session of the Second Parliament of the Fourth Republic of Ghana,* No. 5. Accra: Parliament of Ghana.

———. 1996. *Summarized Report of the Fouth Session of the First Parliament of the Fourth Republic of Ghana,* No. 4. Accra: Parliament of Ghana.

———. 1993–1996. Register of Members of Parliament. Accra: Parliament of Ghana.

———. 1995. *Summarized Report of the Third Session of the First Parliament of the Fourth Republic of Ghana,* No. 3. Accra: Parliament of Ghana.

———. 1994. *Summarized Report of the Second Session of the First Parliament of the Fourth Republic of Ghana,* No. 2. Accra: Parliament of Ghana.

———. 1993a. *Standing Orders.* Accra: Parliament of Ghana.

———. 1993b. *Summarized Report of the First Session of the First Parliament of the Fourth Republic of Ghana,* No. 1. Accra: Parliament of Ghana.

Ghana, Republic of. 1992. *Constitution of the Republic of Ghana.*

Green, Daniel. 1998. "Ghana: Structural Adjustment and State (Re)Formation." In Leonardo A. Villalón and Philip A. Huxtable, eds., *The African State at a Critical Juncture.* Boulder: Lynne Rienner, 185–211.

A Guide to the Parliament of Ghana. 2004. Accra: Assemblies of God Literature Centre.

Gyimah-Boadi, Emmanuel. 2001. "A Peaceful Turnover in Ghana." *Journal of Democracy* 12 (1): 103–104.

———. 1999a. "Ghana: The Challenges of Consolidating Democracy." In Richard Joseph, ed., *State, Conflict and Democracy in Africa.* Boulder: Lynne Rienner, 409–427.

———. 1999b. "Six Years of Constitutional Rule in Ghana: An Assessment and Prospects of the Executive and Legislature." In *Six Years of Constitutional Rule in Ghana.* Accra: Friedrich Ebert Foundation and Ghana Academy of Arts and Sciences, 1–16.

Hopkins, Raymond F. 1971. *Political Roles in a New State.* New Haven, CT: Yale University Press.

Hughes, Tim. 2005. "The South African Parliament's Failed Moment." In M. A. Mohamad Salih, ed., *African Parliaments.* New York: Palgrave Macmillan, 224–246.

Huntington, Samuel. 1991. *The Third Wave: Democratization in the Late Twentieth Century.* Norman: University of Oklahoma Press.

Jackson, Robert H., and Carl G. Rosberg. 1982. *Personal Rule in Black Africa*. Berkeley: University of California Press.

Jeffries, Richard. 1998. "The Ghanaian Elections of 1996: Towards the Consolidation of Democracy?" *African Affairs* 97: 189–208.

Jorgensen, Jan J. 1981. *Uganda: A Modern History*. London: St. Martin's Press.

Joseph, Richard A. 1998. "Africa, 1990–97: From Abeatura to Closure." *Journal of Democracy* 9 (2): 3–18.

———. 1987. *Democracy and Prebendal Politics in Nigeria: The Rise and Fall of the Second Republic*. Cambridge: Cambridge University Press, 1987.

———. 1981. "The Ethnic Trap: Notes on the Nigerian Campaign and Elections 1978–79." *Issue: A Journal of Opinion* 11 (1–2) (Spring–Summer).

Karl, Terry. 1986. "Imposing Consent, Electoralism and Democratization in El Salvador." In Paul Drake and Eduardo Silva, eds., *Elections in Latin America*. San Diego: University of California.

Kasfir, Nelson. 1999. "Démocratie de 'Mouvement,' Légitimité et Pouvoir en Ouganda." *Politique Africaine* 75 (October).

Kasozi, A. B. K. 1994. *The Social Origins of Violence in Uganda: 1964–1985*. Montreal: McGill-Queen's University Press.

Kayunga, Sallie Simba. 2001. "The No-Party System of Democracy and the Management of Ethnic Conflict in Uganda." Ph.D. diss. submitted to the Graduate School of International Development, Roskilde University, Denmark.

Kazoora, John Bashaija. 2005. *Decision-Making in Parliamentary Democracy: The Case of Uganda 1996–2004*. M.A. diss., Makerere University, Kampala.

Kenya, Republic of. 2000a. *The Constitution of Kenya (Amendment) Act*. Nairobi: Government Printer.

———. 2000b. *The Parliamentary Service Act*. Nairobi: Government Printer.

———. 1998. *The Constitution of Kenya*. Nairobi: Government Printer.

Kenya National Assembly. 2001. *Strategic Plan of the Parliament (2000–2012), "The Blue Print."* Nairobi: Parliamentary Service Commission.

———. 1997. *Standing Orders*. Nairobi: Government Printer.

Kim, Chong Lim, Joel D. Barkan, Ilter Turan, and Malcolm Jewell. 1984. *The Legislative Connection: The Politics of Representation in Kenya, Korea and Turkey*. Durham, NC: Duke University Press.

Krafchik, W., and J. Wehner. 1998. "The Role of Parliament in the Budgetary Process." *The South African Journal of Economics* 66 (4): 512–540.

Krehbiel, Keith. 1991. *Information and Legislative Organization*. Ann Arbor: University of Michigan Press.

Laakso, Markku, and Rein Taagepera. 1979. "'Effective' Number of Parties: A Measure with Application to Western Europe." *Comparative Political Studies* 12 (April): 3–27.

Levitsky, Steven, and Lucan Way. 2002. "The Rise of Competitive Authoritarianism." *Journal of Democracy* 13 (2): 51–65.

Lewis, Peter. 2003. "Nigeria: Elections in a Fragile Regime." *Journal of Democracy* 14 (3) (July): 131–144.

———. 1999. "An End to the Permanent Transition?" In Larry Diamond and Marc Plattner, eds., *Democratization in Africa*. Baltimore: Johns Hopkins University Press.

———. 1994. "Economic Statism, Private Capital, and the Dilemmas of Accumulation in Nigeria." *World Development* 22 (3) (March): 437–451.

Lindberg, Staffan I. 2006. *Democracy and Elections in Africa*. Baltimore: Johns Hopkins University Press.

———. 2003. "It's Our Time to 'Chop': Do Elections in Africa Feed Neopatrimonialism Rather Than Counteract It?" *Democratization* 10 (2):121–140.

Lindberg, Staffan I., and Minion K. C. Morrison. 2008. "Are African Voters Really Ethnic or Clientelistic?: Survey Evidence from Ghana." *Political Science Quarterly* 123 (2): 95–122.
Linz, Juan J., and Alfred Stepan. 1996. *Problems of Democratic Transition and Consolidation.* Baltimore: Johns Hopkins University Press.
Loewenberg, Gerhard. 2007. "The Development of Comparative Legislative Research: Surmounting the Obstacles." Unpublished paper presented at the conference on Measures of Legislators' Policy Preferences and the Dimensionality of Policy Spaces, Washington University, St. Louis, MO, November 30–December 1.
Loewenberg, Gerhard, and Samuel C. Patterson. 1979. *Comparing Legislatures.* Boston: Little, Brown.
Lyons, Terrence. 1997. "A Major Step Forward." *Journal of Democracy* 8 (2): 65–77.
Mackintosh, John P. 1966. *Nigerian Government and Politics.* Evanston, IL: Northwestern University Press.
Maforikan, A. 1999. *Le parlement béninois en marche. La troisième législature de l'Assemblée Nationale, 1999–2003.* Cotonou: Friedrich Ebert Stiftung.
Mattes, Robert. 2002. "South Africa: Democracy Without People." *Journal of Democracy* 13 (1) (January): 22–36.
Mayhew, David. 1991. *Divided We Govern.* New Haven: Yale University Press.
Mezey, Michael L. 1993. "Legislatures: Individual Purpose and Institutional Performance." In Ada W. Finifter, ed., *Political Science: The State of the Discipline II.* Washington, DC: American Political Science Association, 335–364.
Michels, Robert. 1962. *Political Parties.* Translated by Eden Paul and Cedar Paul. New York: Collier-Macmillan.
Morris-Jones, W. H. 1957. *Parliament in India.* Philadelphia: University of Pennsylvania Press.
Mozaffar, Shaheen, James R. Scarritt, and Glen Galaich. 2003. "Electoral Institutions, Ethnopolitical Cleavages, and Party Systems in Africa's Emerging Democracies." *American Political Science Review* 97 (3) (August): 379–390.
Murray, Christina, and Lia Nijzink. 2002. *Building Representative Democracy: South Africa's Legislatures and the Constitution.* Cape Town: Parliamentary Support Program.
Museveni, Yoweri. 2003. "Address by H. E. Yoweri Kaguta Museveni, President of the Republic of Uganda, at the Movement National Executive Committee." Kyankwanzi, Uganda, March.
National Assembly of Nigeria, House of Representatives. 2003. *Bills Progression Chart.* www.nassnig.org/house/bills_progression.php.
National Democratic Institute. 2007a. *Toward the Development of International Standards for Democratic Legislatures.* Washington: National Democratic Institute.
———. 2007b. "Statement of the National Democratic Institute International Election Observer Delegation to Nigeria's April 21 Presidential and National Assembly Elections." Abuja, April 23, 2007. www.accessdemocracy.org/library/2151_ng_election_statement_042307.pdf.
Nigeria, Federal Republic of. 1999. *Constitution of the Federal Republic of Nigeria.* www.nigeriacongress.org/resources/constitution/Constitution%20of%20the%20Federal%20Republic%20of%20Nigeria.pdf.
Nijzink, Lia, Shaheen Mozaffar, and Elisabete Azevedo. 2006. "Parliaments and the Enhancement of Democracy on the African Continent." *Journal of Legislative Studies* 12 (3–4) (September): 311–335.
Nijzink, Lia, and Jessica Piombo. 2005. "Parliament and the Electoral System: How Are South Africans Being Represented?" In Lia Nijzink and Jessica Piombo, eds., *Electoral Politics in South Africa.* New York: Palgrave, St. Martin's Press.

Ninsin, Kwame A. 1998. "Elections, Democracy and Elite Consensus." In Kwame A. Ninsin, ed., *Ghana: Transition to Democracy.* Dakar: CODRESIA.
Nkwazema, Stanley. 2008. "Power Sector—Obasanjo Spent $16bn, Not $10bn—Bankole." *This Day* (Lagos), February 7.
Nugent, Paul. 2001. "Winners, Losers and Also Rans: Money, Moral Authority and Voting Patterns in the Ghana 2000 Election." *African Affairs* 100: 405–428.
"Obasanjo and the Survival Game." 2002. *Vanguard,* November 10.
O'Donnell, Guillermo. 1998. "Horizontal Accountability in New Democracies." *Journal of Democracy* 9 (3): 112–126.
Ogbu, Chijama. 2000. "Dangers of Another Delayed Budget." *Post Express* (Lagos), November 6.
Okanlawon, Semiu, Tony Amokeodo, John Alechenu, and Mudiaga Affe. 2008. "Senate Passes Eight Out of 120 Bills in 2008." *Punch* (Lagos), December 23.
Olson, David M. 1994. *Democratic Legislative Institutions: A Comparative View.* Armonk, NY: M. E. Sharpe.
Olum, Yasin A. A. 2002. "The Relationship Between the Parliament and the Executive: The Case of the No-Party System in Uganda." *Mawazo* 8 (June): 95–104.
Oquaye, Mike. 1995. "The Ghanaian Elections of 1992: A Dissenting View." *African Affairs* 94: 259–275.
O'Regan, Davin. 2005. "Debt Relief Critical to Development and Democracy, Senators Say," allafrica.com, May 6. http://allafrica.com/stories/200505060031.html.
Osaghae, Eghosa. 1998. *Crippled Giant: Nigeria Since Independence.* Bloomington: Indiana University Press.
Ottaway, Marina. 2003. *Democracy Challenged: The Rise of Semi-authoritarianism.* Washington, DC: Carnegie Endowment for International Peace.
PAFO (Parliamentary Advocacy Forum). 2002. "Together We Must Defend Constitutionalism and Democracy in Uganda." Kampala, Uganda, May.
Polsby, Nelson W. 1975. "Legislatures." In Fred Greenstein, ed., *Handbook of Political Science.* Reading, MA: Addison-Wesley.
Posner, Daniel N. 2005. *Institutions and Ethnic Politics in Africa.* New York: Cambridge University Press.
———. 2004. "The Political Salience of Cultural Differences: Why Chewas and Tumbukas Are Allies in Zambia and Adversaries in Malawi." *American Political Science Review* 98 (4) (November): 529–545.
Sabiti-Makara, Geoffrey B. Tukahebwa, and Foster Byarugaba, eds. 2003. *Voting for Democracy in Uganda: Issues in Recent Elections.* Kampala: LDC Publishers.
Salih, M. A. Mohamed. 2005. *African Parliaments.* New York: Palgrave Macmillan.
Sandbrook, Richard, and Jay Oelbaum. 1999. *Reforming the Political Kingdom: Governance and Development in Ghana's Fourth Republic.* Accra, Ghana: Center for Democracy and Development.
Sater, James N. 2007. "Changing Politics from Below? Women Parliamentarians in Morocco." *Democratization* 14 (4) (Fall): 723–742.
Schedler, Andreas, ed. 2006. *Electoral Authoritarianism: The Dynamics of Unfree Competition.* Boulder: Lynne Rienner.
Schrire, Robert. 2008. "Parliamentary Opposition After Apartheid: South Africa." *Journal of Legislative Studies* 14 (1–2) (March): 190–211.
Schumpeter, Joseph. 1950. *Capitalism, Socialism and Democracy,* 3rd ed. New York: Harper and Brothers.
Shepsle, Kenneth A. 2007. "Assessing Comparative Legislative Research." In Gerhard Loewenberg, Peverill Squire, and D. Roderick Kiewiet, eds., *Legislatures: Comparative Perspectives on Representative Assemblies.* Ann Arbor: University of Michigan Press, 387–398.

Sklar, Richard. 1963. *Nigerian Political Parties: Power in an Emergent African Nation.* Princeton, NJ: Princeton University Press.
Slade, Humphrey. 1969. *Parliament in Kenya,* 2nd ed. Nairobi: East African Publishing House.
South Africa Parliament. 2004. *National Assembly Guide to Procedure.* Cape Town: Creda Communications.
Squire, Peverill. 1992. "The Theory of Legislative Institutionalization and the California Assembly." *Journal of Politics* 54 (4): 1026–1054.
Squire, Peverill, and Keith E. Hamm. 2005. *101 Chambers: Congress, State Legislatures, and the Future of Legislative Studies.* Columbus: Ohio State University Press.
Tamale, Sylvia. 1999. *When Hens Begin to Crow: Gender and Parliamentary Politics in Uganda.* Kampala: Fountain Publishers.
"The Third Term Agenda: The Gathering Opposition." 2005. *This Day* (Lagos), July 31.
Thomas, Melissa A., and Oumar Sissokho. 2005. "Liaison Legislature: The Role of the National Assembly in Senegal." *Journal of Modern African Studies* 43 (1): 97–117.
Transition Monitoring Group. 2007. "An Election Programmed to Fail: Final Report of the April 2007 General Elections in Nigeria." Abuja, Nigeria, July. www.tmgnigeria.org/publications/anelectprgmedtofail-141107.pdf.
Tripp, Aili Mari. 2006. "Women in Uganda's Parliament: Whom Do They Represent?" In Gretchen Bauer and Hannah Evelyn Britton, eds., *Women in African Parliaments.* Boulder: Lynne Rienner, 179–205.
Twebaze, Stephen Hippo. 2008. "Legislative Resources and Effective Performance: The Case of the Ugandan Parliament." Unpublished paper.
Uganda Bureau of Statistics. 2002. *Uganda Population and Housing Census. Provisional Results.* Entebbe: Government of Uganda.
Uganda Constitutional Commission. 1993. *The Report of the Uganda Constitutional Commission: Analysis and Recommendations.* Entebbe: Uganda Printing and Publishing Company.
Uganda Parliament. 2005a. *Report of the Parliamentary Budget Committee on the Indicative Preliminary Revenue and Expenditure Framework of the Government for FY 2005/06,* Report PBa. Kampala. May 13.
———— 2005b. *Report of the Parliamentary Budget Committee on the Three Years Macroeconomic Plan and Programmes for Economic and Social Development for Fiscal Years 2005/06–2007/08,* Report PBb. Kampala. May 13.
————. 2004a. *Report of the Sessional Committee on Presidential and Foreign Affairs,* Report PFA. Kampala.
————. 2004b. *Hansard.* Seventh Parliament, 3rd session, 3rd meeting. Kampala. February 10–26.
————. 2002. *Rules of Procedure of the Parliament of Uganda.*
————. 2001. *A Directory of Uganda's Seventh Parliament, 2001–2006.* Albany: State University of New York.
————. 1999. *Hansard.* Sixth Parliament, 4th session, 1st meeting. Kampala. November 1–30.
————. 1996. *Rules of Procedure of the Parliament of Uganda.*
Uganda, Republic of. 1995. *Constitution of the Republic of Uganda.* Kampala: Government Printer.
Uganda Sessional Committee on Presidential and Foreign Affairs. 2004. Report PFA.
Ugbolue, Henry. 2000. "8 Months After Inauguration, National Assembly Members Still Idle." *Tempo* (Lagos), March 15.
————. 1999. "Why I Donated My Furniture Allowance." *Tempo* (Lagos), September 9.

UNDP (United Nations Development Program). 2001. *Rapport sur le développement humain au Bénin 2001. Le développement régional et les défis de la décentralisation.* Cotonou: Imprimerie Tunde.

———. 2000a. *The Contribution of the Parliamentary Process in Strengthening Good Governance in Africa.* Fourth Africa Governance Forum (AGF IV). New York: United Nations.

———. 2000c. "Inventaire des programmes de gouvernance en Afrique." Présentation des résultats de la collecte de données sur les initiatives de gouvernance au Bénin. Cotonou: Processed.

———. 2000d. "La contribution du parlement au renforcement de la gouvernance au Bénin." Cotonou: Processed.

———. 2000e. *Programme d'appui à l'Assemblée nationale du Bénin* (prepared by N. Motabar and N. Kassa). Cotonou: Processed.

———. 2000f. *Rapport sur le développement humain au Bénin.* Cotonou: Imprimerie Tunde.

USAID (US Agency for International Development). 1999. *Benin National Assembly Strengthening Program.* Request for Application Number 680-00-002, November.

Uwugiaren, Iyobosa, and Henry Ugbolue. 1999. "Setback for Obasanjo as Senators Throw Out His Bill in Abuja." *The News* (Lagos), December 20.

Wight, Martin. 1947. *The Development of the Legislative Council: 1606–1945.* London: Faber and Faber.

The Contributors

Joel D. Barkan is professor emeritus of political science, University of Iowa, and senior associate, Center for Strategic and International Studies, Washington, DC.

* * *

Ladipo Adamolekun, an independent scholar, formerly was lead specialist in the Public Sector Reform Unit at the Africa Region of the World Bank. He was awarded the Nigerian National Order of Merit in 2005.

Nelson Kasfir is professor of government, Dartmouth College.

Mouftaou Laleye is currently the Republic of Benin's ambassador to Nigeria. He has also served as director of the Policy Analysis Unit of the National Assembly of Benin.

Peter M. Lewis is associate professor of political science and director of the Africa Program at the Paul Nitze School of Advanced International Studies, Johns Hopkins University, Washington, DC.

Staffan I. Lindberg is assistant professor of political science, University of Florida, Gainesville.

Fred Matiangi is chief of party for the State University of New York/USAID mission to the Kenya National Assembly.

Stephen Hippo Twebaze is an independent scholar affiliated with the Centre for Basic Research, Kampala, Uganda.

Yongmei Zhou is senior institutional development specialist in the Sustainable Development Department at the South Asia Region of the World Bank.

Index

Abacha, Sani, 183, 189
Abubakar, Abdulsalami, 189
Abubakar, Atiku, 196–197
Access to Information Bill (Uganda), 84
Accountability: legislatures promoting vertical and horizontal accountability, 1–2
Action Group (AG; Nigeria), 183
Administration of Parliament Act (APA; Uganda), 79, 90, 106
African Legislatures Project (ALP), 246–247
African National Congress (ANC; South Africa): centralization of power, 209–211; free press coverage, 219–220; institutional resources, 222; need for oversight expansion, 224; policy objectives, 211–212; political culture, 213–214; portfolio committees, 216–218; proportional representation, 208–209; Reconstruction and Development Program policy, 228(n10); reformers' agenda, 226–227
Afrobarometer, 147
Age: composition of Kenya's Ninth and Tenth Parliaments, 53(table 2.1); Ghana's MPs, 163, 165(table), 166; profile of Benin's National Assembly members, 120, 125; Uganda's MPs, 96, 97(table 3.1); Uganda's reformers, 99(table)
Akuffo-Addo, Nana, 147
Ala Djetey, Pete, 149, 155–156, 160, 163, 168, 172, 174

Alliance for Democracy (AD; Nigeria), 190, 191(table 6.3)
Allowances: Benin, 122; comparisons by country, 240–241; Ghana's MPs, 166, 168; Kenya's MP compensations, 55–56; Nigeria, 192, 201; South African constituency allowances, 221. *See also* Salaries and emoluments
All People's Party (APP; Nigeria), 190, 191(table 6.3)
Ambiguous regimes, 24(table 1.1)
Amendments, legislative: Benin's budget process, 130–132; Ghana, 152–154, 174; Kenya's constitutional review, 49–50; Kenya's establishment of Parliamentary Service, 239; Kenya's legislative-executive delinking, 45–46; Kenya's resumption of multiparty politics, 38–39; Kenya's 2008 revision, 69; Museveni's repeal of term limits, 84–85; South Africa's legislative autonomy, 214–215; Uganda's MP pensions, 92
American Journal of Political Science, 5
American Political Science Review journal, 5
Amin, Idi, 76–77
Anglican Church, 43
Anglo-Leasing scandal, 52, 72(n18)
Anglo-Nigerian Defence Pact, 185
Angola: postcolonial legislative development, 12; regime classification, 24(table 1.1)
Annan, D. F., 160, 174

Apartheid: South Africa's political legacy, 205–206, 228(n13)
Apraku, Kofi Konadu, 174
Aringo, Peter Oloo, 44, 46, 54, 66, 72(n10)
Arms Deal (South Africa), 224, 229(n21)
Aspiring democracies, 24(table 1.1)
Atta-Mills, John, 147, 173–174
Auditors and audit functions: Benin, 133; Ghana, 157–158; Uganda, 79–80, 85
Authoritarian rule: Ghana, 148–149; Kenya under Kenyatta, 35–36; Nigeria, 182–183
Autonomy, legislative: Benin's budget process, 130–132; difficulties in measuring, 245; Nigeria's constitutional provisions, 182; Parliament of Ghana's decline in, 155–156; South Africa, 214–226; Uganda during the Sixth and Seventh Parliaments, 78–86, 92–96; Uganda's committee system, 89–91
Awolowo, Obafemi, 183, 186
Ayume, Francis, 88
Azikiwe, Nnamdi, 183, 186

Babangida, Ibrahim, 183, 188–189
Backbenchers: coalitions for change, 20, 237; Kenya, 36; salaries, 14; Uganda's Administration of Parliament Act, 90–91k; Uganda's Budget Bill 2000, 82
Bagbin, Albin, 158
Bamford-Addo, Joyce, 174
Banking sector: privatization of Uganda Commercial Bank, 79–80
Bankole, Dimeji, 200
Belgian Congo: postcolonial legislative development, 12
Benin: achievements, constraints, and future directions, 141–144; conference of presidents, 116–117; core function performance, 126–130, 242(table 8.2); demographic profile of National Assembly membership, 119–121; deputies' views on issues, 123–124; distribution of ministries and departments among the five permanent commissions, 113(table 4.1); Fourth Legislature, 2003–2007, 124–126; Freedom House scores and democratic progress, 22; history of political instability, 110; incentive structures for deputies, 121–123; institutional resources, 241; lack of reformers, 233; lawmaking and policymaking, 128–130; legislative calendar, 117; legislative organization and administration, 111–118; legislative relationships with national institutions, 118–119; legislative relationships with the executive, 118; legislative weakness, 3; measuring and evaluating legislative performance, 243, 245–246; multiparty systems and competitive politics, 16; 1990 constitutional provisions, 110–111; nomenclature of parliamentary terms, 26(table 1.2); oversight and control of the executive, 130–136; oversight and control of the parliamentary executive, 136–137; parliamentary staff, 117–118; political parties and parliamentary groups, 115–116; public opinion of the National Assembly, 137–141; regime classification, 24(table 1.1); research methodology, 25; salaries and emoluments, 240, 240(table 8.1); social responsibility and constituency service, 121; state collapse leading to reform, 109
Big men, 12–13
Bills passed. *See* Legislation passed
Blue Print, Kenya's, 47–48
Boni, Thomas Yayi, 113
Botswana: regime classification, 24(table 1.1)
Bribery: Obasanjo's "third term" agenda, 177
Britain: colonialism retarding Kenya's legislative development, 36–37; colonial legislative history, 9–12; Kenya's LEGCO, 35–36
Budget Act (2001: Uganda), 78–81, 85–86, 90, 93, 106, 106(n10)
Budget Office (Uganda), 91–92
Budget process: Benin, 111, 130–132; colonial legislatures' minimal participation, 10–12; committee capacity and quality, 217; Ghana, 151(fig. 5.1), 154–156, 160, 172, 175(n3); Kenya's Blue Print, 47; Kenya's committee system modernization, 49; Kenya's executive setting, 37; Kenya's Standing Orders revision, 67; Kenya's transformation, 43–44; Nigeria's tensions with Obasanjo over, 193; South Africa's National Assembly, 224–225; Uganda's Budget Act, 81–83
Buhari, Ibrahim, 188, 192
Burkina Faso: regime classification, 24(table 1.1)
Burundi: regime classification, 24(table 1.1)

Index   265

Business sector: views of Benin's National Assembly, 139–140

Cabinet ministers: Benin's appointment mechanism, 112; Benin's legislative commission functions, 113–114; colonial legislative history, 10; Francophone and Lusophone colonies, 11–12; Museveni sacking, 103; Parliament of Ghana's declining influence on presidential appointments, 158–159, 169–171; privatization of Uganda Commercial Bank, 79–80; South Africa, 210; Uganda's selection mechanism, 107(n15); views of Benin's National Assembly, 137–138
Calendar, legislative, 117
Cameroon: regime classification, 24(table 1.1)
Campaign finance: Benin's deputies' views on, 123–124; Ghana's, 175(n5); Kenya, 57–59; Uganda's MPs' debts fueling patronage, 101, 105
Campaigns, electoral: Uganda, 101–103, 108(n29)
Capacity building: South African National Assembly's portfolio committees, 216–217
Cape Verde: postcolonial legislative development, 12; regime classification, 24(table 1.1)
Cash handouts, Ghana's, 171
Catholic Church, 43
Caucuses: Benin's parliamentary groups, 111, 125; coalition organization in Uganda's Parliament, 93–95; Nigeria's factions, 184; South Africa, 210, 228(n9); Uganda, 107(n23)
Central African Republic: regime classification, 24(table 1.1)
Centralization of power: South Africa, 209–211
Centre for Governance and Development (CGD; Kenya), 42–45
Chad: regime classification, 24(table 1.1)
Chief administrative officer, 235. *See also* Clerk
Chief Presiding Officer, 235–236; South Africa, 212–213. *See also* Speaker (chief presiding officer)
Chief whip, South Africa's, 210–211, 213
Chiluba, Frederick, 16
Civil society: coalitions for change, 19–20; criticizing Kenya's salary increases, 57; driving democratic reform, 233–234; Kenya under Kibaki, 52; reformers advancing change through partnerships with, 248; role in South African legislative autonomy, 218–219; transformation of Kenya's House, 42–45; views of Benin's National Assembly, 140
Class politics, South Africa's, 205
Clerk (chief administrative officer): Kenya, 40–41; Kenya's Blue Print, 47; Kenya's legislative-executive delinking, 45–46
Clientelism: Nigeria, 178, 180–181
Closed list system of election, 208
Coalition formation: Nigeria, 190; Uganda's no-party system, 93–94
Coalitions for change, 17–21; Ghana, 173; importance of political parties, 236–237; Kenya, 34, 41–42; as requirement for institutional development, 247; six variables affecting viability of, 232–238; Uganda, 75–76, 82. *See also* Reformers
Collective action, 8
Colonialism: historical context of African legislation, 9–12; Kenya's political structures, 71(n1); Kenya's post-independence parliamentary system, 35; neopatrimonial rule emerging from, 12–15; retarding Kenya's legislative development, 36–37
Committee systems: Benin's permanent commission, 111–115; Ghana's budget process, 154; Ghana's weakening oversight performance, 156–158; Kenya after independence, 37; Kenya's modernization, 48–49; Kenya strengthening, 59–61; measuring legislative performance, 245; Nigeria's Fourth Republic, 194, 197, 199–200; South African Parliament, 210–211, 223; South Africa's race and generational politics, 229(n18); types of, 25–26; Uganda's Budget Bill, 82–83; Uganda's change in constitutional powers affecting, 86–89; Uganda's coalition organization, 93–95; Uganda's creation of, 89–91; Uganda's legislative-executive compromise, 84–85; Uganda's performance, 104. *See also* Portfolio committees
Common Fund (Ghana), 168–169
Comoros: regime classification, 24(table 1.1)
Comparative legislative studies, 3–6, 244

Comparative political studies, 6
Competitive authoritarian regimes, 22–23, 24(table 1.1)
Competitive politics: Third Wave of democratization, 15–17
Conference of presidents (Benin), 116–117
Conflict management, 30(n1)
Congo, Democratic Republic: multiparty elections and competitive politics, 16; regime classification, 24(table 1.1)
Congo, People's Republic: regime classification, 24(table 1.1)
Congress of the People (COPE; South Africa), 208
Consensus voting: Uganda's Parliament, 88
Constituency Development Fund (CDF; Kenya), 58–59, 59(table 2.3)
Constituency service: assessing legislative performance, 244; Benin, 121, 123, 126–128, 138–139, 142; changing incentives for MPs, 17–18; core functions of the legislature, 7–8, 242(table 8.2); Ghana, 166–169; incentives through salaries and emoluments, 239–241; Kenya, 34, 37–38, 44–45; postcolonial neo-patrimonialism, 14; PR countries, 30–31(n3); South African emoluments, 221; Uganda, 101–103
Constitutional legacy of colonialism, 17–18
Constitution of Kenya Review Act (2000), 49–50
Constitution of Kenya Review Commission, 50
Constitutions: Benin's history of political instability, 110; Benin's new democratic order, 109; evolution of Nigeria's legislative politics, 182–183; Ghana's hybrid constitution allowing legislative co-optation, 148, 169–171, 173; Uganda's balance of powers, 105; Uganda's 1995 constitution, 86–89; Uganda's Constitutional Commission, 106(n2)
Consultative Group (CG), 71(n4)
Core functions of modern legislatures, 6–8; Benin's representation and legislation, 126–130; coalitions for change, 18–19; comparative performance of the four core functions by country, 242(table 8.2); country studies, 22; identification and analysis of, 30(n1); Kenyan MPs' increasing involvement, 34; Kenya's transformation, 43–44; measuring legislative performance, 244–247; Moi's manipulation of Kenya's House, 41. *See also* Constituency service; Legislative-executive relations; Oversight of the executive; Representative governance
Corruption: ANC members, 209–210, 229(n22); Benin's acts of omission and commission, 135; Benin's deputies' views on declaration of assets, 124; as essential element in Nigerian politics, 181–182; Ghana's ministry appointees, 159; Kenya's Grand Regency Hotel sale, 68–69; Kenya under Kibaki, 52; Nigerian Assembly's investigation of, 199–200; Nigerians' perception of MPs, 201–202; Nigeria under Obasanjo, 196; Obasanjo's "third-term agenda," 177; Uganda, 79, 81, 83–84, 107(n14), 243
Côte d'Ivoire: regime classification, 24(table 1.1)
Coups d'état: Benin, 109; Ghana, 148–149; neopatrimonial systems, 13; Nigeria, 182–183, 185, 188; Uganda, 76–77
Critical mass of committee membership, 216

Declaration of assets: Benin, 124
Democratic Alliance (DA; South Africa), 208, 211–212, 216, 222
Democratic centralism, 220
Democratic reform, civil society driving, 233–234
Democratic studies, 3–6
Democratization: ANC relations with the opposition, 211–212; Benin's National Assembly contributing to democratic consolidation, 141–142; coalitions for change, 19–20; democratic opening of Uganda under no-party rule, 76–78; democratic studies and legislative studies, 3–6; expansion of legislation power driving, 1–2; international community's role in Kenya's, 71(nn3,9); measuring legislative performance, 244–245; multiparty systems and competitive politics, 15–17; Nigeria's hesitance following military rule, 194–195; reformers' commitment to, 233; regime classification, 24(table 1.1); removing constraints to Kenya's, 45–47; Third Wave of, 1, 4; transformation of Kenya's House, 42–45
Democratization journal, 4–5

Demographic features of African society, 17–18
Departmental committees, 27, 49, 156
Department for International Development (DFID; UK), 47
Deputies (Benin), 109–110. *See also* National Assembly (Benin)
Developing areas, politics of, 6
Development, economic, 123
Distributional politics: Nigeria, 179
Djibouti: regime classification, 24(table 1.1)
Domestic Violence Bill (Ghana), 152
Droop method of proportional representation, 208

Economic Community of West African States (ECOWAS), 145(n5)
Economic concerns: as a driver of South African politics, 205–206; role of civil society in South African legislative autonomy, 218–219
Economic performance: Benin's collapse, 109; Ghana's growth under Rawlings, 149; Kenya's growth under Kibaki, 52; Uganda's post-independence economic decline, 76
Education: ANC MPs, 216–217; composition of Kenya's Ninth and Tenth Parliaments, 53(table 2.1), 54; Ghana's MPs, 163, 165(table 5.6), 166; South Africa's race politics, 225, 229(n17); Uganda's MPs, 96, 97(table 3.1); Uganda's reformers, 99(table 3.2)
Elections: Benin's contested elections, 115; Benin's Fourth Legislature, 124–125; Benin's presidential elections, 113, 144(n3); under colonial rule, 11; Ghana's boycott, 149; Ghana's irregularities, 175(n1); Ghana's multiparty election history, 147; Kenya's election of Kibaki, 51–52; Kenya's election of Moi, 71(n6); Kenya's ethnic polarization, 63–64; Kenya's turnover in the Ninth and Tenth Parliaments, 52–55; Moi's manipulation of Kenya's, 37–38; Nigeria's abortive electoral reform, 193; Nigeria's coups pre-empting, 183, 188–189; Nigeria's fraudulent 2003 elections, 195–196; Nigeria's fraudulent 2007 elections, 197–198; postcolonial neopatrimonial rule, 13–14; South Africa's proportional representation, 208–209; term limits, 31(n6); Uganda's changes in constitutional powers, 87; Uganda's contested elections, 106(n4); Uganda's no-party system, 73, 93; Uganda's presidential intervention, 83; Uganda's resumption of multipartyism, 104. *See also* Term limits
Electoral authoritarian regimes, 24(table 1.1)
Electoral Bill (Nigeria), 193
Electoral system: impact on legislative development, 11–12, 39, 208–209, 237–238
Enwerem, Evan, 192–193
Equatorial Guinea: regime classification, 24(table 1.1)
Eritrea: regime classification, 24(table 1.1)
Ethiopia: multiparty elections and competitive politics, 16; regime classification, 24(table 1.1)
Ethnicity: Kenya's coalitions, 35–36, 51; Kenya's polarization, 63–64; Nigeria's Parliament, 183–184, 189; South African politics, 227(n3)
Executive branch: coalitions for change, 19–21; entrenched neopatrimonialism maintaining presidential dominance, 234–235; Nigeria's rent-seeking politics, 179
Executive power: Benin's budget process, 130–132; Benin's Fourth Legislature, 126; Benin's lawmaking and policymaking, 128–130; Benin's legislative bureau, 111; Benin's legislative commissions, 112–115; Benin's oversight and control of the parliamentary executive, 136–137; controlling Ghana's MP salaries, 166; co-optation of Ghana's legislature, 148, 169–171; Kenya's balance of power, 33; Kenya's Constituency Development Fund, 59; Kenya's constitutional review, 49–50; Kenya's legislative transformation, 44–45; Kenya's resumption of multiparty politics, 39; Kenya under Kibaki, 40–41, 51–52; legislative weakness and, 2; measuring legislative performance, 245; Museveni's resumption of multipartyism, 104–106; Nigeria's federal parliament, 183; Nigeria's legislative scope, 182; Nigeria's Second Republic, 186–187; Obasanjo's second term and consolidation of power, 195–198; retarding institutional development, 247; rewriting formal rules to curb, 238–239; term limits, 31(n6); Uganda's

268   Index

changes in constitutional powers and rules of procedure, 86–89; Uganda's no-party rule, 74–75, 77–78, 93–95. *See also* Legislative-executive relations
Expired bills, 153

Federal parliamentary systems, 189; Nigeria, 183
Finance Commission (Benin), 113–114, 130
First past the post electoral system, 11, 39
Fiscal Management Act (Kenya), 67–68
Floor crossing, 207–208, 228(n5)
Formal rules, 238–239
Francophone colonies' failure to develop post-independence legislatures, 11
Fraud: Nigerian MP, 192
Freedom House index: Ghana, 147; Kenya under Kibaki, 52; reflecting legislative autonomy, 31(n10); regime classification, 24(table1.1); scales, 22, 31(n7)
Freedom of Information Bill (Ghana), 152
French language proficiency, 120
French National Assembly, 11

Gabon: regime classification, 24(table 1.1)
Gambia: regime classification, 24(table 1.1)
Gariyo, Zie, 83–84
Gender: composition of Kenya's House, 55; composition of Kenya's Ninth and Tenth Parliaments, 53(table 2.1); Ghana's MPs, 165(table 5.6); Uganda's reformers, 99(table 3.2). *See also* Women
Ghana: campaign finance, 175(n5); coalitions for change, 20; comparative performance of the four core functions of the legislature, 242(table 8.2); democratization success, 147–148; evaluating legislative performance, 243; Freedom House scores and democratic progress, 22; institutional resources, 241; LEGCO, 9; legislative co-optation, 148–150; legislative weakness, 3; military neopatrimonialism, 13; multiparty elections and competitive politics, 16; nomenclature of parliamentary terms, 26(table 1.2); portfolio committees, 216; reformers in legislature, 233; regime classification, 24(table 1.1); research methodology, 25; salaries and emoluments, 240, 240(table 8.1); Speaker appointment and approach, 40; Speaker curbing reformers, 235–236; term limits, 31(n6)
Gichohi, Patrick, 65

Ginwala, Frene, 212, 223–224
Goldenberg scandal, 52
Gowon, Yakubu, 185
Grand Regency Hotel, Nairobi, 68–69
Great Nigeria People's Party, 186, 187(table 6.2)
Growth, Employment, and Redistribution (GEAR) program, 228(n10)
Guerrilla insurgencies, 16
Guinea: regime classification, 24(table 1.1)
Guinea-Bissau: regime classification, 24(table 1.1)

HIV/AIDS, 90, 224
Houphouet-Boigny, Félix, 11
Housekeeping committees, 25, 37, 48–49
House (Kenya). *See* National Assembly (Kenya)
House of Representatives (Nigeria), 184–185; composition in the First Republic, 184 (table 6.1); composition in the Second Republic, 187 (table 6.2); composition in the Fourth Republic, 191(table 6.3)
Hughes, Ebenezer S., 163, 172, 174
Human resource development: Ghana, 163
Hybrid constitution, Ghana's, 169–171, 173

Igbo people, 183
Impeachment, 111, 178, 192
Incentives for democratization: Benin, 121–123; cash handouts for Ghana's MPs, 171; formal rules, legislative powers, and internal rules, 238–239; Ghana's reforms, 174; institutional resources, 241; shaping legislative development, 17–18. *See also* Allowances; Salaries and emoluments
Individualism: Uganda's no-party system, 93
Individual merit system: Uganda, 73, 80, 88, 92–93, 102, 104, 237
Information technology, 125, 145(n5), 220, 241
Inkatha Freedom Party (IFP; South Africa), 208, 227(n3)
Institute for Economic Affairs (IEA; Kenya), 42–44
Institute for Education and Democracy (Kenya), 43
Institute of Certified Public Accountants of Kenya, 43–44
Institutional development, 74, 247

Institutional memory: Benin, 120; Ghana, 157; Kenya, 37, 57, 61; Nigeria, 190–191; South Africa, 222
Institutional resources: Benin, 114, 117–118, 142; committee capacity and quality, 217; as incentive for legislative development, 241; South Africa, 220–222; Uganda, 91–92
Interest groups: committee interactions with, 217; reformers advancing change through partnerships with, 248; South Africa's legislative autonomy, 218–219
Internal rules, 238–239. *See also* Règlement Intérieur; Standing Orders
International community: Kenya's Blue Print reform, 47–48; Moi's control of Kenya's House, 41; need for local partners and ownership, 247; pressure for Kenyan reforms, 38–39; role in Kenya's democratization, 71(nn3,4,9); transformation of Kenya's House, 43; views of Benin's National Assembly, 141
International Monetary Fund (IMF), 148, 193
Internet, 125, 220, 233, 241
Interpellation (queries), 127, 134, 145(n12)

Journal of Democracy, 4–5
Journal of Legislative Studies, 5
Journal of Politics, 5

Kaparo, Francis Ole, 40, 46–48, 65
Karuiki, J. M., 36
Kenya: budgetary process, 225; campaign finance, 57–59; civil society driving democratic reform, 234; coalitions for change, 19–20; colonial history, 71(n1); committee system modernization, 48–49; comparative performance of the four core functions of the legislature, 242(table 8.2); Eighth Parliament, 42–50; Freedom House scores and democratic progress, 22; history of Kenyan MP emoluments, 1993–2008, 56(table 2.2); institutional resources, 241; LEGCO, 9; legislative development and democratization from 1963–1992, 34–38; legislative independence, 2; measuring and evaluating legislative performance, 243, 245–246; multiparty elections and competitive politics, 16; nomenclature of parliamentary terms, 26(table 1.2); portfolio committees, 216; postcolonial neopatrimonialism, 13; quick wins supporting complex reforms, 248; reformers and opportunists joining forces for change, 232; regime classification, 24(table 1.1); research methodology, 25; resumption of multiparty politics, 38–39; rewriting formal rules, 239; salaries and emoluments, 240, 240(table 8.1); Seventh Parliament, 39–42; Speaker containing reformers, 235–236; term limits, 31(n6); turnover from Eighth to Ninth Parliaments, 52–55. *See also* National Assembly (Kenya)
Kenya African Democratic Union (KADU), 35
Kenya African National Union (KANU), 33, 35, 39–40, 51, 71(n6), 71(n8)
Kenya Law Society, 43
Kenya Private Sector Alliance, 43–44
Kenyatta, Jomo, 13, 35–36
Kérékou, Mathieu, 113, 125–126, 130, 235
Kibaki, Mwai, 51–52, 64, 72(n14)
Kiraso, Beatrice, 82–83
Kufuor, John, 29, 147, 149, 155, 159–160, 172, 175, 235
Kuta, Idris, 192

Laakso-Taagepera index, 207
Language proficiency, 120
Law Commission (Benin), 114
Left-right politics, 206
Legal and Parliamentary Affairs Committee (Uganda), 84–85, 90
Legislating in the broad sense. *See* Legislative-executive relations
Legislation passed: Benin's lawmaking and policymaking, 128–130; executive dominating Nigeria's Second Republic, 186–187; Kenya's Ninth Parliament, 61–63; legislative-executive compromise in Uganda's Seventh Parliament, 84–85; measuring and evaluating legislative performance, 243, 246; Nigeria's inefficient National Assembly, 194; Nigeria under Yar' Adua, 200–201; South Africa, 214–215, 228(n15); Uganda's Budget Act, 78–81
Legislative Bureau (Benin), 111
Legislative Council (LEGCO), 9–11, 35–36
Legislative development: chief presiding officer and chief administrative officer, 235–236; civil society driving democratic reform, 233–234; electoral system, 237–238; lingering neopatrimonialism,

234–235; measuring, 244–247; political parties, 236–237; variables explaining, 232–238
Legislative-executive relations: Benin, 118; Benin's collaborative environment, 114; Benin's separation of powers, 110–111; core functions of the legislature, 7, 242–243, 242(table 8.2); Kenya's House reforms delinking, 45–46; Kenya's transformation, 44; manipulation of Ghana's presiding officer, 172–173; Nigeria's legislative expansion under Yar' Adua, 198–202; Nigeria's tensions with Obasanjo, 193–194, 197; Parliament of Ghana's declining autonomy, 155–156; Uganda's Budget Bill, 81–83; Uganda's constitutional powers and rules of procedures, 86–89, 105; Uganda's increasing presidential intervention, 83–86; Uganda's Movement Caucus, 95–96; Uganda's power struggles, 79–81, 105; Uganda's struggle for independence and autonomy, 78–86. *See also* Oversight of the executive
Legislative performance: Ghana, 150–154; institutional resources as measure of, 241; measuring, 244–247; observations of, 241–244; reformers affecting, 232–233; salaries and emoluments affecting, 240
Legislative Plenary (Benin), 111
Legislative Studies Quarterly journal (LSQ), 5
Leon, Tony, 212
Lesotho: regime classification, 24(table 1.1)
Liberal democracies, 23, 24(table 1.1)
Liberia: regime classification, 24(table 1.1)
Linkage, 30(n1)
Local councils, Uganda, 76–77
Local Government Public Accounts Committee (Uganda), 81
Lusophone colonies: failure to develop post-independence legislatures, 11

Madagascar: regime classification, 24(table 1.1)
Mahama, John, 174
Malawi: multiparty elections and competitive politics, 16; regime classification, 24(table 1.1)
Mali: regime classification, 24(table 1.1)
Mandela, Nelson, 209, 219
Manuel, Trevor, 224
Marende, Kenneth, 65–66

Mauritania: regime classification, 24(table 1.1)
Mauritius: regime classification, 24(table 1.1)
Mbeki, Thabo, 209–211, 213, 219, 224, 228(nn7,8), 229(n22), 235
Mbete, Baleka, 213
Media: criticizing Kenya's salary increases, 57; exclusion from Parliament of Ghana meetings, 156–157; exposé of Nigerian MP fraud, 192; Kenya's Grand Regency Hotel sale, 69; Kenya under Kibaki, 52; reformers advancing change through partnerships with, 248; role of free press in South Africa's legislative autonomy, 219–220; views of Benin's National Assembly, 140–141
Mensah, J. H., 158, 172
Methodology: interviews, 23–28; measuring legislative performance, 244–247; observations of legislative performance, 241–244
Military rule: neopatrimonialism, 13; Nigeria, 182–183; Uganda, 76–77
Mineral wealth: Nigeria, 181
Ministries, departments, and agencies (MDAs; Ghana), 148, 154–155, 158, 171
Mohammed, Murtala, 185
Moi, Daniel arap: attempt to block legislative emergence, 28; contesting legislative development, 235; election results, 71(n6); KADU coalition, 35; Kenya's resumption of multiparty politics, 38–39; Kenya's transformation, 44; Kibaki challenging, 51–52; multiparty elections and competitive politics, 16, 72(n13); neopatrimonialism under, 37–38; term limits, 31(n6)
Movement Caucus (MC; Uganda), 94–96, 107(n24)
Movement system (Uganda): executive-legislative power struggles, 79–81; importance of parties in legislative development, 236–237; introduction by 1967 Constitution, 77–78; origins of no-party rule, 73; Parliamentary composition, 98–99; Parliamentary reforms, 92–96
Mozambique: postcolonial legislative development, 12; regime classification, 24(table 1.1)
Muhakanizi, Keith, 81
Muite, Paul, 42

Index   271

Multiparty politics: Benin's democratic reforms, 109–110; Ghana's conversion to, 149; Kenya's resumption of, 16, 38–40, 72(n13); Kenyatta's consolidation of parties, 35–36; Nigeria's putative Third Republic, 188–189; parliamentary reform, 19; term limits, 31(n6); Third Wave of democratization, 15–17; Uganda's resumption of, 96, 103
Muluzi, Bakili, 16
Museveni, Yoweri: coalition for change, 237; coalitions for change, 20; corruption probe, 243; executive power, 86, 105; Movement Caucus, 95–96; no-party politics, 73; Parliamentary composition, 98; patronage, use of, 74, 105; preparation for resumption of multipartyism, 103; Speaker choice, 88; term limits, 16, 31(n6), 84–85
Musumba, Isaac, 82
Musyoka, Kalonzo, 64
Mutebile-Tumusiime, Emanuel, 81, 106(n7)

Namibia: electoral system, 238; multiparty elections and competitive politics, 16; regime classification, 24(table 1.1)
National Assembly (Benin): core function performance, 126–130; financial incentives for deputies, 121–123; organization and function of, 109–110; oversight and control of the parliamentary executive, 136–137; profile of members, 119–121; public opinion of, 137–141; relationships with national institutions, 118–119; relationships with the executive, 118; social responsibility and constituency service, 121; symbolic incentives for deputies, 122–123
National Assembly (Kenya): Blue Print for reform, 47–48; campaign finance, 57–59; composition of Kenya's Ninth and Tenth Parliaments, 53(table 2.1); Constitution of Kenya Review Act, 49–50; impact of civil society on transformation of, 42–45; Kibaki's election, 51–52; legislative development and democratization from 1963–1992, 34–38; level of development, 33–34; Moi's manipulation of, 40–41; Ninth Parliament, 50–63; removing constraints for capacity building, 45–46; resumption of multiparty politics, 38–40, 72(n13); Seventh Parliament, 39–42; Speaker appointment, 71(n5); Standing Orders revision, 66–68; strengthening the committee system, 59–61; sustaining executive oversight, 68–69; Tenth Parliament, 63–65
National Assembly (Nigeria): institutional deficits of the First Assembly of the Fourth Republic, 190–195; legislative expansion under Yar' Adua, 198–202; Obasanjo's second term and consolidation of power, 195–198; rent-seeking behavior, 179–180; tension between democratization and persistent patronage and corruption, 177–178
National Assembly Remuneration (Amendment) Act (2003; Kenya), 57
National Assembly (South Africa): bills introduced, 228(n15); education level of MPs, 229(n17); emerging system of portfolio committees, 215–218; factors shaping political structures, 206; institutional resources, 220–222; legislation amendments, 214–215; legislative autonomy, 222–223; political culture of the ANC, 213–214; role of civil society in legislative autonomy, 218–219; role of free press in legislative autonomy, 219–220; role of the presiding officer, 212–213
National Consultative Council (Uganda), 77
National Council of Nigerian Citizens (NCNC), 183–185
National Council of Provinces (South Africa), 215, 220–221
National Democratic Congress (NDC; Ghana), 147, 149, 153, 158, 172–174, 175(n2)
National interests, 7; Benin's constituency service and, 127–128, 142
National Party of Nigeria (NPN), 186, 187(table 6.2), 188
National Patriotic Party (NPP; Ghana), 147–149, 153, 157–158, 169, 172–175, 175(n2)
National Rainbow Coalition (NARC; Kenya), 51, 63–64
National Resistance Army (NRA; Uganda), 73, 76
National Resistance Council (NRC; Uganda), 77
National Resistance Movement (NRM; Uganda), 73, 104–106, 108(n32). *See also* Movement system (Uganda)
National Resistance

Movement–Organization (NRM–O; Uganda), 95–96
National Working Committee (South Africa), 210–211, 224
Natural resources: Nigeria, 181
Ndindiri, Samuel, 65
Neopatrimonial rule: entrenchment as obstacle to legislative development, 234–235; incentives for patron-client politics, 17–18; Kenya's failure to transcend, 42; Kenya under Moi, 37–38, 40; ministerial appointments, 10; Nigeria's political context, 180–182; postcolonial history, 12–15. *See also* Patrimonialism
Niger: regime classification, 24(table 1.1)
Niger Delta Development Commission, 193
Nigeria: chief presiding officer as force for reform, 236; comparative performance of the four core functions of the legislature, 242(table 8.2); evaluating legislative performance, 243; First Republic, 182–185; Fourth Republic, 189–202; Freedom House scores and democratic progress, 22; institutional resources, 241; LEGCO, 9; military neopatrimonialism, 13; multiparty elections and competitive politics, 16; nomenclature of parliamentary terms, 26(table 1.2); Obasanjo's "third term" agenda, 177, 197–198; political context, 180–182; quick wins supporting complex reforms, 248; reformers in legislature, 233; regime classification, 24(table 1.1); rent-seeking as political core, 179–180; research methodology, 25; salaries and emoluments, 240, 240(table 8.1); Second Republic, 186–189; term limits, 31(n6)
Nigerian People's Party (NPP), 186, 187(table 6.2)
Nnamani, Ken, 198
No-party system, Ghana, 149
No-party system, Uganda, 105; campaign finance, 101–102; justification for and origins of, 73; legislative development, 74; Movement system and Parliament, 92–96
Northern People's Congress (NPC; Nigeria), 183–185
Nujoma, Sam, 16
Nyerere, Julius, 13
Nyongo, Peter Anyang, 42

Obasanjo, Olusegun: assumption of power, 185; contesting legislative development, 235; executive-legislative tension in the Fourth Republic, 193; MP rivalry, 192; Nigeria's legislative shift, 195; "third-term" agenda, 16, 29, 177, 197–198
Obote, Milton, 77, 106(n4)
Odinga, Raila, 51, 64
Office space, 241; Benin, 114, 123; Ghana, 156, 172–173; Kenya, 48; South Africa's MPs, 220
Oil boom: Nigeria, 181, 187–188
Okadigbo, Chuba, 192
Olubunmi Etteh, Patricia, 200
One-party rule. *See* Single-party rule
Open queue voting, Kenya's, 38
Open voting, Uganda, 88
Opportunists, 18–20, 232
Opposition parties and movements: coalitions for change, 20; Kenya's Kibaki, 51–52; Kenya's opposition MPs, 71(n8); Kenya's Speaker blocking reforms, 41; Kenya's transformation, 44; Nigeria's fraudulent 2003 elections shutting out, 196; Parliamentary composition, 98–99; South Africa's ANC relations with, 211; South Africa's floor crossing, 207–208; Uganda's Parliamentary caucuses, 94–95
Orange Democratic Movement (ODM; Kenya), 64–65
Oversight committees, 27
Oversight of the executive: assessing legislative performance, 243; Benin, 130–136; core functions of the legislature, 7, 30(n1), 242(table 8.2); dimensions and indicators of Ghana's legislative impact, 151(fig. 5.1); effectiveness of Uganda's PAC, 104; Ghana's weakening performance, 156–158; Kenya's committee system, 60, 68–69; Kenya's committee system modernization, 49; Kenya's House, 33, 41; Nigeria's expanding legislative scope, 200; South Africa, 224–225; tension between representation and legislation, 8; Uganda's Budget Act, 78–81
Owusu-Adjapong, Felix, 172

Parliamentary Advocacy Forum (PAFO; Uganda), 94–96
Parliamentary groups (Benin), 111, 115–116, 119–120, 125

Parliamentary Monitoring Group (PMG; South Africa), 228(n4)
Parliamentary Pension Bill (Uganda), 92
Parliamentary Powers Index (PPI), 245; comparative performance of the four core functions of the legislature, 242(table 8.2)
Parliamentary Service Act (Kenya), 46
Parliamentary Service Commission (PSC; Kenya), 45–50, 54, 56, 239
Parliamentary systems: colonial history of, 9–10; nomenclature of parliamentary terms by country, 26(table 1.2). *See also* National Assembly (Benin); National Assembly (Kenya); National Assembly (Nigeria); National Assembly (South Africa); Parliament (Nigeria); Parliament of Ghana; Parliament (Uganda)
Parliament (Nigeria): political evolution, 183–185
Parliament of Ghana: characteristics of MPs, 163–166, 165(table 5.6); compensation and constituency service, 166–169; decline in autonomy and performance, 148; declining influence on presidential appointments, 158–159; dimensions and indicators of legislative impact, 151(fig. 5.1); executive co-optation of, 169–171; indicators of financial strength, 161(table 5.3); institutional capacity, 160–163; lack of influence on budget process, 154–156; legislative and policy impact, 150–154; manipulation of the presiding officer, 172–173; number of seats and seat shares by party, 149(table 5.1); professional staff salaries, 164(table 5.5); weakening oversight performance, 156–158
Parliament (Uganda): changes in constitutional powers and rules of procedure, 86–89; composition of, 96–101, 97(table 3.1); creation of the committee system, 89–91; independence under 1995 Constitution, 76–77; institutional nature of, 86–92; institutional resources, 91–92; Movement system and changes in, 73–74, 92–96; naming of, 106(n3); preparation for Uganda's resumption of multipartyism, 103; reformers' characteristics, 99–100(table 3.2); Uganda's MPs' debts fueling patronage, 101
Parties, political: Benin's deputies' views on campaign finance reform, 123–124;
Benin's fragmented parties, 115–116, 118; British ban on Kenyan party formation, 35–36; impact on legislative development, 236–237; Nigeria's Fourth Republic, 189–190, 191(table 6.3); Nigeria's Second Republic, 186; no-party systems, 73–74, 92–96, 101–102, 105, 149; as South African political driver, 205–206; South Africa's ANC's centralization of power, 209–211; South Africa's constituency service, 221; South Africa's floor crossing, 207–208; South Africa's proportional representation, 208–209
Party of National Unity (PNU; Kenya), 64
Patrimonialism: allowing co-optation of Ghana's legislature, 148; corruption in Uganda's Sixth Parliament, 81; Kenya's ethnic coalitions, 36; neopatrimonial rule emerging from, 12–15; Nigeria, 178; Nigeria's neopatrimonial history, 180–182; South Africa's lack of, 226; strengthening Uganda's executive power, 74; term limits combating, 239; Uganda's MPs' debts fueling, 101; Uganda's no-party system, 76–78; undercutting Uganda's legislative independence, 105. *See also* Neopatrimonial rule
Pattni, Kamlesh, 68
Pensions, 92
People's Democratic Party (PDP; Nigeria), 189–190, 191(table 6.3), 195–199
People's Redemption Party (Nigeria), 186, 187(table 6.2)
Permanent commission (Benin), 111–115, 113(table 4.1)
Permanent committees, 27
Plenary, 111
Policymaking: Benin, 128–130; Parliament of Ghana, 150–154
Political Committee (South Africa), 210–211
Political culture: African National Congress, 213–214
Political declaration, 115
Political economy: Nigeria, 181
Politically closed regimes, 24(table 1.1)
Political Reform Conference (Nigeria), 197
Politics of the belly, 13
Pork-barrel politics, 13, 138, 168–169, 171
Portfolio committees: described, 27; Kenya's Blue Print, 47; Kenya's expansion of, 239; Kenya's Ninth Parliament legislation, 62–63; Kenya's

Standing Orders revision, 66–67; South Africa, 210–211, 214–218, 223–224
Portugal: failure to develop colonial legislatures, 12; Third Wave of democratization, 4
Post mortem committees (Kenya), 49
Poverty levels: Benin, 145(n15)
Poverty reduction, 123
Prebendal politics, 13, 181, 188
Presidential power: Benin's presidential elections, 113; chief presiding officer and chief administrative officer containing reformers, 235–236; Constitution of Kenya Review Act, 49–50; dominating Kenya's House, 45; dominating Kenya's post-independence parliamentary system, 35; measuring legislative performance, 245; Nigeria's Second Republic as presidential system, 186; Parliament of Ghana's declining influence on presidential appointments, 158–159. *See also* Executive power
Privatization: Benin, 127; Uganda, 79–80
Procedural committees, 25
Professional staff: Benin, 114, 117–118, 128.134, 142; Ghana, 157, 160, 162–163; Kenya, 46–47; South Africa, 207, 223; Uganda, 92
Proportional representation (PR): Benin, 115; constituency service and national interests, 238; impact on South African politics, 207–209
Provincial National Defense Council (PNDC; Ghana), 148
Public accounts, law on, 132–134
Public Accounts Committee (PAC): Ghana, 156, 158; Kenya, 49, 61, 68–69; Nigeria, 185; oversight, 243; Uganda, 79–80, 85, 104, 106(n6)
Public Investments Committee (PIC; Kenya), 49
Public opinion: approval of Kenya's House, 33; Nigeria's legislature, 201–202, 201(table 6.4)
Public Service Commission (Kenya), 37

Quick wins, 247–248

Race politics, South Africa's: ANC agenda, 211–212; committee membership, 229(n18); floor-crossing, 208; political challenges resulting from, 225; political culture of the ANC, 213–214; portfolio committees, 218; race and class as dominant factors, 205
Rawlings, Jerry, 16, 31(n6), 147, 158–159, 235
Reconstruction and Development Program (RDP) policy, 228(n10)
Recruitment of legislative leaders, 30(n1)
Reformers: affecting legislative performance, 232–233; chief presiding officer and chief administrative officer containing, 235–236; coalitions for change, 18–20; incentives for Kenyan reforms, 55–57; Kenya's Blue Print, 47–48; Kenya's committee system modernization, 48–49; Kenya's House, 34; Kenya's Ninth Parliament legislation, 61–63; Kenya's Parliamentary Service Act, 46; Kenya's Speaker blocking, 41; Kenya's Standing Orders revision, 66–68; Nigerian reformers offsetting Obasanjo's executive power, 196; Parliamentary composition, 98; as requirement for institutional development, 247; South Africa, 226–227; strengthening Uganda's legislative independence, 105; transformation of Kenya's House, 42–45; turnover in Kenya's Ninth Parliament, 54; Uganda's, characteristics of, 99–100(table 3.2); Uganda's committee system, 89–91; Uganda's executive-legislative power struggles, 88–89; Uganda's no-party system, 75, 93–94. *See also* Coalitions for change
Regime classification, 24(table 1.1)
Règlement Intérieur (Benin), 11, 111, 119. *See also* Internal Rules; Standing Orders
Rentseeking, Nigeria: legislation in spite of rentseeking behavior, 192; obstructing democratization, 194–195; as political core, 179–180; Second Republic legislature, 188
Representative governance: assessing legislative performance, 243–244; Benin's deputies, 111, 126–128; Benin's parties, 115; comparative performance of the four core functions of the legislature, 242(table 8.2); South Africa, 207–208
Rubber-stamp legislation, 7, 36, 214, 222
Rules of procedure: Uganda, 86–89. *See also* Standing Orders
Rural reach of Kenya's civil society, 43
Ruzindana, Augustine, 106(n6)
Rwanda: multiparty elections and

competitive politics, 16; regime classification, 24(table 1.1)

Salaries and emoluments: annual compensation for members of parliament, 2008, by country, 240(table 8.1); Benin, 122; Ghana's MPs, 166, 168–169; Ghana's professional staff, 163, 164(table 5.5); history of Kenyan MP emoluments, 1993–2008, 55–57, 56(table 2.2); importance as incentive, 239–241; Kenya's, 55–57; Kenya's legislature, 55–57; Nigeria, 184, 187, 192; as ongoing issue, 248; reformers' "quick wins," 247–248; South Africa, 209, 220–222; Uganda, 92. *See also* Allowances
São Tomé and Príncipe: regime classification, 24(table 1.1)
Select committees, 27
Semiauthoritarian regimes, 22–23. *See also* Competitive authoritarian regimes; Electoral authoritarian regimes
Senegal: regime classification, 24(table 1.1)
Senghor, Léopold, 11
Separation of powers: Benin, 110–111; Ghana's need for, 174; Nigeria's constitutional provisions, 182; Uganda, 77
Seroney, John Marie, 36
Sessional committees, 27, 89
Seychelles: regime classification, 24(table 1.1)
Sierra Leone: LEGCO, 9; regime classification, 24(table 1.1)
Single-party rule: ministerial appointments, 10; postcolonial neopatrimonial rule, 13; South Africa, 207–208
Social responsibility: Benin's deputies, 121
Soglo, Nicéphore, 130, 135
Somalia, 105; regime classification, 24(table 1.1)
South Africa: ANC policy objectives, 211–212; ANC political culture, 213–214; centralization of power within the ANC, 209–211; civil society driving democratic reform, 234; coalitions for change, 20; comparative performance of the four core functions of the legislature, 242(table 8.2); constituency service, 30–31(n3); electoral system, 238; evaluating legislative performance, 243; factors retarding legislative development, 29–30; Freedom House scores and democratic progress, 22, 24(table 1.1); impact of parties on legislative development, 237; institutional resources, 241; legislative independence, 2; nomenclature of parliamentary terms, 26(table 1.2); one-party dominant system, 207–208; Parliamentary Powers Index, 245; political issues driving legislative development, 205–206; reformers and opportunists joining forces for change, 232; regime classification, 24(table 1.1); role of the presiding officer, 212–213; salaries and emoluments, 240, 240(table 8.1); Speaker appointment and approach, 40; Speaker containing reformers, 235. *See also* National Assembly (South Africa)
Southern African Development Community, 145(n5)
Speaker (chief presiding officer): coalitions for change, 20; containing reformers, 235–236; dissolving Nigeria's committees, 200; Ghana's institutional capacity, 160, 174; Kenya, facilitator of reform, 65; Kenya, obstacle to reform, 45–48; Kenya's appointment mechanism, 40, 71(n5); Kenya's Blue Print, 47–48; Kenya's Parliamentary Service Act, 46; manipulation of Ghana's, 172–173; Nigeria's allowances investigation, 192; role in South African politics, 212–213; South Africa, 223, 228(n12); strengthening Ghana's legislature, 149–150; Uganda's Administration of Parliament Act, 90–91; Uganda's Parliament, 25, 88
Special interest constituencies, 87, 103, 238
Ssekandi, Edward, 88
Standing Committee on Public Accounts (SCOPA; South Africa), 211, 224, 229(n21)
Standing committees: described, 25; Kenya, 37; Uganda's change in constitutional powers affecting, 86–89
Standing Orders: Benin's Règlement Interieur, 111; Ghana, 156; Kenya, 48–49, 66, 72(n12), 239; Nigeria, 185; research methodology, 25
State failure: Uganda, 76
State University of New York at Albany (SUNY–Albany), 47, 60–61
Study groups, 210
Sudan: regime classification, 24(table 1.1)
Swaziland: regime classification, 24(table 1.1)

Symbolic incentives, 122–123

Tanzania: coalitions for change, 20; postcolonial neopatrimonialism, 13; regime classification, 24(table 1.1); Speaker appointment and approach, 40; term limits, 31(n6)
Tension between representation and legislation, 8
Term limits: Benin's lack of, 109–110; containing executive power, 239; Kenya, 72(n13); Nigeria, 177, 197–198; Rawlings and Moi manipulating, 31(n6); Uganda's repeal, 74–75, 84–85, 103, 107(n19)
Togo: regime classification, 24(table 1.1)
Transparency International, 43
Tumukunde, Henry, 81
Turnover rate: Benin, 120; Ghana, 165(table 5.6), 166; interrupting legislative development, 247; Nigeria, 198–199; Uganda, 83

Uganda: Budget Act, 78–83; budgetary process, 225; civil society driving democratic reform, 234; coalitions for change, 20; colonial Parliament, 10; committee system and parliamentary autonomy, 89–91; comparative performance of the four core functions of the legislature, 242(table 8.2); constituency service and electoral campaigns, 101–103; electoral system, 238; evaluating legislative performance, 243; Freedom House scores and democratic progress, 22; institutional resources, 91–92, 241; legislative independence and autonomy in the Sixth and Seventh Parliaments, 78–86; Movement system and Parliamentary reforms, 92–96; multiparty elections and competitive politics, 16, 103–106; nomenclature of parliamentary terms, 26(table 1.2); Parliamentary composition, 96–101, 97(table 3.1); Parliament as an institution, 86–92; party organizations, 106(n1); patronage, 76–78; political parties and legislative development, 236–237; portfolio committees, 216; quick wins supporting complex reforms, 248; reformers, 99–100(table 3.2), 232–233; regime classification, 24(table 1.1); research methodology, 25; rewriting formal rules, 239; salaries and emoluments, 240, 240(table 8.1); Seventh Parliament, 83–86; term limits, 31(n6), 239
Uganda Commercial Bank (UCB), 79–80
Uganda People's Congress, 77
Uganda Peoples' Defence Forces (UPDF), 107(n17)
Unicameral system: Benin, 109; Uganda's Parliament, 87
United States: democratic studies and comparative legislative studies, 3–5; Kenya's Blue Print, 47–48
Unity Party of Nigeria (UPN), 186, 187(table 6.2)
USAID, 41, 43, 47, 67, 71(n9), 141, 234

Vice president: Uganda, 25
Violence: Kenya's ethnic conflict, 63–64
Volume of legislation, South Africa, 217–218, 228(n15)
Voter turnout: Kenya under Kenyatta and Moi, 37–38

Wabara, Adolphus, 196
Wapakhabulo, James, 88
Westminster model parliaments, 77, 183
Withdrawn bills, 153
Women: demographic profile of Benin's National Assembly, 119, 145(n6); Ghana's MPs, 165(table 5.6); Parliamentary composition, 98; Uganda's Parliamentary composition, 97(table 3.1), 103–104, 107(n18); Uganda's special interest constituencies, 87
Workshops: Kenya's legislative transformation, 44–45
World Bank, 71(n4), 133, 148

Yar'Adua, Umaru, 198–199
Yoruba people, 183
Young Parliamentarians Association (YPA), 94, 102, 107(n24)

Zambia: multiparty systems and competitive politics, 16; regime classification, 24(table 1.1); term limits, 31(n6)
Zimbabwe: regime classification, 24(table 1.1)
Zuma, Jacob, 209, 228(nn7,8,9), 229(n22)

About the Book

A puzzle underpins this groundbreaking study of legislative development in Africa: Why are variations in the extent of legislative authority and performance across the continent only partially related, if at all, to the overall level of democratization? And if democratization is not the prime determinant of legislative authority, what is?

Exploring the constraints that have retarded the development and power of legislatures across Africa—and how members of some legislatures are breaking free of those constraints—the authors shed new light on the impact of the legislative branch on the political process in six emerging African democracies.

Joel D. Barkan is professor emeritus of political science at the University of Iowa and senior associate at the Center for Strategic and International Studies in Washington, DC. A long-time student of democratization and political economy across Anglophone Africa, his numerous publications include *Beyond Capitalism and Socialism in Kenya and Tanzania*.